UNRESTRICTED
WARFARE

UNRESTRICTED WARFARE

How a New Breed of Officers Led
the Submarine Force to Victory
in World War II

James F. DeRose

Foreword by Roger W. Paine Jr.

CASTLE BOOKS

Grateful acknowledgement is made to the following for permission to reprint previously published material:

Forest, J. Sterling: Quotations from *Wake of the Wahoo*, by Forest J. Sterling, copyrighted 1960, 1997, and 1999.

Little, Brown and Company: Quotations from *Warfish*, by George Grider and Lydel Sims, copyrighted 1958.

Presidio Press: Quotations from *Clear the Bridge* and *Wahoo*, both by Richard H. O'Kane, copyrighted 1977 and 1987.

William R. McCants: Quotations from *War Patrols of the USS Flasher*, by William R. McCants, copyrighted 1994.

This edition published in 2006 by
CASTLE BOOKS ®
A division of Book Sales, Inc.
114 Northfield Avenue
Edison, NJ 08837

This edition published by arrangement with and permission of
John Wiley & Sons, Inc.
111 River Street
Hoboken, New Jersey 07030

Design and production by Navta Associates, Inc.

Library of Congress Cataloging-in-Publication Data:

DeRose, James F.
Unrestricted warfare: how a new breed of officers led the submarine force to victory in world war II / James F. DeRose.
p.   cm.
Includes bibliographical references and index.
1.   Wahoo (Submarine). 2. World War, 1939—1945—Naval operations—Submarine. 3. World War, 1939-1945—Naval operations, American. 4. World War, 1939-1945—Campaigns—Pacific Area. I. Title.

D783.5.W3 D39 2000
940.54'41—dc21   00-024299
ISBN-13: 978-0-7858-2182-3
ISBN-10: 0-7858-2182-1

Printed in the United States of America

CONTENTS

Foreword   vii

Acknowledgments   ix

Introduction   1

Prologue   7

PART I   FIRST-YEAR FAILURE   15

    1   Day of Infamy   17

    2   A Stumbling Start   26

    3   Warriors Gather   35

    4   Frustration   44

    5   Intrigue   53

PART II   MORTON LEADS THE WAY   67

    6   Everything Clicks   69

    7   Success and Excess   77

    8   Days of Fury   96

    9   Luck Falters   111

   10   Luck Vanishes   121

   11   Loss of *Wahoo*   135

PART III   WAHOO's WAR CONTINUES   141

12   O'Kane in Charge   143
13   The New Avenger   150
14   Reluctant Lifeguard   158
15   Prize Patrol   169
16   New Preparations   185
17   Torpedo Troubles
         in Ashcan Alley   189
18   Fortune's Crest   201
19   Catastrophe   212
20   Submarine Sweep   226
21   Final Victory   243

Afterword   261
Appendix I: Top Skippers of World War II:
    Tonnage Credited   273
Appendix II: Top Skippers of World War II:
    JANAC Assessment   275
Appendix III: Top Skippers of World War II:
    Tonnage Percent Overestimated   277
Appendix IV: *Wahoo* Sinkings and
    Tang Sinkings   279
Chapter Notes   285
Sources   293
Index   297

FOREWORD

Ex communi periculo, fraternitas
(From common peril, brotherhood)

For those who may wonder how members of the submarine community manage to achieve the high morale and unity of purpose that are so characteristic of the "silent service," the above credo of the U.S. SubVets (U.S. submarine veterans of World War II) provides at least one answer. The close, even claustrophobic living conditions, the lack of privacy, and the sacrifice of family relations inherent in submarine living all militate against such a commitment. Two things make it not only possible but even desirable. First: inspirational leadership, often (and in fact, usually) from one man, the ship's captain. And second, the realization that you and each one of your shipmates are mutually dependent on each other for your very life.

The Navy's ground warriors, the U.S. Marines, successfully stress the dependency factor in their "boot camp" indoctrination, so much so that over the years a remarkable number of marines have chosen to mask the explosive effect of a live grenade with their own bodies to protect other marines nearby. "Greater love hath no man than this . . ."

Important though the "brotherhood" concept may be, in the submarine service the inspirational leadership of the captain is vital. Besides relating directly to each crew member, he must exude self-confidence; his wisdom and determination must be beyond the doubt of any observer. The best submarine skippers are "born that way"; those who are not must learn how by taking lessons from a "pro" in action, or by direct exposure to events that lead to lasting impressions of quality leadership.

The younger officers portrayed in this book were fortunate to have learned their lessons from some of the finest pros in the business. In my case, I was off to a fast start with Lew Parks and Slade Cutter in *Pompano*. Then followed Mush Morton, Dick O'Kane, and George Grider, all with stellar leadership qualifications and, as time progressed, with command records to prove it.

The first skipper of *Wahoo*—very much a product of the prewar emphasis on caution—lacked self-confidence, yet tended to trust few judgments but his own; as a result he literally burned himself out in the course of two patrols. The tragedy is that he had the finest talent in the submarine force at his disposal but did not know how to use it. To the surprise of everyone, the same ship, with the same cast of characters, under new and inspiring leadership, proceeded to open the door to new heights of the kind of unrestricted warfare that had been mandated more than a year before.

When the leadership crisis was solved, one other stumbling block remained: malfunctioning torpedoes. Whatever could go wrong with them, did. They ran deeper than set; they often exploded prematurely; when set for contact, they were often duds; and worst of all, they could and did make circular runs to come back and hit the firing submarine. The damage to morale and the number of ships lost because of these faults are both beyond calculation. The war was surely prolonged needlessly because of this material deficiency.

To tell the story of how this cast of "young studs" learned their lessons from the pros, as well as from direct experience in the crucible of war, the author has traced their careers through their interactions with each other, and with the common enemy and the associated peril. Mr. DeRose did not serve in submarines, but he has been very near those who did. It is fascinating to follow his exposition of how we grew through the war years. He has listened carefully to our story, independently read and studied a great deal, and uncovered much information that was new and fresh to me. More than a story of men who rose to great challenges, this is also serious history. I hope that you will enjoy the experience of reading it as much as I have.

Roger W. Paine Jr.
Rear Admiral, U.S.N. (Ret.)
El Cajon, California
November 1999

ACKNOWLEDGMENTS

This book grew slowly, its genesis in the many letters, phone discussions, and occasional meals with surviving participants in the only successful submarine campaign of World War II. When I tentatively decided to craft a story that linked the lives of my correspondents, the support from them was enthusiastic. Foremost among the men who encouraged me to continue was Roger W. Paine Jr., now a retired rear admiral, on December 7, 1941, the torpedo and gunnery officer on *Pompano*. A plank owner (a member of the original crew assigned to a submarine while it was being built) of *Wahoo*, he became her penultimate executive officer (XO), narrowly surviving her loss because of an unexpected, but correctly timed, case of appendicitis. He went on to become the youngest submarine captain of the war *(S-34)*, executive officer of *Tinosa*, and commanding officer of a new-construction boat, *Cubera*. Roger read the earliest half dozen chapters, gently setting me straight from the outset. He has continued to read and comment on ever larger manuscripts. Without his encouragement this book would never have been completed.

Many other men carefully proofread various versions of the work in progress. Special thanks must be shown to the those members of the crew of *Tang* who read the developing text as closely as it is possible for humans to do. Foremost among these are Clay Decker, the late Jesse DaSilva, Murray Frazee (executive officer), Bill Leibold, and Larry Savadkin. If I didn't get it right, it is my fault and none of theirs.

Other submariners also gave their time to this project, notably John B. Alden, whose knowledge of World War II submarine attacks is truly encyclopedic. I am also indebted to the late Richard H. O'Kane, who expanded on details of the texts of both his books and generously shared additional information on *Wahoo* and *Tang* with me. He also steered me to others who could provide additional help.

And there are the "associate submariners": George Logue, whose brother was killed on *Wahoo* and who gave me every assistance, from copies of Robert's diary to translations of Japanese attack reports with accompanying maps; Dr. Frederick Milford, whose analysis of the torpedo problem was instrumental in my understanding of this scandalous weapons failure; Steve Finnigan, curator of the Force Museum in Groton, who got me copies of everything from TDC manuals to *ONI 208-J* recognition manuals; and Akiro Kado, chief of the International Cooperation Division of the National Diet Library in Tokyo. He led me, in particular, to the files on *Buyo Maru,* and more generally to the existence of *Senji Sempaku Shi (Wartime Ships History)* and *Senji Yuso Sendan Shi (Wartime Transportation Convoys History).*

This book also owes a debt to those who were there and who wrote their story long before I even thought of this book, particularly George Grider and Forest J. Sterling.

Finally, I would like to acknowledge the debt I owe to my wife, Judy, who encouraged me in this pursuit and patiently listened to—in all certainty—far too many submarine anecdotes for one wife to endure.

JFD

INTRODUCTION

Many critics unfairly believe that prior to the attack on Pearl Harbor the U.S. Navy was completely unprepared for a war with Japan. But at the close of World War I, U.S. naval staff officers saw that Japan was uniquely vulnerable to submarine attack, a fact that the Japanese themselves failed to fully appreciate until too late. In 1920 the navy made an estimate of the number of submarines it would need to blockade Japan if war was conducted from bases in Guam and Manila. The quantity, 144 if Manila were to fall, was considered unacceptably high; the principal reason why "so many" would be needed was the low endurance of the newest submarine, the S-boat.

Technical planning began at once for a new submarine with great range, high reliability, and good surface speed that could get on station quickly, stay on patrol for weeks, and need only a short refit cycle between patrols. This new boat also had to be able to deliver a heavy torpedo load to make its voyage across the vast reaches of the Pacific worthwhile.

For nearly twenty years the search for the right boat was pursued incrementally. Enormous political barriers such as the Washington Treaty (1922), which outlawed submarine blockades, the Geneva Disarmament Conference, and the London Treaty (1930) held down both submarine construction and physical size to stay within permissible tonnage limits. Congress, in the grip of the 1930s Depression, would have been happy with small defensive boats, but the Naval War College successfully defended the logic of the long-range submarine for use in a potential Pacific war.

Congress, however, did block the use of foreign, especially German, engines in American submarines. The navy's Bureau of Engineering struggled for years to find an acceptable American design. From 1927 to 1934 a total of only six submarines were commissioned by the navy, all of them essentially special-purpose or one-of-a-kind vessels. All had engine problems.

In 1932 an agreement was reached with Charles Kettering of General Motors for the use of fast locomotive diesel-electrics in submarines. Three years later two new boats of the Porpoise class were delivered using GM's Winton diesels. These boats were precursors to what would become the World War II "fleet" boat.

Each fiscal year thereafter, production of steadily improving submarines began to rise: four in 1936, five each in 1937 and 1938, ten in 1939. At the outbreak of war in Europe the number of submarines authorized jumped. With the fall of France in May 1940, it was determined that 120 new fleet submarines would be needed if Britain also went under. Fleet boat production was immediately frozen on the Gato design, the boat then under construction. This class of submarine, and its modestly redesigned sisters, the high-tensile steel, deep-diving Balao and Tench boats, would fight and win the Pacific submarine war. Nearly 240 were commissioned between June 1940 and August 1945.

Although the German-type VII-C U-boat is often described as having the best World War II submarine design, compared to the American fleet boat, it was an also-ran. Its endurance on the surface at ten to twelve knots was 6,500 nautical miles; a Gato's round-trip capability was 11,500 miles at comparable speeds. The VII-C constantly struggled with dangerous, often fatal, problems of refueling at sea to conduct patrols in the Americas after traveling the 3,000 miles from Lorient on the French coast to New York. American submarines were able to prowl Japan's coast for weeks without support from the more distant base of Pearl Harbor.

The VII-C's top surface speed was seventeen knots, just enough to out-run a distant corvette. A Gato's speed of twenty-one knots permitted repeated slashing end-around attacks on escorted convoys without calling in assistance from other submarines.

The VII-C U-boat, essentially an improved World War I design, had only five torpedo tubes, four forward and one aft. The Gato had ten tubes, six forward, and four aft. Gatos carried twenty-four torpedoes; the Germans typically carried about half that number inside the boat but often lashed spares in "coffins" on the deck; these could be manhandled below at the risk of being caught helpless on the surface by a searching enemy.

American submarines had air conditioning by 1936, installed over the fierce objections of many traditionalists. Crew comfort was a leading factor, with major emphasis on the expected area of operations, where interior hull temperatures often reached 110 degrees; German U-boat crews were sometimes driven to total exhaustion when patrolling the Caribbean in their unbearably hot, sticky vessels.

But air conditioning also was installed for a second purpose. Americans were betting on new technologies, some yet to come, that demanded air conditioning: the torpedo data computer (TDC); active and passive sonar; search radar, which was quickly installed and fiercely exploited; enemy radar detection gear; and multiple radio communication devices.

American boats also had a number of other crew comfort features designed to ensure reasonable living conditions on extended patrols, including vapor compression stills to provide enough fresh water for the crew to keep themselves and their clothing clean. There were also an adequate number of heads, or toilet spaces, for the crew, unlike U-boats, which had such poor toilet facilities that the boats always reeked. Except under special circumstances, every man on an American submarine had a private bunk; there was no deliberate "hot bunking," or rotating shared sleeping space, as on German submarines; sleeping on deck plates, as was the design in some British boats, was unacceptable.

In addition to the good technical characteristics of the boats, American submarine crews at the beginning of the war were excellent. This was a wholly volunteer, extra-pay, *corps d'élite*—with special food privileges. Reenlistment rates were very high. Due to the intimate living conditions, the officers knew the small, tightly knit crews well. Training opportunities were exceptional, and most men took advantage of their chances. More than half the enlisted crew who took *Gudgeon* on her first war patrol in December 1941 were commissioned officers by war's end.

But there were two glaring weaknesses in U.S. submarines: torpedo performance and overcautious commanding officers.

The torpedo problem was a sickening organizational scandal, deep and fundamental, marked by politically motivated and thoroughly entrenched turf wars. A series of unrelated problems, based on slipshod design and testing, each tending to mask the other, were gradually fixed—some only with the aggressive leadership of the fighting crews as opposed to the Bureau of Ordnance—but a fully reliable, mass-produced torpedo was never truly achieved, leading to needless American deaths and an incalculable prolongation of the war with Japan.

An eerily similar series of problem had occurred in Germany early in the war. There, Admiral Doenitz took dramatic steps to get at the root of the problem. All officers at the German Torpedo Experimental Institute responsible for the problems were court-martialed and convicted for dereliction of duty. The U.S. Navy took no punitive action against those officers responsible for its torpedo problems.

In contrast, the navy's "skipper problem" was tackled ruthlessly. For at least a decade prior to the war, men who became commanding officers in submarines shared at least one common characteristic: they were superb technicians, formally trained as engineers. But in wartime, as Jasper Holmes, an astute participant and historian of the Pacific submarine war remarked, it was "like sending the design section of General Motors out to race their cars in the Indianapolis Speedway races." Some would do well—but that was simply chance at work.

All of the early skippers, typically thirty-six to thirty-eight years old, were trained for a war against combat vessels, not commerce raiding. They were expected to stay at deep submergence and fire at warships on sound bearings alone. The idea of a night surface attack was unknown; the concept of an "end-around" to gain position in front of an oncoming target was only a dream. There was no "war shot" practice with real torpedoes.

Fear of antisubmarine aircraft was instilled in the captains. As part of their training, most were flown over a submarine operating submerged. Sometimes, under good conditions, it was visible at depths of 125 feet. Small noise-making bombs were dropped to drive home the point that submarines were easily detectable.

Delegation of responsibility was nonexistent. If anything went wrong on his submarine the skipper was responsible and took a career hit. Thus the captains grew cautious and stayed on the bridge or in the conning tower at all times. This was endurable during peacetime drills, but unsustainable in war. Subordinates were improperly developed, and the commanding officers (COs) simply wore out.

Career caution was reinforced even during tactical exercises. The captain of a submarine that was detected making an approach was reprimanded. One who never got to the target, but was unobserved, was commended.

Thus it is no surprise that during the first year of the war skipper performance was generally abysmal. During this period one-third of all captains were replaced for lack of aggressiveness or failure to sink ships. Their replacements were typically younger men, about thirty-two years old, only ten years out of the Naval Academy. The "youth experiment" COs leapfrogged over many officers patiently waiting their time for command but who were tainted by peacetime training. Purging unproductive captains continued throughout the war, and the age of the replacement captains continued to drop.

This book deals with a new breed of risk-taking leadership that began to make its energy felt during the second half of 1942. These men made the American submarine a major instrument of victory. The principal focus is on five skilled officers—George W. Grider, John B. Griggs III, Dudley W. Morton, Richard H. O'Kane, and Roger W. Paine Jr.—a group thrust together for the first time aboard *Wahoo*.

There are also three key supporting characters: Duncan C. MacMillan and John A. Moore, who passed through *Wahoo*'s wardroom on the way to commands of their own, and most especially Murray B. Frazee. Frazee joined Dick O'Kane as executive officer of *Tang* by way of *Grayback*, not *Wahoo*.

While each of their ranks rose during the war, these men initially ranged from ensign to lieutenant commander. Seven of the eight became wartime submarine COs, though only five saw combat in that role. Just these five accounted for the loss of at least sixty-six Japanese steel-hulled merchantmen and more than 260,000 gross tons of shipping, nearly 6 percent of all U.S. submarine sinkings in the war of attrition against the Japanese merchant marine.

This wartime success came at a terrible cost. The submarine war was unforgiving. Seven G-named Tambors were commissioned in 1941. Five— *Grampus, Grayback, Grayling, Grenadier,* and *Gudgeon*—had been sunk by May 1944. Fifty-two submarines are generally counted as total U.S. war losses, but this count excludes boats the Japanese damaged so severely they were unfit for further combat, such as *Halibut, Porpoise,* and *Salmon*.

An even higher casualty rate was experienced by our protagonists. Two of the eight were killed in action, and a third taken prisoner by the Japanese. All of them lived with death as a constant companion, and often escaped only because of a providential transfer. As shown in the drawing of six lost boats, Frazee, who had left *Grayback* two patrols before she was sunk, left *Tang* only thirty days before her loss; Paine survived the loss of both *Pompano* and *Wahoo;* Griggs left both *Wahoo* and *Shark* thirty days before their respective losses. These three survived the war physically unscathed. O'Kane also transferred from *Argonaut* and *Wahoo,* but his luck ran out on *Tang*.

In aggregate, these men experienced virtually every facet of the war. Some were present at Pearl Harbor, and most participated in early patrols with faulty torpedoes, inept skippers, or both.

The "*Wahoo* Five," under Morton, began the experimentation that made the U.S. submarine so formidable a weapon. Always struggling with torpedo problems, they made slashing, repeated attacks by day or night. High-speed night surface strikes became a specialty, along with skilled use of radar to keep in touch with targets during end-arounds, and exploitation of the TDC for out-of-position shooting. Surprise gun attacks were conducted on smaller targets. Support for air corps and naval air actions—

"lifeguard duty"—was perfected. As the Japanese recoiled, penetration of harbors and guarded shorelines in shallow water, including threading of minefields with new detection devices, was daringly conducted. And refit cycles were always short, to increase time spent in contact with the hated enemy.

Were mistakes made? You bet. These were very young, very real men, not fictional movie heroes. But their story is richer than any movie. It deserves telling and retelling because of all they risked, and the terrible price they paid, that we might enjoy the wonders of this great nation.

Often Deadly Transfers: Six Lost Boats

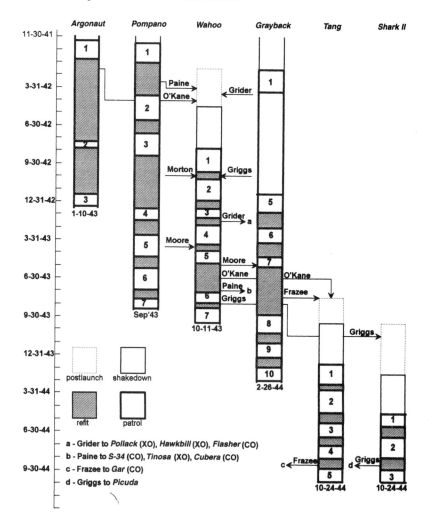

PROLOGUE

Adjust speed, if possible, to permit daylight reconnaissance
vicinity Wewak Harbor, New Guinea Lat 4°S–Long 144°E.

—Wahoo *operational order, third patrol*

Wahoo's brand-new captain, Dudley "Mush" Morton, was determined to alter his submarine's mediocre reputation—decisively. This was the thirty-five-year-old Morton's first patrol as CO and he intended to come back a winner, or die trying. The loose guidance offered by his operational orders might give him just the opportunity he sought.

Morton had already worked at bringing his key officers along to the point where his view of "reconnaissance" and theirs matched. His XO, thirty-two-year-old Dick O'Kane, was no problem. Morton and O'Kane had hit it off from the moment they met on *Wahoo's* desultory second patrol. An incredibly tight bond had formed between the two men. O'Kane seemed braver than anyone Morton had ever met before, and it was clear that O'Kane would walk into a blazing inferno if Morton asked.

It was the junior officers who concerned Morton. In the cramped wardroom, sultry from the humid air of the Bismarck Sea, he presided over a meeting of the three "plank owners." These men had been with *Wahoo* since her days on the builder's ways at Mare Island. O'Kane was there, of course, as well as thirty-year-old George Grider, the third, or diving, officer. The youngest of the four, but the one with the most combat experience, was twenty-five-year-old Roger Paine, the torpedo and gunnery officer. Both the junior officers were exceptionally talented, but their skills had been largely wasted by the previous CO.

They were now approaching the northeastern coast of New Guinea, and Morton intended to brace them directly. He began with Grider, asking George to define what reconnaissance meant to him. Grider responded, "We take a cautious look at the area, from far out at sea, through the periscope, submerged."

"No, boy," Morton replied, grinning "The only way you can reconnoiter a harbor is to go right into it and see what's there."

Warming to his subject, it became clear that Morton contemplated a daylight penetration. Grider and Paine exchanged anxious looks. So the rumors were true! Morton was crazy after all! They all knew that Germany's Gunther Prien had penetrated Scapa Flow, by night, in U-47. But at least he had real charts! But Morton was steadfast. They were going to do it. He had given them a chance to back out of this patrol when they were in Brisbane. There was no backing out now.

At 0300 on Sunday, January 24, 1943, Wahoo arrived off Wewak Harbor, two shallow, muddy indentations in the deep jungle coast. The area of greatest interest to Morton was the nine-mile-deep roadstead to the northwest, water sheltered by a complex series of islands and reefs that promised protected anchorages for Japanese ships. There were two large islands, Kairiru and Mushu (instantly abbreviated "Mush" by the crew), and two small ones, Karsau and Unei. Potential targets could be anywhere in the maze of bays, straits, and passages between islands.

At 0330 the last breaths of jungle-perfumed air were taken by the bridge crew, and then Wahoo dove 2½ miles northwest of Kairiru's shore. Morton decided to begin reconnoitering at the western end of Kairiru, circling into Victoria Bay.

As dawn broke Morton and O'Kane, alternating on the periscope, began to distinguish waterborne traffic. They were so close to shore that they could see a Japanese coast watcher cooking breakfast on a rock. Pappy Rau, the chief of the boat, was given a chance to look at their human enemy. He immediately switched the magnification setting and just as quickly called "Down scope!" Two Chidori class antisubmarine vessels were pounding Wahoo's way. Neither had been seen by Morton or O'Kane nor picked up by sound. Morton conned Wahoo out of the way at high submerged speed while O'Kane poked the periscope eye a few inches above the surface, taking water-lapping peeks at them as they passed.

As they crept around Kairiru Island, landmarks seen by O'Kane through the periscope were plotted on the charts, along with the water depth and sound bearings to the surf tumbling on the beaches. An escape route had to be drawn for their nearly blind, groping submarine.

Victoria Bay was empty, and Wahoo withdrew to round Kairiru and enter the strait separating it from Mushu. The set and drift of the current were carefully plotted, along with the light patches of water marking the shallows. The masts of a ship were spotted to the southwest, possibly behind Karsau Island; it was hard to be sure in the hazy, humid air. Because the best approach was blocked by a tug and a barge, Morton tried to con *Wahoo* around Unei Island and its shoals to get at Karsau. *Wahoo* began to rock from the shore swells striking a reef. Grider remembered that O'Kane said "Captain, I believe we're getting too close to land. . . . All I can see is one coconut tree."

"Dick," Morton replied, "you're in low power."

O'Kane, already embarrassed by Pappy Rau's sighting of the Chidoris, flipped the handle to high power. "Down periscope," he yelped. "All back emergency! My God, all I can see is one coconut!"

This near-disaster was treated lightly by Morton, whom Grider felt "was in his element. He was in danger and he was hot on the trail of the enemy, so he was happy. . . . The atmosphere in the conning tower would have been more appropriate to a fraternity raiding party. . . . Mush even kept up his joking when we almost ran aground."

Morton slowly backed *Wahoo* away from Unei while Grider struggled to maintain depth control in the shorebound swells. They headed back toward the strait, and at 1318, ten hours after the dive and the start of this long search, O'Kane picked up the bridge of a ship in the bight of Mushu Island, a few miles deeper into the harbor. Gunther Prien's acclaimed penetration of Scapa Flow had consumed a single hour.

Now, in glassy, calm conditions where periscope exposure was a real risk, *Wahoo* crept forward at three knots—human walk speed. O'Kane periodically raised the tip above the seas, which rose and fell like the breathing of a sleeping tiger. Soon he thought he could see a moored destroyer with several nested RO-class submarines through the haze. A destroyer it was, *Harusame*. But Morton, who had been trading peeks through the periscope with O'Kane "like a couple of schoolboys," Grider wrote, was not that sure about the submarines. The patrol report notes that "The objects alongside may have been the tug and barge first sighted at dawn."

Morton decided to attack the destroyer. He told Grider, crouched at the top of the control room ladder into the conning tower, "We'll take him by complete surprise. He won't be expecting an enemy submarine in here." Grider hadn't expected to be there either.

Wahoo was rigged for silent running, and the temperature and humidity both began to climb. Morton decided to con *Wahoo* to a position 3,000 yards away from the presumably sitting-duck destroyer. They would make a long-range shot from reasonably deep water and escape. When Paine called out 3,750 yards range generated from the TDC readings, O'Kane took a quick look through the periscope.

"Destroyer under way, angle ten port."

The prudent decision would have been to let *Harusame* go. They were miles inside a harbor of inadequate depth, with very little maneuvering room. But Morton decided to continue the attack, a reckless move, for now the destroyer had to be sunk or *Wahoo* would be exterminated.

The entire fire control party operated at peak efficiency in the muggy 100-degree interior of the conning tower. The sound man detected muffling of the propeller beat, indicating a target zig. O'Kane took a swift look and called out the new course. Morton conned *Wahoo* to a better firing angle. A count of propeller turns indicated a speed of thirteen knots; Paine set fifteen knots into the TDC to allow for the continuing acceleration of the destroyer. At 1441 fifteen words were spoken:

Morton: "Anytime, Dick."

O'Kane: "Stand by for constant bearings" as the scope eye surfaced.

O'Kane: "Constant bearing—Mark!"

Hunter: "Three-four-five," the target bearing.

Paine: "Set." The TDC solution checked.

O'Kane: "Fire!"

Three torpedoes were on their way within fifteen seconds, aimed to strike the destroyer in the stern, amidships, and bow. O'Kane left the scope up and saw that they would all miss astern. The destroyer's true speed was clearly greater than fifteen knots. Quickly Paine set the TDC to a new target speed: twenty knots. A fourth torpedo was fired. But *Harusame* had been alerted by the wakes of the first three torpedoes. She turned to evade the fourth, kept on turning, and charged straight down the lingering torpedo wakes toward *Wahoo*. Forest Sterling, the yeoman, was in the crew's mess, where he "felt an almost uncontrollable urge to urinate." O'Kane ordered "Down scope!"

But Morton intervened. "Leave it up, by God! We'll give that son of a bitch a point of aim, all right!" was the way Edward "Ned" Beach, then engineering officer of *Trigger*, later heard the story. It was "as subtle as a duel with shotguns at five paces," Jasper Holmes wrote later. For this down-the-throat shot to succeed, the oncoming *Harusame* had to be less than 1,200 yards away before firing began, or she could maneuver to avoid the torpedo. She could not be less than 700 yards away or the torpedo would not have time to arm before contact. O'Kane stayed glued to the scope, watching *Harusame* grow in the eyepiece, a great "V" bow wake streaming, rising even to the anchors, as she roared in for the kill.

O'Kane kept the hairline of the scope centered on *Harusame*'s bow as Morton conned *Wahoo* into alignment with the oncoming destroyer. O'Kane called the scope's telemeter divisions from waterline to masthead, and they were quickly converted to range. At 1,400 yards Morton passed control of the boat to O'Kane, who coached the helmsman with simple commands: "Right a hair" or "Left a hair" to keep the scope steady on the destroyer's bow.

When the range reached 1,250 yards Morton gave a calm, confident command: "Anytime, Dick." O'Kane coached the helmsman for a few more seconds, then called "Fire!" The range was 1,200 yards. The torpedo was going to miss. When the distance shrank to 850 yards Morton gave his permission to fire when the destroyer filled four divisions in low power. Grider heard O'Kane say "Captain, she already fills eight." Morton was visibly jarred, but O'Kane coached the helmsman four more times. At 1449, range 750 yards, he fired their last shot. Sterling was suddenly ". . . calm with the cool certainty that I was going to die. I wondered, How can this be happening to me?"

The last torpedo expended, Grider dropped into the control room and took *Wahoo* down to 90 feet, as deep as he dared without knowing the water depth. He "remembered with relief that I had left my will ashore at the beginning of the patrol." Everyone grabbed onto something, not meeting the eyes of the other men, as they awaited the death-dealing depth charges.

"The first explosion was loud and close," said Grider. Sterling wrote, "a terrific explosion shook *Wahoo* and all her inhabitants." For O'Kane, "the first depth charge was severe. . . . A mighty roar and cracking, as if we were in the middle of a lightning storm, shook *Wahoo*. The great cracking became crackling . . . that of steam heating a bucket of water, but here amplified a million times." *Harusame*'s boilers had exploded.

Realization that they had actually hit the destroyer flooded downward from the conning tower. "We hit the son of a bitch!" screamed Paine and the fire control party. "By God, maybe we did," said Morton, who ordered Grider to bring *Wahoo* back up to periscope depth. O'Kane grabbed the handles as the scope started up the tube and reported to all hands that *Harusame* was broken in half just forward of the stack. Her crew, in dress whites, were climbing the masts to get out of the way of an expected seventh torpedo. Jubilation reigned inside *Wahoo*.

Grider shot up the ladder, happy to be alive, his father's Graflex in hand, to begin photographing the extraordinary sight. He saw *Harusame* "broken in two like a match stick, her bow already settling. . . . Her crew swarmed over her, hundreds of men, in the rigging, in the superstructure, all over the decks." In celebration, Morton let the entire crew cycle through the conning tower to take a look at their stricken victims, whom he called "those slant-eyed devils in the rigging."

Blood lust satisfied, *Wahoo* began to thread her way out of the harbor. Mindful of the Chidoris they had seen earlier, Morton risked only a single ping of the fathometer. The water depth was 150 feet; Grider eased her down to 100 feet. With their record of entry as a guide, and with the sound man listening for surf, *Wahoo* crept toward the sea without exposing the periscope. At 1700, 14 hours after arriving off Wewak, all beach noises were behind them. For insurance they crawled seaward for another 2½ hours. At 1930 O'Kane ordered *Wahoo* to "surface in God's clean air" well clear of Kairiru Island.

With four engines on line, *Wahoo* ran north away from Wewak, radar sweeping sea and sky for expected Japanese countermeasures. After half an hour, confidence in their total escape permitted them to return to normal two-engine speed and begin a battery charge.

Morton had the pharmacist's mate pass out the "depth-charge medicine" to the crew: brandy. Sterling remembered it as Three Star Hennessy; Grider recalled it as rotgut. But they all drank it. Morton ordered the exhausted O'Kane, who had been on his feet for nearly thirty-six hours, to bed, then joined the crew in their mess. They excitedly talked their way down to calmness while the pharmacist's mate massaged Morton's tight neck muscles.

One man stood out clearly to everyone: Dick O'Kane. Sterling remembered the crew describing O'Kane in a new way: ". . . the coolest cucumber you want to see in an emergency. . . . Man, he stayed right on that periscope and looked right down their throats with that destroyer coming in plenty fast and shooting right at us. I never seen anything like it."

Grider was also dumbfounded. "I found . . . myself marveling at the change that had come over Dick O'Kane since the attack had begun. It was as if, during all the talkative, boastful months before, he had been lost, seeking his true element, and now it was found. He was calm, terse, and utterly cool. My opinion of him underwent a permanent change."

Beach recorded that when Morton was asked how he had managed to keep his nerve in the face of the attacking destroyer he replied: "Why do you think I made O'Kane look at him? He's the bravest man I know!" In the patrol report Morton wrote: "Lt. R. H. O'Kane . . . is cool and deliberate under fire. O'Kane is the fightingest naval officer I have ever seen and is worthy of the highest praise. I commend Lt. O'Kane for being an inspiration to the ship."

It was a new *Wahoo,* with an incredibly tightly knit crew, that made her way toward Palau. More than one man reflected on the long journey that had brought them together on this day. . . .

Wahoo's Penetration of Wewak Roadstead: January 24, 1943

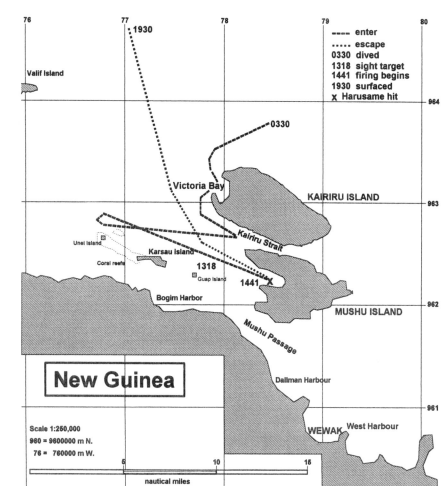

13

PART I

FIRST-YEAR FAILURE

1

Day of Infamy

AIR RAIDS ON PEARL HARBOR. THIS IS NOT DRILL.

—Rear Admiral Patrick Bellinger, Ford Island,
December 7, 1941, 0758 hours

DAWN. *Pompano* would be late for her scheduled 0800 arrival off the entrance buoys at Pearl Harbor. All night she and two sister "P-boats," *Plunger and Pollack,* had pounded through head seas, the black water broken only by the white foam of swells rushing across her deck to crash against the conning tower. Even the good surface performance of her dory bow, and the power of four diesel engines, were not enough to maintain schedule in this weather. All of *Pompano's* variable ballast, including the normally flooded safety tank, had been pumped dry in an effort to lighten the boat and improve her speed. This helped, but all three submarines were still 175 miles northeast of Diamond Head after their week-long transit from San Francisco.

Roger Paine, *Pompano's* twenty-three-year-old officer of the deck (OOD) standing the 0400 to 0800 watch, was particularly anxious to make landfall—and home. He had been gone for much of the year, more than two months on just this San Francisco refit. Paine's wife, "Bebe," was now well into the sixth month of her first pregnancy, and Roger was anxious to spend some normal time with her at their rented home overlooking Diamond Head.

New to submarines, the dark-haired Paine, the son of an admiral, called Fort Smith, Arkansas, home. Graduating from Annapolis in 1939, he was assigned to the battleship *Arizona,* based at Pearl Harbor. Ambitious, Paine did not envision a lifetime career of working himself up to command of a major gun turret. Still, his stay on the *Arizona* had led the slender,

17

handsome, quiet, and very personable ensign to deep friendships with fellow Academy graduates who had chosen to follow the step-by-step career paths of the peacetime navy.

But command came early in submarines, Paine's overriding goal. In January, as soon as the mandatory eighteen months of surface duty plus OOD qualifications had been met, he left for three months' sub school in Groton, Connecticut. In April he was assigned to *Pompano*, home-ported at Pearl.

On June 1, in the minimum elapsed time permitted for newly graduated Academy graduates, he and Bebe were married on Coronado Island, California, where Roger was attending sound school. There was no time for a honeymoon. In mid-June Roger headed for Pearl Harbor as the OOD of an oiler, there to join *Pompano*; Bebe followed on the civilian liner *Lurline*. They moved into quarters found by his executive officer (XO) and neighbor, Earle "Penrod" Schneider. It would be good to be home.

While *Pompano*'s OOD scanned what was to be the last peaceful dark horizon for nearly four years, the air crews of the Kido Butai, the Imperial Japanese Navy's carrier strike force, now 230 miles north of Pearl Harbor, were clambering into the cockpits of the first-wave aircraft.

For more than twenty minutes they sat in their planes on the pitching decks of the carriers. The same weather system that slowed the U.S. submarines was felt by the Japanese. The winds had eased to a speed perfect for takeoff, but the seas were still high. The great carriers' decks pitched fifteen degrees as the waves crashed over their bows, lifting spray over the flight decks. It was not optimum launch weather, but this was war.

0600 The six Japanese carriers swung into the wind. On *Akagi*, signal flags fluttered up, green signal lamps flashed, and the first Zero began its roll down the bucking deck. It dipped perilously low over the waves, seeming to touch them, caught itself, and clawed skyward. More and more fighters rushed to takeoff, followed by the torpedo planes, then the dive bombers. Within twenty minutes 183 aircraft had assembled; the formation headed due south. Pearl Harbor was only an hour and a half away.

0745 On *Pompano*, Paine's relief, Lieutenant (J.G.) Dave Connole, came to the bridge early, as was the custom. Roger dropped down the ladder into the conning tower to make a simple deck log entry: "4–8 Underway as before." It had been an uneventful watch.

Ninety miles to the south, in the Maui submarine sanctuary at Lahaina Roads, the brand-new Mare Island P-boat *Gudgeon* finished pulling in fifty-five fathoms of anchor chain and got under way with one engine. *Gudgeon*, commanded by Lieutenant Commander Elton "Jumping Joe" Grenfell, was off to practice visual recognition signals with navy patrol planes to avoid "friendly fire" incidents. Some of the crew grumbled at this unwanted Sunday-morning duty.

0749 Approaching Pearl Harbor, Commander Mitsuo Fuchida, leader of the first-wave air strike force, gave the signal to attack: "To . . . to . . . to . . . to." The dive bombers came in from the northwest, twenty-seven of them wheeling in a great arc to strike Pearl Harbor from the northeast. The forty torpedo bombers split near Ewa so that many came in from the southeast, the sun at their backs. Fifty high-level bombers flew northeast right up Pearl Harbor channel, past the only U.S. ship under way, the destroyer *Helm*. Fuchida knew that total surprise had been achieved. At 0753, from his holding position off Barber's Point, he radioed Rear Admiral Ryunosuke Kusaka, chief of staff to Admiral Chuichi Nagumo, on *Akagi:* "Tora . . . tora . . . tora." The attack would be successful.

0817 "AIR RAIDS ON PEARL HARBOR. . . ." The stunning Pearl Harbor attack bulletin, transmitted in the clear, reached the four submarines with jolting, immediate effect. Paine heard the unbelievable news in the conning tower. The radioman passed the message up the hatch to Connole, now the OOD.

Pompano's skipper, Lew Parks, gave Penrod Schneider, the XO, the order "Rig ship for dive and compensate. Get the water back in so we can dive." *Pompano's* prior efforts to improve her surface speed now made her a vulnerable target, unable to hide in the depths.

But reballasting the boat was not an instantaneous task. Many tons of water could not suddenly be poured into the forward trim, after trim, and safety tanks without making the boat dangerously unstable. Even fuel consumption since the last dive had to be accounted for to calculate neutral buoyancy.

Minutes later, on orders from *Plunger,* which carried the submarine division commander, all three boats began to zigzag on a base course still aimed at Oahu.

0850 The dive bombers of Lieutenant Commander Shigekazu Shimazaki's second wave began to rain new death on Pearl Harbor, selecting targets that had been missed during the previous hour. They were to keep at this task for the next forty minutes. One of the first targets was the battleship *Pennsylvania,* squatting in empty drydock no. 1, her decks so low that the high sides of the drydock obscured the view of attacking aircraft. A young boatswain, Bill Leibold, whose long-term goal was a career in submarines, was aboard the beleaguered battleship. Her five-inch guns were served so rapidly their barrels sagged with heat. At 0906 the first five-hundred-pound bomb found its mark.

Everywhere stunned men were fighting back. One was Fire Controlman Robert B. Logue. His submarine, *Dolphin*, had been rushed to sea when Hideki Tojo, "the razor," became Japan's prime minister on October 16. *Dolphin* had returned less than four days ago from a bone-wearying forty-seven-day patrol off Wake Island. Virtually all of the crew were on liberty, but Logue had the duty. He was jolted into action when he heard the topside anchor watch on the submarine *Tautog*, tied up next to *Dolphin*, shout down the forward torpedo hatch, "The war is on, no fooling!" The Japanese planes were roaring by Merry Point on their way in to strike Battleship Row.

Logue broke out a Browning .50-caliber machine gun from its locker and raced to the cigarette deck as ammunition was passed up from below. Already *Tautog's* crew had put rounds into one Japanese plane. In a few moments a fiery whip of bullets struck a second Japanese plane, downing it. Now, as Shimazaki's dive bombers plunged toward the harbor, every gun from Quarry Loch, across from the tethered submarines where Logue held sway, to the 1.1-inchers on the battleship *Maryland* returned fire. Three dive bombers were instantly destroyed.

0923 A lone plane appeared from the direction of Pearl Harbor, about a mile ahead of *Plunger*. Its strange appearance caused *Plunger* to flash the "quick dive" order to the other boats. Aboard *Pompano*, full reballasting was incomplete.

Parks and Connole dropped down the hatch to the conning tower, Parks pulling the lanyard to close it after him, pressing down hard two times on the diving alarm. "Dive! Dive!" Ready or not, *Pompano* was headed under.

The dive was nearly catastrophic. Improperly trimmed, *Pompano* submerged with a sailboat's heel to starboard. The list rapidly worsened as the waves closed over her. At twenty-five degrees heel, equipment began to clatter noisily against steel bulkheads; frantic counter trimming to port did not help. At thirty degrees items secured for heavy weather broke free; men fell or hung precariously to pipes, valves, table edges. At thirty-five degrees heel *Pompano* was on the verge of capsizing underwater—certain loss of the boat and everyone aboard—when Slade Cutter, the diving officer, was finally able to "catch" her.

0930 Inside *Plunger*, the P-boats division commander had not seen the aircraft; he was not really sure it was Japanese. U.S. aircraft insignia had a red ball in the center; it might have been a "friendly." He ordered *Plunger's* skipper to surface. Dave McClintock, *Plunger*'s OOD, leaped to the bridge and sighted a two-float monoplane five hundred yards to starboard. The plane roared in at two hundred feet, fired four machine-gun bursts at *Plunger*, then continued northward. *Plunger* stayed on the surface.

This plane was likely not a member of the Japanese air strike force. Those aircraft were reassembling off Kaena Point, the extreme western side of Oahu, for their return flight north to the waiting carriers. The three P-boats were not in their path. The attacker was probably a scout plane from either the cruisers *Chikuma* or *Tone*, whose planes had been ordered to make a reconnaissance of Lahaina Roads. On its return to the Kido Butai the scout had encountered the three diving submarines east of Oahu. It had been able to wait ten minutes for *Plunger*'s return to the surface, but its fleeting attack was probably an indication of low fuel.

Plunger's commanding officer desperately wanted to report the attack, for it indicated the probable direction of the Japanese fleet. Lew Parks on the now-surfaced *Pompano* chimed in. He raised the division commander on the voice radio and said, "You should tell Pearl Harbor we were attacked by enemy aircraft." But the senior officer, probably in a state of denial from the fury of war so suddenly thrust upon him, refused. He still believed it was a U.S. plane trying to signal the submarines with its gunfire.

0944 Surfaced after the near-disastrous dive, all four of *Pompano*'s engines went on line for a full-speed drive toward Pearl Harbor, where the attackers had just vanished. Now the notoriously troublesome HOR, the "whores," diesels began to betray her. In less than an hour the supercharger was out on engine three, the beginning of a series of problems that would vex *Pompano* throughout the day. Speed dropped by a third.

There were also growing doubts about the wisdom of trying to approach Pearl Harbor where every finger was resting against a ready trigger. For the next three hours a series of course changes had the effect of placing all three submarines in a holding pattern. A little before 1300 the decision was made to continue toward Pearl on a zigzag course. Group progress was impeded by continuing engine failures aboard *Pompano* and by the arrival of a new threat: U.S. Navy aircraft, their pilots crazed with anger. Two crash dives were needed to get out of the way of U.S. planes.

1400 Admiral Thomas Withers, commander of U.S. submarines in the Pacific, received a dispatch from the chief of naval operations in Washington. It was simple and blunt: "Execute unrestricted air and submarine warfare against Japan."

1700 With Oahu still fifty miles over the horizon, new orders from Admiral Withers at Pearl Harbor caused a redirection of the submarines to the Lahaina Roads sanctuary, and a rendezvous with *Gudgeon*. Running on the surface and, increasingly separated from her pelagic companions, *Pompano* drove to the northeastern corner of the island of Molokai. At 1950, with Paine again the OOD, *Pompano* turned south through Pailolo Channel, between Molokai and the island of Maui, for her rendezvous.

1705 Some eleven hundred miles to the west of Oahu, *Argonaut* was preparing to surface after a long day submerged off Midway. She had departed Pearl Harbor on November 28 to begin a simulated war patrol endurance test, and had been plagued with mechanical troubles from the outset. A serious problem occurred on December 2, with a saltwater leak into distiller no. 1, forcing the crew onto a strict water ration. Now the new dehumidifier plant had failed. *Argonaut* was an old, riveted-hull boat with no air conditioning. An increase in electrical problems that had already shorted out the trim pump armature was expected if the problem could not be fixed.

As soon as *Argonaut* surfaced, radio station KGMB in Honolulu was turned on in the chief petty officer's quarters to pick up some music. Instead the crew received the stunning news of the war, to which it had been oblivious during the all-day submergence. Fifteen minutes later, *Argonaut* received the message of the commander in chief, Pacific (CinCPac) announcing the start of hostilities. *Argonaut* began to cruise along an east to west line south of Midway to reduce her massive silhouette in the bright moonlight, charging her depleted batteries and her air banks.

The third officer aboard *Argonaut* was a complex, prickly man: Richard Hetherington O'Kane. New Hampshire–born, O'Kane was almost jingoistically patriotic. O'Kane was short, fiercely aggressive, even reckless, and uncommonly hardworking; his talkative manner and constant stream of ideas came across as overly garrulous and boastful. Contemporaries thought of him as potentially unstable.

Thirty years old, O'Kane had been aboard *Argonaut* for more than three years and loved his ship. His first reaction to the news was to propose to Captain Stephen Barchet that they immediately set sail for Japan to lay mines—for *Argonaut* was a minelayer, the only one in the navy. There were seventy-eight mines, as well as four hundred rounds of armor-piercing six-inch shells for her two guns, ready. All the necessary charts for empire waters were aboard. O'Kane felt they should "take advantage of their thirteen-hundred-mile head start, lay mines, bombard shore installations, and maybe sink an unwary merchantman or two."

Barchet was appalled. On an emotional level the captain was opposed to his assigned role of minelaying, feeling that it was a task better suited to airplanes. On a more practical level he doubted that *Argonaut* could actually cover the great distance to Japan, given the electrical problems already plaguing the boat while submerged. When O'Kane recommended that they run for Japan on the surface, the bold proposal did not endear him to the cautious Barchet.

2144 *Argonaut*'s lookouts sighted what appeared to be gunfire west of Midway. Nine minutes later, a radio message was received from Midway that reported enemy ships south of the reef, shelling the island with great effect. *Argonaut* was readied for an attack.

No more unlikely vessel could have been purposely selected to make the first U.S. submarine attack of the war. Launched in 1927, she was considered a technical failure. *Argonaut*'s submerged displacement was twice that of the newest fleet boats. She was nearly four hundred feet long, with a high profile made worse by large radio antenna A-frames on deck. With only two six-cylinder, low-horsepower "rock crusher" engines, she was extremely slow; the average *surface* speed from Pearl Harbor to take station off Midway had been 8.6 knots—even though engine rpm's had been advanced to increase the pace. She could not outrun a determined ferryboat, let alone a destroyer. There was no radar—nor could its electronics have withstood the high internal humidity of the boat. Her turning radius was abysmal; the *maximum* rudder movement was only fifteen degrees; it took four minutes to turn 180 degrees.

Argonaut dove slowly and clumsily, hindered by two large deck guns and lack of a negative tank for quick flooding. The large planing surfaces made it hard to drive her under when heading into the sea or with a following sea. Standard practice was to turn into the trough of the seas with the swells abeam. This made for faster but horribly sidewise dives. While patrolling off Midway she recorded dive times longer than 2½ minutes.

Depth control was difficult to maintain, and she had short periscopes, which increased the risk of broaching. *Argonaut* was poorly armed for submerged action, with only four torpedo tubes forward—period. There was no torpedo data computer; all attack calculations had to be made manually.

Yet she lumbered in, her crew stricken with anxiety, and quickly and correctly spotted just two enemy ships—not the much larger invasion force of cruisers and destroyers reported by the marines on Midway. The enemy vessels were identified as "good-sized destroyers or small cruisers." Actually they were the destroyers *Akebono* and *Ushio*—the worst possible foes of even the sleekest submarine.

At about three miles' distance, *Argonaut* dove for a sonar attack. O'Kane wanted to stay on the surface, but a submerged approach was standard U.S. submarine doctrine in 1941. In this case it was prudent, given that *Argonaut* was such a moonlit, visibly large surface target. The Japanese likely sighted, or perhaps heard, her. Loose peacetime gear, even a small boat used as a launch, was rattling around in the superstructure. One of the destroyers came over to investigate.

The destroyer moved down the port side of *Argonaut*, pinging. The dread sound ended the widely held belief that the Japanese had not yet mastered the technical intricacies of sonar.

From the propeller sounds overhead, *Argonaut's* officers concluded that the destroyer was small. The hunter moved across *Argonaut's* stern as the crew held their breaths, then up the starboard side, did a loop across the bow, and started down the starboard side again, pinging steadily. The search was methodical, but with *Argonaut* at a depth of 125 feet, the destroyer did not make positive contact; no depth charges were dropped. By midnight neither the destroyer's screws nor searching sonar could be heard.

So ended the first enemy ship encounter by a U.S. submarine in World War II. The Japanese moved on, their shore bombardment having thoroughly damaged Midway's installations without interference.

December 9, 1941

After rendezvousing with *Gudgeon* and the other two P-boats the night of December 7, *Pompano* killed time on the surface in Lahaina Roads. At 0546 on the eighth, as planned, Paine ordered her under—but not before being spotted by army air corps planes.

The contact report for "enemy" submarines was relayed to the headquarters of Admiral Husband E. Kimmel commander in chief of the Pacific Fleet (CinCPac), at Pearl Harbor. Kimmel, certainly exhausted after the disaster of the preceding day, forgot the sanctuary nature of Lahaina Roads; he immediately ordered the submarines bombed. Fortunately Withers heard about, and blocked, Kimmel's order.

Pompano spent all day of the eighth moving submerged along a north to south line before surfacing at 1822 that evening; Paine took the con to begin the gradual move toward Pearl Harbor. For the rest of the night the four-submarine pod milled about on the surface, edging ever westward in Kalohi Channel, until a rendezvous with an escorting destroyer, *McFarland*, could be arranged. This was not a casual precaution; the submarine *Thresher*, fifty miles to the northwest of Oahu, had been bombed repeatedly on the eighth as she tried to make port, contributing to the death of one of her crew.

Now, on the morning of the ninth, the four submarines began their final move to Pearl Harbor, in column. At 0939 *Pompano* entered the channel and its crew began to see the true carnage of the seventh.

First to appear was the battleship *Nevada*, now beached on Waipo Peninsula. She had backed off her grounding at Hospital Point during a valiant attempt to make the open sea while under fierce bombardment. As *Pompano* bore to starboard to pass east of Ford Island, the ruins of the destroyer *Shaw* and her new floating drydock came into view. Bodies bobbed in the water, possibly blown from *Shaw* when her magazines erupted. Then the damaged battleship *Pennsylvania*, caught in her drydock along with two destroyers; *Cassin* was not completely sunk only because she had rolled over on top of *Downes*.

Before reaching ten-ten dock (named for its 1,010 foot length), the battleship *California* was seen resting on the bottom, her main deck underwater. Rounding the dock for the turn into Southeast Loch and the submarine base, new horrors appeared. Paine's sentimental favorite, the battleship *Oklahoma*, on which he had taken one of his midshipman's cruises, had capsized. The visual image was stunning. *Oklahoma*'s upturned bottom was covered with workers desperately trying to cut through to reach four hundred men still trapped in the interior. Beside her the *Maryland* was a shambles.

Next in Battleship Row was the battleship *West Virginia*, sunk in the mud, her decks awash. Just behind *West Virginia* was Paine's prior ship, *Arizona*, gone along with eleven hundred of her crew—a deep personal tragedy for the young ensign.

Everywhere, oil-soaked bodies were being fished from the debris floating in the harbor and gathered for mass burial; some of *Pompano*'s young deck crew were sickened to the point of vomiting. Anger and dismay welled up in all of them at the human loss, the destructive waste, the lack of preparedness that had led to this disaster.

At 1020, *Pompano* nosed into berth S-9. Paine was on the forecastle to supervise the line handling. *Pompano*'s deck crew were dazed, as were the base personnel. A former *Pompano* crew member who had been left ashore two months earlier for disciplinary problems grabbed the mooring line. *Pompano* was finally home.

2

A Stumbling Start

Every beginning is hard.

—German proverb

Argonaut continued on station at Midway following her nervous, tentative introduction to war. On December 8 she was attacked by U.S. Marine aircraft while on the surface charging batteries. Usually a slow diver, the crew got her under in fifty-two seconds—a record. Additional sound contacts were reported, but the Japanese were not sighted again. The sound contacts may have been targets or simply gregarious sealife; Captain Barchet was not about to verify it by exposing the periscope. This lack of aggressiveness led to a bitter quarrel between Barchet and his executive officer. O'Kane, the third officer, was as ready for combat as ever. As late as Christmas Eve he still hoped for the order to proceed to empire waters.

Nearing forty, Barchet was a product of the peacetime navy. He may have been a superb technician, but he was not a warrior. Like many of his contemporaries, Barchet's priority was to concentrate on ship handling and avoid mistakes, not to do battle. He was interested in methods and procedures to be developed for long war patrols, his current mission. The war he fought was an engineer's war—one with *Argonaut* herself.

The winds remained brisk at twenty-five knots, kicking up broad seas. *Argonaut* dove especially poorly under these conditions. Even though pinging and screw noises were heard on December 11, *Argonaut*'s war patrol report for that day would focus on the foul smell of the boat and successful repairs to the dehumidifier—technician's concerns.

As the days ground on, the patrol report was filled with continuous complaints about poor-quality binoculars (true), compressor burnouts, transmitter motor generator breakdowns, and the innovative techniques employed to restore service: placing parts in the oven or using heat lamps to dry them out, and rewinding armatures.

Argonaut was now one monstrous list of deficiencies. All-day submergence and attendant high humidity caused electrical grounds throughout the boat. Small fires were routine. Much of her major equipment became inoperative. With a boat that was quick to broach at periscope depth, and underpowered for surface running, the fear of detection dominated Barchet's thinking. He deeply resented Pearl Harbor's requirement to break radio silence, fearing it would lead the enemy to him. He was not pleased when President Roosevelt reported to the nation that *Argonaut* was on station at Midway, defending them. This was worse than breaking radio silence!

Through it all O'Kane swallowed his fighting instincts and focused on the boat's many technical problems. He thought of Ernestine, his childhood friend and wife of five years, and their children, and worried about their safety in Honolulu.

Back at Pearl Harbor, feverish activity was under way to get *Gudgeon* and the newly arrived P-boats ready for patrol. *Gudgeon,* still on her shakedown cruise, was quickly loaded with torpedoes, ammunition, food, and fuel. She departed for the Bungo Suido, the southern entrance to Japan's Inland Sea, at 0900 on December 11, fewer than forty-eight hours after arrival at the sub base mooring, and in the midst of yet another false air raid alarm. *Plunger* departed on the twelfth for the Kii Suido, the northern entrance to the Inland Sea, *Pollack* on the thirteenth for the waters off Tokyo Bay.

Pompano's departure was delayed by temporary repairs to her hated HOR engines. There was one bright moment for Roger Paine in the incessant, round-the-clock effort to get *Pompano* ready. He was able to leave the boat on the evening of December 15 for a meal at home with Bebe.

At 0900 on the eighteenth *Pompano* backed away from her mooring en route to the Marshalls by way of Wake Island. Key personnel changes made Slade Cutter the new XO; Penrod Schneider was detached to become XO of the new-construction boat *Trigger,* which would be commissioned at Mare Island six weeks later. Paine was the torpedo and gunnery officer, and he manned the sound gear, located in the forward torpedo room on *Pompano.* Dave Connole manned the TDC.

The TDC had been developed secretly, starting in 1932, as a means of exploiting a World War I capability of U.S. torpedoes. These early "fish" were capable of having their internal gyrocompasses set to turn as much as ninety degrees after firing. It was thus theoretically possible for a submarine running parallel to the target to fire a broadside salvo. Practically speaking, this was impossible because the gyro settings had to be worked out manually, and could never be recalculated quickly enough if the target changed course. Further, there was no way to automatically, instantaneously reset the gyros once the torpedoes were loaded in the tubes.

Struggling to solve these problems, the Bureau of Ordnance conceived of an all-mechanical fire control computer—really multiple special-purpose, but interconnected computers—that could keep track of the submarine's course and speed, project the future target position, and automatically adjust the torpedo gyros while in the tubes through a mechanical "umbilical cord." With the TDC it was not necessary for the submarine to reach a position on the firing track; superior torpedo speed and directional control permitted successful snap attacks against poorly positioned, high-speed targets.

A small Brooklyn company, ARMA, designed and built the devices, geared wonders that would have been the envy of Charles Babbage. The first unwieldy unit was delivered to the fleet in the spring of 1938, but *Pompano* had been built with the latest, very much smaller unit—the Mk3—in the conning tower.

The TDC was data-hungry. The course and speed of "own ship" was automatic, of course. Some key torpedo characteristics could be manually entered before the attack: speed (which varied by torpedo type), and running depth. But even here there were variations; steam torpedoes were forced to operate at very much slower speeds if the range were long, and then were vulnerable to "creep angle" errors as the earth rotated during the long run to the target. The TDC made all this figuring possible, including calculating the turning radius of the torpedo as it exited the tubes and swung to its selected gyro angle.

The TDC operator had to begin with very imprecise initial target data, perhaps just the stick of a mast on the horizon, and make estimates of range, course, and speed. These estimates were refined based upon intermittent observations from the attack officer, supplemented by passive sonar returns, which fed the sound bearing converter. A single-ping active sonar beam might be used to confirm range. Once the operator had the "correct solution" light he passed the results to the angle solver, which moved the torpedo gyros in the tubes. As the submarine or target continued to change course and speed, the torpedoes were kept aimed at the target.

After *Pompano* cleared the Pearl Harbor channel and reef, Cutter ordered, "Secure the maneuvering watch. Station the sea detail. On deck first section."

Paine was standing by the anchor and lead line with the forecastle crew. Taking a last look at Oahu, he went below as the lookouts climbed to their perches on the periscope shears. *Pompano* began to run for the open sea on course 261 degrees true.

Almost immediately, irritating engine problems began to occur. *Pompano* stayed on the surface all day, zigzagging, as work on these new troubles progressed.

At 1715 the first dive was ordered—necessary for the diving officer to "catch a trim," to check and adjust *Pompano's* weight and balance so she could submerge quickly and safely in an emergency. Paine took a last look around the submarine, a small island over which waves broke, alone in the world and dwarfed by the sky and the vast expanse of the Pacific. Then came the order "Lookouts below" followed by "Dive! Dive!" *Pompano* began to slide down into the cold and unfriendly ocean depths.

The dive revealed yet another problem. The after battery hatch was leaking badly around an area that had previously been patched. Surface again; temporary repairs; a new dive; problem not fixed; surface again. Finally, at 1944, after 2½ hours of work, the repair seemed good enough, but now main engine no. 3 was out of commission with a defective exhaust supercharger valve. *Pompano* stayed on the surface all night as this new plague was fought.

The following morning brought a real enemy: U.S. Navy air patrols. *Pompano's* crew knew that in a submarine they were on their own, every man's hand turned against them. The navy pilots were relentless, and *Pompano* was forced to dive five times during the day to escape their unwanted attention.

Just before the third dive, main engine no. 4 had to be stopped because of excessive noise. Worse, the engine exhaust valves were leaking, and power to close them had been lost. To top it off, the after battery hatch leak had returned. Pompano again ran on the surface all night, repairing problems.

At 0705 hours on the twentieth, four hundred miles from Oahu, a U.S. plane returned—this time on a bombing and depth-charge run—and scored a near-miss. As soon as possible *Pompano* was on the surface again, running toward Wake, hoping to shake the "friendly" pursuer. But the antisubmarine patrol aircraft, near the limit of its effective range, radioed the carrier *Enterprise* about its contact.

At 1410 *Pompano* dove again as three *Enterprise*-based dive bombers attacked. Passing a hundred feet, *Pompano* was shaken by very close, well-placed explosions. Lightbulbs broke, circuit breakers tripped, and, not yet known to *Pompano's* crew, fuel tank seams were strained. Putting distance between herself and Oahu's land-based aircraft clearly was not going to be a total solution. On the twenty-first, in the face of continuous air attacks by U.S. carrier forces, *Pompano* switched to submerged running by day and surfaced only by night, greatly slowing her progress to the patrol area.

Each night, all night, the battle with the HOR engines continued: flooding of engines, grinding exhaust valves, broken piston rings, stuffing box leaks, and piston rod seizures. And now a new problem: the fuel tank seams strained by the navy air attacks began to leak. By the Christmas Eve dive seventy-seven hundred gallons of fuel oil had oozed out, its rainbow trail visible from the periscope and, of course, from the air. Wake Island had fallen on the twenty-third; it was too late for *Pompano* to make any contribution to its defense.

The fuel tank leaks worsened. All forward tanks were seeping fuel, leaving prominent slicks. Diesel oil even drained into the negative tank; the fumes caused the boat to reek.

On New Year's Day *Pompano* finally arrived off Wake, nine days after the marines had surrendered. Parks nosed *Pompano* nearly ashore; thoughts of rescuing marine stragglers went through his mind. But while he could see Japanese troops manning the newly captured gun emplacements, there were no targets for the submarine. A south-southeast course was set for the Marshalls and the Ratak chain where, headquarters feared, the Japanese were assembling a new invasion force.

At 0514 on the twelfth *Pompano* submerged five miles southeast of Wotje and proceeded toward Schischmarev Strait. Eleven men were crammed into the conning tower, so crowded that as Parks walked the scope around he had to pull in his butt at each station. Connole stood by the TDC, Slade Cutter beside him with the backup "is-was," a sort of circular slide rule for manually computing angles, slung around his neck on a lanyard.

At 0554 Parks sighted a patrol ship three miles away, ignored it, and kept working up the strait. At 1058 a large transport—he thought it was the sixteen-thousand-ton transport *Yawata Maru*—was sighted standing out of the channel on a southerly course, at slow speed. This was it!

Parks maneuvered *Pompano* into firing position, noting that the big target was picking up speed. At 1123 he commenced firing with a four-torpedo spread, the first torpedo aimed a quarter length ahead of the target, the next three at successive quarter-length intervals to account for the accelerating target speed, now thought to be fifteen knots.

Parks left the scope up to watch the first hit, which seemed disappointingly small. As *Pompano* went deep, another hit was heard. Fifteen minutes later Parks took another look and saw the target he believed to be damaged. It was lying to, about three miles away, with a heavy sea on the port beam, and settling. The forward tubes were reloaded for a second attack. During the reload loud noises were heard from the target, which Paine identified as "breaking-up noises": collapsing compartments, rushing water, exploding boilers. When *Pompano* returned to periscope depth, no target was in sight. The crew was exultant. A major ship sunk on their first attempt, without so much as a single Japanese counterattack! Parks privately harbored dark thoughts about the torpedoes.

Since other masts had been seen in Wotje Harbor, *Pompano* waited—for days—to see what new target might present itself. On the seventeenth, Parks saw a patrol craft, which, perhaps in boredom, he decided to attack. He fired two torpedoes, which blew up shortly after leaving the tubes, the first possibly countermining the second. The shock was terrible and frightening—and the explosions were seen by the patrol boat, which now came racing directly for *Pompano*.

Parks was cool under fire. He decided on a "down the throat" shot, zero gyro angle on the torpedoes, at close range: a thousand yards. Submarine theory taught that the oncoming attacker would see the wakes and turn, thus catching a torpedo in the side. If it did not turn, the magnetic influence exploder would detonate as the target passed. This patrol craft did not turn; the torpedoes did not explode. The Japanese captain deftly "split the wakes" and commenced to pound *Pompano* with depth charges.

The hushed and expectant crew could hear the splash of falling depth charges as they struck the surface of the water. After several seconds, the time for the charge to sink toward them, came the detonation click—two small pings, almost as if nuts had been dropped on the hull—then BLAM! Water rushed violently around the hull and superstructure with a physical force that can only be understood by those who have experienced it.

Pompano was rigged for depth charge: all internal sea and hull valves closed, external vents opened, all machinery save the electrical propulsion motors stopped. There was no refrigeration, air conditioning, air recirculation. All fans, even battery blowers, were stopped. The hydraulic plant was secured; steering and operation of both bow and stern planes was done by hand—that is, by brute strength. All unnecessary lights were extinguished, and all personnel were required to remain silently in place. Those not on watch went to their bunks and turned in.

For thirty minutes the patrol craft worked over *Pompano*. Six separate attacks were made with careful husbanding of depth charges, sometimes only one, never more than three at a time. One of the attacks was truly damaging. The starboard propeller shaft was bent and developed a shrill, howling noise. The noise, coupled with the continuous oil trail on the surface, promised big trouble. But at 1550 the attack was broken off—to the relief of everyone.

Pompano stayed on station for another week, then, running low on fuel and down to one main engine operating with cannibalized parts, began the long trip home—diving for aircraft every day.

Throughout December and much of January, *Argonaut* held station off Midway. On January 22 she arrived off Pearl Harbor to greet her escort, the destroyer *Litchfield*, at 0600. Her patrol had been fifty-six days in length, then a new endurance record, with forty-seven days submerged. *Argonaut's* only battles had been with equipment failures, many caused by the intolerable humidity. Mildew was everywhere inside the boat, and many crew mattresses simply had to be thrown away.

Argonaut docked at West Loch and unloaded her mines; she was going to return empty to the U.S. for a complete modernization. O'Kane's work was done at 1700 hours, and he was released to find his family. Ernestine and the children were fine, living with their former landlady in Kahala, near Diamond Head, and waiting for transport to the mainland.

The weary old *Dolphin*, Bob Logue aboard, departed for the Marshalls on Christmas Eve. This one-of-a-kind, reduced-tonnage V-boat (a category of boats first proposed in 1912 and last built in 1931) was in no condition to make a patrol. She was barely seaworthy. Another submarine captain saw her departure and wrote, "She should never have been sent on patrol without an overhaul, which she had not had in six months. She had too many deficiencies."

Dolphin began to break down at sea—and so did her captain, Gordon "Dizzy" Rainer. The XO took command and fought seventeen major mechanical failures and countless minor ones. *Dolphin* did learn that the major Japanese forces were concentrated at Kwajalein, a significant intelligence finding that was quickly passed on to Admiral William F. Halsey, then commander of the carrier task force built around *Enterprise*. *Enterprise* began punishing air raids on February 1.

On January 24 the XO radioed Pearl Harbor requesting permission to return in the face of overwhelming mechanical and command problems, which Withers granted.

On January 28 *Dolphin* staggered into Pearl and was immediately sent to an overhaul area for work on her engines.

In the days that followed, *Gudgeon* and the other two P-boats also returned. The crews were excited; all had seen action and claimed multiple sinkings. Grenfell, aboard *Gudgeon*, only claimed damage to a surfaced Japanese submarine he had ambushed, courtesy of Jasper Holmes and the Pearl Harbor codebreakers. Like Parks in *Pompano*, he neither saw nor heard anything other than the dullest of explosions and believed the torpedoes had not detonated. This could be true, but there were no propeller noises after the attack. The codebreakers knew that *I-173* had indeed sunk, perhaps by being rammed with a dud, the first warship ever downed by a U.S. submarine.

A review of these first patrols was made by the squadron and division commanders as well as by Admiral Withers. The claimed sinkings were credited; this was the good news. For the rest of the war Paine was proud to have been a part of the destruction of the *Yawata Maru*. After the war the Joint Army-Navy Assessment Committee (JANAC) found no evidence that any ship had really gone under. Perhaps she, too, had only been damaged by duds or prematures and made her way back to Wotje Harbor for repairs.

Now the bad news began. The soft-spoken, usually kindly Withers was unsatisfied with his captains. All prewar doctrine and training were trashed, and criticisms levied for those who followed them. He was even angered that the subs going to Japan honored his orders and made their transit at the most economical speed, and thus were slow to arrive on station.

Barchet was criticized for a sonar approach without exposing the periscope. Further, Withers felt as O'Kane did. Withers wanted *Argonaut* to act like a nimble German U-boat and attack on the surface by night. The fault for the superstructure noise was laid at Barchet's door: "The loose gear should have been removed at clear ship." Even the length and tone of Barchet's report was criticized. The division commander unsuccessfully attempted to defend Barchet, who faded into history.

Rainer, *Dolphin*'s sick captain, was reprimanded and relieved of command. Withers refused to accept that *Dolphin*'s "matériel casualties . . . [were] a true reflection of the condition of the ship." Rainer was returned to the United States, a mental institution, and medical retirement in 1943.

Parks was faulted for his recommendation that *Pompano*'s HOR engines should be replaced as unsuitable for wartime operations. Withers's endorsement snipped that "despite remarks of the CO and the division commander, the performance of the HOR engines is vastly improved over what it was a year ago."

This was preposterous. The HOR engines were totally unreliable in any submarine unlucky enough to have them. HOR's chief engineer, noted by the navy as a "young, capable, and sincere individual," worked so desperately hard to fix the problems that he suffered a fatal stroke. The HOR problems were simply uncorrectable. Every submarine using HORs had to be reengined at great cost, especially in reduction of boats available to the fleet.

But the really bad news was not yet understood. Every captain and crew who had fired torpedoes during December and January had misgivings about their performance. In truth, some problems should have been expected. The number of torpedoes fired in just the three weeks of December 1941 far exceeded the total number of torpedoes fired in the entire previous history of the U.S. Navy. Hidden problems were bound to exist.

But Withers quickly dismissed the concerns. His endorsement to *Pompano's* patrol report said that "corrective measures have been taken to avoid future premature explosions." This was nonsense. No actions were taken, nor did Withers think it necessary. He had been at Newport when the Mark VI exploder was developed and believed in it without question. Freeland Daubin, the commander of Squadron 4, wrote that "If the torpedoes were unreliable, *Pompano* had plenty of time to find it out before the torpedoes were fired."

The stage was now set for eighteen months of tragic refusals by naval ordnance to face an authentic problem.

TABLE 1

U.S. Submarines versus Merchant Shipping, December 1941 to January 1942

	December	January	Total
Offensive patrol days	281	322	603
Merchant ships attacked	31	33	64
Torpedoes expended	66	78	144
Merchant sinkings claimed	17	11	28
Merchant sinkings (JANAC)	7	3	10
Tonnage sunk (JANAC)	28,233	13,993	42,226

3

Warriors Gather

... the stern joy which warriors feel ...

—Sir Walter Scott, "Lady of the Lake"

On February 7, 1942, new orders came for Dick O'Kane aboard *Argonaut*. Upon arrival at Mare Island O'Kane would become the executive officer of the new-construction boat *Wahoo*. *Argonaut* departed Pearl Harbor for San Francisco the following morning and spent the next twelve days struggling toward home, diving frequently to avoid friendly aircraft. On the twentieth she picked up an escort, the old four-stack destroyer *King*, and pounded along at good speed to the California coast. At 1005 on February 22, 1942, *Argonaut* passed under the Golden Gate Bridge and headed for Mare Island. On the way in she passed the newly launched *Wahoo*. O'Kane, the first officer of the new crew to see her, could hardly contain his excitement about serving aboard this "dandy-looking sub."

New orders also reached Roger Paine aboard *Pompano* in the Pearl Harbor repair area. The new lieutenant (junior grade) was to become the gunnery and torpedo officer aboard *Wahoo*. His departure date for Mare Island was March 4. There was one complication: Bebe's "birthing" date was March 1. Nature, with its own schedule, might easily cause Paine to miss this major milestone in their lives. On February 26 Roger and Bebe began marching up and down Wilhelmina Rise. The effort was successful. At 0500 on February 27, Roger Paine III was born at Kapiolani Hospital.

Traveling by navy transport, the new father was the first officer to reach *Wahoo*; O'Kane had not yet arrived. He had diverted to find a home for Ernestine and the children, who were being evacuated from Hawaii by ship. One was found near Hamilton Field, twenty miles from Mare Island. Paine was soon joined by *Wahoo's* new third officer, Lieutenant George Grider, up from San Diego, where he had been serving aboard an old S-boat.

Grider was born in Memphis and possessed an unforgettable expressive face resembling Robin Williams in his *Mork and Mindy* days. Grider was an energetic extrovert, forever sticking his nose into anything new. As a battleship catapult officer he soon talked his way into taking rides in scout aircraft; as a destroyer officer he was hitching rides on submarines. He took private flying lessons, became an accomplished amateur photographer, and loved to party.

Grider had qualified for an appointment to Annapolis as the son of an officer killed in World War I. No scholar, he had to go to prep school to pass the entrance examination. But he graduated in 1936 nearly in the top quarter of his class and immediately celebrated with a secret, against-regulations, marriage to his sweetheart, Ann. Grider volunteered for submarine school and graduated at the close of 1939. This twenty-nine-year-old, lean, sandy-haired, "sweet-talking Southerner" seemed lighthearted, even improvident, but he was an excellent engineering officer and a skilled sonarman.

Grider, as was his way, immediately began talking up the new crew of *Wahoo's* sister ship *Whale*, being built alongside. He learned that some of the officers had made an S-boat patrol from the Aleutians that, in Grider's mind qualified them as "gods . . . , they had encountered the enemy." Paine, forever modest, never told Grider that he had not only gone on a war patrol but also had made two attacks. Fifteen years later Grider was still none the wiser.

Now the senior officers arrived, O'Kane first. He expected to be serving under Duncan MacMillan, who had been the XO of *Argonaut* in 1939 and 1940 and whom O'Kane liked. O'Kane immediately busied himself with shipbuilding tasks, including the creation of a homemade target-bearing transmitter (TBT), which would permit *Wahoo* to make night surface attacks. He had taken Withers' criticisms of *Argonaut's* first patrol to heart.

But MacMillan was instead diverted to Fairbanks-Morse to supervise the building of new diesel engines. The new captain was Lieutenant Commander Marvin "Pinky" Kennedy, a tall, thin man with unusually fair skin, an excellent reputation in fire control and tactics, and a history of running taut ships. He had last been on staff duty, a nose-wrinkling recommendation for an action-oriented man such as O'Kane. Prior to that, however, Kennedy had been the XO of *Narwhal*, one of two giant 1920s cruiser submarines built a year after *Argonaut*.

This shared experience of having served on similar ships might have been the foundation of a personal bond between Kennedy and his new exec, but their personalities didn't click. O'Kane found Kennedy "gentlemanly, but more formal than my previous captains." It was also clear to everyone, though Kennedy was too courteous to speak of it, that the new captain did not have complete confidence in his energetic but sometimes erratic XO.

Wahoo was a modern wonder to her new officers. She far surpassed any submarine in which they had served; she was faster, and had the great range required by the vast reaches of the Pacific. In attack or flight situations she could make nearly twenty-one knots on the surface. At ten knots she could travel four thousand miles from Pearl Harbor to Tokyo, patrol three thousand miles in empire waters, and return. This was accomplished using four reliable Fairbanks-Morse engines, much to Paine's relief, who was heartily sick of the HORs.

With six tubes forward and four aft plus fourteen reloads, she was far more heavily armed—given reliable torpedoes—than the German U-boat workhorse, the type VII-C. Her design depth had been improved to a bit more than three hundred feet, one of the few parameters in which she lagged behind the Germans (periscope optics was another). *Wahoo* had the latest TDC and a brand-new innovation to cram into the already tight conning tower: search radar.

In addition, living conditions—habitability, in naval parlance—was greatly improved. There was air conditioning, of course, but also Kleinschmidt stills to produce fresh water for crew showers, and washing machines for their clothes.

Crew training commenced the moment the first small group of men arrived. Now construction supervision was constant. The officers were determined to know every inch of their boat and where every valve, line, and wiring conduit was located. Modifications to *Wahoo* beyond the Gato design, revised as a result of war patrol reports, became fixations with the officers; they were made on the spot.

From the war's first month Admiral Withers had required that war patrol reports be disseminated widely: to other submarine divisions and squadrons—thus to all boats—but also to support arms such as the naval shipyards and the Bureau of Ordnance. This was an excellent, highly useful way to broadcast the very latest war experience. But this cautious man was in trouble. He had abandoned his prior emphasis on submerged sonar attacks and now favored the more aggressive night surface strikes that the Germans were exploiting only too well. Unfortunately, to date he had seen few positive results from this new stance.

Withers' Pearl Harbor boats had been able to mount only seventeen war patrols during the first three months of 1942. These patrols accounted for just fifteen Japanese ships sunk, though Withers believed it was twenty-two. Meanwhile, the Germans had begun an all too comparable offensive, code-named Paukenschlag (Drumbeat), against shipping along the eastern coast of the United States.

On December 16, 1941—two days before *Pompano* began her first patrol—the first U-boat had departed Lorient, France, for the arduous transatlantic crossing to Nantucket. More soon followed. Husbanding fuel in the relatively low-endurance U-boats, the first attack was made on January 12, 1942, the same day *Pompano* attacked *Yawata*. The result was a publicly visible slaughter. With only a handful of U-boats on station, twenty-five Allied ships were sunk in the first two weeks of the offensive.

As more U-boats assembled at the undefended convoy concentration points, the fearful sinking rate increased. The relatively few German submarines departing France between mid-December and the end of March sank 244 Allied ships in American waters. Admiral Doenitz was able to report to the German people that "our U-boats are operating close inshore along the coast of the United States . . . so that bathers and sometimes entire coastal cities are witnesses to the drama of war, whose visual climaxes are constituted by the red glorioles of blazing tankers."

Withers did not seem to have an overall strategy. There was no concentration of U.S. boats against Japanese shipping choke points. Too many submarines were diverted to unproductive patrols in barren areas such as the Marshalls, even though the codebreakers knew that the Japanese had returned to empire waters. Given the fiasco of Pearl Harbor, Withers did not trust their advice and, in general, did not seem to know how to exploit intelligence information.

Short of the drop-by visit of *Pompano*, Withers did not really go to the defense of Wake Island. He easily could have assembled the first boats there to engage the large Japanese fleet concentration. As the marines continued to resist, a buildup of Japanese ships, including two carriers, arrived to break the U.S. hold on the island. The codebreakers correctly identified this target opportunity. Withers dispersed his boats to other, unproductive areas instead. He was proud that no Pearl Harbor–based boat had been lost to date, a grim signal that his submarines—and some of their skippers—were not going "in harm's way."

But the worst headache continued to be torpedoes. Withers was obsessed with an authentic problem. There were not enough torpedoes to go around; Pearl Harbor had only 101 in reserve. Production was not likely to improve before July. Thus he favored single-round "rifle" shots with no wasteful "spreads." He wanted to exploit the new, secret Mark VI magnetic exploder.

Almost to a man, the submarine captains had begun to distrust their torpedoes. They urged Withers to order deactivation of the magnetic exploder. Withers was adamantly opposed. Contact exploders would require two to three torpedoes per target, whereas the magnetic exploder would require only a single fish below the keel.

In spite of Withers' opposition, some skippers began secretly to deactivate the exploders once on patrol. *Tuna*'s captain, John DeTar—who had many quirks, some of which were to reappear in Pinky Kennedy—openly gave up on the magnetic exploder after getting no hits on a freighter. In a subsequent attack he sank a good-sized ship. Withers was outraged at the brazen defiance of his orders; the other skippers thought DeTar naive or foolish to confront the admiral in the now public war patrol reports.

The magnetic-exploder argument became deeply personal when, in March 1942, George Crawford took command of Submarine Division 43. Crawford had just returned from Charles Lockwood's naval attaché staff in London. Lockwood and Crawford had known since early September that both the Germans and the British had abandoned their own magnetic exploders. They offered the Mark VI to the British, but were turned down with an exquisite written riposte: "The extreme ingenuity of this instrument rather blinds one to its utter uselessness."

Now Crawford ordered the submarine commanders in his division to deactivate the Mark VI. Withers lost control, ordered the exploders reactivated, and threatened to remove him. Since Withers had served as the Newport Torpedo Station commander when the magnetic exploder was developed, all his objectivity was lost. The Mark VI just had to be good, tested or not.

Complicating the torpedo problem was the fact that many of the skippers began reporting their belief that the torpedoes were running too deep. Withers rejected these assertions even when he knew better. *Tambor* left Pearl Harbor in March for a fifty-eight-day patrol. Upon returning in April, her captain blamed much of his trouble on the torpedoes and recommended that they be set to run shallower. By then Withers had been informed by Rear Admiral William Blandy, chief of the Bureau of Ordnance, that Newport tests confirmed that the torpedoes were running at least four feet too deep. However, the squadron commander rejected *Tambor*'s recommendation and insisted that Withers' instructions be followed. Withers refused to conduct confirming tests.

In April Charles Lockwood was promoted to rear admiral and summoned from London to take over the Asiatic Fleet submarines centered in Perth,

Australia. He made stops on the way. In Washington he called on Admiral Ernest J. King, the chief of naval operations, and opened a back channel of communications with an old friend, Admiral Richard Edwards, now King's right-hand man for submarines. At Pearl Harbor Lockwood met with Admiral Nimitz, whom he had known since earlier days in primitive submarines.

Upon reaching Australia Lockwood began a whirlwind tour of the scattered submarine bases. A hands-on leader, he boarded every submarine returning from patrol, interviewed their captains, and, more importantly, believed them. He suspected that the torpedoes were running far too deep, and wrote of his beliefs to the Bureau of Ordnance.

Admiral Nimitz relieved Withers on May 14 in what was described as "a routine command change." Others saw it differently. Some thought the final straw was the failure of Pearl Harbor submarines to intercept the damaged Japanese carrier *Shokaku* following the Battle of the Coral Sea. The "wounded bear" had been reported and tracked—even seen—by nine Pearl Harbor submarines since May 7, but none got in a shot. Characteristically, the self-centered O'Kane believed Withers was fired for embracing, and losing, O'Kane's argument to use *Argonaut* as a minelayer.

On May 14 Nimitz was convinced by the Hypo codebreakers that the Japanese were planning to invade Midway. He ordered a state of "Fleet Opposed Invasion," replacing Withers with Admiral Robert English, another member of Newport's "gun club." Pete Galantin later wrote that English, who had graduated in the bottom 15 percent of his Naval Academy class, "was not an inspiring, imaginative, or bold . . . leader and did not have the confidence or high regard of his skippers." English blamed torpedo failures on officers and crews. He, like Withers, insisted that Pearl Harbor boats rely on the magnetic exploder.

English and his submarines were quickly tested in combat. At 0904 on June 3 the crew of a navy Catalina flying boat spotted the first elements of the Japanese fleet 470 miles northwest of Midway. English had managed to assemble twenty-five submarines; eleven were deployed in the general area of the aircraft contact report, arranged in a fan formation. But after receiving position information from continuous aerial reconnaissance, he was slow to order them into the precise positions of the oncoming Japanese.

Because of this delay, only two boats positively saw elements of the Japanese fleet on June 4. The captain of the new boat, *Grouper*, failed to press home attacks on possibly damaged carriers. He did not report his contact but remained at deep submergence, firing two useless torpedoes on sound bearings. He was later described in the endorsements to the patrol report as "evasive, not aggressive" and was relieved of command.

The second boat was the old *Nautilus,* built in 1927 and best suited for transport duty. But its captain, William Brockman, had courage to spare. He spotted the Japanese ships, and quickly they spotted him. After seven hours, in spite of fierce aircraft strafing runs and destroyer depth charge attacks, Brockman got *Nautilus* into attack position on the damaged carrier *Kaga.* He fired four torpedoes—all the old boat carried forward. One torpedo failed to leave the tube, the second passed ahead of *Kaga,* the third astern.

But the fourth struck the carrier amidships—and was a dud. The warhead snapped off and sank. The buoyant body of the torpedo bobbed on the surface and was used as a life raft by Lieutenant Commander Yoshio Kunisada, *Kaga's* assistant damage control officer.

On June 5, based on a poor contact report from *Tambor,* English incorrectly rerouted every other submarine to the wrong location. The Pearl Harbor submarines had played no useful role at all in the great victory at Midway. English and his captains were at loggerheads, each blaming the other for the disappointing results.

In Australia, the Bureau of Ordnance gave Lockwood a "stiff reply that our submariners [were blaming the torpedoes] as an alibi for poor marksmanship." This was too much for Lockwood. On June 20 he ran his own tests using nets strung in a remote area outside Fremantle harbor. The torpedoes were actually running *eleven* feet too deep. When the Bureau of Ordnance was told of the findings, they scorned Lockwood's unscientific approach. Lockwood ordered the depth settings changed anyway. He also kept Admiral King in the loop through his back-channel correspondence with Edwards.

All during these military and political actions, Pinky Kennedy at Mare Island was meticulous and exacting in preparing *Wahoo*—"a perfectionist and a slave driver," wrote Grider. Kennedy pushed his new officers hard. The training he enforced on approach techniques was excellent and was to stay with O'Kane, Grider, and Paine for the rest of their lives.

But Kennedy had Queeg-like quirks that rattled both officers and crew. He decreed that all of *Wahoo's* lights were to be red except for one in the tiny ship's office. Only here, with an automatic trip switch on the door, could charts be read so that the red danger marks could be seen. Errors, some serious, occurred in the unnatural lighting. The red magazine flood valve wheel was not seen in the red interior. During a practice dive it was inadvertently cracked, and the magazine flooded. Kennedy yielded slightly, permitting one white light per compartment, but it was red mashed potatoes, black vegetables, and specially marked playing cards for the crew's mess.

Kennedy shared another quirk with *Tuna*'s John DeTar. The Kleinschmidt stills, and by extension the showers and washing machines, were not to be used. Buckets were distributed for the officers' staterooms, several more for the crew spaces. O'Kane was ordered to rig holding tanks to capture the air-conditioning distillate so the men could take sponge baths; there was to be no washing of clothes.

The eccentric DeTar dragged a mattress into the conning tower to sleep on. Kennedy did him one better, having a fold-down bunk built against the TDC; he intended to use this temporary bunk in place of the more comfortable one in his own cabin. Paine felt that the presence of the captain asleep in the conning tower was bizarre, but he could deal with it. Others were not so philosophical.

On May 15 *Wahoo* was commissioned, and underway testing was started in San Pablo and San Francisco Bays. The officers were good, and they knew it. Grider's first dive was a smooth success. Responsibilities were rotated so that any man acting as OOD could take the dive.

Quick diving is a complex task requiring a smoothly functioning team. With the Ahooga! Ahooga! blasts of the Klaxon, the lookouts scramble out of the periscope shears and plunge down the ladder into the conning tower. Simultaneously, the chief of the watch opens all the vents on the ballast tanks, which flood in nine seconds. In the engine rooms the diesels are killed. The chief waits for the "engines stopped" indication, then closes the main induction, which supplies air to the diesels.

At nearly the same moment two of the lookouts, who continue their descent into the control room, man the diving planes. The bow planes are rigged out to control the downward angle. The conning tower hatch is dogged shut within fifteen seconds of the alarm. In the control room the last vent opening indicator light on the panel called the "Christmas tree" switches from red to green to indicate that all hull openings are closed. "Green board," says the chief to the diving officer. At the high-pressure manifold, air is bled into the boat while the diving team watches the barometer. It rises and steadies. "Pressure in the boat" says the chief, confirming that the submarine is truly sealed. It took *Wahoo* about thirty-five seconds to submerge totally.

After diving, the trim was managed with such precision that it was rock steady when the periscope was raised or lowered. The slight additional volume of the periscope barrel exposed to the sea increased *Wahoo*'s displacement, making her slightly more buoyant. The diving officer and the crew would offset these tendencies with tight control of the bow planes, even the trim tanks. They were very, very good.

On July 15 *Wahoo* departed on her shakedown cruise to San Diego. Ann Grider, along with their son Billy, had shifted north to Mare Island to be close to George. She now returned to Coronado to milk the last few days of togetherness. Bebe Paine had returned to Arkansas with Roger III "for the duration," they thought.

At San Diego the training grew even more intensive and exhausting. For two grueling weeks, night and day, there were repeated torpedo attacks, using dummy warheads, on zigzagging escorts. Kennedy's target approaches were exceptional; Paine and the entire fire control party were honed to excellence. Finally, a "counterattack" on *Wahoo* was staged, using live depth charges so the crew would know how it felt (Paine already knew). This was the signal that training was over.

Wahoo returned to Mare Island for a final touch-up on her mechanical systems, the fitting of a pitifully small three-inch deck gun, and last liberty for the crew. At 0930 on August 12, 1942, she started for Pearl Harbor. Ernestine O'Kane was on the Golden Gate Bridge to wave to Dick as *Wahoo* passed below, headed to sea and the war with Japan.

4

Frustration

... incessant expectation, and perpetual disappointment.

—*Arthur Young:* Travels in France, *1787*

Almost immediately after clearing the Golden Gate, small irritations began to worsen the relationship between the captain and the executive officer. Kennedy had made specific watch list assignments, normally the XO's responsibility, without telling O'Kane. This action left O'Kane scrambling to train a novice seaman, Fertig B. Krause, as assistant navigator. As a result the first sun sight, at noon, was a few minutes late reaching Kennedy, irritating him.

The relentless training, emergency drills, battle stations, and surprise dives continued as *Wahoo* made her way toward Pearl at seventeen knots. O'Kane's typical day ended at midnight; at 0430 he was called for morning star sights and never returned to his bunk. He, all the officers, and much of the crew were exhausted. The work schedule was akin to an endurance test to weed out the weak.

At 0330 on August 18 *Wahoo* picked up her escort, *Litchfield*, by radar in the dark. She was exactly where plotted, for O'Kane was an excellent navigator and took pride in the task. Kennedy ignored this achievement and, perhaps to demonstrate that the crew must always be in a state of combat paranoia, or perhaps because he was in that state already, ordered the crew to their battle stations. All the forward torpedo tube doors were opened in case *Litchfield* was really a Japanese destroyer just hanging around Pearl Harbor to trap the unwary.

Wahoo docked alongside Pier 2 early that morning, welcomed by Admiral English, to whom Kennedy had once reported. There was no break after the six-day crossing; Kennedy gave orders to the crew that the remainder of the day would be spent working. Paine immediately began the task of inspecting the final torpedo adjustments in the shop, then supervising their loading into *Wahoo;* Grider set about getting the fuel tanks topped off. O'Kane was left with the duty as the captain went ashore with the admiral to scout up additional junior officers for the boat.

Kennedy, perhaps because of his excellent connections with Admiral English, received the full cooperation of Personnel. Two new officers, including Lieutenant (J.G.) Richie Henderson, whose battleship had been sunk beneath him on December 7, were assigned and reported aboard. Henderson, was to stay with *Wahoo* to the end. Now, with seven officers and sixty-five enlisted men aboard, *Wahoo* was ready for her first war patrol. The only unfilled billet was yeoman, a skill shortage that particularly affected O'Kane.

At 0900 on August 23, 1942, *Wahoo* backed from her slip to begin her first patrol, to Truk, in the Carolines. Three hours later Kennedy had new surprises for O'Kane. He would require two officers for each watch. O'Kane was to stand the four-to-eights, with the navigational fixes due to Kennedy promptly at the end of the morning watch. And—oh, yes—a noon fix was also required, which, of course, Kennedy said would be "no problem." Exactly how O'Kane was to function as XO was left unsaid. In addition, the illumination compromise was over. *Wahoo* was to be converted to all red lights again, with only the tiny ship's office sporting a white light to read charts.

They plowed on toward Truk, almost always surfaced, the captain ever present on the bridge or in the conning tower. A tense Kennedy rejected the intertwined notions of delegation of responsibility and conservation of his own personal energy. He got very little rest, and a cold virus now made itself a force within the boat. The schedule given O'Kane prevented him from even eating a hot meal with the other officers.

On August 29, after a run of 3,109 nautical miles, *Wahoo* reached her station near Piaanu Pass, west of Truk. Kennedy's apprehension rose. *Wahoo* was to be submerged all day, with a periodic periscope check once every thirty minutes, with two exceptions. Kennedy followed surface-ship doctrine and manned general quarters in the twilight half hour before dawn and after sunset. During this time "Paragon" Paine, as Richie Henderson jokingly called him, manned the periscope for continuous observations. Kennedy always accepted Paine's view of the absence of danger, and his recommendation that the crew could stand down. Kennedy never bothered to check "outside" for himself.

Otherwise, *Wahoo* was to be slowed before every exposure to minimize the chance of a "feather," the telltale wake of a moving periscope. The scope was never to be raised higher than three feet, constraining its useful range to perhaps six thousand yards under ideal conditions. The captain would sleep in his conning tower bunk each night, forcing all crew there, even those turning the balky radar antenna by hand, or going on and off watch to the bridge, to remain silent—and not bump his bunk.

Since the boat was submerged all day, its physical atmosphere was stifling. The surrounding water temperature down to 150 feet was eighty-five degrees; the air-conditioning units, struggling with the heat of newly idled diesels, operational electrical motors, galley stoves, electronic equipment, and seventy-two men, could maintain the internal temperature of the boat at about ninety degrees if all units were operating. Required maintenance on an A/C unit caused the temperature to rise to truly uncomfortable levels. Internal air pressure rose continuously throughout each submergence, particularly bothersome to the ears of those with colds. The steady depletion of oxygen gave many men headaches by the end of the day.

The first target appeared on the baleful snake's eye of the periscope just after dawn on September 6. Its masts rose over the horizon to reveal a small, unescorted freighter headed *Wahoo*'s way. It would be an easy shot at a range of 1,430 yards, duck soup for this superbly trained crew. But all three torpedoes missed.

Thirty seconds after the calculated one-minute run time had elapsed Kennedy could still see the torpedoes leading the target's track. *Wahoo* went deep and shortly turned away. Two explosions were heard after two minutes and 20 seconds, more than a mile beyond the target, but Kennedy did not come to periscope depth to see what had happened. The foamy torpedo wakes in glassy seas, and proximity of airfields, ruled out contemplation of a second attack for him. The psychological letdown on the entire crew was profound.

It seems likely that this finely honed fire control party choked in their first real attack. The range had been visually estimated by Kennedy using a somewhat arbitrary masthead height of 50 feet; a sonar ping was not used as an independent check, since Kennedy feared detection. The target speed was set at 10 knots; passive sonar had not been used to count propeller turns to get another estimate of speed.

The postmortem was unsatisfying. Later examination of *ONI-208J*, the *Japanese Merchant Ship Recognition Manual*—a copy of which was not in the conning tower for the fire control party—revealed that the masthead height for similar ships was 85 feet. If this was the more accurate value, the range was closer to 2,400 yards than to 1,400 yards. But a 1,000-yard range error would have added only another 40 seconds to the run, not an extra minute and a half. Why did the explosions occur so late? The interval between shots had been only 6 seconds. A lead torpedo running 1½ knots slower could be overtaken in the 3,600 yard run to the time of explosion. Had countermining occurred?

ONI-208J also indicated that vessels of this class could make 13 knots. A 3-knot difference over just a 1,400-yard range meant that the target would have moved forward an additional 300 feet in the 60-second run time of the torpedo. Since the target was probably only 250 feet long, such a speed error would guarantee that all torpedoes missed astern. But why did Kennedy see them leading the target?

To his credit, Kennedy did not blame the torpedoes. They were, of course, set to run under the target; a faulty magnetic exploder could easily have betrayed him. Instead, he blamed himself for a faulty estimate of the mast-head height. The fire control party blamed themselves for mismatches between the plot and the TDC, and began to train even harder. The whole experience had been a depressing anticlimax.

Eight days later, a second chance appeared. Kennedy had pulled away from Piaanu Pass, the entrance to Truk Lagoon. Wahoo was now submerged nearly 100 miles to the west. Propeller noises were picked up on sonar at 1025. A quick periscope check revealed a small freighter coming their way, about 6 miles distant. Kennedy also believed he saw an escorting aircraft and immediately reverted to the now discredited prewar tactic of a submerged sonar approach. For 32 minutes he attempted to steer Wahoo toward the target by sound alone. When a second peek was finally dared, the target was 4,000 yards beyond them, fading away.

That evening O'Kane, as usual, was locked away with the only white light, plotting the position of the boat. Roger Paine bypassed the overworked XO and asked Kennedy's permission to test the torpedo tube firing valves. The captain agreed without a second thought. A blunder by a torpedoman resulted in a live torpedo being fired with the outer torpedo tube door closed, not the harmless water slug from an empty tube. The torpedo lunged against the door, jamming it, its whining motors finally stopped only by an automatic safety device in the torpedo itself. O'Kane leaped up from his navigation work, darted into the control room, and ordered all propulsion stopped.

Paine, the torpedo officer, after understanding what had happened, climbed to the forward deck, went over the side with Ed Smith, a seaman volunteer, and swam to the bow to inspect the damage. He found the shutter intact, but the outer door had sprung about 1½ inches. Could they get the torpedo back in? If not, would the torpedo arm itself as *Wahoo* moved forward in the water? Would an armed magnetic exploder be triggered by *Wahoo*'s own hull?

The answer to the first question was no. For hours the torpedomen struggled to retrieve the jammed weapon. Since the damaged tube was in the highest position relative to the waterline, and the outer door was not fully open, it was possible to open the inner door and not be swamped. The pumps could keep up with the steady stream of water into the boat. But even a 1½-ton chain fall could not budge the force-fitted fish.

The answer to the last two questions was probably not. Paine could feel the torpedo and believed that the paddlewheel activator on its nose was protected enough not to be turned by a flow of water. Still, everyone held their breath as propulsion was restored and *Wahoo* moved forward.

They would simply have to continue the patrol with one tube out of commission, and with the cracked outer door making *Wahoo* more vulnerable to depth charge attacks forward of the boat. And they would have to learn to live with the possibility that at any instant the torpedo could really arm itself, destroying them all. Kennedy was, quite naturally, furious at "this piece of gross carelessness," even though his isolation of O'Kane, and acquiescence in Paine's request for testing, had played at least a part in the mishap.

The beautiful night of September 20 found *Wahoo* on the surface, charging batteries. There was a bright moon, and the clear sky produced no wind to ruffle the flat sea. Just before 2300 one of the lookouts standing watch with George Grider sighted a column of smoke in the moonlight. For thirty minutes *Wahoo* ran toward this new opportunity on the surface, then submerged for a night periscope attack.

At battle stations, now with *ONI-208J* in the conning tower, the target was identified as a modern, respectably large freighter of the Keiyo Maru class. The oncoming ship made halting progress, at times as high as 12 knots, then stopping to lie to, as if waiting for something.

Kennedy was convinced it was waiting for an escort, and was furious that the sonar man could hear no approaching screws that would have proven its presence. Afraid of being surprised by the enemy, he made the snap decision to relieve the sound man and bring George Grider to the conning tower to man the sonar. Grider was an excellent sonar officer and had taught at sonar school, but now there was no diving officer. O'Kane, who should have been working on the attack approach, was sent below to relieve

Grider. O'Kane had never personally handled a dive on *Wahoo* and was uncertain of the trim. As torpedoes are fired, a submarine has a tendency to rise, or broach, as the heavy weights leave the end. Precise counterflooding must be employed to compensate and maintain depth control. O'Kane, out of the conning tower, concentrated on this task.

Now, with no assistant approach officer to help him, Kennedy botched the attack. "Lost in the box," he was unable to keep mental track of where the target was relative to *Wahoo;* they came too close to the freighter, and on a parallel, not perpendicular track. Just after midnight, target and stalker passed each other at a distance of two hundred yards. Kennedy turned away to get in a stern shot.

The first torpedo was fired at such short range that it could not arm. The second was fired at a poor angle, which caused the torpedo to run down the side of the target, not into it. The freighter saw this shot and began to turn left and pour on speed. Kennedy passed new setup information to Paine at the TDC, where gyro angles were being frantically calculated. A third torpedo was fired without a hit. Finally, as the freighter continued her turn, Kennedy had a ninety-degree shot with the last torpedo left in the stern tubes.

Torpedo number four hit at a range of two thousand yards. Kennedy shared the scope with Grider, Paine, and a few others in the conning tower. The freighter had a port list of fifty degrees and was down by the stern. *Wahoo* turned away from the target and did not maneuver for a follow-up shot.

About fifteen minutes after the torpedo explosion, strange, new, and loud sounds were heard from the freighter, now four thousand yards away. All of *Wahoo's* crew believed these were the breaking-up noises of a sinking ship and, indeed, when Kennedy took a quick periscope look, no target could be seen. They had their first victim!

Wahoo surfaced and ran from the area at speeds up to twenty-one knots. A lookout spotted a "fuzzy bump" on the horizon, which Kennedy believed was a chasing escort. O'Kane, now relieved of his diving duty, was back on the bridge but could see nothing. Nevertheless, Kennedy ordered evasive action, and after an hour of many course and speed changes ended up in a rain squall to hide from the pursuer.

In this shelter Kennedy demanded to know from O'Kane *Wahoo's* current position, including the plot of how they got there. He would not accept the current position stated by the dead-reckoning indicator (DRI). O'Kane was forced to work up a plot from the DRI position upon surfacing, and subsequent orders to the helmsman recorded in the quartermaster's log. This dubious additional proof would be augmented by a dawn star sight on O'Kane's 0400 to 0800 watch.

Unfortunately, postwar analysis indicates that the freighter attacked by *Wahoo* did not sink. While it seemed damaged to Kennedy and crew, there is no Japanese record of a ship hit off Truk on that day. No matter. *Wahoo* was to be credited with sinking a sixty-four-hundred-ton freighter; the unknowing officers and crew were exultant, since they could now wear the submarine combat pin!

Days drifted by with no ship sightings, but Kennedy would not expand the search horizon by raising the periscope more than his rigidly prescribed three feet. In keeping with his aggressive personality, O'Kane favored daylight surface searches, which must have struck Kennedy as insanely reckless. Resentment over Kennedy's extreme caution began to grow in O'Kane, Grider, and some of the crew. They began to conspire to get around the restricted-visibility problem.

Once each half hour during daytime hours *Wahoo* was raised from ninety to sixty-four feet for a quick periscope check. With O'Kane manning the scope, Grider had ensigns being trained as diving officers come gradually to fifty-four feet, then ease down to the normal sixty-four-foot periscope depth. The crewmen operating the bow planes cooperated in this trick. If the captain were to notice the fluctuation, the trainee would accept the blame for not yet being able to maintain good depth control. Meanwhile, O'Kane would search the horizon with an extra ten feet of periscope exposed. Care was taken to try this ploy only when Kennedy was dozing in his conning tower bunk, or absent.

On the second day of intrigue O'Kane spotted a target on the horizon that might be reachable. He rang battle stations and turned toward the prey at a high, battery-depleting, underwater speed. Meanwhile, Grider eased *Wahoo* back down to her normal depth. Kennedy raced to the conning tower, slowed *Wahoo* so as not to risk a "feather," then searched with three feet of periscope. He saw no ship. O'Kane proposed raising the scope higher. Kennedy refused; no target existed for him. O'Kane's intrigue had failed.

September 30 dawned with high winds that stirred the seas to whitecaps, good cover for an extended periscope. Kennedy still refused to go beyond the standard three feet. At 0545, just after diving for the day, an unescorted warship was sighted coming their way at high speed. It had the distinctive profile of a Chiyoda class seaplane tender, an extremely attractive target. But the ship had been seen too late. *Wahoo*'s best short-term underwater speed, nine knots, was no match for this twenty-knot zigzagging opponent. The opportunity for an attack was lost.

Kennedy later wrote in the patrol report: "There were no screens or escorts, no planes sighted. The Japs were just begging someone to knock off this tender, but it was not our lucky day." No postmortem was held in *Wahoo* on this missed opportunity, but O'Kane and Grider conferred privately; they knew that more periscope exposure would have picked up the target earlier.

Five days later O'Kane was at the scope again after the morning dive. At 0654 he spotted two destroyers escorting an aircraft carrier! Excited, he called for battle stations, turned to the normal approach course, fed the preliminary speed and angle information to Paine at the TDC, and increased *Wahoo*'s underwater speed toward its maximum nine knots. The carrier was fast; *Wahoo* would have to move to intercept it.

Now Kennedy arrived and called for one-third speed, which O'Kane hoped was only to quiet *Wahoo*'s propellers to get a better sound bearing. But Kennedy let *Wahoo*'s speed drift down to three knots and took a quick periscope observation of his own. It seemed clear to O'Kane that Kennedy did not trust him. The captain's observations, and a check by the sonar operator, confirmed the settings that Paine already had in the TDC.

O'Kane urged full speed at once; at fourteen knots the carrier clearly could outrun *Wahoo*'s best effort once she got past. He also urged Kennedy to back the motors down to quickly kill headway for the next periscope observation. Kennedy did neither of these. Instead, he made a slow approach, and each succeeding observation showed that the carrier, mistakenly thought to be the *Ryujo*, was leaving them behind. When it was clear that the underwater race had been lost, Kennedy left the conning tower for his cabin.

But O'Kane had not given up. *Wahoo* could make nineteen knots on the surface in the current poor weather. With this slight speed advantage *Wahoo* could overtake, and get in front of, the carrier. They would keep her under observation by using *Wahoo*'s extended periscopes, their eyes high above the water. *Wahoo* would be able to see the enemy, but not herself be seen.

The proposal was made. Kennedy hesitated, then agreed, but delayed surfacing for an hour. Finally, at 0915 all engines were put on line as *Wahoo* ran an interception course under overcast skies, with shifting winds and seas. The many rain squalls reduced visibility: three thousand yards at best, sometimes only a hundred yards. O'Kane hoped to see the carrier within two hours and then would begin to plot the attack course.

Once on the bridge, Kennedy assigned O'Kane to the after sector. Out of position, he could not see the gyro repeater and *Wahoo*'s actual course. The sun briefly broke through the clouds, giving O'Kane his first crude knowledge of their heading. He realized at once that *Wahoo* was not on an interception course; *Wahoo* was running parallel to the carrier. They might be abreast of it, but they certainly were no closer. O'Kane recommended a course change to intercept. Kennedy, uneasy about being on the surface in daylight, even though the weather nullified air observation, disagreed. He ordered *Wahoo* to dive. The chase was over.

The missed opportunity on the aircraft carrier ruined the self-confidence of officers and crew. Grider was "brooding and discouraged." For an aggressive man like O'Kane the failure to attack was a grinding, hateful, searing frustration. Secretly he began to read the navy regulations governing assumption of command; he was contemplating a legal mutiny.

As October 7, the scheduled day of departure from their patrol area approached, O'Kane met privately with Kennedy. He proposed that *Wahoo* stay on station another week. They had plenty of food, fuel, and fresh water—the latter an immense irritant, since all hands were still permitted only sponge baths. Kennedy refused. In a candid admission of failure, he told O'Kane that *Wahoo* needed a new captain.

5

Intrigue

Something attempted, something done . . .

—Longfellow, "The Village Blacksmith"

Dick O'Kane consoled himself with one redeeming thought: Marvin Kennedy was sure to be replaced as *Wahoo*'s captain. The "Remarks" section of the patrol report guaranteed it. Referring to the missed carrier, Kennedy wrote:

> The remainder of the patrol was a fiasco. . . . Had I but required a more rigorous and alert watch, we might have picked her up sooner. Had I correctly estimated the situation and made a more aggressive approach, we could have gotten in a shot. Had I taken up the surface chase without allowing over an hour to elapse we might not have lost the target. Had I continued to search through the rain squalls until dark we might have picked her up again. None of these happened and the second target proceeded unharmed.

O'Kane was annoyed at the "rigorous and alert watch comment," feeling it reflected on him; he certainly had *tried* to get the captain to be more aggressive in his searches. But the overall tone of the patrol report was that of a beaten man. O'Kane departed for his break at the pink-stuccoed Royal Hawaiian Hotel confident that he had seen the last of his captain. Kennedy did not join his crew at the hotel but, private and distant as ever, left them and went to stay with his own friends.

Wahoo's patrol was viewed dimly by the division commander, whose endorsement read: "It is very unfortunate that attack positions were not attained on either [the] *Chiyoda* or *Ryujo*. . . . The situation upon sighting indicated that attack position . . . could be gained only by the most aggressive kind of approach. It is regrettable that the need for such immediate action was not recognized."

The squadron commander's criticisms, signed on October 20, were broader. For the missed opportunity on the small freighter he wrote: ". . . to resort to an approach wherein no periscope observation is made for 32 minutes invites failure." As for major missed opportunity: "To get in an attack on such a valuable target as an aircraft carrier calls for the greatest degree of aggressiveness. The fact that *Ryujo* [sic] was not sighted until at a range of 11,000 yards bears out the CO's statement that a more alert watch could have been kept."

Admiral English's endorsement was critical of Kennedy, but relatively mild considering the missed opportunities. They were ranked roughly in the same class as excessive torpedo usage:

1. "More time . . . should have been spent in close proximity to Piaanu Pass."
2. "It is unfortunate that *Wahoo* failed to press home an attack [on the carrier]."
3. "The firing of 4 single torpedoes [on the freighter that was hit] . . . undoubtedly resulted in . . . needless expenditure."

These endorsements were widely circulated, and Grider, for one, felt "a little ashamed." However, he was relieved to be back at Pearl Harbor and was enjoying his off time. An expert swimmer, swim team captain at Annapolis, and an All-American water polo player, Grider swam often. Taking a break from the Royal Hawaiian beaches, he went to the pool at the submarine base, where he chanced to meet a man with a personality much like his own. This was Dudley "Mush" Morton, formerly a football star at the Naval Academy. Grider and Morton hit it off immediately, playing in the water like little boys.

As a lieutenant, Morton had been in command of the ancient *R-5*, the "nickel boat," based in Groton. *R-5* was laid down in 1917, decommissioned in 1932, and reactivated in 1940 as the navy began to prepare for the coming war. *R-5* patrolled the imaginary line between Nantucket and Bermuda. On February 10, 1942, Morton spotted a German U-boat running on the surface and struggled to close for a submerged attack. At maximum underwater speed *R-5* quickly depleted its small battery but could not gain on the far faster U-boat. Morton tried a desperation four-torpedo salvo, but there were no hits. He was criticized for failing to surface in pursuit of the far more effective German submarine.

Following *R-5,* Morton had been moved to the Pacific Fleet and given command of the antique *Dolphin,* on which Bob Logue still served. Morton's task was to mend this wretched boat. He quickly concluded that *Dolphin* was beyond repair and should never again be sent on patrol. Morton was relieved of command, under a cloud, but saved from banishment to surface duty by a friend who was the operations officer for Admiral English. Morton had been returned to the prospective commanding officers (PCO) pool, or the "makey-learn." He was waiting for another chance to redeem himself.

During the Pearl Harbor refit cycle a new crew member arrived on *Wahoo.* It was Forest "Jim" Sterling, the long-awaited yeoman. Unlike much of the crew, Sterling was career navy. He had joined in 1930, and served as a radioman aboard the tender *Canopus* on the China Station through 1937. Curiously, he had reported to Grider's new friend Mush Morton, then an ensign, when both were in Manila.

Sterling was a slender, cigarette-smoking, hard-living sailor. He liked to keep busy and did not consider himself as exclusively a yeoman. He was open to other jobs, from lookout to radar or sonar, and was willing to stand extra watches to learn the new tasks. This work ethic greatly impressed O'Kane.

In turn, O'Kane's well-developed sense of self struck Sterling, who noted that the XO "could get alarmingly purple in the face whenever his work did not receive precedence over all other matters." Roger Paine, however, was expert at laying on the charm in a way that softened up the yeoman. When Paine's work was done out of sequence he never forgot a thank you and a compliment. More than fifty years later Sterling would recall Paine as "foremost of the many fine officers I served under."

O'Kane's dream of a new captain for *Wahoo* was dashed a few days before they were ready to return to sea. Standing in the crew's mess examining charts, he heard words emanating from the control room that drove a knife into his heart: "Guess who's come on board as our new skipper . . . Lieutenant Commander Kennedy."

O'Kane shot up the ladder from the crew's mess, avoiding Kennedy altogether, and raced for headquarters. There he met "Jumping Joe" Grenfell, who had left *Gudgeon* and been assigned to a staff job after a nearly fatal airplane accident. O'Kane asked Grenfell to intercede—to have Kennedy removed. Grenfell had not read *Wahoo's* patrol report but was well aware of the politics at work. He knew that Kennedy was Admiral English's boy, and told O'Kane so.

But as O'Kane filled Grenfell in on his view of Kennedy, the captain's private confession that a new skipper was needed, and his lack of aggressiveness, he began to have a receptive audience. Together, O'Kane and Grenfell collaborated on a plan to have a PCO assigned to *Wahoo* to "help" Kennedy. That PCO was to be Mush Morton.

As a finishing touch, young John B. "Duke" Griggs III, son of Admiral English's chief of staff, would join *Wahoo* as the most junior officer on the boat. Kennedy would have had to be supremely confident not to wonder what inside information might be passed along, father to son. For his part, young Griggs was unsure of the political dynamics. He had been told that Morton's PCO assignment was his last chance to make good in submarines.

Dudley Morton was Kentucky-born and Miami-raised. He was tall and very broad-shouldered, with huge hands. Childish in many ways, Morton could be a roughhousing bully. He wrestled with Grider in the wardroom, popping his neck in a vicious half nelson. Nor were the enlisted men off-limits. Morton pounded Sterling on the back so hard he knocked him into his typewriter, then dared him to retaliate. At heart he was still the young ensign from Manila who raised fighting cocks.

But his personality was such that a room seemed illuminated when Morton walked in. He was more than genial; his enthusiastic vitality was magnetic. Most men were willingly drawn into his sphere of commanded loyalty, including the enlisted men, whom he took pains to cultivate. Some of his techniques were masterful for this insecure crew: dressed only in skivvies he washed his clothes in a bucket, as they had to do, and probed for details of *Wahoo*'s first patrol. He also demonstrated his special trick: talking while simultaneously holding four golf balls in his mouth—hence "Mushmouth." Morton made no bones about conveying his eagerness to be the skipper, not just the PCO, of *Wahoo*.

Morton bonded tightly to his fellow officers, especially O'Kane. Grider noted that O'Kane "clearly had no reservations about Mush. The two were in agreement on everything." They began playing cribbage virtually as soon as Morton joined the ship. In these moments of play, and while on duty, Morton sounded out O'Kane for his views on *Wahoo*'s first patrol and Kennedy's performance. At mealtimes the wardroom was filled with Morton-generated laughter, an enormous change from the quiet meals the captain preferred. Even before the start of the second patrol it was clear that Morton and O'Kane were linked in ways that isolated Kennedy.

Twenty-two days after *Wahoo*'s arrival in Pearl Harbor she began her second patrol, fitted with a four-inch gun taken from *S-19*. On the morning of November 8, 1942, with Admiral English there to salute him and the strains of the Hawaiian War Chant to cheer him, Kennedy began to back *Wahoo* from the dock. The engines roared as the propellers dug into the water and suffocating diesel exhaust swept over the boat.

Turning smartly in Southeast Loch, *Wahoo* headed for the main channel. It was still marked with a mourning band of oil from the ships sunk there less than a year ago. The band now played Aloha; the well-wishers called out "Good luck, good hunting." For Sterling it was a stomach-churning moment of excitement. He stood at attention as *Wahoo* passed the wreckage of *Arizona* and *Oklahoma* and hoped that some moment of vengeance would come to them. Their course: 238°T; their destination: Bougainville, in the Solomons, three thousand miles away—a week's run.

Kennedy made small but important changes for this patrol. To his great relief, O'Kane was freed from the requirement to stand the 0400 to 0800 watches. Further, the officers' wardroom and crew's mess were fitted out with white lights. Food would now look normal. Officers and crew going on watch would wear red glasses for thirty minutes prior to taking station. Kennedy did not relent on the parsimonious use of fresh water, however. Morton broke this prohibition when Kennedy slept, subtly enlisting the crew in his conspiracy by having them stand watch should the captain rise from his fitful slumber.

On November 16, after crossing the international date line, *Wahoo* reached her patrol area in stormy weather. Gale winds and heavy seas swept the surfaced boat by night, making it impossible for the lookouts to spot targets. When submerged by day, sheets of rain beat on the surface of the sea and blocked the use of sonar. *Wahoo* was blind and deaf, groping as she tried to keep on station.

Kennedy returned to his bunk in the conning tower, where he slept restlessly. One night, while Sterling manned the sound gear, Kennedy had a nightmare, leaped up, and grabbed the whispering yeoman by the shoulders. He screamed into the shocked Sterling's face, "Where? Where away? What bearing?" Coming to his senses, Kennedy went below, but not before everyone in the conning tower exchanged glances of tense uneasiness.

After a week of fruitless effort, a lookout spotted smoke between lightning flashes during Grider's 2000 to 2400 watch. O'Kane, peering through the squalls, thought it was a convoy. A lightning flash exposed one large ship with escort. The range was ideal for a sudden, slashing night surface attack. In this weather *Wahoo* would never be spotted in time for retribution. But

Kennedy rejected surface action and submerged instead. O'Kane remembered how *Argonaut* had lost its targets when switching from a night surface to submerged attack. History was replayed for him. Neither Kennedy at the periscope, with its poor night vision characteristics, nor the sonar men could reliably track either target. The Japanese got by them. O'Kane seethed; Morton was silent.

Kennedy held no postmortem but returned to his conning tower bunk. At midnight, after Grider came off watch, he, Morton, and O'Kane convened in the wardroom to discuss the blown opportunity. All three agreed they should have stayed on the surface. But given Kennedy's seeming aversion to surface combat, they could have made an end-around to get in front of the targets, then dived at dawn for a daylight periscope attack. O'Kane also involved the crew in this analysis by having the chief of the boat privately interview all lookouts to get a better idea of just how many targets were in the convoy.

Another week dragged by. Then, on November 30, the codebreakers intervened to warn of a very large tanker coming their way at high speed. O'Kane did the navigation work to plot the interception track. They would be in front of this high-priority target at 0200, two hours away. With a full battery charge *Wahoo* moved into position and began to search with extra lookouts, the SJ radar, and sound.

Surprisingly, sound won. The telltale ping of a searching destroyer was heard to the north. Now the radar focused in just this sector, picking up the target at eighteen thousand yards—nine nautical miles away. *Wahoo* was maneuvered on the normal approach course and dove when the range shrank to ten thousand yards. The priority target was coming on as planned; they would fire when the range contracted to twenty-five hundred yards.

"Echo ranging on our starboard quarter!" called the sonar man, a position exactly opposite of where the escort should be.

"Reciprocal! Reciprocal!" shouted Morton.

The sound man had mistakenly called the opposite bearing. Morton's clarification was too late or, possibly, Kennedy decided to take no chances. He instantly ordered the negative tank flooded and deep submergence. The huge tanker passed overhead, its propellers throbbing as it pulled away.

Morton went below to avoid an open argument with Kennedy, who, shaken, left for his own cabin. O'Kane angrily shouted "Secure from battle stations!" over the loudspeaker, the furious tone in his voice clearly detectable by Sterling, who was in the crew's mess. The mess room quickly filled with frustrated crew, all critical of the lost opportunity. O'Kane was too agitated to turn in, his mind racing with "what ifs?" for the remainder of the night. Up early for star sights, he brought his copy of the *Navy Regulations* to the conning tower and opened it to the pages concerning assumption of command. In what O'Kane later called "one of life's touchy moments," Kennedy came to the conning tower, found the book open, and read it while O'Kane stood nearby. The full depth of O'Kane's disgust, even hatred, was now clear to Kennedy.

Ten days passed, and *Wahoo* was in the center of the thirty-mile-wide passage between Buka, Bougainville's northwestern tip, and the Kilinailau Islands. Kennedy agreed to some changes in the daytime search procedure. O'Kane had pressed for continuous periscope observations. Kennedy did not go that far, but did agree to a look every fifteen minutes. Like camels with their noses in the tent, O'Kane and Morton worked out a tandem observation. Upon reaching periscope depth the OOD would make a quick sweep for aircraft. As he retracted his scope, the watch quartermaster would simultaneously extend the search periscope for a more thorough target scan. Total periscope exposure time was thus greatly extended over that of the first patrol.

On the afternoon of December 10 Roger Paine was in the control room as acting dive officer. He was practicing the depth control art as the new observation protocol forced *Wahoo* to rise to sixty-four feet, then return to the depths every fifteen minutes. Above him, in the conning tower, a crewman on the search periscope calmly announced "Heavy smoke on the horizon" and the relative bearing.

A flurry of job changes followed. Grider took the dive as Paine climbed to the conning tower and his post at the TDC. Kennedy was alerted quietly to give him a chance to get in position before the inevitable mob scene when battle stations was sounded. O'Kane took a second observation and began to sketch in the target's probable course on a chart.

Kennedy made several observations of his own, his faced flushed after each one. They had a three-ship convoy, guarded by a single escort, headed their way! In his excitement Kennedy initially flooded Paine with too many target settings for the TDC. O'Kane, ever more assertive, asked the captain to pick a single target on which they could concentrate. Kennedy picked the largest, a heavily laden freighter in the center of the column.

The fire control problem for the freighter was straightforward. The trick was to avoid the escort, identified by Kennedy as an Asashio class destroyer, which was roaming in front of its charges. Kennedy contemplated attacking the escort first to rid himself of this menace. But its patrolling plan, and good echo ranging, persuaded him to let her pass. The freighter was very close, only seven hundred yards away, when the firing began. The first three torpedoes struck home—or were at least such close prematures that *Kamoi Maru* was observed to sink later that night. After the war JANAC found the record of her sinking. *Wahoo* had truly taken her first victim.

And now the escort wheeled in to extract her revenge. The wakes from the steam torpedoes were markers leading to *Wahoo*'s firing position. The first depth charges exploded just astern of *Wahoo* as she passed 120 feet, swimming for the depths.

As Grider blew the negative tank to level *Wahoo* at the planned 250 feet, the vent's gasket carried away. Water flooded in before the vent could be closed manually, and Wahoo sank to 350 feet—below her test depth. This was likely a fortunate accident since, in 1942, Japanese charges could not be set to explode below 250 feet and might have caught *Wahoo* at exactly the wrong place.

Sterling was in the crew's mess. This was his first experience with depth charges fired in anger and skillfully placed. He was "totally unprepared. The shock shook the boat . . . lights went out, followed by audible *pops* that sounded like a rifle firing in the compartment. I was shaken so hard my head snapped. Small loose objects whistled through the pitch darkness, and huge segments of overhead cork propelled downward on my head and shoulders."

The closeness of the explosions momentarily sprang the main induction valve that brought air to the voracious diesels when on the surface. The valve was forty inches in diameter, and copious amount of seawater flooded in till the valve reseated. There was minor damage throughout the boat. The escort came back for twenty more attacks over the next ninety minutes. Sterling was repeatedly slammed bodily into vibrating mess tables before taking to his dust-covered bunk.

The sheer number of depth charges was a matter for debate. Grider counted forty, O'Kane forty-odd. These somewhat low tallies may have been macho accounts of only the close ones. The crew count was seventy-eight, the figure entered in the ship's log. This higher count indicates that if there was only one escort it was likely a frigate, which could carry as many as three hundred depth charges. Japanese fleet destroyers carried only thirty.

Grider wanted to go in for another attack immediately; the second freighter was stopped in broad daylight, taking on survivors from their first victim. Morton and O'Kane both favored a second attack after dark, using the SJ radar to define the target. But the vigilant, patrolling escort cooled that notion for Kennedy.

The crew hated the depth charging but were elated with their success. Kennedy grew in stature in their eyes, especially when he ordered a shot of brandy for all. Sterling heard one say, "I never saw the old man so brave." O'Kane was also pleased at the victory, attributing it to his confrontations with the captain. He was sure he had forced Kennedy to "show that whippersnapper"—himself.

O'Kane's cautious hope of a new leaf was dashed fewer than two days later. Once again the codebreakers vectored *Wahoo* toward a target. Kennedy ordered single-engine speed that theoretically could get *Wahoo* to the interception point in time. Just as for the missed tanker, the sonar man picked up distant echo ranging first. O'Kane had left orders to be awakened before the captain and was on the bridge when contact was made. It was 0130, December 12, 1942.

Visual sighting of the large freighter was made before radar picked her up at ten thousand yards. Roger Paine manned the TDC and began working out the fire control problem. Battle stations were not sounded; most of the crew slumbered on. The freighter was fast. Only her zigzag pattern slowed her progress. With only a single engine on line, *Wahoo* was not gaining. She needed more power.

O'Kane lost it. In front of the bridge watch he railed at the captain "rather strongly," demanding more speed and insisting that *Wahoo* had to go after this unescorted target. Kennedy shouted back angrily, "Don't be stupid; you can't attack a ship from here!" The freighter steamed on, unmolested. Only the crew had something to talk about in subsequent bull sessions.

O'Kane smarted from this embarrassing humiliation and became "broody," lashing out unpredictably. Grider noted that "Dick had grown hard to live with, friendly one minute and pulling his rank on his junior officers the next. One day he would be a martinet, and the next he would display an overlenient, carefree attitude that was far from reassuring." Sterling was in the conning tower when O'Kane ordered Krause, the seaman who helped him with his navigation, to get him some coffee. Much to Sterling's surprise Krause's firm response was "I am not a mess attendant, sir, but I'll tell James you want a cup." Surprisingly, O'Kane shrugged his shoulders and let it slide.

Sterling was in the conning tower on sonar, honing his skills. In the middle of his watch he heard an extra-heavy rain squall beating on the surface of the sea. He told George Grider, the periscope watch officer, that it must be hailing it was so noisy. Grider asked Sterling to switch the sound to the loudspeakers so he could listen. The noise was so unusual that Grider decided to bend the captain's orders and take an early periscope search.

He ordered *Wahoo* to periscope depth, pressed the "pickle," the tethered pushbutton that raised the scope, and rose with the eyepiece as soon as the periscope cleared its well. He steadied on the direction of the sound, started, then immediately retracted the scope. Grider now did three things almost simultaneously. He rang "battle stations," shouted for the outer torpedo doors to be opened, and jumped to the TDC to begin putting in the critical speed and bearing information of the target he had just sighted.

Kennedy leaped up into the conning tower, followed by O'Kane and Paine, to hear Grider's report of a submarine about to cross *Wahoo*'s bow at a range of a thousand yards. The rising sun and numerals still painted on its conning tower identified it as *I-2*, a large Japanese attack boat. With the TDC already cranking, Paine entered tuning adjustments as Kennedy made two more low-elevation looks, honing the fire control solution. At eight hundred yards range, three torpedoes were fired. Kennedy raised the scope ten seconds before the calculated impact and saw a hit forward of the conning tower. Sterling had a flash of doubt, thinking it might be a premature. Kennedy reported the submarine was sinking, with crew still on the bridge.

Two and a half minutes after the initial firing, there was a second explosion. O'Kane described it as "a great muffled WHOMP with an intensity far greater than the detonation of a warhead"; to Grider it was "a crunching noise, the sound of metal collapsing inwardly"; Sterling became "aware of another noise outside the hull, explosions and breaking-up sounds." They were all absolutely convinced that the submarine had gone down, and easily, morbidly pictured how easily *Wahoo* could have been the victim instead.

If the target was indeed *I-2*, then Sterling's doubt was valid. The Japanese submarine must have encountered a frightening, bone-shaking premature and dived to live on for eighteen more months. She was finally sunk on April 7, 1944, by the destroyer *Saufley*. In later years O'Kane came to believe that their target was really *I-15*. That submarine is thought to have been sunk on November 11, 1942, by the destroyer *Southard*, but there is some imprecision about the date and slayer. In any case, neither JANAC nor subsequent Japanese records recorded any Japanese submarine sunk on this date.

On the morning of December 15, *Wahoo* was well down the eastern coast of Bougainville off the tropical port of Kieta. A routine periscope sweep picked up the masts of a large unescorted ship running parallel to *Wahoo*. She could be intercepted if they surfaced now, ran at full speed for an hour to get in front, then dove for a submerged attack. O'Kane thought this plan reasonable. Kennedy thought he was nuts. The captain's rationale was that *Wahoo* would be spotted on the surface by shore lookouts, who would call for an air attack. O'Kane argued that the nearest Japanese airfield was on Rabaul, two hundred miles away. Even if there were a closer plane, *Wahoo's* thirty-five-second diving speed would ensure that they could get under before being spotted. O'Kane's arguments lost; there was no pursuit. Kennedy made the decision to head for Australia instead.

Morton had lost some of his jokester's edge now that *Wahoo* was returning to Brisbane. The patrol would be an acceptable one on the books, but he was only too aware of the many missed opportunities. He wanted one more chance. Morton and O'Kane were standing the afternoon watch together on December 18 when smoke was sighted on the horizon. Kennedy was napping in his cabin. O'Kane put *Wahoo* on an interception course and advanced her speed to ensure success. He then sent a seaman to awaken Kennedy and sounded battle stations.

O'Kane explained to the captain "an approach in progress that could not fail" and showed Kennedy the plot of target and attacker on the chart. Kennedy did not accept O'Kane's observations and slowed *Wahoo* for a look of his own. After lowering the scope Kennedy was silent for more than twenty minutes, working on the chart with dividers. He then ordered that the crew secure from battle stations and told Morton and O'Kane that *Wahoo* would be in *Grouper*'s area when the attack was made—a legalistic argument for not engaging the enemy.

O'Kane blew up. He and Kennedy were headed for an ugly confrontation. Morton circled behind the captain and used hand signals to warn O'Kane to shut up. Swallowing his fury, O'Kane complied. The freighter passed unmolested. That night Morton presided over a wardroom meeting with the off-duty officers while Kennedy slept fitfully in the conning tower. With what was judged excessive bravado, even by Dick O'Kane, Morton told them he was going to report Kennedy for cowardice when they reached Brisbane.

In the days that followed, O'Kane spent much time in his cabin, catching up on paperwork but also thinking through his dilemma. He wanted Kennedy out, and he wanted to stay with *Wahoo*. But above all had resolved that he would never again go to sea as Kennedy's XO: "A blowup would be inevitable."

As luck would have it, the two men chanced to meet privately on the conning tower cigarette deck. Kennedy criticized details of the draft war patrol report submitted by O'Kane, then suddenly turned away and said, "You'd probably make a good submarine captain." He may have had O'Kane's pending fitness report in mind; Kennedy was conscientious about the administrative part of his job.

O'Kane was not the only morose soul aboard. Grider wrote: "We put into Brisbane . . . more discouraged than we had been at the end of the first patrol. . . . *Wahoo* . . . was not making much of a record and we knew it. We had excuses [but] . . . we still felt thoroughly discouraged. We didn't want good excuses; we wanted a good record."

The tension spilled over to the crew. O'Kane relieved Sterling of normal watch duty so he could concentrate on completion of the patrol report, his normal yeoman's job. But O'Kane was tardy in telling the chief of the boat of this action. When called to stand watch, Sterling refused with an oath, then guessed that the chief didn't know about the change in orders. He went into the control room to explain and was met by the furious CPO's fists and nearly knocked unconscious.

Lieutenant Roger Paine supervising *Wahoo's* docking (Rear Admiral Roger W. Paine Jr.)

At 0300 on December 26, Kennedy stationed the special sea detail, which handled docking and mooring, even though it was at least five hours from the river entrance to Brisbane. This included Sterling, who had just finished the patrol report. At the entrance an Australian pilot came aboard to guide *Wahoo* up the ninety winding miles to Brisbane. The special sea detail was held in place. Kennedy went below and turned the con over to Morton. At 1215 *Wahoo* tied up alongside the tender *Sperry,* and the special sea detail was relieved after more than nine hours on watch.

Now began five days of hardball political maneuvers by Morton and O'Kane. In Brisbane Kennedy came under command of Admiral Lockwood, not his mentor and protector Admiral English. Lockwood's second in command, the icy-cold James Fife, and Lockwood's best friend "Gin" Styer would decide Kennedy's fate.

On paper, *Wahoo*'s second patrol could be made to appear successful. But Kennedy had had enough. He told Roger Paine that Morton and O'Kane were against him, and he was "going to turn in his suit."

Duke Griggs reported a different version: "As was the custom, upon our arrival . . . [Morton] accompanied the C.O. up to the Commodore's cabin . . . and listened while the C.O. was debriefed. After the C.O. was finished, Cap't Styer turned to Mush and asked 'Well, Mush what do you think?' [Morton replied] 'Commodore, he is a yellow-bellied S.O.B. and ought to be relieved. If you doubt my word call the Exec up and ask him.' This was done and Dick O'Kane confirmed Mush's statement. . . ."

Kennedy was formally relieved on December 31, 1942—a New Year's Eve present for O'Kane. *Wahoo*'s new captain was Dudley Morton.

As this political maneuvering was occurring, thousands of miles to the northwest, in Singapore, events were unfolding that would soon involve *Wahoo.* Approximately five hundred Indian prisoners of war were assembled in the Serangoon Road Camp on December 28. While men of other units, including British medical personnel, were present, these soldiers were mostly from the 2nd Battalion, 16th Punjab Regiment. All had been captured by the Japanese on February 15, 1942, when Singapore fell.

Since that time they had been marched from camp to camp—Bidadari, Neeson, Tingah, Seletar, Buller—all the while subjected to lectures from representatives of the Indian National Army (INA). The INA was the brainchild of Subhas Chandra Bose, the Indian nationalist leader who had broken away from Gandhi and been repeatedly jailed by the British. He recruited new soldiers for the Japanese Army from the huge POW pool created by the fall of Singapore. Bose was committed to the defeat of the white race, and to independence for India.

These men, mostly from the "5/2 Punjab," were those who would not yield to Bose. They were loyal to the British Empire. The Japanese tried to turn the tide with "lectures, moral and physical training" from Major General Fuke, who doled out increasingly harsh conditions to those men who refused to comply.

Captain O. A. V. Sen, of Indian 12th Brigade headquarters, was suddenly ordered to assemble a force of 500 of the most recalcitrant prisoners—some of whom had refused to listen to the Japanese "lectures"—for shipment to New Britain. They would be forced laborers in the fighting zones, where they would "be treated in accordance with Japanese military law."

In the frenzied haste to break camp at dawn, the Japanese sentries miscounted the group and refused to let the last three soldiers pass. Sen reported this to the Japanese but was ignored. When recounted at the docks the Japanese came up with only 497 men. Major Yamanouchi, who commanded the 26th Field Ordnance Depot garrison troops, demanded an explanation from Sen. Before Sen could answer he was set upon by Lieutenant Hiro Goto and beaten savagely on the head with a three-foot-long staff.

This was only the beginning. The 497 men were jammed into the unlit hold of a ship, just above the engines, with no air circulation, no room to lie down, and with only two latrines. Planks were placed across the top of the hold, and trucks loaded on the planks. It was to be a hellish voyage. Japanese ordnance troops were also loaded aboard the ship, 200 to a hold, three holds' worth, all with circulating fans. The transport's name was *Buyo Maru*.

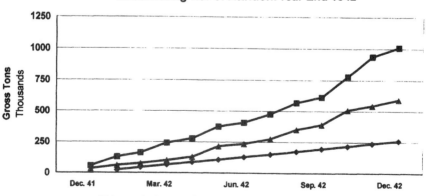

Accelerating War of Attrition: Year End 1942

PART II

MORTON LEADS
THE WAY

6
Everything Clicks

Your luck changes only if it's good.

—Ogden Nash, "Roulette Us Be Gay"

Morton began to stamp a new identity on *Wahoo* the moment Kennedy left the boat, trailed by several pieces of his tan leather luggage. "Mush" grabbed the first enlisted man he met, all of whom he knew by name, and asked him to move through *Wahoo*'s interior tearing down every silhouette of Japanese ships that Kennedy had posted—even in the heads. In their place went Morton's private "girlie" pictures, which he had somehow obtained during a short stopover in Hollywood. O'Kane contributed an autographed picture of Olivia DeHavilland for the crew's mess.

The physical reminders were next: Kennedy's bunk was ripped from the conning tower; the condensate holding tanks were pulled from below the air-conditioning units and replaced with crew's lockers. From now on, *Wahoo*'s crew would use the installed washing machine for their clothes, the showers for their bodies.

Morton told Sterling to "somehow get the Captain's Mast book lost. We won't be needing it on my boat." He also instructed the yeoman to call him "Mush." Grider marveled at how the crew took to Morton, even loved him. Morton wandered the boat restlessly; like Grider, he did not sleep well aboard. But Morton had a built-in authority that survived his bull sessions with the crew even while dressed only in skivvies. He understood their anxieties, was never stiff. Grider thought "he was as relaxed as a baby. The men were not merely ready to follow him, they were eager to."

Sterling said "the men felt differently. There was more of a feeling of freedom and of being trusted. . . . A high degree of confidence in the capabilities and luck of our ship grew on us and we became a little bit cocky. It was a feeling that *Wahoo* was not only the best damn submarine in the . . . Force but that she was capable of performing miracles." Jasper Holmes believed Morton exercised a "discipline hardly recognizable as such" but "her crew responded perfectly to their captain's will and for him reached peaks beyond . . . maximum performance or their ordinary capabilities." Morton was a clear hit.

Griggs wrote that Morton, a nonsmoker and essentially a nondrinker, required each of his officers "to buy his ration of 4 fifths of whiskey from the Club. But little of this was consumed during the rest period. . . . When we departed on patrol the officer's ration of whiskey would go in the ship's safes and would be dispensed to the crew after an attack or other suitable occasions." This did not mean that *Wahoo* was a drunkards' boat. It did mean that at critical times each man could enjoy about ten ounces of booze, disseminated slowly over the course of a patrol—a great lift.

The sudden jump in morale was not limited to the crew. For Grider, "meals in the wardroom took on the nature of parties; instead of staring at our plates and fretting . . . as we had grown accustomed to doing, we found ourselves led along by a captain who was constantly joking, laughing, or planning outrageous exploits."

O'Kane was stuffier about his hero. Unlike the enlisted men, he never called Morton "Mush," but Dudley. He remarked on the change in the officers, but in a superior, pursed-lip manner intended to convey maximum dignity to this luminary: "The change in our wardroom was heartening, perhaps best described as a combination of pleasant, proper etiquette, with an overriding camaraderie. Morton was the president of the mess and set an example by recognizing the junior officers, so they were no longer hesitant about entering into any of the conversations. . . ."

But Morton was not just Dr. Feelgood. He made profound, deep changes in the way *Wahoo* would patrol and attack. The most startling was his decision to make O'Kane his "coapproach officer." That is, O'Kane, not Morton, would man the periscope on submerged attacks and the TBT on the surface. Morton would con the boat to the best attack position; O'Kane would make the all-important angle-on-the-bow, range, and speed estimates—and call the torpedo firing instant.

Mechanically, O'Kane was an ideal choice. In addition to excellent vision, he possessed a trigonometric mind. He did not just visually estimate the angle on the bow, a surprisingly difficult task through the single eye of the periscope, he also observed the ship's length. If it was, say, half its full length, the angle on the bow was thirty degrees, since the sine of thirty degrees is one-half (O'Kane's mind actually functioned this way).

Morton honed this talent by requiring O'Kane to practice an hour a day on flash cards, photos of ships of all types, shown in all aspects. Griggs and other junior officers would pull random cards from a box and flash them at O'Kane, who would call the all-important angle on the bow. Later, they built a homemade simulator: ships' models on a lazy Susan that he would view backward through a single binocular tube. O'Kane, competing with the other officers, became very good indeed. Griggs wrote that "he could call angles to 2° even on a beam observation."

Emotionally, O'Kane as coapproach officer was a questionable choice, but Morton showed remarkably prescient judgment of O'Kane's coolness under fire. Grider still thought O'Kane a "petulant adolescent." Morton saw something more; his confidence and trust would be rewarded.

Morton scrapped tradition by assigning officers to the job they could do best, regardless of rank. George Grider was an excellent tactician, and Morton depended on his advice. Griggs wrote that "Roger Paine was perhaps the premier TDC operator in the force.... Mush himself knew the fire control problem as no other one did.... With his ever present 'Is-Was' it was amusing to observe [Morton] and Roger Paine arguing over 5° of target course and ¼ knot of speed."

Morton delegated well. He junked Kennedy's requirement to always have two officers on the bridge. Now only one would stand watch. He left no doubts that the OOD "was on his own, that he was trusted, and that he was thoroughly in command unless . . . he asked for help." Morton would go below to sleep, projecting total confidence in the officer who had the con. And he reestablished O'Kane's authority as executive officer. Now all administrative reports went first to O'Kane, who was quite capable of handling them without involving the energies of the captain.

To keep the crew interested and alert, Morton continually rotated tasks during the watches. The number of lookouts was reduced, the better to clear the bridge in a dive. But the lookouts stayed on station for only an hour, then rotated to radar or sound, the helm, or even messenger duty. Morton wanted to break the monotony that often dulled alertness. He also held out "alertness bait." Any lookout who made enemy contact on a watch that resulted in a ship sunk would be promoted on the spot.

Small details were not overlooked. Since *Wahoo* would be diving faster, a spare Mae West was attached to the periscope shears. Any lookout who did not clear the shears in time would at least have a chance to grab a flotation device before the waters closed over him. Morton encouraged the crew to come up with more new tricks. Sterling said the "initiative fever was catching and we all began to have ideas. . . . We had the best morale I had ever experienced aboard a ship. . . ."

In the midst of this miraculous rebirth O'Kane received devastating news. On January 11 he was told that his beloved old boat, *Argonaut,* had been lost the preceding day southeast of New Britain. The sinking was observed by an army air corps bomber returning to Australia with its bombs already expended. There were no survivors.

Argonaut had been modernized after O'Kane's departure, including new engines and two after torpedo tubes. The minelaying gear had been removed and the huge ship given a new mission for which she was suited: special operations for General MacArthur. She had already served as a transport for the 2nd Marine Raider Battalion to Makin.

But Admiral Fife, new to his command and discontented with the poor showing to date of U.S. submarines, wanted Japanese ships sunk. *Argonaut* was en route from Pearl to Brisbane to take on the special missions task when Fife intervened. He ordered her instead to attack shipping in the hazardous area south of St. George's Channel, a task for which she was not fit. A convoy of five Marus escorted by three destroyers was sighted. Her new captain, Jack Pierce, apparently decided to attack the destroyers first. An American airplane flying overhead reported one hit, possibly as many as three, on the destroyers, but no evidence exists to support this gallant claim.

Now *Isokaze* and *Maikaze* had come boiling to the attack and trapped the old, slow boat. Crippled from the depth charging, *Argonaut* tried to surface. Her great bow broke the water at a steep angle and the two Japanese destroyers circled, pumping shells into it. *Argonaut's* crew was large—105 men—many of whom O'Kane knew very, very well. Already stung by Pearl Harbor, O'Kane could not help his desire to seek revenge for his friends whose deaths he felt were needless.

At reveille on January 15, 1943, Morton called the crew to quarters. Sterling remembered that Grider's and Paine's faces were expressionless as Morton quietly told the crew: "*Wahoo* is expendable. . . . Our mission is to sink enemy shipping. We are going out there . . . to search for Japs. Every smoke trace on the horizon, every contact on watch will be investigated. If it turns out to be the enemy, we are going to hunt him down and kill him. . . . If anyone doesn't want to go along under these conditions, just see the yeoman. I am giving him verbal authority now to transfer anyone who is not a volunteer. . . ." The crew was given thirty minutes to consider this offer.

Sterling waited in his tiny office, smoking and drinking coffee while he thought about what he had just heard. At the end of the allotted time Morton stuck his head in and asked "Any customers, Yeo?" Sterling replied in the negative; Morton was elated. "That's the kind of stuff I like in a crew. We're going to sink some Jap ships this trip."

But while peer pressure was too great for anyone to step forward, second thoughts crossed many minds. Chief Ralph Pruett, career navy, was "wary of men like Morton. . . . I don't think he had a postwar plan, which I did have . . . to come back from the war alive. [I don't] think Morton thought that far ahead."

Several of the other chiefs, including Chief of the Boat Pappy Rau, asked Sterling to meet with them privately in the CPO quarters. Because of his prior service with Morton on the China Station, they thought Sterling might have special insights into Morton's thinking. The chiefs feared he might be a little crazy and pumped the yeoman for details that would confirm their forebodings.

Grider and Paine were also uneasy as they discussed their captain's attitude. Grider remembered, ". . . there had been times on the second patrol when [Morton's] casually expressed opinions suggested the absence of any reasonable degree of caution. It is one thing to be aggressive, and another to be foolhardy, and it would be a mistake to think that the average man . . . never thought of his own hide. Most of us, in calculating the risk, threw in a mental note that we were worth more to the Navy alive than dead—and to our wives and children as well. But when Mush expressed himself on tactics, the only risk he recognized was the risk of not sinking enemy tonnage."

Misgivings hidden, *Wahoo* departed Brisbane at noon with a seaman's flourish. Morton, in his first display of boat handling, was closely watched by both his crew and the crew of submarines tethered on either side. With a loud command "All back full," *Wahoo* lunged stern first into the Brisbane River, as if shot from a cannon. With the starboard screw still backing, Morton ordered "Port ahead two-thirds" and "Left twenty degrees rudder." *Wahoo* pivoted neatly. "Rudder amidships, starboard ahead two-thirds" and the accelerating submarine neatly split the channel markers. The Australian river pilot was most impressed, as was O'Kane. Fortunately, Morton was accustomed to river currents from prior duty in the Thames at Groton. Otherwise his departure could have been embarrassing.

Within ninety minutes *Wahoo* was into the bay. Morton immediately began intensive training with the destroyer *Patterson*, which would accompany them on a twenty-four-hour run toward the Coral Sea. Morton's relaxed management techniques may have been a wonder to the officer corps, but this relaxation did not extend to training. While surfaced he kept *Wahoo* at full power, running the turbos constantly to blow a constant stream of bubbles along her skin in an effort to increase her speed. *Wahoo* flashed through the seas at twenty-one knots.

All dives, even routine trim dives, were executed with bone-crushing speed. Lookouts simply dove for the conning tower hatch, not necessarily hitting a ladder rung on the way down. If they didn't roll out of the way quickly enough, the next lookout landed on top of them. But *Wahoo* trimmed three seconds off her average dive time. Morton planned to use this ability to get under quickly to stay on the surface longer, even in the presence of reconnaissance aircraft.

When surfacing for gun action, seven tons of water were blown from the safety tanks first. Lighter, *Wahoo* would try to rise while Grider forcibly held her down with bow planes and increased speed. At the command "Battle surface" Grider blew the main ballast and put the planes on hard rise. *Wahoo* popped to the surface like a cork, the ready gun crew streaming out through the conning tower after door to man the "new" four-inch deck gun.

During practice submerged attacks on *Patterson*, Morton concentrated on perfecting the down-the-throat shot. He had a prior agreement with *Patterson*'s skipper that the destroyer could charge the periscope if it was seen. Deliberate short exposures prevented *Patterson* from spotting the scope until the last simulated attack. Then O'Kane deliberately held the periscope high out of the water as bait. *Wahoo* got off four simulated shots during the charge. The fire control party's technique seemed to work. Paine was concerned about Morton's battle philosophy, since this technique had failed *Pompano* on her first war patrol.

Because of the high-speed running, *Wahoo* had advanced more than four hundred miles farther on her course than expected during the training period. After exchanging farewells by signal lamp, *Patterson* turned back to Australia. *Wahoo* proceeded on the surface for Vitiaz Strait, separating New Guinea from New Britain.

Morton decided to bring the crew up to speed by posting *Wahoo*'s operational orders for all to read. O'Kane thought this improper. We're "all in the same boat. Why not?" Morton replied. One order of interest read:

"Adjust speed . . . to permit daylight reconnaissance vicinity Wewak. . . ."

The first problem was to locate Wewak, which did not appear on any charts. Morton's trust in the crew and encouragement of their initiative paid off. Dalton "Bird Dog" Keeter, a chief motor machinist's mate, had purchased a school atlas in Australia for his children. Knowing Wewak was the goal, he pored over a large fold-out map of northeastern New Guinea, spotted it, and took the atlas to his officers. The map was the wrong scale but quite detailed, showing both the harbor and its protective islands. Grider used his father's World War I Graflex camera and an Aldis lamp as a projector, adjusting the height until correctly scaled harbor details could be traced onto the sea charts.

Next Morton, with the flair of a ham actor, hooked the crew. Sterling was present when he shuffled into the crew's mess room dressed in "an old red bathrobe and go-ahead slippers. He . . . had a navigational chart under one arm and a bucket of soapy water in the other hand." The chart was the projection of Keeter's school atlas.

After dramatically thumbtacking the chart to the bulletin board, he played the role of Kentucky farmer, washing his khaki shirt in the pail as he engaged the crew in small talk about the mission. When the trigger word "reconnoiter" was uttered, Morton asked the crew, "Would you guys like to go in and look around? Maybe we'll find a submarine tender with a lot of submarines alongside. I sure would like that."

As the crew's interest grew, Morton wove a fairy tale: "By the way, I'm forming a group of commandos. Pass the word around that, if anybody wants to volunteer for it, to come see me in my stateroom." The younger crew members were hooked, even if the chiefs were skeptical.

Wahoo pounded toward Vitiaz Strait mostly on the surface, pausing only for gun drills whenever a large enough piece of wreckage could be sighted in the sea. One afternoon when Grider had the watch, Morton climbed to the bridge to talk. Their eyes and the radar simultaneously picked up a Japanese plane about eight miles away. Grider turned to head for the conning tower hatch when "Mush's big hand landed on the back of my collar just as I reached the ladder."

Morton said, "Let's wait till he gets in to six miles." The plane closed the range to 6½ miles while Grider's heart pounded. Then, not having sighted the submarine, the plane opened its range and faded from view. Morton had averted a dive, with its attendant slow underwater progress, but Grider was now convinced he was "under the command of a madman."

As they neared New Britain, with Japanese airfields only thirty miles away, Morton continued *Wahoo*'s daylight surface run. Now Morton added two more lookouts, one fitted with special binoculars to sweep the area near the sun. After an hour of this brazen run Grider, to demonstrate his aplomb, sent for his sunglasses. Another hour passed. Grider sent for his suntan lotion. His bravura performance impressed the captain. After fifteen more minutes Morton said, "All right, George, you can go ahead and take her down now." Even O'Kane "welcomed the security below."

And so it was that now supremely confident officers and crew found themselves capable of the long, hazardous penetration of Wewak Harbor. The daring task complete, *Wahoo* cruised northwest along the coast of New Guinea after sinking *Harusame*. She crossed the equator during this leg, and the "shellbacks" staged an enormous initiation party for the "polliwogs."

This was actually the second crossing for many, including George Grider, but no one had dared to suggest a party when Kennedy was captain.

Morton went all out, and the initiation extended to the officers. Roger Paine, already a veteran, dove the boat while King Neptune and his advisers held court. Grider had his hair shaved in spite of growing a decoy mustache, which he hoped would be a suitable sacrifice. There was much kissing of the fattest, suitably greased bellies. A gauntlet of swinging paddles had to be traversed on hands and knees. Medical inspections resulted in Mercurochrome tongues followed by Tabasco sauce, iodine, vinegar, soap powder, and castor oil dough "pills." Finally, no slimy, sneaky, leprous polliwogs remained in the crew.

But it was not all boyish play. A somber reminder of the harshness of life came when *Wahoo* encountered a native banca carrying six living men of indeterminate race and language. Paine manned the foredeck as *Wahoo* came alongside. The crew of this little boat was in ghastly condition. One was blind, all were covered in sores that O'Kane and Grider felt were indications of scurvy. They were near death, three of their number having already died. Morton took pity on them and had as much fresh fruit, canned goods, bread, cigarettes, and water as could be spared transferred to the banca. O'Kane had Krause mark a spare chart for the sailors' guidance; then *Wahoo* pulled away to continue her search as the banca crew weakly waved back.

7

Success and Excess

All actions beyond the ordinary limits
are subject to a sinister interpretation.

—Montaigne, "Essays II"

Buyo Maru was a good-size cargo ship of 6,447 tons. Before the war she was operated by the Tamai Steamship Company, but had long since been commandeered by the Japanese Army. In company with the 5,900-ton *Pacific Maru* and the much smaller freighter *Fukuei Maru 2*, she was now making good progress on her two-thousand-mile-run from Ambon, Indonesia, to Rabaul, on New Britain.

The first part of the journey from Singapore to Surabaya had been horrible. The Indian prisoners, already weakened by nearly a year's captivity, had not fared well. The vomit from their seasickness, and the overflow from the dysentery cases lined up to reach the two latrines, had made the hold a stinking cesspool. It was so foul that the Japanese finally jury-rigged two more "heads" for the captives. After several days at sea Captain Sen managed to persuade the Japanese Army officers to let fifty men at a time be rotated on deck for fifteen minutes of fresh air. The Japanese soldiers were disgusted by this stinking rabble and shouted to Sen to send them below. There was scant food and water, though the Indians complained less of this than did the very few British on board.

Buyo Maru stayed in the port of Surabaya for five days. The Indian prisoners were not permitted to leave the hold. The trucks were replaced with four "barges," dead shellfish still sticking to their sides. The odor of decaying seafood overwhelmed the hold. Upon reaching Ambon the condition of 6 prisoners was so grave they were disembarked. There were now 1,126 men aboard, 491 of them Indian POWs.

Buyo Maru left Ambon on January 21 to sail north-northwest through Manipa Strait, the Ceram Sea, then into the Molucca Sea. Her course then became northerly, passing Halmahera. She finally turned east into the Pacific Ocean, toward Rabaul, after rounding Morotai.

Now, on this morning of January 26, *Buyo Maru* was making ten knots in excellent weather, in company with the two other ships of the convoy. She was still nine hundred miles from her destination, but at this pace, with no zigzagging, all three ships would be in Rabaul in four days. They were soon to pick up an escort that would guard them during their passage through the Bismarck Sea.

At 0757 Grider was about to go off watch, sadly rubbing his newly bare pate and consoling himself with thoughts of breakfast. On his last scan of the horizon he spotted smoke and rang battle stations. Morton sent lookouts high in the periscope shears to see more as *Wahoo* cranked up to full speed to get ahead of this prospective target. Soon the highest lookouts could see the tops of masts of one ship coming over the horizon, then another. Morton and a rested O'Kane were pleased, since neither of the masts resembled that of an escort.

JANUARY 26, 1943. Roger Paine (right rear) and Dudley "Mush" Morton working on fire control program during attack. (National Archives)

The targets were not zigzagging, a surprise to *Wahoo*'s fire control party, and the plot of their course was quickly calculated. Paine already had the TDC humming with angle-on-the-bow and range information. *Wahoo* quickly reached a position dead ahead of the targets and at 0845 slid silently down into the sunless sea to await their arrival.

The general plan was to get into position thirteen hundred yards off the target's track, with all six bow tubes pointed at the enemy. Exploiting the capability of the TDC, they would let the first ship pass, then fire a spread of three torpedoes each at both targets, with different gyro settings.

At 1030, on the final periscope observation, O'Kane saw that the targets had adjusted course toward *Wahoo*. They would be too close for the torpedoes to arm. Morton immediately conned *Wahoo* into a U-turn. They would use the same strategy, but fire the four stern tubes as *Wahoo* moved away to open the distance.

But now they had to move fast, the targets were making speed, and the TDC—a mechanical computer—took measurable time to complete its calculations and transmit the new gyro angles to the stern tubes. At 1041 O'Kane commenced firing. Two torpedoes struck home in *Fukuei Maru 2*. One of the two torpedoes for the second target missed ahead; the gyro setting generated by the TDC had not been fully completed on the new setup. But the second torpedo seemed to slam home in what was later identified as *Pacific Maru*. Morton immediately swung *Wahoo* around again. Now he would use the six bow tubes to finish off the two cripples.

As *Wahoo* turned, O'Kane was sweeping the area with the periscope. He stopped in his tracks. He had just sighted a third target, the POW ship *Buyo Maru*.

Morton said, "You're on the wrong bearing."

"That may be, but I've got a big one coming at us with a zero angle," O'Kane replied.

Grider remembered "a feeling of annoyance at Dick's words. . . . He had distinctly mentioned three ships, [and] all of us knew there were only two up there."

Morton instructed O'Kane to go for a down-the-throat shot on *Buyo Maru*, but in the excitement Krause accidentally fired a torpedo prematurely. The transport turned away from this scattershot and inadvertently presented her whole side to *Wahoo*'s fire control party. Two more torpedoes were purposefully unleashed, both of which struck *Buyo*. She stopped in her tracks.

O'Kane now turned his attention back to *Pacific Maru*. While the ship was clearly damaged, her captain had been lumbering toward *Wahoo*'s periscope with the intent to ram. Damaged, she was too slow even to produce a bow wave, but she had greatly narrowed the distance between the two combatants. Morton conned *Wahoo* around and ordered O'Kane to fire two more torpedoes down the throat. O'Kane, after his experience with the destroyer at Wewak, "had hoped never to hear those words again." The sound man heard the first torpedo strike without detonating—a dud. The second torpedo did explode, though it was probably a premature, since *Pacific Maru* kept on coming.

Grider wrote later that he had ". . . a higher regard for the captain of that freighter than for any other enemy skipper we ever fought." The civilian skipper of the damaged *Pacific Maru* was about to ram *Wahoo*'s conning tower; Grider dove the boat to a hundred feet to escape. Morton had increased underwater speed and twisted *Wahoo* out of the way in case the freighter was about to roll depth charges over the side.

Fukuei Maru 2, now sank with a great cacophony of sea noise and crumbling bulkheads, leaving coal dust and debris to mark its going. Sonar was useless in the underwater din. Eight minutes later, after torpedo tubes were reloaded and the noise level had subsided, the sound man had *Pacific Maru* and *Buyo Maru* sorted out. *Wahoo* returned to periscope depth, and Morton decided to go after *Buyo* first.

Dead in the water, she did not present much of a fire control problem for Paine to solve. But *Buyo* fought back. The Japanese were firing at *Wahoo*'s periscope, and O'Kane could not help flinching at the water splashes. At 1133 two torpedoes were fired; one was a dud, bouncing off the transport's side. The second blew an enormous hole in *Buyo,* and she began to sink. Lifeboats and rafts were launched for the Japanese; their troops began to pour off the doomed vessel into their new havens in the sea. The Indian prisoners all had life belts but were not permitted in the rafts. They simply jumped in the water.

Once again Morton turned his attention back to *Pacific Maru*. The valiant ship was struggling away at a speed *Wahoo* could not match submerged. In fact, she had either repaired her damage or put another boiler on line; she was now making six knots, climbing back toward ten. To complicate matters, Chief Pruett stuck his head into the conning tower to tell Morton that the four hours of high-speed underwater running had depleted the batteries. Morton decided to take a break; feed the crew, which had missed breakfast; then go after *Pacific Maru* on the surface while simultaneously charging batteries.

The watch officer, tracking their game adversary through the search scope, now saw a fourth ship come over the horizon. The thick masts of target number four at first led O'Kane to believe it was a light cruiser. But as she turned away to join *Pacific Maru* he caught sight of a large stack aft and identified her as a tanker. She wasn't, but may have been *Ukishima Maru*, a 4700-ton armed merchant cruiser. No matter. *Wahoo* had enough torpedoes for both of them. It was going to be an interesting afternoon.

Dudley Morton had been born in the first decade of the twentieth century. Like most white men of that time, he thought his race uniquely superior to all others. This opinion was probably reinforced by his Florida upbringing and his years in the navy, where no man of color was allowed any but the most menial of duties, typically as steward. World War II had not changed this rigidly racist structure.

Morton viewed the Japanese, in particular, as subhuman. The Pearl Harbor attack had hardened his heart. He felt no compassion, and the brutal Japanese conquest of East Asia had reinforced his hatred. While in Brisbane he had heard fresh stories of the Japanese attack on Darwin.

On February 19, 1942, Admiral Chuichi Nagumo's fast carrier group launched 242 aircraft against Allied shipping packed in the northern port of Darwin, Australia. When the successful bombing raid was over, the Japanese pilots machine-gunned the lifeboats and helpless survivors struggling in the water, killing 170 men. Even an Australian hospital ship, clearly marked with red crosses, was bombed and strafed. With incidents like these as part of his emotions, Morton developed what Grider called an "overwhelming biological hatred" of the enemy. In every compartment in *Wahoo* he had had Sterling post 8½ × 11 placards, printed in glaring red, that said:

SHOOT THE

SUNZA

BITCHES

Morton was determined that the horrors the Japanese had visited on the United States would be returned a thousandfold.

Morton and O'Kane ate sandwiches in the conning tower, alternately keeping watch on the two targets retiring to the north, away from the coast of New Guinea. By now O'Kane and the fire control party had identified the fourth ship as a 6,500-ton Manzyu Maru class tanker. This was an important target, but Morton had his mind on *Buyo Maru*'s "Jap" troops, now floating in lifeboats of all descriptions. He "decided to let these two ships get over the horizon while we surfaced to charge batteries and destroy the estimated twenty troop boats now in the water." Grider's memory was blunter. With "fierce joyousness" Morton said, "Let's finish him off."

As Paine readied the gun crews, Grider eased *Wahoo* closer to the surface. Her periscope rose higher and higher, O'Kane glued to the eyepiece to track the retiring vessels. At 1315, satisfied that the sea and the sky were empty of all but *Buyo Maru*'s survivors, O'Kane gave the order "Battle stations—surface." Morton called, "Bring her up quick, George."

Moments later *Wahoo*'s bow broke the surface at a sharp angle, followed by the low, black hull cascading water from her decks and sides. The great sea monster plowed forward quietly under the power of her electric motors. The conning tower hatch banged open. O'Kane, Morton, and Roger Paine, who was responsible for the gun crews, leaped to the bridge, followed by the lookouts. Sterling took his position on the starboard platform, about six feet above the bridge. He had already stuffed cotton in his ears. "Adrenaline was pouring into my bloodstream and I felt a primitive instinct to do battle."

"Open the main induction!" was followed by the loud clang of the hydraulically operated valve opening its huge mouth to breathe for the engines. The explosive roar of a starting diesel shattered the relative peace and was followed by three more roars as all engines were brought on line. *Wahoo* moved faster now, engines rumbling, their exhausts half submerged in the sea. Grider turned on the low-pressure air blowers to completely cleanse the ballast tanks of seawater. Their high-pitched screaming sound could be heard across the water by the *Buyo Maru* survivors, six miles away.

Because of the lunchtime pursuit of the fleeing ships, *Wahoo* had to reverse course. She closed the distance at two-engine speed, perhaps a twenty-minute run. O'Kane reported Morton's explicit instructions to Paine and the gun captains: "I'll order a single four-inch round at the largest craft, and we'll continue in to see if we draw any return fire. Keep your crews in any protected area until I commence firing. Machine guns, it'll be your job to chase the troops out of the boats, and Chief [Carr, the four-inch-gun captain] . . . you smash up the boats."

Wahoo's crew could not see the deadly struggle among survivors taking place in the sea. The Japanese had placed a flag on one of the lifeboats as a rallying point. Only Japanese were permitted to occupy lifeboats and rafts, but there still was inadequate space for all of them. Many Japanese troops were in the water, and were engaged in deadly fights with the Indians over possession of debris. Captain Sen "warned those men near me to keep away from the Japanese who were hunting for floating wreckage. . . ." So did Subedar Hussain Shah Mohd of the 2/16 Punjab. But Sep. Abdulla Khan of the 5/2 ignored the warning, fought with, and killed, a Japanese soldier who tried to take a plank away from him. The Japanese would later wreak horrible vengeance on Khan for this action, beating him to death after the most horrible torment, including putting out Khan's eyes.

Wahoo was now near the survivors. As Paine moved his gunners into position behind the conning tower he "could hear the 'zing' of overhead shots and the 'thunk' of bullets into the superstructure." They were receiving counterfire.

The four-inch gun fired once at the largest craft, and a near-miss drove all its occupants into the sea. The Indian survivors did not report this initial round. *Wahoo* churned closer. O'Kane recorded that ". . . about two minutes later, the [largest] craft returned a long burst from a machine gun." Again, no Indian survivor reported this event, but evidently Morton heard it. It was all the excuse he needed. "Commence firing" was his exultant order.

The Indians were dismayed. Subedar Mohd testified: "The submarine came to the surface and began to machine-gun the boats. At this all the Japs at once jumped into the sea." Captain Sen elaborated: ". . . the submarine . . . started to shell the boats and machine-gun also. Many of us shouted out to the submarine that we were Indian POWs. . . ."

Wahoo's four-inch gun, two twenty-millimeter machine guns, and two Browning automatic rifles (BARs) opened up. O'Kane thought the firing was quite ". . . methodical, the small guns sweeping from abeam forward like fire hoses cleaning a street."

He wrote that ". . . no individual was deliberately shot in the boats or in the sea." Not everyone agreed. Chief Pruett recalled that he ". . . was there . . . as Morton gave the order for the deck guns to open fire on several thousand Japanese troops left swimming in the water" and commanded, "Anyone who doesn't get up here and load the deck guns, I'll court-martial." Pruett obeyed.

Captain A. K. Daw, a British doctor from the 40th IGH, remembered that the "boats were destroyed by the submarine which . . . started shelling them and also opened machine-gun fire on the men." Sep. Ahmad Khan of the 5/2 reported that "the submarine . . . opened fire on us and a few died." Sep. Ghulam Mohd, also of the 5/2, swore that ". . . the submarine . . . opened fire on us. We shouted and said we were Indian POWs but with no result."

Sterling could see that "the water was filled with heads sticking up from floating kapok life jackets. They were scattered roughly within a circle a hundred yards wide. Scattered among them were several lifeboats, a motor launch with an awning, a number of rafts loaded with sitting and standing Japanese fighting men, and groups of men floating in the water where they had drifted together. Others were hanging onto planks or other items of floating wreckage. A few isolated individuals were paddling back toward the center in search of some human solidarity."

Grider was diving officer, but with twenty-five to thirty of the crew on deck, and with several deck hatches open, it was clear *Wahoo* was not about to make a quick dive. He came up through the conning tower and went to the cigarette deck behind the bridge to watch.

He saw "... a sea of Japanese. They were on every piece of flotsam, every broken stick, in lifeboats, everywhere, and as we cruised among them, they looked at us with expressions beyond description. . . . The water was so thick with enemy soldiers that it was literally impossible to cruise through them without pushing them aside like driftwood."

That may have been an exaggeration, but *Wahoo* was clearly very near to the men in the water. Captain Daw wrote: "The submarine was quite close as I could see the painted number on it and also the men on board. . . ." Many of the Indians tried to convey to *Wahoo*'s crew that they were prisoners. Captain Sen testified after the war that ". . . some men waved white clothes or handkerchiefs," and Subedar Mohd said that ". . . our men . . . started shouting and waving handkerchiefs or towels saying we were Indian POW but evidently it was not heard by the crew of the submarine."

Sterling, with cotton-plugged ears, could hear nothing over the roar of the engines and the din of gunfire. But he misunderstood the visual signals. "I . . . took another quick look at the Japs in the water. Some had drifted in to about twenty-five yards of *Wahoo* and I could see the close-cropped skulls of those without campaign visors. They all stared without expression at *Wahoo*'s hull. . . . I saw one Jap standing on a raft waving a large piece of canvas in the air. 'I didn't think the Japs ever surrendered,' I said over my shoulder."

Morton and O'Kane also had their perceptions altered by what they expected to see, not reality. Pumped by the gun action, they were not analyzing the scene with detachment. They huddled below Sterling.

"What do you think? They look like marines to me," said O'Kane.

"Yuh, damn right they are. They're part of Hirohito's crack Imperial Marine outfit. I run into some of them before the war at Shanghai," Morton answered.

Thus were ordinary Japanese ordnance depot soldiers and Indian prisoners of war elevated to the ranks of justly vanquished supermen.

Years later Jasper Holmes wrote of Morton, "There is no doubt that this remarkable man became intoxicated with battle, and when in that state of exhilaration he was capable of rash action difficult to justify under more sober circumstances." Grider was more emotional. These were "nightmarish minutes," he wrote.

Sterling felt that O'Kane was inclined to keep shooting as he said to Morton, ". . . if those troops get rescued, we're going to lose a lot of American boys' lives digging them out of foxholes and shooting them out of palm trees."

But Morton was beginning to regain mission priority. "I know," Sterling heard him say, "and it's a damn stinking shame . . . when we've got them cold-turkey in the water. . . . But . . . there's still that oil tanker and cargo ship out there. We're going after those babies as soon as we get a battery charge."

O'Kane asked Sterling if he could still see the fleeing Japanese ships. "Yes, sir. I can still see smoke on the horizon and they are hull down." After fifteen to twenty minutes at the site of the *Buyo Maru* sinking, *Wahoo* turned to a north-northeast course, ignoring the men in the water, and set off in pursuit at flank speed. At 1530 they were in perfect position to plot the targets' course and speed—now back to a full ten knots—with ample daylight hours left to make an end-around and get in front of their prey. At 1721 *Wahoo* dove in front of the oncoming ships.

The "tanker"—though O'Kane now thought it could be an engine-aft freighter—was to be first. The assumption was that *Pacific Maru* was hurt, though a speed of ten knots was a clue that the wound could not be severe. Thus the undamaged ship had the first priority.

At 1830 three torpedoes were fired from the bow tubes at the engine-aft ship—possibly *Ukishima Maru*. *Wahoo* immediately began to turn to bring its stern tubes to bear on *Pacific Maru*. In the midst of the turn there was a great flash and subsequent explosion from a single torpedo, which the crew of *Wahoo* believed to be a hit on *Ukishima*. However, her speed did not slacken. The indomitable *Pacific Maru* turned away as a result of the blast and ruined *Wahoo*'s fire control setup.

Morton was now faced with a practical problem. *Wahoo* had only four torpedoes left, all in the stern tubes. There could be no underwater maneuvering that would permit a shot at these rather swift "cripples." Morton decided to surface and pursue the targets at high speed, hoping to get in a shot.

At 1841 *Wahoo* was racing at full surfaced speed after *Ukishima Maru*. This ship was ably handled, with good lookouts. Every time *Wahoo* turned to present her tail to the target, *Ukishima* would turn away, with excellent high-speed evasion tactics. Morton was unable to con *Wahoo* into firing position. In desperation, he attempted to run at the target, full speed, in reverse. As anyone who has backed a sailboat into a slip knows, the force of the sea on the rudder is tremendous. Just as *Wahoo* reached full speed, the hydraulic steering mechanism yielded to the pressure against the rudder, throwing *Wahoo* into a wild backward turn.

For an hour and a half Morton struggled to get into firing position, with the Japanese crew anticipating his every move and evading. Meanwhile, Paine and the fire control party had solved the basic zigzag pattern. Morton placed *Wahoo* in an anticipatory position for the next zig. At 1,850 yards range two stern torpedoes were fired, one of which hit. Morton believed they had broken *Ukishima Maru*'s back. O'Kane could see a sharp list and considered this "Manzyu Maru tanker" sunk. At 2036 *Wahoo* passed the gravely wounded target: "Only the bow section was afloat."

Wahoo now began her third approach on *Pacific Maru*, which was firing back with excellent flashless powder—better than anything possessed by the U.S. Navy. The Japanese gunnery accuracy was very good, and Morton was forced to dive again, ". . . grinning in . . . admiration of the job the freighter was doing," Grider wrote, as "a shell fell almost on the bridge." One lookout was so frightened by the near-misses, Sterling wrote, that "his teeth were chattering, his face pale under a lookout's tan, and his eyes were dilated." A new approach plan was settled, and *Wahoo* resurfaced at 2058 to see that *Pacific Maru* was about to receive aid.

A searchlight beam swept the surface of the sea, its rays ". . . just clearing our periscope shears." This was *Choku Maru 2*, an armed merchant cruiser, coming to the aid of the savaged convoy. Rather than break off the attack, Morton concluded that *Pacific Maru* would head toward this beacon of relief. He put *Wahoo* on an interception course and prepared to fire at comparatively long range—three thousand yards.

The plotting party did heavy algebra to calculate where and when *Pacific Maru* would rendezvous with *Choku Maru*. It was imperative that *Wahoo* get there first. O'Kane called constant bearings on *Pacific Maru*'s stack from the TBT. All alone, Roger Paine continually updated each new data point into the TDC. Grider climbed into the conning tower and noted that "the thinking was being left to the mechanical brain built into the computer."

Wahoo raced at emergency speed to get between target and rescuer, then turned off the track and presented her stern to *Pacific Maru*. Morton decided the time had come.

"Anytime, Dick."

O'Kane called out, "Constant bearing—mark!"

Paine, manipulating the spread control, responded, "Set."

The last two torpedoes were fired.

"Lieutenant Paine," said Grider thoughtfully, "if either one of those torpedoes hits, I will kiss your royal ass on Times Square at high noon."

This declaration of intent was followed by two on-time explosions. Paine did not bother to drop his pants.

It was 2026, and *Wahoo*'s crew were certain they had sunk their fourth ship of the day. Sterling, on starboard lookout, saw "the freighter turn . . . slowly over and split into two dark sections before one end tilted up and then slid out of sight. The other end just faded into blackness."

A course was set due north for Fais Island, leaving *Choku Maru* behind, searchlight still sweeping. Every man knew that Pearl Harbor and the Royal Hawaiian was just days away. Morton and all his officers, except those on watch, gathered in the wardroom to celebrate their success. He was lavish in his praise of them and told O'Kane, "Tenacity, Dick. Stay with 'em till they're on the bottom!" He was absolutely right—for those with enough courage—and O'Kane never forgot the lesson.

Wahoo had maintained radio silence to date. Since they had gotten such an enormous running start, both Brisbane and Pearl Harbor likely assumed that *Wahoo* was only now approaching Palau. In fact, she would never even go there now that all torpedoes had been expended. *Wahoo* had sunk five ships (they truly believed)—which at the time was an unprecedented single-patrol tally. Morton crafted a message to Pearl with just the right touch of swashbuckler:

SANK DESTROYER IN WEWAK SUNDAY AND IN A

FOURTEEN HOUR RUNNING GUN AND TORPEDO

BATTLE TODAY SANK CONVOY OF ONE TANKER

TWO FREIGHTERS AND ONE TRANSPORT

DESTROYING HER BOATS TORPEDOES EXPENDED

PROCEEDING PEARL HARBOR VIA FAIS ISLAND

The stunning bulletin electrified Pearl Harbor. It was wonderful news for a submarine force that had had too little to show for their 1942 efforts. Admiral Griggs, whose son was aboard *Wahoo,* began to arrange a spectacular reception for the return.

Admiral English would not be there. He had already departed for a San Francisco conference and, on January 27, his plane was reported long overdue. English was dead, along with nine other officers. On February 5 Admiral Nimitz detached Admiral Charles Lockwood from the Australian submarine command; he was to return to Pearl Harbor as commander of submarines, Pacific Fleet (ComSubPac).

Grider slept the deep sleep that often follows prolonged, intense emotional strain—especially when the pleasant outcome is one's personal safety and the prospect of "home." He turned out of his bunk early for his 0400 to 0800 watch and was now fewer than thirty minutes away from relief and breakfast. At 0720, just under twenty-four hours since his fateful sighting of the now sunken convoy, Grider again saw smoke on the horizon. *Wahoo* was essentially toothless and Grider said to the lookouts, "We can't do anything about it this time, but I'll call the captain. Might as well let him know what's going on."

Wahoo dove at 0800. By 0830 six ships were in sight through a periscope raised ten feet above sea level. This was the largest concentration of enemy shipping they had ever seen. They were unescorted, and *Wahoo* was impotent!

Morton reasoned that while *Wahoo* had no torpedoes, the Japanese did not know that. Further, the ships seemed lightly armed and, better yet, one of them was straggling near the rear of the column. Morton concocted a daring plan. They would pop to the surface using their practiced technique; then two of the gun crew would run forward, free the gun, train it toward the target, and return to safety inside the conning tower while *Wahoo* raced in to intercept the straggler. Morton reasoned that the other ships would pour on the coal, thus increasing the isolation of their target. They would sink the freighter with *Wahoo*'s deck gun.

Wahoo surfaced about twelve thousand yards—nearly seven miles—away from the convoy and started in at full speed. For ten minutes they were undetected, but the targets responded as Morton predicted when the submarine was spotted. Smoke belched from stacks as the convoy headed for a rain squall and visual cover. Two of the ships opened fire, but their range was far too short. In the scramble for safety a tanker became easiest for *Wahoo* to cut off, and Morton bore in, reasoning that it might be filled with aviation gasoline. Only one good deck gun hit would be enough for that kind of cargo.

At 1000, with a range seventy-five hundred yards, Sterling spotted the mast of a seventh ship—an escort—coming their way. The surface attack would have to be aborted. Morton ordered the gun crew below, gun still canted toward the enemy, abandoning the ammunition on deck.

O'Kane, Grider, and Paine insisted the newly discovered escort was a destroyer; Morton was convinced it was a Chidori—a 550-ton torpedo boat—and *Wahoo* could outrun any old Chidori. *Wahoo*'s patrol report records that she "turned tail at full power to draw the escort as far as possible away from the convoy in case we were forced to dive, as this would greatly shorten the time he could remain behind to work us over."

Now began a race for life. In the beginning, *Wahoo* led the way. She pounded along at twenty knots (Grider claimed twenty-one) and in twenty minutes opened the distance from her pursuer to thirteen thousand or fourteen thousand yards. Morton was now in a "see, I told you it was only a Chidori" mood. But the pursuer was issuing more and more smoke. Morton mistook the significance. He yelled at O'Kane, "Why, that anti-quated coal-burning corvette! What a hell of a thing to have escorting a six-ship convoy. The Emperor deserves to lose every ship he's got!"

But the smoke was really a clue that more and more boilers were coming on line. In fifteen more minutes the pursuer, now clearly a destroyer, had closed the range to seven thousand yards and was gaining rapidly. O'Kane could see the "V" of the bow wave rising as high as her deck. Suddenly the destroyer turned right. "Hot dog," said Morton, "she's giving up. . . . We've dragged her a good thirty miles from her convoy. . . . She can't afford to leave it unprotected."

This bravado was answered by a full broadside from the destroyer, the reason she had turned. Morton instructed O'Kane to watch for the splashes, which he believed would fall short. O'Kane wrote that ". . . 3 seconds later a mighty clap of thunder to port and starboard sent me towards the hatch with ringing ears. I saw the shell splashes a half ship's length ahead; she had straddled our shears horizontally." Sterling recalled, "At that moment I moved out into space, hit the deck with a jarring thud . . . skated on the slip-pery deck past the Captain. . . . The next thing I remember I was standing in the mess hall."

Grider heard Morton shout, "Where's that damned diving alarm?" and called up to him "Come on down, Captain." He had already opened the div-ing vents and flooded the negative tank without orders. Morton paused, confused at the absence of lookouts. O'Kane said, "Hell, they dived for the hatch on the flash of the gunfire! It was *Wahoo's* fastest dive . . . ; the next salvo whacked overhead as our shears went under."

Morton instructed Grider to take *Wahoo* deep. Her test depth was 250 feet, but they had already operated at 350; Grider soon had her below 300 feet. There were six teeth-shaking depth charges, the first three terrifying to Sterling: "We were plunged into complete darkness, and a loose piece of metal shooting through the void struck my left ear, causing it to sting sharply. Dishes stacked on the tables were lifted and thrown about. Loose knives and forks flew about at random, their screaming lost in the blasts of the depth charges. Patches of cork showered down, followed by a ventila-tionless room full of choking dust."

The destroyer broke off the search at 1120. It was a long way back to her flock, who had presumably kept on sailing, though O'Kane believed that the destroyer may have also feared a counterattack from *Wahoo*.

Morton was a bit subdued after this excitement, ordering *Wahoo* to stay submerged till 1400 while everyone wound down and had a shot of medic-inal brandy.

After surfacing, *Wahoo* resumed its run to Fais Island. That evening the radio sprang into operation. At nightfall the radio began working in both directions. *Wahoo* sent out a contact report with unusual wording:

ANOTHER RUNNING GUN BATTLE TODAY . . .

WAHOO RUNNIN DESTROYER GUNNIN

In response to *Wahoo's* earlier transmission, radioed congratulations had begun to pour in from the brass. Admiral Griggs, of course, sent accolades representing ComSubPac. But more important was one from Nimitz himself, which was copied to all submarines at sea and included praise from Admiral Halsey. After many laurels it closed:

WAHOO LT COMDR MORTON COMMANDING TWO

DAYS AFTER SINKING DESTROYER AT WEWAK

ENCOUNTERED UNESCORTED CONVOY WHILE

ENROUTE PALAU X WAHOO SANK ENTIRE CONVOY

TWO FREIGHTERS TANKER AND TRANSPORT

DESTROYING HER BOATS. . . .

Miles behind *Wahoo*, the floating survivors of *Buyo Maru* simply concentrated on staying alive. At about 1800 on this same January 27, *Choku Maru 2* and *Pacific Maru*—only damaged, not sunk—churned to the rescue.

One of the first prisoners saved was Captain Daw, who had been in the water about thirty-five hours. He was fortunate. Subedar Mohd testified that "the Japs were rather reluctant in picking up Indians. They directed their energies towards rescuing their own men." But the Japanese did trail ropes in the water, and nets hung from the sides of the ships. Those prisoners strong enough to help themselves lived.

The two rescue ships searched through the night and well into the twenty-eighth. But between 1300 and 1500—accounts vary—they abandoned the recovery effort. Many Indians were left in the water to die. One of the last to be picked up by other Indians, after more than forty-eight hours in the water, was Sep. Ahmad Khan. He was hauled aboard at about noon on the twenty-eighth. "I could hear voices of our men in the sea crying for help to be rescued but they were left behind." Captain Sen knew when the rescue ships sailed that ". . . many of my men who were still alive had not been picked up." Captain Daw saw ". . . twenty men scattered over

FEBRUARY 7, 1943. *Wahoo* arrives at Pearl Harbor at the close of the third war patrol with a broom attached to the periscope signifying "clean sweep." Dudley Morton is at the con, Forest Sterling is starboard lookout, and Dick O'Kane is on the fairwater afterdeck. (U.S. Naval Historical Center)

the sea between 150 . . . [and] 200 yards away . . . struggling to swim up to the ship in spite of exhaustion but they were all left behind."

While the rescue operation proceeded on January 28, *Wahoo* reached Fais Island and completed her reconnaissance. Morton hatched a plan to shell the phosphate works at night, but his aggressiveness was cooled by the arrival of an interisland steamer with two gun mounts. Grider said, "All of us talking together finally convinced Mush that *Wahoo* had done its duty and that the best plan now was to go back and get some more torpedoes."

With Grider navigating, practicing skills in anticipation of a possible promotion and transfer, *Wahoo* arrived at Pearl Harbor at 0830 on February 7. Grider missed his rendezvous with the escort, earning O'Kane's disdain, but could hardly miss Oahu. Allowing for the date line crossing, it had been fewer than twenty-two days since she left Brisbane.

Morton, ever the showman, had a broom affixed to the periscope shears, the old Dutch Navy's symbol of "clean sweep." As *Wahoo* rounded ten-ten dock it was clear that the navy had gone all-out. The Hawaiian War Chant boomed over speakers. Dignitaries abounded. The press was given uncommonly free rein, even taking photographs belowdecks. The *Honolulu Advertiser* headline proclaimed WAHOO RUNNING JAPS A'GUNNING. Morton and O'Kane were celebrities. Morton was interviewed repeatedly and even appeared in the newsreel series *The March of Time*. Morton's wife was interviewed by the Los Angeles press. The acclaim was sensational.

Lockwood arrived from Australia on February 14 and immediately nicknamed *Wahoo* "The One-Boat Wolf Pack." Morton was awarded the Navy Cross. Personal adoration aside, it was clear that Morton's combativeness had ended the prewar stealth philosophy of submarine attacks. From now on, daring aggressiveness would be rewarded; nonperformers would be eliminated.

Wahoo received full wartime credit for the five claimed sinkings. After the war JANAC reduced this total sharply, but these official credits are a muddle.

No credit was given for the sinking of the destroyer *Harusame*, in spite of Grider's pictures, since she was not broken in half, as O'Kane reported. *Harusame* was beached, repaired, and lived to fight another day.

Fukuei Maru 2 did go down permanently—but JANAC gave her size as 1,900 tons. The Imperial Japanese Navy (IJN) monograph published in 1952 trimmed this further, to 1,700 tons. *Wahoo* had claimed 7,200 tons. Part of the size estimate problem was a result of the distorted magnification caused by poor U.S. periscope lenses, but throughout his very active career O'Kane had a subconscious tendency toward oversizing targets.

FEBRUARY 7, 1942. Dick O'Kane (left) and Dudley "Mush" Morton on the bridge of *Wahoo* as she arrives at Pearl harbor at the close of the successful third war patrol. (U.S. Naval Historical Center)

Buyo Maru absolutely sank, but the survivors recalled only two torpedo hits. It is likely that some of the explosions were prematures. Perversely, JANAC gave *Wahoo* credit for only 5,447 tons; IJN claimed 6,446. A transcription error is one possibility.

Pacific Maru was not sunk in spite of the most diligent efforts to bring her down. IJN reported light damage. Possibly this was also caused by prematures.

JANAC did give *Wahoo* credit for a third sinking, a 4,000-ton cargo ship simply labeled "unknown." This was the afterstack "tanker" that more than one witness believed was certainly sunk. A later German publication reported that *Ukishima Maru*, a 4,730-ton armed merchant cruiser, was heavily damaged on January 26, in the right location. However, Roger W. Allan, a 1980s researcher who independently analyzed Japanese wartime shipping losses, says that *Ukishima Maru* was alive and well at Tsingtao on the twenty-sixth. We will likely never know the truth; JANACs "unknown maru" is the most optimistic assessment.

Hidden by the credit given for five sinkings was almost certainly a high mixture of premature explosions caused by the faulty magnetic influence warhead. Lockwood had long been disposed to discontinue this marvel of American engineering, but Morton's life-saving sixth shot on *Harusame* stayed his hand. Lockwood later wrote that ". . . the magnetic exploder, when bad, was horrible; but when it was good it was wonderful." This delay caused many missed opportunities for all submarines over the next year.

Numerous estimates were made as to how many Japanese troops had been killed after the destruction of *Buyo Maru*'s lifeboats. Morton was the most aggressive in attributing large body counts to this action. The annotation on the photograph of the sinking *Buyo Maru*, inspired by Morton, reads: ". . . the transport sank quickly taking with her from 1,500 to 6,000 enemy troops."

MacArthur awarded Morton the *Army* Distinguished Service Cross for ". . . his attack on a hostile convoy proceeding to reinforce the enemy forces in New Guinea . . . he destroyed completely [the] enemy vessel of the convoy. . . ." *Wahoo* later received a Presidential Unit Citation that lauded the submarine for ". . . destroying the entire force [including] . . . one transport and their personnel." The bigger the death toll, the better.

Paine was easily the most conservative. He had counted shell expenditures, and his "personal estimate [was] that between 25 and 75 Japanese troops were killed by *Wahoo*'s gunfire, and perhaps twice that many wounded. Anyone familiar with statistics from wars of this century on how many rounds of gun ammunition it takes to kill a single enemy soldier is aware that to kill, say 50, soldiers with 2,257 rounds of ammunition would have to be remarkably efficient shooting."

Paine rejected subsequent reports that Morton had claimed "most of the troops" were destroyed. Paine was also directionally accurate in assessing what might have happened after the gun action. He was wary of the huge troop counts that had come to be associated with *Buyo Maru*'s sinking: "There were a lot of heads in the water, but nobody was counting them. There could very well have been only one or two thousand." But if the number were very large ". . . a few thousand may have drowned before a rescue ship could have reached the scene. Except indirectly . . . that can hardly be blamed on Morton. It is simply proof once again that 'war is hell.'"

Recent research has uncovered the fact that Captain O. A. V. Sen took a head count of Indian survivors after they were landed at Palau. There were only 296—a loss of 195 after departing Ambon. The Japanese Diet Library states the Indian losses to be 269. This number may include those who subsequently died in captivity, which, for them, was uncommonly cruel. The Japanese lost 87 men, the lower number clearly a reflection of their rescue priorities. *Wahoo* had 2 wounded, 1 only slightly, when a twenty-millimeter shell exploded in a hot, jammed gun barrel that had been placed on the deck.

Little time was spent by top U.S. commanders reflecting on the moral values associated with destroying lifeboats. After all, it was hardly new.

Japanese submarines had been known to surface in an attempt to kill survivors of sunken merchant ships. As early in the war as January 2, 1942, all but 3 of the 94 crew of the *Langkoeas* were machine-gunned to death by *I-58*. In October 1942, off Guadalcanal, Japanese ships had destroyed all the lifeboats filled with American survivors of the sinking of *YP-284* and *Seminole*. This was to be a long and cruel war.

8

Days of Fury

To be furious is to be frighted out of fear.

—*Shakespeare*, Antony and Cleopatra

O'Kane was hunched over, watching the smoky, circling target through a partially extended periscope. He had been there since 0814 on this Saturday morning, March 13, 1943. It was now 1640. Morton was seated on a swing-out stool beside O'Kane, moody and unenthusiastic. "I don't like it," Sterling heard him say. "She could be a Q-ship. . . ."

Wahoo had arrived on station in the "wading pond," the shallow Yellow Sea, two days prior to sighting this small ship. The turnaround at Pearl Harbor had been unusually swift. The crew had had only eight days free of duty while the refit unit swarmed over *Wahoo,* repairing a damaged main engine and moving the four-inch gun from the afterdeck to a position forward of the conning tower. A third twenty-millimeter gun was mounted in the vacant position—a harbinger of possible surface action in "sampan alley." A number of the torpedo reloads contained new high-explosive Torpex heads.

Morton was supremely confident, even arrogant, during refresher training. The division commander, aboard in a supervisory role, saw that *Wahoo* was running submerged with main vents open—standard Morton doctrine. The division commander ordered Roger Paine, now the diving officer, to close the vents. Morton immediately countermanded the instructions. He ordered Paine to reopen the vents and, as Griggs remembered, told "the division commander that *Wahoo* was his ship and he would not abide others telling him how to run it." Morton was not tested again.

FEBRUARY 8, 1943. George Grider (left) and Roger Paine at Marble Beach, Hawaii. This was an arm's-length self portrait taken by Grider, who became XO of *Pollack* the next day. (Courtesy of Roger Paine)

Three days after arriving at Pearl Harbor, George Grider was transferred. Morton broke the crushing news to him personally. He was to be the XO of the old *Pollack*, one of *Pompano*'s companions on December 7. Grider had his heart set on a new-build in the States. Instead he was to be going on patrol again immediately in a leaky, riveted-hull boat whose keel had been laid down in 1935 and that had a reputation for infirmities.

Pollack was lightly armed, with only four tubes forward and two aft— about the same as a German VII-C U-boat. But the welded-hull U-boat's test depth was 400 feet; *Pollack*'s was only 250 feet.

Grider's view was that "it was a promotion, but it wasn't worth it." His obvious disappointment prompted Morton to say, "Never mind, George. With you aboard she'll burn up the Pacific."

"Yes, but who's going to keep you and Dick out of trouble?" Grider replied.

Grabbing Grider in a wrestling hold, Morton replied, "Don't worry. Roger is almost as big a sissy as you are. He'll take care of us."

Grider dragged himself to *Pollack* to replace his friend and classmate Gus Weinel, who had received the coveted assignment: to the States to help commission the new-build boat *Cisco*. Weinel was gone in minutes, and Grider ached with envy.

Sixteen days after arriving in Pearl, *Wahoo* was under way again, first to Midway, then to the East China Sea—"Tung Hai" to old-timers—gateway to her patrol area between China and Korea. The transit weather was foul. Morton made up for it by running the entire distance from Midway, thirty-nine hundred miles, on the surface, without once sighting so much as a patrol plane.

With an average depth of 90 to 120 feet, the Yellow Sea was a poor spot in which to dive or hide. There had been twenty prior war patrols in neighboring Tung Hai. Most captains found Tung Hai to be shallow, with poor

Lieutenant Commander Dudley "Mush" Morton in his stateroom aboard *Wahoo*. (National Archives)

sonar conditions, and afflicted with glassy seas, which readily disclosed a periscope. But Japanese maritime traffic there was abundant; at least forty-two ships had been credited to these early patrols. *Triton* alone had sunk five ships on her second patrol there, one by gun action. Five ships became Morton's not-so-private goal for *Wahoo*'s fourth patrol into the as-yet-untapped Yellow Sea.

George Grider had not been cleanly replaced. Roger Paine had moved up to engineering officer and now controlled the dives. But Morton wanted Paine to man the TDC during attacks. His fire control party skills were too good to lose. Paine would share the depth control responsibility with Richie Henderson during attacks.

Some of the staffing problems were eased by the presence of a prospective commanding officer. The new PCO was Duncan MacMillan, whom O'Kane had originally expected to be the first captain of *Wahoo*. Now O'Kane felt awkward with the wartime narrowing of ranks between them, and switched to the formal address of Commander. Soon he would unjustly feel that "old man" MacMillan—he was thirty-nine—was short of the aggressive temperament required aboard *Wahoo*.

The usual personality traits persisted or intensified. Sterling made the necessary accommodation to O'Kane: "We get along fine. I always get the last word in. I say 'Yes, sir,' and he walks away." Morton turned on the charm with new crew members, memorizing their first names, encouraging them with arm-around-the-shoulder pep talks, keeping everyone in the picture by personally posting the chart of the Yellow Sea in the mess hall. He also organized a commando group, with U.S. Marine–provided Molotov cocktails stored in the conning tower fairwater, for potential ship boardings.

The only troublesome area of the boat was technical. *Wahoo* had been constructed with an experimental battery that was intended to better withstand depth charge attacks. But the shock-absorbing hard rubber jars surrounding each cell had an internal temperature of 120 degrees F and tended to crack where they touched against the cold hull of the boat. About a quarter of the cell capacity had already been lost.

Now the circling "smoky Maru" turned toward the submerged *Wahoo*, causing O'Kane to press Morton to attack. The ship had been speculatively reidentified all day long. O'Kane was now convinced it was a lightship and had Sterling retrieve the identification book that would prove his point. Morton remained doubtful. At O'Kane's repeated urging Morton finally agreed, ". . . anxious to shoot something." However, he severely limited the attack: ". . . it was the type of target worth one torpedo if you sink him, but not worth two torpedoes under any conditions."

The single stern shot failed. Morton had been sitting downcast, head in hands, during the torpedo run. O'Kane watched the torpedo porpoise ahead of the target, a range error attributed to an incorrect masthead height setting. Immediately he pressed for a second attack. Morton flatly refused: "Hell, no, I'm not going to waste any more shots. . . ."

Sterling saw O'Kane turn purple with frustration: "Captain, we ought to sink that son of a bitch. Let's don't let him get away with that."

Now it was Morton's turn to be angry. In "a cold, brittle voice" he told O'Kane: "That's enough, Dick. Goddamnit, when you get to be a captain in your own sub you can shoot all the torpedoes you want, at whatever you want." He ordered Paine, controlling the TDC, to break off the attack. Morton also ordered a new course and instructed O'Kane to secure from battle stations.

O'Kane later wrote that "the captain and I had continued to vent our frustrations and help the adrenaline subside . . . by a game or two of cribbage." As luck would have it, a few nights later O'Kane drew a perfect hand of twenty-nine—with odds of about one in a quarter million. Exultant, he had all the officers autograph one card each of the winning hand, proof of his triumph. A day later Morton dealt O'Kane a twenty-eight and exploded. "Why, I'll never play another game with you," O'Kane reported with self-satisfaction. Morton tore the cards to bits and threw them through the pantry window.

On March 19 Wahoo's luck suddenly changed for the better. A seemingly endless supply of targets began to appear. In the eleven days ending March 29 Wahoo delivered nine torpedo attacks and engaged in four individual gun actions. Eight ships were claimed as sunk. JANAC was to credit nine, though seven sinkings is the number that can be verified today. One target, which took a single Torpex hit on the nineteenth, was thought to have been only damaged. The patrol report noted: "We certainly hated to see this one go over the hill." But Kowa Maru had, in fact, been fatally gored, and sank on the twentieth. Wahoo easily set the record for the number of sinkings on a single patrol, a record that would finally be beaten, by one more ship, only late in the war—by Commander Richard H. O'Kane.

The attacks were nearly continuous; Sterling wondered ". . . when the officers got any sleep." They were also unusually aggressive. Daytime patrolling was carried out with fifty feet of keel depth and seventeen feet of periscope exposed. On the twenty-third, in the Gulf of Pohai, the water was so shallow that the attack scope was manually disconnected and dropped from the conning tower down into the control room to reduce the exposure somewhat.

Torpedo failures continued to plague *Wahoo*. There were four dangerous prematures and a fifth dud on contact, which infuriated Morton. But O'Kane, who conducted all the periscope attacks, was very, very good at estimating the all-important angle on the bow and target speed. Eight of *Wahoo*'s remaining nineteen torpedoes hit, and seven of the ten ships attacked by torpedoes went under. Fewer than 10 percent of the torpedo attacks by other U.S. submarines resulted in sinkings.

O'Kane, generally the only person to actually see the target, persisted in his tendency to overestimate target size. Contrary evidence did not deter him. On the final attack O'Kane thought he could conceivably be tracking the old tender *Holland* because of the target's distinctive clipper bow. But the estimated tonnage for clipper-bowed ships was too low. O'Kane later identified this target as the *Kimishima Maru* even ". . . though the drawing didn't show the clipper bow. . . . We would accept her [5,200 tons] just the same." She was actually the *Yambato Maru*, of 2,556 tons.

In all, *Wahoo* claimed eight ships for 36,700 tons. JANAC later credited *Wahoo* with nine ships for 20,000 tons. In 1952, Japanese records revealed that the actual tonnage was closer to 27,000. However measured, this was a brilliantly successful patrol.

Morton's emotions seesawed throughout these days of combat. Sterling remembered him as animated, always with an eager look on his face. He especially loved the surfaced, close-range gun actions: "Anyone who has not witnessed a submarine conduct a battle surface with three twenty-millimeter and a four-inch gun in the morning twilight with a calm sea and in crisp and clear weather, just 'ain't lived.'"

His racial hatred easily penetrated to the receptive crew. After a gun action they roared by Japanese survivors in the frigid water while the crew merrily called out, "So solly, please." He was fighting "Nips" and "monkeys," up close and personal. The Japanese were no cowards, refusing to be rescued from certain death in the cold seas, mooning *Wahoo*'s crew in defiance.

And yet there were flashes of pity. After one swift sinking four Japanese could be seen through the periscope, floating on scattered debris. Morton stared at them through the eyepiece and muttered, "It's colder'n hell up there. Those poor devils are really shivering." After a few more observations Morton said, "Next thing I know they'll be calling me 'Mush' Morton and his widowmakers."

Morton ordered *Wahoo* battle-surfaced and unsuccessfully tried to persuade the Japanese to come aboard as prisoners. They refused, resolutely keeping their backs to *Wahoo* no matter how she turned around them. The patrol report notes that "After a few minutes of this indifference we said to hell with them and went after something worth salvaging."

Morton's fury at unpredictable torpedo behavior grew, increasing his aggressiveness. On March 24 a target was sighted shortly after surfacing that evening. In a clockwork attack, with O'Kane at the bridge TBT, three stern torpedoes were fired. The first premature in eighteen seconds, possibly countermining the second, which also exploded. The third torpedo vanished in the uproar. The Japanese ship immediately returned fire with deck guns and scored several near-misses before *Wahoo* could get under.

After examining the charts, Morton was certain that the target was headed for Dairen. Since its top speed was believed to be only twelve knots, Morton knew that *Wahoo* could beat the Japanese ship to its place of refuge if they surfaced and did a high-speed end-around.

As luck would have it, Duncan MacMillan was now the OOD and would go topside first. In what was essentially a battle surface, *Wahoo* exploded from the sea while MacMillan whirled the handle opening the hatch. Holding the lanyard, he called down to Morton, "They're still shooting at us!"— a reasonable observation. Morton gave the signal to the enlisted man poised on the ladder below to goose MacMillan. The thumb plunged home, and PCO MacMillan shot to the bridge.

At flank speed *Wahoo* raced on the surface, circling the target, and diving in front of him just four miles off the Dairen breakwater. A single torpedo hit just under the stack, apparently sinking what O'Kane believed to be the large oiler *Syoyo Maru*. Postwar analysis indicates the unidentified ship survived; *Syoyo Maru* would be sunk by *Trigger* the following September.

Three and a half hours later *Wahoo* picked up another, smaller target heading into Dairen, with navigation lights burning. Once again there were two premature torpedo explosions. "Goddamnit, it isn't hardly worthwhile to risk our necks bringing these goddamn failures all the way out here for nothing," Morton raged.

O'Kane observed, "She's going to get away, Captain."

"Like hell she is. Pass the word battle stations surface."

In a furious gun action *Wahoo* raked and sank the hapless cargo ship *Takaosan Maru* in minutes. As light illuminated the morning, a second, even smaller ship, *Satsuki Maru,* was sighted and similarly sunk by gunfire.

These successful gun actions inspired Morton to surface in the midst of fishing fleets, small sampans he called "fishi Marus." With twenty-millimeter guns blazing and his "commandos" throwing Molotov cocktails, Morton was emphatic: "Every time we sink a sampan, we help shorten the war. We cut down on the Japanese supply of food and they get that much hungrier."

As *Wahoo*'s predations took her back into Tung Hai, Morton's impatience and aggressiveness grew. On the twenty-eighth he proposed to lay in wait off Kagoshima Wan, at the southern tip of Kyushu. Even O'Kane finally blanched. He pointed out to Morton that they had but two torpedoes—perhaps of dubious value, only emergency levels of deck gun ammunition, the battery was ailing, and the currents around the end of Kyushu were fierce for a submerged submarine with a sick battery. It was the first time O'Kane had not supported one of Morton's plans.

Oddly enough, O'Kane's plea for a more conservative approach seemed to please Morton. He agreed to postpone his plan for "a day or so" and—perhaps more important—to again play cribbage with O'Kane. Fortunately, Morton won. An attack off Kagoshima Wan was shelved.

On the next day Wahoo sank her ninth ship with her last two torpedoes and headed for Colonet Strait—on the surface, in daylight, with Japanese ships clearly visible in the distance—and home.

On March 29 O'Kane was awakened by Krause with news from the evening "Fox"—Pearl Harbor's nightly coded radio transmission. He was now Lieutenant Commander O'Kane. His own command would be coming soon—certainly this year. He was thirty-one.

Passing into the Pacific, Wahoo encountered heavy seas. On the evening of the thirtieth, with O'Kane on the bridge, a rogue wave passed over the conning tower. O'Kane believed it came from the stern—a classic "pooping." Sterling, acting as lookout, remembered it came from ahead. No matter. Wahoo's main induction was flooded, killing the engines. As the water poured into the engine rooms, the sea valves were closed from the inside. This overwhelmed the valves to the maneuvering room, flooding it and shorting out all electrical power.

Wahoo wallowed on the surface, dark and powerless, while emergency repairs were made. One engine was started to "take a suction," clearing the smoke from the after compartments. Water was run into the after torpedo room sumps, then pumped over the side. After 1½ hours, power could be applied to the port shaft, getting Wahoo in motion again. By dawn, both shafts were turning from the power supplied by main engine 1. By 1100, with one dive to avoid a low-flying plane, three engines were operational.

Now Wahoo plowed straight for Midway. She did not dive at the next plane contact. In fact, except for short trim dives, she continued on the surface all the way home.

As soon as empire waters were cleared, Morton composed and sent a message to Pearl Harbor:

ONE SURFACE RUNNER ONE DUD FOUR PREMATURES ONE
TANKER SUNK ONE FREIGHTER HOLED AND BELIEVED SUNK

FIVE FREIGHTERS SUNK BY TORPEDOES TWO FREIGHTERS

TWO SAMPANS SUNK BY GUNFIRE AND LARGE TRAWLER

WRECKED. . . .

This was stunning news at ComSubPac. *Guardfish* had been credited with sinking six ships (it was actually five) in August 1942, an event worthy of an impressive press conference. In just eleven patrol days *Wahoo* had sunk half again as many! In a message that all boats could copy, ComSubPac radioed *Wahoo:*

CONGRATULATIONS ON A JOB WELL DONE

JAPANESE THINK A SUBMARINE WOLF PACK

OPERATING IN YELLOW SEA

ALL SHIPPING TIED UP

Morton's public broadcasting of poor torpedo performance did not seem to trouble Lockwood. The admiral had been struggling with the Bureau of Ordnance over a decision to deactivate the magnetic exploders. Morton's prior success at Wewak, in which it was widely believed the magnetic exploder had worked correctly in the sinking of *Harusame,* had tended to stay Lockwood's hand. Now that psychological barrier began to crumble. In fewer than ninety days Lockwood would have Nimitz's agreement to disable the principal source of premature explosions. Unfortunately, this action would reveal yet another torpedo design deficiency.

While *Wahoo* was on patrol, Admiral Lockwood, new to his job, had visited Midway and decided to use that harbor for submarine refit, at least part of the time. Roughly twenty-four hundred miles of time, fuel, and wear and tear would be eliminated from every round trip to the hunting grounds. Unfortunately for the crew, *Wahoo* would be one of the first to be routed there, not to Pearl Harbor, for refit. One and all were bitterly disappointed; their faulty battery alone seemed a good enough reason to return to Pearl.

But it was not to be, and everyone made the best of it. Morton occupied some of his time by hand-sewing large battle flags. A master pennant flew from the raised periscope. A yardarm had been constructed from brooms, from which hung two streamers of flags. The top flag of each string was the house flag of a ship sunk on this patrol. Next there was a rising sun on each, signifying the destroyer and submarine kills. This was followed by fourteen white flags—seven per string—each with a red "meatball" for a merchant ship sunk.

The grand entrance was on April 6, 1943—and it was wasted. There were no admirals and press photographers to greet them, as at Pearl Harbor, only bored line handlers. Sterling missed the attention. He ". . . decided that they were so used to successful submarines coming in off war patrols that *Wahoo* was just another break in their humdrum life. . . ." But the crew was intensely proud of their ship and themselves.

Morton received a jolt at the squadron commander's debriefing. In a reprise of his earlier evaluation of Kennedy, he learned that the PCO, Duncan MacMillan, "had developed grave reservations about the manner in which the *Wahoo* conducted a war patrol." MacMillan took "exception to what he called a lack of planning, poor coordination, and an absence of discipline in the conning tower during attacks." Morton seethed, but the outstanding success on this patrol gave him bulletproof protection.

Midway was a far cry from Oahu and the Royal Hawaiian Hotel. Initially, there were no billets for *Wahoo*'s officers at the "Gooneyville Lodge"—the renamed Pan American Airways prewar structure for overnight stops of the *China Clipper.* They slept aboard *Wahoo,* grateful for a stable platform and the ability to go ashore at will and walk the beach. There were no fresh vegetables, and only beer for recreational drinking—which the officers had to pay for.

The crew fared even worse at the Gooneyville. They were bunked six to a room and spent their spare time bored, drinking a lot of beer, tormenting gooney birds, playing softball, and watching movie reruns. It was too cold to swim.

There was a meeting room at the Gooneyville reserved for officers from all boats to have their beer, play poker, and swap war stories. Here, O'Kane reported, he overheard MacMillan "belittling most everything that *Wahoo* had accomplished on patrol and including some disparaging remarks about me." Morton also overheard MacMillan's comments and, in cold fury, prepared to fight. O'Kane later claimed that the room was cleared without further incident.

Sterling wrote that the next day O'Kane sported "one of the most beautiful black eyes . . . that I had seen. . . ." Naturally Sterling, who didn't care for O'Kane, tried to find out what had happened, only to learn it was "the best-guarded secret the navy ever had." Probably O'Kane had done something relatively common such as banging his face on a hatch, but the black eye was the genesis of a dozen stories. O'Kane had his revenge. He ordered all of MacMillan's "effects gathered up and set on the dock, and when [MacMillan] arrived to pack, he discovered that orders had been left that he was not to be allowed aboard."

APRIL 6, 1943. *Wahoo* at Midway with battle flags flying. Foreground: BM3c (later BM1c) Donald O. Smith, who was lost with *Wahoo* the following October.

The officers moved into the Gooneyville with the departure of another submarine on patrol, but Morton got only one night of rest there. He was called back to Pearl Harbor the next morning for his first meeting with Lockwood, a briefing on his attack style, as well as torpedo problems encountered. Briefly hospitalized, he was visited by his friend from the codebreaking unit, Jasper Holmes, who caught an earful of Morton's frustration with torpedo performance.

At Midway O'Kane was now in charge and drove the refit crews hard. There were incessant air raid alarms, and one night the urgent cry "Emergency, all boats under way!" rang through the corridors of the Gooneyville. Rumors flying, O'Kane backed *Wahoo* away from the slip into the lagoon, only to learn that it was simply a drill. This was a cruel exercise to play on exhausted crews.

As *Wahoo* was readied for duty, Morton still had not returned from Pearl Harbor. O'Kane, the acting CO, took the crew through its sea training. He used the Morton approach to fire control, moving Roger Paine to the periscope, Richie Henderson to the TDC, and a young ensign, John Campbell, to diving officer. The squadron commander, along to pass judgment on *Wahoo*'s sea readiness, protested this arrangement. O'Kane held his ground and told him "This is the way we do it on *Wahoo*." Paine and Henderson came through; the exercise torpedo passed right under the bridge of the target destroyer.

The next day, at about noon, a violent storm moved in from the south. *Wahoo* headed for Midway, with Paine at the con. The narrow entrance, never easy under ideal weather conditions, was treacherous in forty-knot tailwinds and high seas. Roger threaded the needle, with lookouts calling out the coral heads.

Wahoo was now inside the lagoon, but had to make berth on the north, or downwind side of an east–west pier, which was punctuated with fifty feet of rocks at its head. O'Kane stood silently beside Paine, who made two tries at landing, approaching at standard speed, then backing at full. On the first attempt a line was put over but soon parted in the wind. On the second try two lines were secured; both broke in about thirty seconds.

Paine, knowing the danger to both ship and crew, and the disastrous effect on both their careers should *Wahoo* strike the rocks, turned to O'Kane and said, "Would you like to try it now, Dick?" O'Kane was completely supportive. "No, I wouldn't have done anything any differently. Try it again." On the third try Paine succeeded in making a successful landing. Multiple lines were put over—and held. *Wahoo* was safe.

Finally, there was a moment of glory. Morton quietly returned from Pearl

Harbor; Paine did not even know he had arrived. He had decorations for officers, some chiefs, and a few other enlisted men. A hasty honors ceremony was arranged, with *Wahoo*'s crew receiving their "eyes right" from marine and Seabee battalions while themselves dressed in dungarees. Morton was conspicuously absent, so O'Kane did the honors, wearing a long-sleeved khaki shirt and combination cap—and his new lieutenant commander's gold leaves.

After the gratifying ceremony, Sterling returned to *Wahoo* alone and discovered that Morton was, indeed, present and aboard but too ill to participate in the ceremony. His explanation to Sterling was that "My damn kidneys bother me every now and then, and I get some bad headaches. I didn't feel up to the review today."

This may have been Morton's cover story. He actually suffered from prostatitis, with the attendant back pains, chills, and fever. He had to urinate frequently and urgently, and there was blood in his urine. The affliction was well known among the officers but rarely spoken of. John Griggs, Captain Griggs's son, wrote later that "during our periods in port [Morton] would be hospitalized and on patrol he had to have semiweekly prostate massages." Morton was not a well man, but Paine observed that "his medical problems did not affect his performance of duty at sea."

On April 18 there was both a reunion and a parting. *Pollack*, ending her sixth war patrol, put in at Midway a day late because of foul weather. Morton and O'Kane were standing on the dock waiting to greet Grider.

"What happened, George?" Morton called innocently. "Forget about the international date line?"

"Aw, Captain," O'Kane called loudly, "he just got lost again."

In fact, Grider had missed *Pollack*'s initial outbound destination, Makin, by a day and had been ridden unmercifully by his fellow officers. He decided not to give Morton and O'Kane a clue concerning this small navigational misstep.

Another submarine, *Seal*, put in that same morning. One of its young ensigns was a classmate of Duke Griggs. This officer, he wrote later, ". . . had a reputation at the Naval Academy of being something of a goldbrick, came down with a supposed case of appendicitis." The ensign was detached, and Griggs was immediately transferred to *Seal* to take his place. *Seal* pulled out at 1615 with a very unhappy, and incompletely rested, Griggs aboard.

Sterling had been temporarily relieved by a extremely competent yeoman second class named W. T. "Bill" White, who proposed a trade. White would go on patrol, and Sterling would become a member of the relief crews.

APRIL 20, 1943. Awards ceremony at Midway: (left to right) Ensign John "Sugar" Campbell (KIA), Lieutenant Roger Paine, Ensign George "Dugong" Misch (KIA), Lieutenant Commander Richard O'Kane, Lieutenant Chandler "Jack" Jackson, Ensign John "Duke" Griggs III, Lieutenant Richie "Hank" Henderson (KIA). (U.S. Navy, courtesy of Roger Paine)

Sterling bristled at the suggestion, insisting that he wouldn't consider a transfer until he had made five war patrols aboard *Wahoo*.

White switched to a more subtle approach. When Sterling returned to *Wahoo,* White had left a Navy personnel book open on his desk with key sentences underlined in red. By this means Sterling learned that the navy would begin a stenography school in San Diego the next November—more than six months away. Attendance at such a school was key to Sterling's career plan to make chief petty officer.

He pondered this potential opportunity for some time, then decided to act. Sterling made out the application for steno school and took it to O'Kane for the necessary initials before submission to Morton. O'Kane was uncommonly negative. Sterling wrote that he snarled "What the hell? Don't you like the officers on the *Wahoo*?," thus personalizing the Yeoman's effrontery. Sterling backpedaled, defending himself from O'Kane's wrath, but the executive officer was adamant. "I'm not going to initial this. The captain won't sign it anyway."

"What won't the captain sign?" It was Morton, in the corridor, and he had overheard just enough. O'Kane explained the request in such a way that Morton would not be inclined to go along with Sterling's long-term request. But Morton heartily overruled his exec, praised Sterling generously, and signed the request with a flourish. O'Kane was furious, his eyes sparkling dangerously. Sterling hurriedly mailed the request ashore, then forgot all about it, since he believed his chances were exceedingly slim.

9

Luck Falters

... fortune is a fickle gypsy ...

—W. M. Praed, "The Haunted Tree"

Wahoo turned away from the ice floes nearly encircling her in the approach to Matsuwa Harbor, in the Kuriles. The bitter-cold seas, with temperatures as low as twenty-eight degrees Fahrenheit, were kept from freezing only by their high salinity and the restless currents flowing from the Sea of Okhotsk. Sterling could not really adapt to the Arctic cold. On successive watches, in sleet and snow, he shivered, teeth chattering, until the new ensign took pity and let him obtain shelter in the lee of the cigarette deck. They couldn't see much anyhow.

The crew's stay in Midway had been restless and unsatisfying. There had been no sharp, clean break from ship's duties as at Pearl Harbor. Fifteen days after their arrival they were at sea again, for training exercises.

Significant personnel turnover had occurred while in port. Gone was Duncan MacMillan, on his way to take command of *Thresher*. In his place as PCO was the extraordinarily aggressive John Anderson "Johnny" Moore, from the same mold as Morton and O'Kane. Moore was driven by a personal vendetta. His younger brother had been captured in the fall of the Philippines and was a prisoner of the Japanese.

The chief of the boat, Pappy Rau, had been relieved, and Jack Griggs was already aboard *Seal* with a promise to rejoin *Wahoo* at the conclusion of that submarine's patrol. Eugene Fiedler, fresh from Brooklyn, was the new junior officer of *Wahoo*.

These changes were absorbed seamlessly. While Roger Paine would be retained on the TDC during attacks, he was now the true third officer. His ship-handling skills, always good, now improved. Even O'Kane could comfortably acknowledge on trim dive exercises that "again Roger's compensation was right on." *Wahoo* was diving beautifully and routinely in forty seconds.

The United States had finally decided to dislodge the Japanese from the Aleutians. More than two hundred army scouts would be landed on Attu by *Narwhal* and *Nautilus,* followed by conventional amphibious landings of major infantry units. The navy knew from a surprise surface engagement that the Japanese had moved four cruisers and six destroyers to a base at Paramushiru, in the northern Kuriles.

Wahoo, along with three other submarines, was given an initial covering task before departing for the hunting grounds: scout the Kuriles for a possible Japanese counterattack on the Aleutians. To maintain the reconnaissance location secret, *Wahoo's* crew loaded foul-weather gear by night; she departed Midway on April 25 on a westward course until passing over the horizon. No civilian contractor routinely moving in and out of Midway would be given the opportunity of an educated guess as to *Wahoo's* first destination. Then the turn was made to the northwest and Onnekotan, just southeast of Paramushiru.

On May 2 the screening part of the patrol began—on the surface—in hail and snow, with only Onnekotan's snow-covered peak as proof that *Wahoo* was on station. *Wahoo* prowled southwestward down the Kuriles chain, always nursing her greatly diminished battery capacity.

At Matsuwa a major airfield was discovered that seemed to be as large as the one on Midway. Photographs were taken and positions plotted. O'Kane urgently pressed Morton to surface and shell the airfield hangars, but Morton declined in spite of continued pressure from O'Kane to attack the "secret air base that SubPac doesn't know anything about." But Morton, noting that no aircraft had been sighted—perhaps because of the miserable weather—did boldly order *Wahoo* to proceed on the surface toward Honshu, Japan's main island.

As *Wahoo* moved southwest, Griggs, and *Seal,* were already in action. On May 2, south of Palau, an attack was made that *Seal's* captain thought was a failure. It wasn't. The 2,054-ton *Unyo Maru 5,* seeking protection against the coastline, ran aground and sank. No credit was given *Seal,* but her attack surely contributed to the Japanese loss. On the afternoon of May 4 *Seal* struck again, sinking the 10,215-ton *San Clemente Maru,* an impressive trophy.

Just before dawn on May 4 *Wahoo* dived for a submerged reconnaissance of the northern tip of Etorofu Island. Johnny Moore was given the con and, in spite of poor visibility, soon picked up a target. At first neither Morton nor O'Kane could make out what kind of ship they were tracking. As the range closed to 3,000 yards, they could see planes on deck. They appeared to have a large—O'Kane thought she was nearly 16,000 tons—auxiliary plane tender in their sights.

With Paine at the TDC, O'Kane called out the angles for a ship he thought was 510 feet long, drawing 28 feet of water. Three torpedoes were fired. One seemed to hit amidships—the timing was right—but the other two missed. The target clearly reacted. The patrol report recorded that she ". . . tooted her whistle, commenced firing to port away from the *Wahoo*, and then turned away dropping four depth charges." But she didn't slow down—and she got away. *Wahoo*'s fragile battery could not stand a high-speed underwater approach or a determined counterattack from land-based planes. It was only 0600, a poor time to surface and attempt an end-around.

Morton and O'Kane were convinced they had experienced at least one dud torpedo. Their fury spilled into the patrol report: "It is inconceivable that any normal dispersion could allow this last torpedo to miss a 510-foot target at this range." They took some solace in at least damaging a large, important ship.

But this attack was not recorded by the Japanese, a likely sign that only trivial damage occurred. O'Kane may have overestimated the length of the target. At 1,350 yards' range, with a target moving at eleven knots as this one was, the last torpedo could easily have missed a ship that was only, say, 400 feet long. The one "hit" might have been a delayed-action magnetic exploder. Since it was believed to be such a large target, the torpedo was set to run deep. It actually might have passed under, exploding as it left the magnetic field. This would have caused some damage; O'Kane did see a small list. It would certainly explain the target's counterfire and depth charges in the opposite direction. The hunted might simply have been attempting to become the hunter. In any case, the attack left a bad taste in everyone's mouth.

On May 7, at dawn, *Wahoo* arrived at her patrol area south of the fortieth parallel, twelve miles off the coast of Honshu. Targets began to appear within the hour, hugging the coastline. At 1039 two targets, thought to be dead ducks, were spotted at the close range of 900 yards. Six torpedoes were fired. One hit, sinking *Tamon Maru 5*, of 5,260 tons. The second ship successfully threaded a salvo of four torpedoes. These results deeply disappointed O'Kane but pleased the crew. New members would now receive the coveted submarine combat pin, and seasoned veterans another rosette.

Several hours later Morton entered O'Kane's tiny compartment and sat down on the bunk. He had been considering the disappointing results and concluded that he, Morton, was too cautious in patrolling twelve miles at sea. He asked O'Kane to take *Wahoo* right up to the coast at Kone Saki. In the impending night surface run, Morton would rest and await O'Kane's call that a target had been sighted.

O'Kane was overjoyed. As soon as they were on the surface, he and Krause took the necessary round of stars for the desired course. Both men were up again before dawn, and O'Kane conned *Wahoo* to a position a mile and a half off the promontory. The combative Johnny Moore joined O'Kane, and spotted the first prospective target at 0512 on May 8. The Japanese were clearly aware that a submarine was hunting, because this vessel, too small for torpedoes, followed the exact contour of the land, never straying even 1,500 yards from the beach.

Morton arrived much later, seemingly refreshed by an uninterrupted night's sleep. After a routine check of conditions, he returned to his cabin for more rest.

That afternoon a small convoy of three ships came down the coast, also hugging the shoreline. Three torpedoes were fired at the largest. Less than a minute later, roughly halfway to the target, the first torpedo prematured. The second was uselessly diverted by this unwanted explosion. The third torpedo charged on in—and was a dud. The sound man heard the unsatisfying thud, and O'Kane could see the plume of water thrown up by a rupturing air flask.

Morton took *Wahoo* both deep and to full speed, not worrying about battery limitations. The counterattack was perfunctory. Morton and O'Kane's mood was sour. The junior officers went into a funk and argued among themselves as to possible causes of failure. Gloomily, Morton called for a new course farther down the coast.

At 0230 O'Kane, still half asleep, took his coffee to the conning tower. Running on the surface, *Wahoo*'s radar had picked up Kone Saki, resulting in a wake-up call to the XO. Fifteen minutes later the radar picked up two other contacts. Johnny Moore materialized, and together he and O'Kane decided they had fresh targets. O'Kane immediately closed the coast on the surface. By the time Morton was called they had identified "a large tanker and freighter, without escort" and a recommended interception point.

On came the unsuspecting victims. *Wahoo* dove to get her hull, but not radar antenna, underwater. At 0440, when the range closed to 1,200 yards, six torpedoes were fired. Three hit, one in the freighter, two in the tanker. Both ships split in two and were seen to sink. As usual, O'Kane's target-size eye had been off. The identification made by both O'Kane and Johnny Moore was a bit shaky as well. There was no tanker; both were freighters. The ships, each estimated at about 9,500 tons, were actually *Takao Maru*, of 3,204 tons, and the much smaller *Jimmu Maru*, of 1,912 tons.

The now jubilant crew was happy to leave the scene at deep depth. They had been in a near-constant state of readiness for five days and had conducted four attacks. They were tired, and so was Morton. *Wahoo* headed away from the coast for everyone to rest.

The next day, May 10, O'Kane learned via the evening "Fox" that he had been selected to command a new-construction boat now starting its build cycle at Mare Island. This would be his last patrol on *Wahoo*, and twenty-five-year-old Roger Paine would replace him. Within a day Paine began to yield his responsibilities as diving officer to the next officer in line. O'Kane held out a few more days, but it was clear he would have to divest himself of some XO duties. Navigation would now become Paine's responsibility.

Wahoo's repeated attacks led to a marked increase in Japanese antisubmarine patrols; also, aircraft were frequently sighted. Morton decided to revert to normal submarine routines: submerge by day, attack by night. Early on the morning of May 13 O'Kane participated in his last attack on *Wahoo*. Two ships had been spotted the prior evening. One looked very big to O'Kane.

In a night end-around *Wahoo* got in front of her intended victims, submerged, and fired four torpedoes. There was one hit. One torpedo was thought to be a dud. Both ships kept moving, although one was falling behind. Furious, Morton ordered *Wahoo* to the surface and completed another end-around at flank speed to catch the laggard. This time he would go in on the surface. When in the correct firing position the last bow torpedo was fired. It exited the tube and sank to the bottom.

Morton spun *Wahoo* in place, with the port screw backing emergency and the starboard screw ahead full. The last stern torpedo was fired and raced to the target as it was designed. It hit, but produced only a "low-order explosion." There was no satisfying "WHACK," as in a normal hit.

Morton called out the gun crews; determined to engage in a surface gun action and sink this damnable Maru. But now the lead ship returned accurate supporting gunfire, forcing *Wahoo* to dive. With regret, Morton "withdrew, quite helpless to stop the cripple."

At 0336 Morton reported to ComSubPac that *Wahoo* had expended all her torpedoes. That evening came the welcome news: head for Pearl Harbor! *Wahoo* poured on the coal, consuming fuel oil at the rate of nearly 16 gallons per mile instead of the usual 8.5. There were advantages to a short patrol that left large fuel reserves.

Roger Paine assumed the navigational duties and plotted a rhumb line to pass north of Midway. O'Kane, good navigator that he was, noted that the projected track was just ten miles from Kure Reef, which they would pass just after daybreak. He was uneasy with this track but chose to say nothing. However, he and the faithful Krause were on the bridge at 0345, watching.

After Paine took the morning stars, he went below to work them out. Krause crawled higher, onto a lookout station. He soon waved his arm to indicate the telltale coloring of reefs, visible from the light of a brightening sky. O'Kane looked over the side of the bridge and saw coral heads in the water and shouted the order "All back emergency." *Wahoo* slowed, then stopped, then backed down her wake till they were well clear of the reef. O'Kane later wrote, "It would be a lesson that Roger would never forget."

As the miles rolled along, Morton retreated to his cabin to do his ritual sewing of battle flags. On May 17 *Wahoo* crossed the international date line, giving Sterling two birthdays. Morton arranged a surprise party in the darkened mess room, luring Sterling off watch with a plausible ruse. Sterling was so touched by the cupcake and candle, and the crew singing the "Happy Birthday" song, that tears streamed down his cheeks.

South of *Wahoo*'s return course, off the coast of Wotje in the Marshall Islands, *Pollack* hunted. On May 18 she sank the 3,110-ton *Terushima Maru*, with *Wahoo* graduate George Grider playing the traditional XO backup role to the attacking captain. On May 20 the captain gave in to Grider's repeated "This is how we did it in *Wahoo*" entreaties. Grider conducted the attack, and *Pollack* sank the 5,351-ton *Bangkok Maru* with three hits from four torpedoes fired. In his excitement, Grider concentrated fiercely on just the target, to the exclusion of the escorts. This thoughtless oversight cost *Pollack* a severe depth charge counterattack. The *Wahoo* coapproach technique was not tried again.

Everyone in *Pollack* thought "Grider's ship" was a routine sinking. But *Bangkok Maru* was carrying 1,200 troops to Tarawa. Most of them were rescued and taken to Jaluit, but all their equipment and armament intended to reinforce Tarawa were lost. The troops stayed on Jaluit for the duration of the war, withering on the vine. Had they reached Tarawa to augment the 4,000-man garrison, they might have been instrumental in suppressing the assault, which was twice in doubt. Had the marines prevailed, by statistical averages these 1,200 additional soldiers would have killed or wounded nearly 1,000 U.S. Marines, who lost 990 dead and 2,311 wounded against the entrenched garrison.

At dawn on May 21, 1943, Paine's precise navigation revealed the escort *Litchfield* waiting dead ahead on the horizon. By 1000 *Wahoo* was tied to Pier 1 within the Pearl Harbor submarine base.

There was no grand entrance, and some of the crew thought that Morton was ashamed to have sunk only three ships. In fact, during the ten days that *Wahoo* had been on station, ten U.S. submarines made a total of seven gun and twenty-six torpedo attacks. These attacks accounted for seventeen Japanese ships downed, some as small as the 164 ton schooner *Gar*, sunk by gunfire. Only *Snook* sank more ships—four—but she claimed less tonnage. *Wahoo* was thought to be the tonnage leader, at 25,000 tons. Although the true score was only a bit more than 10,000 tons, it was still the second-highest score of any submarine during this short period.

Everyone was having torpedo problems. In late 1942 "Red" Ramage had convinced Lockwood that there was something wrong with the magnetic exploder, based on his *Trout* experience. But now Lockwood had gone to Pearl Harbor; the Australia-based Ramage had a new admiral, Ralph Christie, who simply would not accept any insults to his beloved design. In March 1943 "Moke" Millican, CO of *Thresher*, criticized the torpedoes in his patrol report. He had "clinked 'em with a clunk." Millican bad-mouthed torpedo design and was backed by his division commander. Christie immediately relieved Millican, and ordered the division commander to never again criticize the torpedoes in writing.

Christie then came down to *Trout* to see Ramage off on patrol. He jokingly told Ramage he expected one ship sunk for every torpedo. Ramage blew up. "If I get 25 percent reliable performance on your torpedoes, I'll be lucky, and you will bless me." The ensuing argument between admiral and lieutenant commander was exceedingly tough. Ramage went on patrol and had fifteen misses or duds. Christie relieved him, too.

In April Lockwood finally acted. He flew to Washington and attacked the Bureau of Ordnance directly for the dud/premature problems. He saw the naval commander in chief, Ernest King, and forced the inspector general to begin an inquiry into the late production of electric torpedoes. Lockwood was fighting everyone, but he was beginning to win. It didn't hurt to have the solid political backing of Admirals Nimitz and King.

Shortly after *Wahoo* tied up, Lockwood came aboard. After a quick tour of the boat he took Morton with him to headquarters. Everyone knew that Morton would try to persuade Lockwood to send *Wahoo* back to Mare Island for refit—if only to replace the batteries. Only Krause and Sterling left the boat to deliver the patrol report and track chart. With crossed fingers the rest of the crew awaited Morton's return. There were no buses waiting to take them to the Royal Hawaiian—a good sign. Those topside saw Morton come hustling back, a broad grin on his face: there would be payday and an awards ceremony tomorrow, with departure for San Francisco the following day.

At once some of *Wahoo*'s crew began to off-load gun ammunition and extra stores, while others turned out to clean ship. Fumigant was applied to trouble spots; even small interior scuff marks were painted. Dress whites were readied, with the latest rank badges sewn on.

On May 22 Admiral Nimitz arrived like the head of a comet, the tail a cluster of other admirals and captains, as well as photographers. Roger Paine commanded the assembled crew, which was augmented by personnel from other boats who were also to be recipients of honors.

Wahoo received a Presidential Unit Citation that all the crew could wear with their combat pins. Morton received his second Navy Cross, and discipline momentarily broke; Nimitz's "congratulatory handshake was accompanied by a spontaneous, muted, heartfelt cheer" from the crew, wrote O'Kane, who received a second Silver Star, "without fanfare." Sterling was deeply moved by the entire ceremony, the band, the speech. Ten years earlier he had served under Nimitz and greatly admired him: "Here was a man who understood that it is the cogs in the wheel that make the success. . . . Here was a man to be respected."

After the dignitaries left, Morton uncharacteristically began a full-scale inspection of the boat, beginning in the forward torpedo room. While he was lighthearted, O'Kane was grim and efficient, pointing out deficiencies to be written up. Still, everything was proceeding beautifully. The cooks had prepared hams with cloves, and were making doughnuts as Morton passed through the galley.

When he reached the after sleeping compartment, Morton paused to joke with the pharmacist's mate. O'Kane, unseen by Morton, slipped behind him, ordered the floor hatches to the battery compartment opened, and lowered himself in. Morton turned, unaware of the open hatch, stepped forward, and fell partway through. His leg was jammed, and his chest and stomach badly bruised by the impact of the hatch edge.

Sterling helped extricate the shaken Morton, who angrily called off the inspection and stalked out of the compartment. O'Kane popped up from below and hurriedly raced after Morton to make amends. This painful incident was gossip fodder for the entire crew.

The next morning Admiral Lockwood and the division commander came to see them off. Johnny Moore was gone, to take command of *Grayback*. But everyone else was there, ready for the U.S. of A. Morton graciously gave the con to O'Kane, since it would be his last trip on *Wahoo*. Morton gave the nod, and O'Kane had lines cast off with an extended blast from the horn. *Wahoo* pivoted in the channel, then moved out at two-thirds speed past the ruined hulk of *Oklahoma*, now being slowly righted to clear space in the harbor.

Morton had committed to be at Mare Island by noon on May 29, only five days away. *Wahoo's* four engines went to full power. O'Kane could hear the reduction gears "whining at close to high C." At dawn on the twenty-ninth, after a run of twenty-one hundred miles, *Wahoo* found U.S.S. *Lawrence* waiting to escort her through the Golden Gate.

Intensely excited by their return home, especially on such a gorgeous morning, the crew dressed ship in style. Up went the jury-rigged yardarm with the flags recording kills. All deck hatches were opened, and every crewman not standing watch came topside in his whites, while *Wahoo* crossed the bay to make her way to the Napa River.

As *Wahoo* approached her mooring the crowd was huge, their cheers drowning out the band playing "California, Here I Come." Both Morton's wife, Harriett, and O'Kane's wife, Ernestine, were waiting—clearly tipped off by a private code from the two officers.

And now Morton revealed his sewing skills first exhibited at Pearl Harbor to the Mare Island onlookers. A pennant, with a sleeve that pulled over the periscope head, had been attached as they passed Alcatraz. When *Wahoo* swung into the wind, moving slowly to her mooring, Morton's pennant—his motto—was unfurled, its words electrifying the mob:

SHOOT THE SUNZA-BITCHES

The crew quickly began to evaporate, half already on leave. Morton vanished in minutes, leaving O'Kane to place *Wahoo* in drydock. O'Kane swiftly worked out an agreement with the navy yard to stand many of *Wahoo's* watches. Even more of the crew vanished, much to the consternation of the older Captain Griggs, who was now ComSubAd at Mare Island—transferred from Pearl when Lockwood brought in his own men.

At least three men were married during the break: Lieutenant Chan Jackson, SM1C Fertig J. Krause—O'Kane's loyal assistant—and Forest J. Sterling.

Sterling's decision was impulsive. On liberty in Vallejo with other *Wahoo* crew, he proposed to Marie Henry in Los Angeles from a telephone booth inside Jim's Place, a bar on Georgia Street. She was in Vallejo within two days for the ceremony.

Sterling took his bride to the now cold, batteryless *Wahoo* to meet Morton and O'Kane. O'Kane was in an expansive, pleasant mood. He not only congratulated Sterling, but also, as a wedding present, promoted him to petty officer first class. The new rank gave Sterling a thirty-day leave, which he instantly seized.

Wahoo was being restored to life: new batteries, overhauled engines, a new prop shaft, new sound gear, improved radar, and a reduced conning tower profile. To strengthen the conning tower, a 2-inch-by-2 inch steel ring was welded around the circumference, and the rear dome of the conning tower was replaced with a high-tensile steel cap 1½ inches thick. The cap had no door, eliminating any future use of the conning tower as an escape chamber, but strengthening the conning tower seemed prudent given the increasing power of Japanese depth charges. *Wahoo* was approaching the state of a new-build boat.

With his impending departure, O'Kane arranged a reward for Krause. He would go to a new-construction boat in Philadelphia: *Escolar*. This would ensure that he stay in the States for months. Now it was O'Kane's turn. In a ceremony that deeply touched him, O'Kane was given an engraved silver cigarette box from the officers and crew of *Wahoo*. He then walked along the waterfront to his own new submarine, still on the ways: *Tang*.

10

Luck Vanishes

Damn the Torpedoes!

−Wahoo *Patrol Report 6*

On July 4, 1943, a week before *Wahoo*'s overhaul was completed, three submarines slipped through La Pérouse Strait at night, on the surface, and into the Sea of Japan. For months Admiral Lockwood had considered making a bold penetration of this large, but essentially landlocked, body of water he reasoned would be crowded with Japanese shipping. Two of the three narrow entrances were almost certainly mined.

La Pérouse might also be mined, especially with deeply set devices meant only for submerged submarines. But the strait marked the boundary between Japan and the Soviet Union. Soviet ships from Vladivostok used it in the summer; it was often frozen solid in winter. U.S. submarines should be capable of following the route used by the Soviet surface ships to gain entry. Lockwood ordered a four-day trial raid. The first boat was *Plunger*, the old boat that had accompanied *Pompano* to Pearl Harbor on December 7. She was joined by her sister ship *Permit*, "cranky and infirm," with officers and crew who had already made eight war patrols, as well as the brand-new boat *Lapon*.

The key problem with this foray was that if targets were encountered, the Japanese would obviously move to close La Pérouse. Lockwood planned a diversion using the huge V-boat *Narwhal*. Fresh from her amphibious action at Attu, *Narwhal* would take her twin six-inch guns to bombard the airfield at Matsuwa To, discovered by *Wahoo* on her last patrol. In theory this would draw Japanese antisubmarine forces northward, permitting the three submarines to escape.

As in most untried ventures, nothing went as planned. *Lapon* was totally enveloped by fog the entire four days "inside," and her search radar—the SJ—was not working. She sank nothing. Much of *Permit*'s crew was racked with an inexplicable illness marked with nausea and vomiting. Still, *Permit* made a successful attack on a two-ship convoy, with the usual situation of some dud torpedoes, sinking one ship and damaging the other. The Japanese now knew there were submarines inside their almost holy waters.

As *Permit* surfaced to do an end-around on her crippled target, she was pooped by a rogue wave. Green water flooded the boat, and only the emergency measures ordered by her captain saved her from certain sinking. The radar was ruined. *Permit* made four more attacks during the raid, but visibility was so poor no accurate range could be obtained without the SJ. All subsequent attacks failed.

Plunger was now commanded by an extremely aggressive skipper, "Benny" Bass. On both his previous patrols he had sunk ships, and the last one was remarkable. For two days he had chased an escorted convoy, sometimes on the surface, in daylight, in close proximity to airfields. He made six separate attacks, had his share of duds, but managed to sink two ships and damage the others. Out of torpedoes, he battle surfaced and engaged in gun action with a cripple until every shell had been fired from his small-bore three-inch cannon. This man was not faint of heart.

On this run *Plunger* was also bedeviled by fog, but damaged one freighter and was driven off by air escorts. Then Bass found another target and sank *Anzan Maru* in spite of maddening duds.

All three boats exited La Pérouse without the planned diversion. *Narwhal* was late on station, and after twelve minutes of firing in the airfield received highly accurate counterfire. So much for that plan.

At Midway the captain of *Permit* went to new construction in the States. The captain of *Lapon* was relieved for his disappointing results and sent to the Bureau of Ordnance to work on torpedo problems. Benny Bass volunteered *Plunger* for another shot at the Sea of Japan.

At Mare Island, *Wahoo* adjusted its personnel to form a new team. Roger Paine replaced Dick O'Kane as XO, and Chan Jackson was now third officer. As promised, Duke Griggs returned from his patrol on *Seal* all the way to the States. Bill Carr, a "plank owner" and friend of Sterling, was made chief of the boat. This was a good, stable organization. With it Morton began to conceive a unique strategy. On his next patrol he would fire a single torpedo at each ship, aimed at the center of the target. Even with duds, he might be able to get fifteen sinkings from twenty-four torpedoes, an unheard-of patrol total.

JULY 21, 1943. Roger Paine and Errol Flynn on the cigarette deck of *Wahoo*, departing San Francisco. (Courtesy of Roger Paine)

After the usual sea trials, the crew was treated to a party by the actor Errol Flynn. Morton's Hollywood contacts were still working. The next morning, July 21, *Wahoo* departed Mare Island with Flynn aboard. He got off with the pilot, some twenty miles out, and returned to San Francisco on the pilot boat. *Wahoo* pounded on, bound for Pearl Harbor. En route Morton received the first personnel hit. Chan Jackson would be detached at Pearl to return to the States as the XO of a new-construction boat. The newlywed was overjoyed; Morton was less happy.

Paine's navigation skills got *Wahoo* to Pearl Harbor on time, in exactly the right location, on July 27. Upon arrival, *Wahoo* was scheduled for a second fumigation; the one at Mare Island had not been successful. While venting the boat, Chief Carr became deathly sick, poisoned from the fumes. A substitute who had served on *Wahoo* on two earlier patrols was hastily dragooned as a replacement.

Then, on July 29, Roger Paine developed acute appendicitis and was transferred to the hospital for surgery. Morton's new team had vanished. That same day Lieutenant Commander Verne Skjonsby was transferred to *Wahoo* as Morton's new XO. Skjonsby came from Lockwood's staff via the Bureau of Ordnance and had never been on a war patrol. On August 2, after three days' sea training to get these strangers used to each other, *Wahoo* departed for Midway.

The tall, thin Skjonsby immediately made a favorable impression on Sterling. He was friendly and eager to learn the *Wahoo* way, coming to Sterling for a rundown on the ship's company. He was in no way a martinet. Still, there were so many new faces. . . .

At Lockwood's request, on June 24 Admiral Nimitz had issued an order to deactivate all Mark VI magnetic exploders on boats under his control. One source of torpedo problems would now be eliminated for *Wahoo*. Morton's resolve to fire single shots grew, even with a largely untried fire control party.

On August 2 Morton visited both Roger Paine and Chief Carr in the hospital. Then *Wahoo* departed Pearl Harbor for Midway. She would participate in a second penetration of the Sea of Japan with the eager Benny Bass on *Plunger*.

At Midway Bass was waiting. He and Morton discussed the conditions *Plunger* had encountered both in transiting La Pérouse and inside the Sea of Japan. Bass believed there were no minefields in place. He told Morton that the Japanese ships had been operating with running lights lit, but this might change now that they had been alerted. The agreement was made that *Wahoo* would precede *Plunger* inside and patrol north of Tsugaru Strait; *Plunger* would patrol to the south. At 1700 on August 6, after a stay of a bit more than nine hours, *Wahoo* departed for the Kuriles and Etorofu Strait.

A thousand miles to the south, *Pollack* was in the Bonins. Grider was on his sixth consecutive war patrol without a break and had uncharacteristically "acquired a reputation for a bad temper," as he later wrote. Bearded now, he was fiercely homesick, obsessed with thoughts of his wife, Ann, and jealous of his friends in *Wahoo* who had gotten home briefly. Just before departing on this patrol, Grider had received news of the loss of yet another friend on *Triton*. His mood was black with depression.

AUGUST, 1943. George Grider while executive officer of *Pollack*. (U.S. Navy)

On August 6, the day *Wahoo* departed for the Kuriles, *Pollack* made a second attack on a freighter. One of its torpedoes dove straight down and exploded beneath them. The concussion was breathtaking, stupendous, frightful. The sea illuminated all around *Pollack;* every circuit breaker and electrical contact opened from the shock. *Pollack* drifted, powerless, on the surface. The convoy boiled away in fright, and Grider and the crew were left to repair the damage and get functional again. They didn't have the stomach for a third attack.

Morton did not spare his newly rebuilt engines and made the transit into the Sea of Okhotsk a day early, just after midnight on August 13. He was so eager to enter the Sea of Japan that he ordered *Wahoo* to run on the surface all day, sometimes in conditions of unlimited visibility. At 1710 *Wahoo* was only sixty miles east of the center of La Pérouse, and dove to wait till nightfall.

The almost slushy water was a bitterly cold twenty-five degrees Fahrenheit, but the circulation of heat from the now stopped engines made the interior of the hull comfortable for the crew. It did nothing for sound conditions, however, and *Wahoo* began to encounter Japanese antisubmarine patrol craft, which were carefully avoided.

At 2030 *Wahoo* surfaced and began the run through the strait under a nearly full moon. The passage was made at one-third speed, which might make the submarine register as a fishing boat to a bored patrol craft. Sterling was a lookout during the transit. At 0133 on the fourteenth, he observed a shore station on Soya Misaki, seven miles south, signaling to *Wahoo.* The signal was ignored, and *Wahoo* continued her transit. At 0442 *Wahoo* dove, comfortably "inside."

Plunger encountered engine problems on her trip from Midway and fell two days behind schedule. Arriving off the entrance to La Pérouse on the morning of August 16, Benny Bass decided to make a submerged daylight transit rather than wait all day. *Plunger* still had to pass south of *Wahoo,* which had already made her presence known to the Japanese.

The excellent fuel reserves and the beautiful, clear day made Morton confident. He was sure this area "will likely reward us with a target during the night." Sure enough, *Wahoo* picked up her first target visually at 2217.

Now began the most frustrating 3½ days of Morton's life. He deliberately executed his one-torpedo-per-target strategy in nine consecutive attacks, weakening just once to fire two torpedoes at a large freighter he had missed on an earlier try. As far as Morton knew, there were no normal hits. He was beside himself in anger and frustration.

With the magnetic influence exploder deactivated, the previously obscured contact exploder problem was now fully revealed. In the second attack Morton—indeed, the whole crew—could hear "the thud of the dud." Skjonsby saw the water column thrown up as the torpedo air flask ruptured against the side of the ship. In the final attack a second torpedo broached and exploded twenty-three seconds into the run. This may have been the fault of Morton's desperate experimentation, trying to get something to go right. It was set to run at only four feet and might have popped out of a large wave.

The other eight torpedoes seemed simply to be misses. It certainly wasn't because Morton didn't close the range. Three of the first four torpedoes fired had an average run of only 780 yards. On the fifth attack Morton deliberately let a range of 600 yards open up, since the only hit he had made so far, the dud, was fired at 1,050 yards. Perhaps the torpedoes were running too deep at short range. The longest run was only 1,200 yards. The average run for all ten torpedoes was under 1,000 yards.

Morton was also not lacking in aggressiveness. Attack, miss, surface, end-around, dive, attack, miss, swing ship, stern shot, miss. The surface runs permitted good radar ranging, far more accurate than the sonar, in addition to visual plots, which were simplified by the excellent visibility of the full moon.

Each problem was reworked backward on the TDC, which could be made to perform like a simulator. All solutions checked perfectly.

By the sixth attack Morton had begun to alter torpedo speeds, firing at low power in hopes it would make them run truer. On the seventh attack he abandoned the TDC and returned to the Mark VIII angle solver, an improved "banjo" he had used in the past, on R-5. Morton took over control of the firing from Skjonsby on this attack; Morton knew, as did the British and the Germans, how to shoot with accuracy using this old-fashioned method. He missed, and noted gloomily that the TDC had come up with the same solution as the Mark VIII.

Skjonsby's background was Bureau of Ordnance, and he had taken postgraduate college courses in torpedo construction. He was uniquely qualified to supervise the close examination of the unreliable tin fish: their gyro steering and depth mechanisms, the vertical and horizontal rudder throws. The only thing that could not be tested was the exploders. Could there be something wrong with the contact exploder as well? Morton became convinced this was true, and even wrote in his patrol report that the magnetic influence exploder should be reinstated as an option.

What Morton and his superior officers would never know is that the sheer weight and speed of two dud hits had been enough to damage two ships: *Ryokai Maru,* a 4,643-ton fish factory, and *Terukawa Maru,* a 6,433-ton Japanese Navy tanker. It seems that *Wahoo's* fire control party had actually been performing quite well. The fault almost certainly lay in the torpedoes themselves.

In a cold fury, Morton surfaced on the afternoon of August 18 and poured on the coals in the direction of Vladivostok. An angry message to Pearl Harbor was transmitted reporting his dismal luck and requesting an early termination of the patrol. As soon as the acknowledgment receipt came in from NPM, the Pearl Harbor naval radio, *Wahoo* reversed course and headed back toward the Japanese coast at emergency speed. After twenty minutes, *Wahoo* dove. Any Japanese pursuers triggered by the radio transmission would search in the wrong direction.

Morton came to the conning tower while Sterling was working the sound gear. The discouraged captain "sat down heavily on a stool . . . assumed a head-in-chin position and sat staring . . . at the bulkhead." At the half-hour mark Sterling gave his report on a patrol craft above them and Morton "grinned wanly." Morton asked Sterling, "How would you like to be interned in Vladivostok for the remainder of the war, Yeo?" In the ensuing discussion over the pros and cons of being interned in the Soviet Union, Morton told Sterling, "If *Wahoo* got depth-charged pretty heavily and there was no other way out, we might have to."

With nightfall, *Wahoo* surfaced. Just after midnight, Lockwood signaled his agreement to terminate the patrol; *Wahoo* was on her way to Midway at once. With extraordinary brass, Morton remained on the surface, diving only once for a potential target that turned out to be a Soviet ship. *Wahoo* resurfaced immediately and continued her all-day run toward La Pérouse, diving just off Soya Misaki, twenty-five miles from the entrance to the strait, a little after 1700. At 2000 she was on the surface again, pounding through the strait, ignoring the blinker-light challenge from the shore station.

Benny Bass was having similar torpedo troubles aboard *Plunger.* Unlike Morton's single-shot approach, he was firing spreads, but his luck was only marginally better. In the first three attacks, eight torpedoes were fired at three different targets. Only one exploded. Closing on this stopped cripple, Bass pumped four more torpedoes into her, one shot at a time. There were no explosions from the first three; the fourth detonated, and the ship finally sank. On August 22 Bass fired two torpedoes at a freighter. One was an observed dud. A third torpedo finally finished off this ship, the only two sinkings *Plunger* was able to make.

When *Plunger* departed the Sea of Japan a few days later, two Japanese destroyers were guarding La Pérouse Strait, obviously alerted to submarine comings and goings by *Wahoo*'s brazen exit.

Morton was clearly grim, and expressed his bitter disappointment to Sterling. Morton's deepest hopes for a record-setting patrol were in ruins. Near the Kuriles Morton found a way to vent his fury. Sterling spotted a sampan at 0900 on the twentieth, within sight of the shore. When the luckless fishermen hid below after a warning shot was fired, *Wahoo*'s gun crew dismembered the sampan.

The submarine nosed up to the wreck and, astonishingly, found six survivors. Five others had already been killed. A rope ladder was thrown over the side and multiple guns pointed at the hapless civilians. One, a boy of about ten, jumped in the water and swam to the ladder. The other five quickly did the same, and all six were interned in the after torpedo room as prisoners of war.

The same afternoon another sampan was destroyed. There were some survivors, but none was picked up. At 1800 a third sampan was dispatched with the same vigorous gun action. Clearly, any Japanese vessel that got in Morton's way now was a disposable target.

A measure of the crew's devotion to Morton came when he was observing the debris left from the sinking of a fishing boat. He muttered, "I'd sure like to have one of those glass fishing balls for a souvenir." Instantly two men dove into the icy water, fully clothed, to get Morton what he wanted. He was dumbfounded, and roared out orders to "get those men back on deck before they freeze to death." When the shivering men were brought to him in the conning tower and explained that they simply wanted to get him the toy he desired, Morton was deeply touched. He had a whiskey ration issued to each, sent them below, and grabbed the rail with both hands to keep his emotions in check.

As *Wahoo* left the Kuriles behind, she continued through Etorofu Strait and on to Midway—all on the surface. At Midway Morton paused for eight hours to unload ten serial-numbered torpedoes, as ordered by ComSubPac. He earnestly hoped they would not be recycled to another outgoing submarine. Then *Wahoo* was gone, arriving at Pearl Harbor at 1035 on August 29, 1943.

Two days earlier *Pollack*, and Grider, had survived a near-death experience. They daringly penetrated a convoy screen to sink the 3,520-ton *Taifuku Maru*, only to be pounced on by a destroyer and two small escorts. *Pollack* dove at flank speed, eighteen knots, but the bow planes refused to rig out.

She sped for the bottom with an incredible, ever-increasing down angle. *Pollack* roared through her test depth, the steepening angle of descent throwing men against compartment bulkheads.

In desperation, *Pollack*'s captain ordered the main ballast blown, but this action made the problem nearly intractable. The air rose, and was compressed in the stern tanks, but not in the much deeper bow. The submarine was nosing over like a dive bomber, headed for the bottom. Men hanging on to watertight door edges, tables, and control panel handles felt their feet swing free in the air. The internal cacophony of equipment, food, and tools spilling from secure stowage only added to the confusion and fear.

In the din the voice of the assistant engineering officer rang out: "For God's sake, Captain, ain't it about time to back?" This sane, desperate alternative was seized. "All back, emergency!" *Pollack* continued her plunge, but now a counterforce could be felt. The submarine slowed, the angle became less insane. The control room depth indicator read 450 feet, 200 more than *Pollack*'s test limit, but the torpedo room in the lowered bow was likely at 600 feet—near crush depth for this old boat.

As the submarine stabilized, the ballast tank air was uncontrollably redistributed. Tanks empty, *Pollack* began to shoot for the surface. The ballast tanks were vented with a swirl of bubbles, but the incoming water was nearly inadequate to the task of slowing her rapid ascent. *Pollack* was about to broach. The diving officer caught her just short of the surface, and just below the keel of the searching destroyer. In all this uproar of sound, air, and shifting target depth, the destroyer could not bring its search sonar to bear. *Pollack* got away. Later, during cleanup, hydraulic oil from overhead drip pans was found in the coffeemaker. Eleventh-grade trigonometry showed that *Pollack*'s down angle had been an astounding fifty-three degrees.

During *Wahoo*'s absence Roger Paine had been offered command of the old training boat *S-34*, in which Pinky Kennedy had long ago served as torpedo officer, based in San Diego. Paine was overjoyed: his first command at age twenty-five! And in the States! Bebe and Roger III could join him! It was a dream come true.

Enter Morton, already furious at his poor results, and smarting from the public, sharply critical endorsements given him by his superior officers. All pounded home one key point. Morton, having full knowledge of the disgraceful reliability of U.S. torpedoes, had chosen to use single shots at each target.

Standard tactics taught that, given completely dependable torpedoes, there was only an 80 ± 10 percent chance of getting one hit on a target with a spread of four torpedoes fired on a broad track. These mathematics assumed that the target speed was correct within two knots and that the range did not exceed a thousand yards.

Morton had experienced this in the real world. Of the seventy-two torpedoes he had been responsible for firing in his prior patrols, only twenty-nine were thought to have struck their target, four of these duds. If this excellent 40 percent useful ratio could be maintained, Wahoo might make nine to ten hits. Naturally, not all hits resulted in sinkings.

The commander of Submarine Division 42 was to write, "Considering all the factors including torpedo performance it is essential that spreads be used to insure [sic] destruction of the target." The commander of Squadron 4 hit harder: ". . . all torpedoes were set for shallow depths . . . unreliable torpedo performance with shallow depth settings has been noted in the past. The decision of the commanding officer to fire single torpedoes . . . is not concurred in. . . ." Lockwood's comments were devastating: "Failure to use torpedo spreads . . . undoubtedly contributed to the lack of success. . . . This patrol is not considered successful. . . ."

Morton came to see the now recovered Paine. He wanted Roger to come with Wahoo on the seventh patrol. Paine would not be the XO; Skjonsby already had that job, but Morton, who "forgot to put himself in my shoes," needed Roger. Paine, with a command in hand, a career in the navy that he hoped would extend decades beyond this war, an assignment out of the war zone, and a chance to be with his wife and child, quite naturally refused the request. Morton was boiling mad and stormed out in anger—the last time Paine was to see him.

Morton had more success with Carr, who rejoined Wahoo as chief of the boat. He also persuaded Sterling to make one more patrol. Upon his return to Pearl, the yeoman had learned he had been accepted to steno school, with classes set to begin in the States on November 1. Probably feeling some guilt, Morton turned on the charm: "Yeo, I'm going to ask a favor of you. Howsabout you making one more patrol with me? We'll be back in October. When we get in, I'll get you plane transportation back to the States. . . . Howsabout it?" Sterling, who truly loved Morton, agreed, telling Morton, "Captain, your word is good enough for me."

This personnel work was exceedingly important. Morton was determined to reenter the Sea of Japan and recover his reputation; the right crew was all-important. But he also needed good torpedoes. He sought an interview with Lockwood for just that purpose.

Since 1915 the navy's Bureau of Ordnance had toyed with an all-electric, wakeless torpedo. When World War I ended, all research was stopped for lack of funds, but one Newport technician continued to work on the electric concept in his spare time. This dedicated man finally produced a single working prototype, which sank during its test firing in 1931. The Bureau left it at the bottom of Rhode Island Sound. Several years later a ship weighing anchor accidentally snagged it and brought it to the surface. With war looming, the Bureau dusted off this old design and began a desultory design effort.

In March 1942 several German electric torpedoes ran up on U.S. beaches during the Paukenschlag slaughter. Stunned by their advanced technical development, Admiral King, commander in chief of the navy, requested that the Bureau of Ordnance expedite development of the electric torpedo for the United States. In a vicious, destructive series of internal political moves, the steam torpedo men worked to kill the electric.

Only the arrival of *Lapon*'s commanding officer, sent to Newport after his unproductive foray into the Sea of Japan, revealed the magnitude of the problem. His and his XO's reports ignited furious personal, and ugly, battles between Lockwood and the head of the Bureau of Ordnance, Admiral Blandy.

By mid-1943 several electric prototypes had arrived at Pearl Harbor, where Lockwood's technicians, one of whom was Bob Logue from the old *Dolphin*, discovered a variety of problems. Logue, working with Westinghouse technicians, learned how to control hydrogen leakage with a simple burning device; how to prevent battery compartment deformation, which ruined the necessary smooth launches; and how to insulate the batteries so that cold northern waters did not reduce battery power. He also understood several structural improvements that were rigged to strengthen the control surfaces.

When Morton braced Lockwood for a new batch of torpedoes, use of the new electrics was proposed. The admiral took Morton on a tour of the torpedo shops, where Logue explained the new weapon to him. Morton remembered Logue from his own short assignment as CO of the wretched *Dolphin*. Logue had just been given orders to go to a new-construction boat in the United States. A deal was struck on the spot: *Wahoo* would carry twenty-four essentially handmade electrics, with the TDC modified to accommodate the better-turning characteristics of the new torpedoes. She would also carry someone else: newly promoted FC1c Robert B. Logue.

Sawfish would also participate in this third penetration of the Sea of Japan. There were only fourteen electrics left for her and, of course, no Bob Logue.

Morton also learned some other news. In July *Tinosa*, operating against a stopped, unescorted target, fired eleven consecutive duds into the side of a

Japanese ship from a perfect ninety-degree angle. On August 31 Lockwood's staff duplicated the problem by firing torpedoes against the vertical cliffs of the Hawaiian island of Kahoolawe. It was undeniable, unbelievable: the contact exploders also were faulty. A stop gap measure was introduced: fire at targets at an oblique angle.

Lockwood was uneasy about his meeting with Morton. "Mush was boiling mad. He had found plenty of targets but a combination of deep running and duds had broken him down." Ned Beach later wrote that Lockwood thought, "I ought to take him off his ship and let him cool off a bit. But I just can't do it."

On September 8, after a stay of only ten days, *Wahoo* left Pearl Harbor, two days ahead of *Sawfish*. There was a last-minute personnel loss. Just hours before departure John Griggs was transferred yet again, this time to Groton and the new-construction boat *Shark II*. He joined her company on October 4, two weeks before launch.

Morton was now a full commander, a promotion performed without ceremony. *Wahoo* was carrying an interesting guest as far as Midway, the ex-boxer Gene Tunney, who would try to organize a physical fitness regime,

SEPTEMBER 8, 1943. The last known picture of *Wahoo*'s crew prior to departure from Pearl Harbor on the seventh, and final, war patrol. (Courtesy of Paul Crozier III)

and suppress beer drinking, on that island. The very notion of this plan was hated by all potential participants.

Wahoo arrived at Midway on the morning of September 13 to top off her fuel. After tying up, Skjonsby left for the tender with Morton, telling Sterling that they would depart by 1600, six hours away. At about 1500 Sterling heard Morton enter the boat and head for the yeoman's office. He announced his presence by slapping Sterling hard on the back, nearly knocking him off his chair.

Morton was in an excellent mood. He asked Sterling, teasingly, "Got your steno school orders made up, Yeo?"

"No, sir, Captain, but I could sure make them up in a damn quick hurry if you gave me the word," Sterling replied.

Suddenly Morton shifted from teasing to serious. "We've got an hour before we sail. Let's go up to the squadron and get you a relief."

Sterling was pop-eyed with shock but wasted no time scrambling after Morton. During the short jeep ride he was sure that Morton was staging an elaborate practical joke. But when they got to the squadron commander's office he learned that Morton was deadly serious.

"I'm giving up the best goddamn yeoman that I ever had working for me. He's got orders to go back to stenography school. I say there's nothing but the best for the best. Have you got a relief you can give me for him?"

The squadron commander motioned to three yeomen, who rushed to the desk. Morton asked Sterling, "Which one is the best, Yeo?"

Sterling picked Bill White. "This man wants the *Wahoo* more than anybody else. He did a damn good job as relief yeoman before."

Morton said, "That's good enough for me." Turning to the squadron commander, he said, "What do we do now? I'm sailing in forty-five minutes."

"We'll have White over there in half an hour."

"Come on, Yeo, let's get moving," said Morton.

Sterling was stunned by the pace of events, but the confusion didn't slow him down. Back at *Wahoo* he typed up his own transfer orders, had them signed by Skjonsby, and ran to his locker to stuff his belongings in a seabag. He left the boat in a flurry of handshakes, catcalls, notes pressed into his hand, and looks of fear, as if his leaving were a jinx. At 1556 a jeep roared up with White, Sterling's official relief.

Sterling stepped ashore and saw all the officers and lookouts on the bridge. He declined the offer of a ride back to *Sperry* and stood on the dock with the line handlers. As the diesels roared, Sterling took the bowline in hand, and threw it off the bollard at Morton's command.

Morton's voice came across the widening water. "Take care of yourself, Yeo."

"Good hunting!" Sterling shouted back, waving to everyone topside. They were all grinning and waving back.

Sterling threw his seabag on the dock and sat down on it. He smoked several cigarettes "before *Wahoo*, a tiny submarine silhouette on the horizon, headed into a rain squall and disappeared from sight. Forever."

11

Loss of Wahoo

Into that silent sea . . .

—*Coleridge, "The Rime of the Ancient Mariner"*

"So it was that the *Wahoo* left on its seventh patrol for waters so perilous they were shortly to be abandoned as a patrol area, and with a skipper so enraged he was ready to take any chance to redeem his boat's proud record, and with a fire control party that did not know him well enough to try and hold him in check." So wrote George Grider fifteen years later, his heart still heavy with the mysterious disappearance of *Wahoo* from the face of the earth.

Sawfish passed through La Pérouse Strait in the early-morning of September 23, 1943, in heavy rain and seas. *Wahoo* had preceded her by two days leaving Midway, but may have lost a little ground. Relatively recent research on Japanese sinkings reveals that on September 21 a large fishing boat, *Hokusei Maru*, was sunk in the Sea of Okhotsk about 150 miles east of La Pérouse Strait. The attack was made by a surfaced submarine employing its deck gun, and thirty fishermen were killed. This was *Wahoo*'s opening attack of her seventh patrol and was surely noticed by the Japanese.

On September 24 *Sawfish* made an unsuccessful attack in the northwest, near the Soviet Union. The seas were so heavy the Japanese appear to have been unaware of this strike. Their first positive knowledge that a submarine was once again inside the Sea of Japan occurred on September 25, when *Wahoo* hit *Taiko Maru* with a torpedo in number-three hold, killing thirteen crew. She sank just south of Tsugaru Strait, forty miles southwest of O Shima. After the sinking *Wahoo* moved west nearly five hundred miles, toward Hungnam, Korea.

On September 28 *Sawfish* made another unsuccessful attack, in daylight, six miles southwest of Motsuta Misaki, near the Hokkaido shoreline. *Wahoo* struck the next day near the Korean coast, sinking *Masaki Maru*, killing thirty-three of the thirty-seven crew. The Japanese now knew that there were two submarines inside; antisubmarine patrolling intensified.

The widely scattered attacks continued, *Sawfish* failing on every attempt with maddening torpedo performance. The new electrics were tried first. Seven ran slow in the cold waters, passing astern of targets. Three failed to eject smoothly, striking the torpedo tube shutters, then the bow of *Sawfish* itself, and running erratically thereafter. Three did not run at all; a fourth ran straight to the bottom, where it was heard to strike in sixty-eight fathoms of water. It did not explode. Switching to steam torpedoes, *Sawfish* had at least one broach; two more made it to targets, only to have the faulty contact exploders produce duds.

Meanwhile, *Wahoo* was scoring repeatedly. On October 5, on the heels of a small typhoon that produced fifty-mile-per-hour winds and twenty-foot waves, *Wahoo* sank the large passenger transport *Konron Maru* in Tsushima Strait, a thousand miles southwest of La Pérouse. This sinking was in the well-traveled sea lanes from Pusan, Korea, to Honshu, known to Morton because of a prewar trip in the Sea of Japan.

Possibly because of the foul weather, the ship sank uncommonly quickly, "after several seconds," the Japanese Domei news agency reported. Loss of life was extremely high, with 554 of 616 passengers perishing. This caused Tokyo Rose to denounce the brutality of the sinking, an event picked up by *Time* magazine and reported in an article titled "Knock at the Door." The intelligence staff at Pearl Harbor had already picked up the news via an Ultra intercept.

On October 6 *Wahoo* sank *Kanko Maru*, farther north along the Korean coast, then moved more than 550 miles to the northeast, sinking *Hankow Maru* off Honshu's Oga Peninsula three days later. Each ship carried 48 crew. There were no survivors from either of these sinkings. Clearly, Bob Logue's knowledge of the peculiarities of the electric torpedo had paid off for Morton.

Plotting the path of the sinkings, the Japanese could see that *Wahoo* was heading back toward La Pérouse. On October 7 *Sawfish* had been spotted and bombed repeatedly by air patrols about 20 miles from Okushira Shima. She slipped out on October 9, while *Wahoo* was sinking *Hankow Maru*. *Sawfish* was detected and challenged by the lighthouse on Cape Soya. Knowledge that a second submarine was on the way must have been certain.

On October 11 the Japanese were vigilantly watching the approaches to La Pérouse. Minesweeper 18, with Shinichi Shibata aboard, was patrolling between Wakkanai and Russian Karafuto. Subchasers 15 and 43 cruised nearby. In the air, two Seiran attack float planes searched, each crew of three scouring the sea for any sign of the desperately sought *Wahoo,* whose transit they expected.

At 0920 Suguru Ichida, the radioman of float plane 32 heard the alarm. Float plane 319 had spotted a small lubricating oil slick, ten meters by five meters, twelve miles off Cape Soya on the Sea of Okhotsk side. This small amount of light surface oil could be generated by the volume of a single water glass. The Japanese airmen had seen them before; they came from submarine propeller shafts.

The cold northern waters were exceptionally clear, and the crew of float plane 319 could see the dark shadow of a submarine's conning tower beneath the sea. Clearly Morton had taken *Wahoo* out submerged by day, as Benny Bass had done on *Plunger* a few months earlier. His proximity to the surface may have been the result of a fatal "look-see."

Float plane 319 bore in and dropped one bomb, which must have gone off underneath *Wahoo.* She momentarily broached so that the Japanese could see "the body and the wake of a propeller." A second bomb was dropped, which clearly damaged *Wahoo*'s fuel oil tanks. The Japanese saw bubbles and heavier oil spouting to the surface.

Trailing oil, *Wahoo* turned to course 315 degrees, toward the Soviet Union. Float plane 32 took its turn. The heavy oil slick was now thirty meters in diameter. Two more bombs were dropped on the sometimes visible submarine silhouette. Shuttling to the city reservoir at Wakkanai, the float planes refueled and rearmed. By the fourth attack the oil slick was two thousand meters long and *Wahoo*'s speed had dropped to nearly zero.

The attacks were continuous and relentless. The Japanese pilots began to distinguish air bubbles leading the oil trail by sixty to seventy meters. These air bubbles became the points of aim. By the eighth attack the oil leaks were enormous, but *Wahoo* still staggered forward at low speed, near enough to the surface to produce a visible wake. Compartments were likely flooding; Morton may have been struggling to surface and scuttle.

Markers were dropped to vector in the patrol ships, which began to drop depth charges at about 1115. At 1207 one pattern of seven charges dropped by submarine chaser 15 blew a piece of one of *Wahoo*'s propeller blades to the surface. The Japanese flew fourteen sorties, and dropped forty bombs, their last at 1630. The surface ships added twenty-three depth charges to the onslaught.

By 1330, and the eleventh air attack, *Wahoo* was stopped a little more than eight miles from Skala Kamen Opasnosti lighthouse, off Sakhalin. She rests there today. Alone and friendless, *Wahoo* had come to the end of the line. The frame-smashing bombs and depth charges broke her hull, and the hydrant flow of ice-cold seawater flooded the boat, ending forever all hope of seeing daylight again.

The Japanese reported, "The submarine had stopped and gushed . . . oil." Roger Paine believes this "most likely resulted from a last-ditch attempt to achieve positive buoyancy by blowing the two main ballast tanks still containing the fuel to get home." The men in the center of the boat could no longer make an underwater escape through the recently strengthened conning tower. If this emergency surfacing was attempted, the effort failed. *Wahoo*, Morton, Skjonsby, Henderson, Carr, Logue, White—eighty men in all—were gone.

Lockwood began to grow uneasy when *Sawfish* reported her passage through the Kuriles, but *Wahoo* remained silent. This uneasiness grew to fear when *Wahoo* did not make a required report by October 26. The thought of Morton's loss was nearly unbearable to the admiral and his staff. Planes were sent out from Midway to scout along *Wahoo's* path in case she was damaged and unable to report her problems. There was, of course, no trace of the submarine or her gallant crew.

Lockwood later wrote, "It just didn't seem possible that Morton . . . could be lost. I'd never have believed the Japs would be smart enough to get him. [*Wahoo*] would never come steaming in again with a broom at her masthead and Mush Morton's fighting face, with its wide grin, showing above the bridge rail."

Shaken, on November 9 Lockwood had the sad duty to report *Wahoo* "overdue, presumed lost." Knowing nothing but silence and, suspecting mines, Lockwood ended all further sorties into the Sea of Japan for the next twenty months.

Of all the original *Wahoo* plank owners, George Grider probably heard the horrible news first. He was at Pearl Harbor, exhausted after months in combat aboard both *Wahoo* and *Pollack*. He was also depressed. Rumors were about that the new-construction boat he had so envied, *Cisco*, was lost. The rumors were true. *Cisco* had been sunk by air attack in the Sulu Sea on September 28. The entire crew, including Grider's friend Gus Weinel, was dead. But *Wahoo's* loss left him bitter and heartbroken.

Grider believed, probably unfairly, that the problem lay in the heavy personnel turnover *Wahoo* had endured—particularly the one-two loss of Dick O'Kane and Roger Paine.

Paine's replacement was, he wrote, ". . . a capable officer, but one who knew Mush by his awesome reputation rather than long association. It was a difference . . . that was to prove fatal. For by now virtually all Mush's old associates in the conning tower were gone, replaced by men who naturally thought of their great and famous skipper as infallible. . . . On previous patrols, Mush had come to rely subconsciously on his officers to tell him what not to do, and with the loss of Roger this safety factor disappeared. Here was a man whose valor blazed so brightly that at times he could not distinguish between the calculated risk and the foolhardy chance, and now the men who knew him well enough to insist on pointing out the difference were gone."

In spite of Grider's palpable grief, the knowable evidence suggests that Morton made only two arguable errors: the sinking of *Hankow Maru* on October 9, which telegraphed *Wahoo*'s coming exit, and (possibly) running too close to the surface on October 11 after successfully passing through La Pérouse Strait. It seems fairer to say that his luck simply ran out. Grider's epitaph remains fitting: "*[Wahoo]* was a mighty warrior, skippered by the most valiant man I ever knew."

In San Diego, Roger Paine was flooded with contradictory emotions, intensely glad to be alive, but also staggering under the hammer blows of widespread death.

Pompano, on which then ensign Paine served during the Pearl Harbor attack, also had not returned from her September patrol off Honshu. Lew Parks, Slade Cutter, and Dave Connole had already been transferred and were alive, but the entire seventy-six-man crew vanished without a trace.

Eighteen of the eighty men on *Wahoo* had been plank owners. *Pompano*, also on her seventh patrol, likely had a similar ratio of men well known to Paine. Ironically, one of those lost, Jesse Appel, had served aboard *Wahoo* for the first five war patrols. He transferred to *Pompano* and nearly simultaneous death.

Lockwood was persuaded by the remarkable intelligence officer Jasper Holmes that *Pompano* had blundered into a relatively new minefield. Developing a defense against mines became Lockwood's obsession, and would influence Paine's coming assignments on *S-34*.

The day after *Wahoo*'s loss *Dorado*, commanded by Paine's former neighbor and XO on *Pompano*, then *Trigger*, Penrod Schneider, was sunk in the Caribbean with the loss of all hands. *Dorado* was a new-construction boat, on the way from New London to the Panama Canal and the Pacific war. There was some uncertainty about what happened, but it appeared that the pilot of a PBM Mariner flying out of Guantánamo Air Station in Cuba, and instructed to provide air cover for a convoy, was given faulty information on *Dorado*'s position. The U.S. submarine would normally have been exempt from attack inside a rectangle with fifteen-mile sides. In any case, Schneider was dead.

Ironically, *Dorado* had been chosen for a series of war paintings by the artist Georges Schreiber, who had ridden with her during the shakedown cruise. Images of *Dorado*'s crew were captured for the Navy Combat Art Collection and can still be seen at the Submarine Force Museum. Schneider, the son of a navy chief radioman, is at the center of the painting *Up Periscope*, which depicts an attack that was never to be made.

The news of *Wahoo*'s loss was a devastating blow. Paine would have had to be inhuman not to be depressed, while simultaneously joyful at living. There were also hidden pangs of guilt, made more poignant by the way he and Morton had parted. It was a hard emotional range for the twenty-five-year-old to span.

At Mare Island Dick O'Kane heard only rumors. But they were believable, and he vowed revenge for the death of his captain, mentor, and friend. For the rest of his life he would fight to have Morton's four Navy Cross awards be superseded with the Congressional Medal of Honor. It would never come, but for now O'Kane devoted his fantastic energy to the creation of an avenging machine: *Tang*.

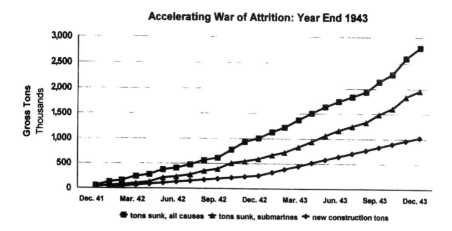

Accelerating War of Attrition: Year End 1943

PART III

WAHOO'S WAR CONTINUES

12

O'Kane in Charge

Old fuds, young studs . . . Lieutenant Commanders run the subs.

—*Richard G. Voge, "Old Fuds, Young Studs*
and Lieutenant Commanders"

An exceedingly tough Pennsylvanian, Lieutenant Murray Frazee, was the new executive officer of *Tang*. He arrived at Mare Island first, straight from *Grayback*, where he had already made seven war patrols under cautious skippers, for disappointing results. *Grayback* would now be commanded by the daring Johnny Moore—the PCO on *Wahoo*'s fifth patrol, and a Morton-trained man. Her productivity would soar.

Frazee was a rarity in the submarine force. He was not a volunteer. He had been dragooned into sub school from a destroyer, and was not impressed by silent-service mystique: "You didn't have to know anything about submarines to be a submariner. After all, it was just another ship. You learned the peculiarities in a hurry."

Frazee was not initially impressed by Dick O'Kane. "I had made more war patrols and had been exposed to more depth charges than he had, so [*Tang's*] men weren't getting any cherry in me. . . ." Five years younger than O'Kane, the short, intense Frazee was a commanding, take-charge individual. O'Kane had the excellent sense to recognize, and act on, this characteristic: "Now when you have someone who is carrying the ball, don't stand in his way. I took my own advice, leaving Fraz in charge. . . ."

O'Kane's typical daily routine began with a 1000 meeting with Frazee, where that day's "to do" list was briefly discussed. Frazee wrote that O'Kane would then "embark on a round of visits to different shops where he knew the leading men and supervisors from *Wahoo* days." O'Kane would "offer suggestions and make requests, the latter usually including a request for speed in completion so he could get to sea." Soon O'Kane began to concentrate on determining the true strength of *Tang*'s new hull with the Mare Island design engineers.

In late 1941 the two leading navy submarine architects proposed a design that would permit U.S. submarines to dive deeper and withstand heavier depth charge attacks. But the sudden onset of the Pacific war forced the existing submarine yards to stick with a proven "thin skin" design.

The new high-tensile steel (HTS) boats were slotted into production at Cramp shipbuilding in Philadelphia, a private yard that had been closed since 1926. The production results were disastrous. Ignoring special-case anomalies such as the 16-year cycle for *Roncador,* Cramp boats took an average of 784 days from keel laying to commissioning, far too long for the wartime emergency. Krause's new boat, *Escolar,* would do a bit better, finishing in 723 days—in June 1944, giving him an extra six months in the States.

Stung by the production problems, at the end of June 1942 the navy laid down two keels for "thick-skinned" boats in its own yards at opposite sides of the continent—*Balao* in Portsmouth, New Hampshire; *Seahorse* at Mare Island. Production leaped forward. *Balao* was commissioned in 223 days, *Seahorse* in 273.

Now Mare Island was building its third HTS boat—*Tang*—and O'Kane was intrigued with the possibility that she could dive well beyond the specified test depth of 438 feet.

Commissioning took place on October 15, 1943. Dick O'Kane had been at Mare Island for only 4½ months. *Tang* was ready for him 14 months ahead of *Manta,* which had been laid down at Cramp shipbuilding on the same day. O'Kane immediately began sea trials, performing true dives from the outset, not simply slow test flooding. *Tang* quickly passed the dive to test depth. O'Kane decided to press farther.

On her combined endurance/shakedown run off San Diego O'Kane ordered *Tang* to 450 feet, where relatively minor lines and hoses blew out. Instead of quitting, Frazee was astonished to hear O'Kane order the lines plugged with raw potatoes until they could be shut off. O'Kane immediately started down again. At 525 feet the sound head rollers cracked under the strain.

O'Kane immediately moved *Tang* to the San Diego destroyer yard facilities, where he had old friends from his days in the "tin can" navy. Here the broken rollers and lines were replaced by heavy-duty rigs. On the next afternoon, O'Kane dove *Tang* again. At 580 feet vent riser pipes sprang leaks.

OCTOBER 15 1943. *Tang*'s crew, officers and men, at Midway. (National Archives)

The destroyer yard worked all the next night, building special tools, to tighten the junctions. At dawn O'Kane was ready again. The crew was stricken with anxiety. Frazee was mightily impressed with his new captain's raw courage.

The 580-foot mark was reached, and *Tang* kept going down. The numbers on the depth gauge dial stopped at 600 feet; its needle pegged three-quarters of an inch beyond that mark. Frazee guessed that they had just made a 625-foot dive.

After docking at San Diego, the chief cook came up to Frazee, who was standing on deck. He wanted a transfer, which Frazee refused, telling the cook he would have to make one war patrol before Frazee would even consider the request. The cook, obviously scared witless by O'Kane's test dives, said, "Well, if you're not going to do anything about it now, I just won't show up tomorrow morning."

That was exactly the wrong way to approach a man as tough as Frazee. He turned to Bill Ballinger, chief of the boat, and said, "Chief, you heard what he said, didn't you?" Ballinger replied, "I sure did!" Frazee wheeled, grabbed the hapless cook by the shirtfront, pulled his face close, and said, "Listen, you son of a bitch, if you're not here tomorrow morning at 0800 when we sail, I'm going to have you shot for desertion in time of war! Now, have you got that straight?" The cook did.

Frazee's explanation was clear and unambiguous. "That was the end of it. I made a believer out of him. He was older than I and had been in the navy longer than I had. But by God, we couldn't fool around like that. We were in the middle of a war." Frazee, no volunteer himself, later remarked that "In the *Tang* with Dick O'Kane, some of the crew occasionally wished they had never volunteered."

One cheerful volunteer was Howard M. Walker—the "Negro" steward. The armed forces were nearly completely segregated during World War II, and the prewar navy had been highly elitist. It took care that its officers would enjoy a prestigious role in society. In keeping with its social norms, a ship of any size had to have stewards for the officers' mess. For decades minorities, especially blacks and Filipinos, were almost automatically named to this post at the completion of boot camp. There would be no technical training for the likes of them.

As individual submarine size and officer counts grew, the scorned "pigboats" became candidates for stewards. By the 1920s the big V-boats each had a recognizable officers' wardroom and a steward. In an ironic reversal of fortune, the most personally and physically intimate ships of the navy became integrated. Drawn by the hazardous-duty pay and the willingness to provide cross training to all crew members once aboard, for many men of color the position of submarine force steward was an entry-level slot.

Walker was not motivated to drive for technical training, but he was hardworking, highly attentive to O'Kane, and a favorite with the crew. His gambling exploits—and winnings—would become the subjects of a hundred crew stories. O'Kane really liked Walker; Frazee didn't, since he was the one required to handle the resulting disciplinary problems.

Although O'Kane had loved and respected Morton, he did not turn *Tang* into a copy of Morton's *Wahoo*. Morton was averse to having too many lookouts, believing the extra time they took to scramble below slowed down the dive. O'Kane liked lookouts, lots of them. He simply didn't intend to dive that much.

From *Wahoo*'s two, O'Kane eventually had shipyards weld enough extra platforms to handle up to seven lookouts. He reasoned that Japanese antisubmarine aircraft had no effective search radar, and a submarine, especially in waves or whitecaps, was so low-lying as to be almost invisible to an airplane fifteen to twenty miles away. But the submarine could always see the plane at that distance and take the necessary next step. O'Kane wanted to be up, lookouts scanning the horizon with binoculars. Frazee said, ". . . on the surface, we . . . could see a ship thirty miles away, long before he could possibly see us. That was the sort of thing O'Kane originated. . . . He revolutionized the science."

O'Kane restructured the bridge layout. Disgusted with the poor night optics of American periscopes, O'Kane intended to fight on the surface, from the bridge. Target-bearing transmitters (TBTs) were positioned on the centerline of the boat, moving the compass repeater out of the way to make an uncluttered nighttime firing space.

He also finessed the acquisition of a wire recorder and captured all the conversations during mock attacks. He then listened to the recorder after each attack, playing back the sound to his officers and crew, pointing out the excess verbiage. When O'Kane attacked he wanted only the words that counted for this particular action.

Most important, he abandoned Morton's coapproach officer approach. O'Kane, not Frazee, would man the periscope during daylight attacks. While he had a rational explanation, including a sense that the *Wahoo* approach would waste his hard-earned observational skills, his ego played a key part in this decision. He wrote later that he "had already found that maneuvering a submarine . . . was greatly simplified once I had command. No longer was I being second-guessed by a senior, and I knew my decisions, with logical follow-through, would bring the desired results. . . . I was able to con our ship to an advantageous attack position."

O'Kane also decided to fire spreads, even though he was partial to Morton's single-torpedo-per-target philosophy. He did not intend to be criticized as Morton had been.

Finally, the loose informality of Mush Morton's *Wahoo* would not prevail in *Tang*. Frazee "never dreamed of calling him anything but Captain."

Quite simply put, *Tang* would be run O'Kane's way. This included the required posting of the "Articles for the Government of the Navy" prominently throughout the boat, and having the Articles read to the crew while he stood stiffly at attention. O'Kane especially liked Articles 4 and 19: "The punishment of death . . . may be inflicted on any person . . . [who] does not do his utmost to overtake and capture or destroy any vessel which it is his duty to encounter." Not surprisingly, after these actions O'Kane discovered that "We had several reluctant sailors." But not to worry: "Fraz and Ballinger would handle this under my instructions." Frazee leaned even harder on a frightened crew.

One crewman who was working out exceedingly well was a young boatswain, a rarity in submarines, named Bill Leibold. He had joined the navy before the war for the express purpose of serving in submarines. Instead, he had been assigned to the battleship *Pennsylvania*, where he was a witness to the December 7 attack.

In 1944 he was at Mare Island and chanced to come aboard *Grayback*, which was undergoing refit, including the installation of the first five-inch gun on a fleet boat. Always entranced with submarines, he declared to *Grayback*'s captain that he was going to *Tang*, then being built nearby.

"Do you have orders for *Tang*?" another officer asked.

"Why, no," replied Leibold, "but I'm still going to serve on her."

"Well, I'm the prospective XO of *Tang*, and I like that attitude," said Murray Frazee, who immediately set to work getting this determined young man the right papers. "Boats," as he was called, would become a key member of the crew, loyal to Frazee and a clear admirer—and later friend—of the captain, Dick O'Kane.

Training was relentless—as hard as Pinky Kennedy had ever dished out. In part this was simply because hard training was O'Kane's style. But there was a practical side. With the exceptions of O'Kane, Frazee, and Lieutenant Bill Walsh, *Tang* had no Naval Academy graduates, and very few experienced submarine men aboard.

Walsh, the engineering officer, had been on two war patrols on *Tautog* and knew how to dive the boat. Hank Flanagan was a mustang from New London, an enlisted man rising from chief torpedoman to ensign who had already made eight war patrols in *Tambor* and *Thresher*. Frank Springer, the TDC operator, was a graduate of the emergency officer procurement program and just out of submarine school. Bruce Anderson, originally from the merchant marine, had made two patrols on *Greenling*, but was not yet designated as qualified in submarines. Ensign Mel Enos, a University of California ROTC graduate, did Anderson one better: Enos had never even been to sea.

Frazee, who thought both Anderson and Walsh lazy, was phlegmatic: "We generally had a good, average bunch of officers, considering we were stuck with whoever was sent to us."

On January 1, 1944, *Tang* left San Francisco for Pearl Harbor, training round-the-clock on the entire passage. Immediately upon arrival the morning of January 8 O'Kane left the boat for courtesy calls. Admiral Lockwood confirmed the persistent rumors of the loss of *Wahoo*.

O'Kane and Frazee also ran into Johnny Moore and *Grayback*, who had preceded them to Pearl by four days. Moore was in a swaggering mood following two very aggressive, very successful patrols. He bragged to Reuben Whitaker, the more cautious—but very effective—captain of *Flasher*, of his daring torpedo attacks and surface gun actions. Whitaker was alarmed by Moore's charged talk and warned him, "Look, I think you've lost respect for the enemy, and unless you learn better, you're not going to come back from one of these patrols." Moore dismissed the danger, saying, "They can't lay a glove on me."

After Lockwood, O'Kane saw "Babe" Brown, head of Training Command.

O'Kane proposed to Brown that *Tang* would be ready to go on patrol in eight days. Brown was astonished, since no submarine had ever been permitted to go on patrol with fewer than three weeks' training at Pearl Harbor.

At the end of the eight days, O'Kane invited Brown aboard to witness late day and night operations. The entire crew, and *Tang*, performed splendidly, and Brown agreed that they would be released for patrol after a four-day ready-for-sea program. Torpedoes, stores, and fuel were loaded on a rotating-shift basis so that one watch section was free for liberty in Honolulu each day. All hands were aboard, and *Tang* was ready, on the afternoon of the fourth day, January 21, 1944.

13

The New Avenger

Vengeance is in my heart, death in my hand. . . .

—*William Shakespeare,* Titus Andronicus

In spite of Babe Brown's positive impression of *Tang*'s readiness, O'Kane was not about to get a hot hunting ground on his first war patrol. After all, O'Kane got command because he was Morton's XO. Would this impulsive hothead really be any good on his own? *Tang*'s first task was to go to Wake Island, six hundred miles to the west, and perform lifeguard duty for two modest air strikes to be executed by Coronado seaplanes from their base at Kaneohe, Oahu.

O'Kane knew the seaplane squadron commander from their days at Annapolis. He and Frazee immediately beat it over to Kaneohe and began to expand *Tang*'s role. They would reconnoiter Wake before the strikes, then surface to act as a night beacon for the incoming planes. Only then would *Tang* be released to go ship hunting.

To increase the submarine's post–air strike range, the safety tank would be filled with fuel oil instead of salt water. The diving officer would simply have to compensate for the lighter weight. O'Kane intended to get on, and stay on, a station filled with shipping.

Tang's periscope began surveying the Japanese installations on Wake Island at dawn on the morning of January 28, 1944. The fuel oil consumed on the outward leg had been replaced with the safety tank reserve; depth control was now normal. For nine frustrating days O'Kane waited, twice acting as a beacon for the incoming Coronado bombers. As far as he could tell, the bombings were ineffectual. Finally came the long-awaited release. *Tang* was on her way to the area of Truk, in the Carolines, before the message from Pearl had even been decoded.

The five-thousand-square-mile patrol area assigned seemed without prospects, well north of Truk and crossed by no shipping lanes. O'Kane was disappointed, but determined to make his own luck: "No one would be telling us what we could do here, or how we should conduct our patrol." O'Kane took his boat to the western edge of the area, killed the engines, and lay on the surface looking, and listening with the passive sonar. Each evening *Tang* shifted another twenty miles south, listening and, looking. There were no daylight dives; O'Kane was literally betting his life on the skill of the lookouts and sonar operators.

On the twentieth patrol day O'Kane's tactics paid off. An Ultra message from Pearl Harbor to *Skate* and *Sunfish* was picked up and decoded. It informed those two boats that a convoy would be leaving Gray Feather Bank at 0800 the following day. O'Kane knew this area well from *Wahoo's* first patrol. "With the Ultra developments, we saw fit to modify [our patrol area]." *Tang* immediately began pounding toward Gray Feather Bank on all four engines, intent on beating the competition to the targets.

This brash drive did not go undetected. Japanese air patrols drove *Tang* under twice, clearly alerting the convoy to the presence of a nearby submarine. Assuming the convoy would either hold up its departure or hide at Mogami Bank, O'Kane positioned *Tang* to cover both areas. Just after midnight on February 17 *Tang's* SJ radar registered a zigzagging contact nearly eighteen miles away.

As O'Kane maneuvered for an attack position ahead, a new Ultra message—actually a few hours old—arrived. It was addressed to *Tang*, which Pearl Harbor thought was still near Truk: *Skate* and *Sunfish* were copied. The message read:

CONVOY WILL DEPART GRAY FEATHER BANK AT

TWENTY TWO HUNDRED FEBRUARY SIXTEEN FOR TRUK

NOTE SKATE AND SUNFISH THIS IS THE CONVOY

YOU WERE TO HAVE ATTACKED BUT ONE OF YOU

WAS SIGHTED AND CONVOY ORDERED TO RETURN

ONTO GRAY FEATHER BANK

O'Kane bristled at the sighting note as a ". . . slurring statement . . . written behind a calm desk ashore." In truth, *Tang* was poaching. O'Kane had stolen the first shooting opportunity from his shipmates and had authentically been spotted, to their detriment. He justified this action by writing, "Sometimes a submarine did get sighted when doing its damnedest to make contact. . . ."

At about 0230 *Tang* was detected on the surface by a radar-equipped destroyer escort, which closed rapidly in spite of *Tang's* flank speed. After a quick dive, *Tang* headed for 500 feet, well below the sonar-reflecting temperature gradient in the water. At this depth she was impervious to sonar detection. Sound captured a protective zig made by the convoy, but O'Kane compensated by going at full speed underwater to penetrate the convoy screen.

At 1,500 yards' range O'Kane fired a full spread of four torpedoes from the after tubes—his first war shots as captain of his own submarine. O'Kane observed three hits starting fifty-five seconds after the first torpedo was ejected, then directed *Tang* to go deep: 575 feet, where the Japanese escorts simply could not hear them.

Exuberant, O'Kane wrote in the patrol report that "The explosions were wonderful, throwing Japs and other debris above the belching smoke." Morton himself would not have penned it any differently. O'Kane identified his victim as a 7,770-ton Mansei Maru class cargo ship. The initial postwar analysis revealed that the stricken vessel was, in fact, the 6,854-ton *Gyoten Maru*. But in 1952 the Japanese prepared a monograph of ship sinkings. The *Gyoten Maru* was clearly listed as sunk on this date and location, but the IJN also tallied the 5,184-ton oiler *Kuniei Maru*. The IJN may be in error, but it is possible that O'Kane sank two overlapping ships with his first salvo.

The next morning *Tang* was boldly running on the surface. A message was picked up on the morning "Fox" from Pearl. Five submarines were being reassigned to Saipan; *Tang* was among them. O'Kane quickly ordered eighteen-knot speed. Unless the other submarines were also surfaced, *Tang* would have a 250-mile head start before they learned about the change in orders on the evening "Fox."

O'Kane's progress toward the Marianas was slowed by continuous air patrols that repeatedly forced *Tang* under. Fed up, he ordered *Tang* not to dive but just to ignore the Japanese "Betty" bomber on the horizon. This worked until the Betty, clearly a spotter decoy, called in two smaller planes, which made life-threatening attacks.

On Washington's birthday *Tang's* radar picked up a convoy of five ships, frequently hidden in rain squalls. O'Kane decided to attack U-boat style, at night, on the surface. The Japanese escorts were doing a good job of protecting their charges, and *Tang* had to turn away twice before finally penetrating their screen. Four torpedoes were fired at a "good-size ship." All four hit; the target simply disintegrated. O'Kane identified the sunken vessel as a 6,486-ton Kenyo Maru class cargo ship. She was actually a converted gunboat, the 3,581-ton auxiliary *Fukuyama Maru*. O'Kane's tendency to see the targets as larger than life had returned.

Within *Tang* the bronze inner doors of the forward tubes were opened and the long torpedoes were silkily thrust inside. The gyro angle umbilicals were connected, the inner doors slammed shut, the outer doors opened. Fully reloaded, O'Kane bore in again and sank what he believed to be the 8,663-ton naval auxiliary *Arimasan Maru* just after midnight on the twenty-third. Four torpedoes were fired. The first two hit in a normal fashion. The third caused a massive explosion that whitened the seas with phosphorescence and stung *Tang* with a monstrous, jaw-dropping explosion. O'Kane wrote in the patrol report that the ship "raised from the sea as you would flip a spoon on end, then plunged by the stern, engulfed in a mass of flames." This was the holocaustal incandescence of the 6,777-ton *Yamashimo Maru*.

Belowdecks all compartments were checked for damage that might have resulted from the horrendous explosion. The forward torpedo room reported that tube five was leaking, but the problem was not considered serious. O'Kane was sure "it would undoubtedly seal tightly with sea pressure on diving."

Sleep was impossible for the adrenaline-charged officers. They tried to relax by playing cribbage, with O'Kane playing Morton to Frazee's O'Kane: "Tenacity, Fraz. Stay with 'em till they're on the bottom!" Like Morton, O'Kane kept losing to his XO. Frazee later recalled that during this patrol ". . . we played a lot of cribbage, and I led him in games approximately 200–125. He never asked me again to play the game."

On the twenty-fourth, after a day-long high-speed chase against an escorted, alert, and competent convoy, O'Kane finally worked *Tang* into position to get a night surface shot at the last ship in the group, what he believed was a 7,064-ton Tatutaki Maru class freighter. Another spread of four torpedoes, again with three hits. "The freighter came to pieces." O'Kane's tonnage eye was deteriorating. He had actually sunk the 2,424-ton *Echizen Maru*.

Exhausted from three straight days of successful attacks, O'Kane went to bed, leaving command of the boat in the hands of the equally tired Murray Frazee. Following O'Kane's instructions, Frazee shadowed the convoy, maintaining position about five to six miles off the port beam. At 0300 Frazee went to three engines to move *Tang* into position ten thousand yards ahead of the convoy by morning twilight. O'Kane intended to attack as soon after dawn as practicable.

O'Kane left instructions to be awakened thirty minutes before morning twilight. As was his habit, Walker, the steward, advanced his own wake-up call to rise before O'Kane. Walker woke the captain with a hot mug of coffee, and O'Kane went to the bridge, refreshed by three or four hours' sleep. "Where are they, Fraz?" was his first query.

"Right back there ten thousand yards, where they're supposed to be" was the blunt, professional reply. This was a factual assertion but masked the very real problems Frazee had encountered during the night in keeping up with, then getting ahead of, the zigzagging convoy.

Tang was heading due east, toward Truk, at reduced speed. Soon the dim shapes of individual ships in the convoy could be discerned behind them. O'Kane ordered "All stop" and *Tang* waited, motionless, as the convoy moved ever closer, on a zigzag track that would overtake the submarine. At that moment an Ultra was received warning of a change in the convoy's base course at dawn. But O'Kane was committed. If the convoy truly zigged due north or south, *Tang* could not close the gap. Maneuvering on battery power, O'Kane chose to stick with the original plan. *Tang* submerged to forty feet, leaving the radar completely exposed, scanning the targets.

The search radar caught the large dawn zig, but it was only a thirty-degree base course change. They could still catch up in a high-speed submerged run. *Tang* slid down to a hundred feet and ran at full speed for fifteen minutes on a course perpendicular to the enemy track. O'Kane was hungry to get what he saw as a very large tanker, one he felt had more value than the other four ships combined.

In glassy seas, O'Kane used the periscope with unusual skill. With his short stature, perfect for the five-foot, four-inch elevation of the scope's eyepiece, there was no need to stoop. Each observation was only three to four seconds, the tip of the scope inches above the surface. O'Kane's trigonometric mind calculated ranges based on deck level to mast height, the angle on the bow by estimating the separation of the masts. He was constantly aware of both the target and her destroyer escort, only eight hundred yards away, between *Tang* and the tanker.

The target appeared enormous to him: "The destroyer was absolutely dwarfed by the length of the loaded oiler." The tanker turned toward *Tang*, too close for the torpedoes to arm. O'Kane pivoted the submarine to open the range and fire from the stern tubes instead. In one of his last observations he saw that "her rail was manned by white-uniformed sailors, an estimated 150 men on our side alone."

With a seventeen-hundred-yard torpedo run, O'Kane commenced firing. The fourth torpedo had just left the tube when the first struck home. He hadn't bothered to lower the scope, since the target did not have time to avoid the incoming fish. O'Kane watched, morbidly fascinated: "On the tanker, the lookouts saw the torpedo wakes and were pointing and waving right up to the explosions. I saw not one of them leave his post." O'Kane then relinquished the scope to Frazee, who watched the tanker go down in four minutes, "a mass of billowing flame and grayish-brown smoke."

Unbelievably, *Tang* had sunk only the puny, 1,790-ton *Choko Maru*, not the enormous Cimarron-type tanker he estimated at 18,276 deadweight tons. Even the gross weight, for which *Tang* received wartime credit, was estimated to be 12,000 tons, and O'Kane was disgusted "to have the estimated tonnage of that great tanker arbitrarily cut nearly in half by the staff." It was one of the worst overestimates O'Kane was to make during the war, and may well be explainable in light of his exhaustion. Four hours' sleep in four days does not make for dispassionate judgment.

After torpedoing this fifth (and possibly sixth) ship, O'Kane took *Tang* deep. At 475 feet the bathythermograph recorded a sharply delineated water temperature gradient, which would provide excellent protection from the escorting destroyer's sonar.

Except that *Tang* kept diving, clearly on a course for the bottom. Alarmed, O'Kane dropped down to the control room and found the diving officer struggling to level off with diving planes and pumps. O'Kane ordered the safety tank blown, but the cautious chief operating the manifold did not act decisively. O'Kane seized control of the dive, hooked up the high-pressure air in series, and ordered, "Blow safety! Blow bow buoyancy!"

Air roared into the tanks, but by now the depth gauge was pinned at its maximum reading: 612 feet. The true depth was unknown; it was impossible to know if they were still sinking.

Possible corrective actions raced through O'Kane's mind. The most obvious—blowing the main ballast tanks—would produce enormous, telltale bubbles on the surface. There were no other signs of unbearable pressure, no lines breaking, no gauges popping. He gambled that *Tang* was stable, albeit very deep. Further action was held up, listening for complaints within the boat. O'Kane waited for "the longest nine minutes of my life," then the depth gauge needle fluttered, then rose off the pin. *Tang* was temporarily safe, but what was wrong?

It was the number five torpedo tube, initially damaged in the enormous explosion of *Yamashimo Maru* two nights earlier. A crown of water, much like the stop-action photography of a rock dropped in fluid, sprayed around the entire inner door of the tube. The torpedo room was flooded knee deep, the pumps running at full speed. O'Kane went to the torpedo room while Frazee supervised the diving officer. It was clear to O'Kane that *Tang* would have to rise sharply, sacrificing water temperature sonar protection in exchange for less water pressure. The pumps could never keep up with the flooding at this depth.

Tang was carefully brought to eighty feet with almost no up angle. The lake in the forward torpedo room, the empty safety tank, and the continually venting bow buoyancy tank caused the boat to be unstable. The risk of an unwanted broach was very real. The destroyer could clearly hear *Tang*'s pumps, which were temporarily stopped each time the escort made a run at them.

For fourteen hours they sweated out the destroyer's incessant searching. Few depth charges were dropped; O'Kane guessed that the escort was getting low on charges and intended to use them sparingly, only on a near-certain contact. And the destroyer must have had its own problems. There was no active pinging, which would quickly have located the submarine running at such a shallow depth. Perhaps its sonar had been damaged by the nearby explosions of the prior attacks.

Tang pumped, evaded, struggled to repair the leak, and waited. At the five-hour mark the torpedomen had forced the extruding rubber gasket well back into its groove. Pumping could be stopped for an hour at a time without danger of flooding the sonar equipment in the torpedo room. The destroyer made fewer passes.

At 2000 it was pitch black outside, and O'Kane had to call evasion courses based on sound alone. But the destroyer had a tactical dilemma. The hunted might now be on the surface, prepared to be the hunter. At 2040 a final run was made, which O'Kane avoided by reversing course and passing down the side of the destroyer. Eight close, powerful explosions rent the surrounding sea. While horribly frightening, none was lethal. And then the destroyer moved quietly away, its speed reduced so as not to become a sonar target for the submarine.

The interior of *Tang* was reeking and foul. In these tropical waters the requirement to shut down air conditioning and fans had caused the internal temperature to soar. Heat from the batteries had no place to go but the inside of the boat, compounding the problem. Oxygen depletion was severe, and CO_2 absorbent only reduced the possibility of poisoning. In addition to the ever-present miasma of diesel odor, the sweating men's anxieties contributed to the smell. "The odor that really assaulted the sensitive nose . . . was the 'Three Fs'—feets, farts and fannies—of eighty-one souls aboard living in close quarters with limited bathing and laundry facilities. Some thought the USS *Tang* was named after the odor . . ." wrote Paul Schratz, XO of *Sterlet*.

Air compressors were run to bring down the alarming internal pressure in the boat. No hatches could be opened until this was complete. Finally a last sonar check and *Tang* surfaced "flat" so the lake in the forward torpedo room would cause no further damage. The entire crew was overjoyed, but for O'Kane "best of all was the aroma of God's fresh air." Frazee had thoughtfully ordered the cooks to begin thawing steaks hours before, and the entire ship's company celebrated as *Tang* moved northward.

After an hour's run, the submarine was halted to enable divers to go over the side to repair the source of the trouble, the damaged outer gasket of the torpedo tube. Within an hour it had been replaced, in the dark, under water, by touch. The outer door was closed and the tube drained. With the source of the problem corrected, repair work was begun on the inner door seal.

Tang pounded north on three engines toward the Volcano Islands, a new area assigned by Pearl Harbor in the belief that *Tang* was having no luck finding ships. Frazee plotted a "cheat course" that kept them about fifty miles off the Marianas, and finally tumbled into the sack for some long-overdue sleep.

On the afternoon of the twenty-fifth, running on the surface abreast of Pagan Island, smoke was sighted by the lookouts. The SJ radar was down, its parts strewn in disarray around the conning tower floor. Frazee's plots convinced O'Kane that a daylight attack was impossible. O'Kane decided they would stay on the surface, abeam of their targets, keeping visual contact by the extended-search periscope. *Tang* would close the convoy by night and make a dawn submerged attack.

Frazee exploded: "Oh, Christ, Captain, then it's so damned long till dark!" Clearly representing the emotions of the entire crew, the XO did not want to endure another long postattack day submerged, miserable in the heat, smell, and lack of oxygen.

O'Kane resisted Frazee's desire to attack more quickly, pointing out that they would not be leaking. But Frazee had caught the mood of the boat. Then the SJ radar came back on line. O'Kane yielded. They would attack on the surface as soon as the moon set. The attack was a failure. O'Kane could see during the firing that the torpedoes were going to miss astern, and tried to compensate for the too-slow target speed setting of the TDC with each succeeding shot. All missed. After reporting the convoy's location by radio, *Tang,* empty of all torpedoes, turned toward Midway.

A postattack critique of this miss astonished O'Kane. By "seaman's eye" he had the target moving at 13 knots. The TDC speed setting was 8½ knots. It was the first attack he had ever made without personal knowledge of the speed setting. It would be the last.

14

Reluctant Lifeguard

EXTRA: SUB RESCUES FLIERS

—Honolulu Advertiser, *May 18, 1944*

Tang arrived at Midway on March 3. Her maiden performance was considered fantastically good. Clearly O'Kane had not just been lucky enough to bask in the glow of Morton. Here was, indeed, a new killer. Babe Brown, writing for Admiral Lockwood, wrote a glowing endorsement: "Six outstanding attacks were made . . . all of which were extremely well planned, determined, and aggressive."

Once ashore, O'Kane learned that his nemesis Duncan MacMillan had taken *Thresher* on patrol in December. "Old Man" MacMillan, at forty the oldest man to command a fleet boat, sank four ships in January, in relentless end-around attacks in foul weather, enduring savage counterattacks. It seemed that there was absolutely nothing lacking in MacMillan's courage. O'Kane's competitive juices began flowing.

The refit crew was driven hard, and the regular crew was not given full relief. O'Kane had his men re-cement the outer door gasket on the number five tube and check all others, not trusting that task to anyone whose life was not on the line. The officers stayed at the Gooneyville, never more than five minutes away from the refit crew.

Because of Midway's great distance from the Bureau of Ships in Washington, O'Kane was able to finesse the installation of a "crow's nest" high in the periscope shears. The lookout manning that position wore leather gloves, and slid to the bridge deck near the conning tower hatch down a cable when the order was given to dive. O'Kane was nearly through with reliance on the SD aircraft detection radar. Its short range, lack of directional capability, and dangerously detectable radio emissions were simply not worth it, he felt. Instead, more and more, he would rely on multiple lookouts, four each covering one-quarter of the horizon, two with specially coated binoculars for sun searches, and one perched high in the crow's nest.

After only eight days at Midway, the refit was completed on March 11. O'Kane informed the division commander that *Tang* would be ready to leave on patrol on the sixteenth. With a few new crew members aboard, she put to sea for refresher training, returning on the fourteenth for final torpedo and fuel loading. *Tang* was to be on station by March 28 to support a carrier air strike. The potential for lifeguard duty existed—a task O'Kane and Frazee detested—and 110,000 gallons of fuel were jammed in every conceivable tank to extend their range.

For the next forty-eight days *Tang* roamed the central Pacific, seemingly without purpose. They cruised through the Marianas, to the Palau Islands, then almost to Mindanao on Davao Gulf. With only one engine on line, often with just the 670 horsepower auxiliary, *Tang* plodded along at 4½ knots. Lockwood's staff at Pearl Harbor moved their chess piece over endless vistas of water. There were a few "maybe, maybe" calls, but nothing materialized. O'Kane seethed.

On April 10, near Palau again, the SJ search radar gave up the ghost. Two more lookouts were posted to the twenty-millimeter gun platform. On an emergency dive they would escape into the gun access trunk but could not enter *Tang* herself. O'Kane reflected that ". . . they didn't like it, but that's the way things are sometimes."

O'Kane felt like a ". . . privateer caught in the doldrums. . . ." He began to make important judgments about his officers. Frazee was simply tops, and it seemed clear that Frank Springer was a comer. He required Frank to prepare a detailed qualification notebook, complete with drawings, when off watch. "I knew that some considered me a stickler in adhering to this peacetime requirement, but Frank's qualification for command would follow quickly." O'Kane was less enthusiastic about Bruce "Scotty" Anderson: "I wished he had more interest in the machinery that surrounded us. He would have to master it all before qualification."

One monotony breaker was a series of rendezvous with *Trigger*, captained by O'Kane's friend Fritz Harlfinger. *Trigger*'s executive officer was the skilled veteran Ned Beach. Harlfinger and Beach used the *Wahoo* technique: Beach was Harlfinger's coapproach officer. This important delegation of responsibility to the XO had been adapted when Dusty Dornin, an admirer of Morton and O'Kane, was captain of *Trigger*. It was extended seamlessly with Harlfinger.

On the night of April 8, in the western Marianas, *Trigger* had attacked one of the largest Japanese convoys ever seen. She was counterattacked by a particularly skilled killing group of six Japanese destroyers. For seventeen hours they pounded *Trigger,* causing extensive damage. With an internal temperature of 135 degrees, the crew continually bailed water from the motor room to the after torpedo room bilges, all the while enduring relentless serial attacks that drove the submarine ever deeper. Harlfinger and Beach decided to battle surface just after evening twilight on April 9 and try to fight their way out. Fortunately, the destroyers temporarily lost their concentration and gave *Trigger* an opening to escape submerged.

Now this battered submarine needed spare parts, and O'Kane was happy to oblige. They also exchanged movies and gossip. *Trigger* continued her patrol, making seven more attacks and sinking three ships.

While *Tang* was seemingly being micromanaged by the Pearl Harbor staff, the great carrier Task Force 58, commanded by Admiral Marc Mitscher, was striking repeatedly at the Marianas. In March the Joint Chiefs of Staff had given the green light to two independent plans: General MacArthur would leapfrog four hundred miles west along the northern coast of New Guinea to Hollandia in April, with TF 58 providing support; Admiral Nimitz would bypass Truk and capture the Marianas in June.

The various units of TF 58 rendezvoused west of the Admiralties and headed north toward the Palaus—*Tang*'s station—to deceive Japanese reconnaissance planes. On April 21, under the cover of darkness, they turned southwest and achieved an unprecedented surprise at Hollandia. Most of the 11,000 dazed Japanese, with no time to organize a defense, faded into the jungle to die of starvation and disease. But 650 Japanese soldiers simply surrendered—an unheard-of event at this stage in the Pacific war, and a sign of deteriorating morale.

With his magazines still filled with unused bombs, Mitscher decided to launch a last strike at Truk on April 30. On April 22 *Tang* was ordered to move from Palau to Truk, a distance of twelve hundred miles, to support this carrier air attack.

To conserve dwindling fuel, *Tang* moved at single-engine speed, with O'Kane heartily cursing the ComSubPac staff at Pearl for their failure to grasp the distance he had traveled in the past seven weeks. The track laid down by Frazee passed Fais Island, where Morton had wanted to shell the phosphate works after running out of torpedoes on *Wahoo*'s third patrol. Since Frank Springer was the gunnery officer, and the gun crew had not fired their weapon since the shakedown cruise, O'Kane decided to use this spot for a gun exercise.

A periscope investigation of Fais Island revealed new gun emplacements. O'Kane took a careful bearing line between the island's lookout tower and the phosphorite refinery. He then circled the island submerged and aligned *Tang* on the reciprocal of the bearing. They would fire from behind the gun emplacements, and could receive no counterfire. The SJ radar, functional once more, was raised, and an exact range of 7,300 yards was recorded.

Using the technique employed by Morton, *Tang*'s safety tanks were blown dry, but the planesmen held the submarine down. Then the main ballast tanks were blown, and *Tang* popped to the surface like a cork. Just thirty-three rounds were pumped into the plant, and the actual results were unknown, but O'Kane had trained a smoothly functioning gun crew.

On the twenty-seventh *Tang* closed Truk, encountering search aircraft that repeatedly drove her under. Even though he had a lifeguard mission, O'Kane took a stab at intercepting some seaborne traffic, to no avail. On the morning of the twenty-ninth *Tang* dove and went to her station east of Truk, surfacing at 1700 just ahead of a flight of B-24 Liberators making a bombing raid. The Japanese quickly discovered her and kept making airborne passes using flares. As soon as the battery charge was complete, and notification given that no Liberators had been hit, *Tang* dived and moved to her assigned spot for the carrier raids of April 30. O'Kane got four hours of shut-eye; Frazee stayed up all night to navigate her into position, southwest of the reef.

As the strike progressed, *Tang* kept edging in closer to the reef. When the first call for assistance came in, they were only ten minutes from the downed fliers, since they ran in at flank speed. Three survivors were picked up from a life raft in a smooth man-overboard operation. Fortified with brandy, they were escorted to a makeshift aviation information center, an AIC, in the officers' wardroom. The airmen were experienced at radio communications, knew all the pilots by name, and many just by the sound of their voices. They would staff this position.

As darkness descended, two more calls for help were picked up by the AIC. One was for a raft inside the reef. *Tang* could not cross, and the men would have to paddle out of the lagoon. The second was some distance away, since *Tang* had to skirt Kuop Atoll. Deck gun blazing with suppressing fire, she skirted Ollan Island and ran for the atoll. In spite of an all-night search and liberal use of the Very pistol flare launcher, the raft could not be located.

At dawn a Japanese RO class submarine was spotted within striking distance. *Tang* dove and, just as O'Kane was about to fire, the target did the same. *Tang* was now vulnerable to a counterattack if she had been spotted. O'Kane took her to 150 feet and turned away to avoid a possible incoming

APRIL 30, 1944. *Tang* rescues downed airmen at Truk. (National Archives)

torpedo. After a short high-speed submerged run, *Tang* surfaced, the diesels were kicked on, and she rolled back toward Truk to try to retrieve more fliers. The officer saved on the thirtieth recommended to O'Kane that he break out his largest colors and display them on both deck surfaces. This was done to avoid a case of mistaken identity from aircraft hunting for the missing Japanese sub.

A little after 0830 the AIC alerted O'Kane to a Kingfisher aircraft that had been damaged in a landing inside the reef. A second Kingfisher, piloted by Lieutenant (J.G.) J. A. Burns, had arrived and towed out the first Kingfisher pilot as well as the raft containing the two men missed the previous evening. The transfer from the Kingfisher to *Tang* was uneventful, and *Tang*'s twenty-millimeter gun crew cheerfully sank the now useless plane. Burns took off, looking for more shallow-water rafts.

Immediately, a smoking torpedo bomber was seen headed for the water. *Tang* roared past Ollan Island again, its suppressing fire holding the Japanese down as the damaged plane ditched just beyond the reef. Three more aviators were picked up, including a full commander—a rank distinction O'Kane instantly noted. He offered the commander the use of his cabin, and was not overjoyed when the hospitality was readily accepted.

Almost without pause, *Tang* was off again for the eastern side of the reef. The improvised AIC had been monitoring aircraft transmissions and knew that there were three new rafts in the water. Because of concern that the morning's RO submarine might be waiting for them, the AIC called their airborne mates and secured close coverage from planes returning from their bomb strikes.

As *Tang* was escorted to the pickup area, O'Kane blew all tanks: safety, negative, the depleted fuel tanks—and kept a low-pressure turboblower streaming air into the main ballast tanks. *Tang* rode high, and the stream of air bubbles venting around the hull from the ballast tanks increased her speed by at least 1½ knots.

The ubiquitous Burns had already landed his Kingfisher near these rafts, and the AIC requested that he tow them to deeper water, where *Tang* could reach them. As the Kingfisher came into view, some men were seen clinging to the floats, the rest being towed to sea on their rafts by Burns.

But planes overhead signaled O'Kane to a more immediate task, the rescue of a single pilot from the previous day's strike who had seen *Tang* signaling with Very stars but who was afraid to respond. This raft was very close inshore, and the escorting aircraft placed murderous machine-gun fire into the Japanese gun emplacements until *Tang* could retrieve the survivor.

The AIC then heard that there was a single swimmer in the water, five miles from *Tang*. O'Kane immediately turned toward this man. An escorting aircraft dropped the swimmer a raft, but he was too weak to pull himself completely in. Very carefully, O'Kane nosed *Tang* up on the beach, sound heads pulled in so as not to strike coral, and pulled the human dishrag aboard.

At last O'Kane could back away, swivel, and head for Burns's Kingfisher. As *Tang* pulled alongside the now damaged aircraft, the nine pilots and crewman "came over like a pack of hounds let out of a kennel."

It was now nearing evening, with one more raft still in the water. Frazee plotted its position and told O'Kane that they could not make it before dark. One of the rescued fliers, a lieutenant, suggested that the new night fighters could locate the raft in the dark. O'Kane's commander guest interjected that "only the task force commander could authorize that." He was stunned when the junior officers working at the AIC post raised Marc Mitscher himself on the radio.

"We'll need two night fighters to locate the last raft, Admiral."

"You'll have three" was Mitscher's crisp reply, which seemed to annoy the commander.

Incredibly, in the pitch dark, the night fighters located the raft, whose occupants had already rigged a sail in a gallant attempt to sail to the Solomons, twelve hundred miles away. With red Very stars to guide them, *Tang* picked up the last two aviators they were to find.

Far to the south, at Satawan, was Slade Cutter. The XO of *Pompano* on Paine's first war patrol, Cutter had been transferred before her loss and was now captain of the new *Seahorse.* Radio reception conditions were ideal, and Cutter could hear all of *Tang*'s AIC chatter with the striking, and ditching, aircrews. He piped the sound throughout *Seahorse,* and the crew listened with rapt attention. "More exciting than any football game ever thought of being," he told O'Kane later.

As the search wound down, O'Kane went below to his cabin to find his bunk occupied by the commander. With all the extra men aboard it was clear that some hot bunking would be required, but O'Kane had no intention of sharing his bed. He was outranked, but intended to fall back on a navy regulation that states that the captain of a ship shall not vacate his cabin for an embarked senior. O'Kane had no intention of being "pushed around, [my] status, prestige, and authority suffer[ing] in the eyes of [the] crew." Fortunately Ballinger, the chief of the boat, solved the problem by sharing his own bunk, the best in the CPO quarters, with the commander.

That night the AIC picked up a message from Mitscher that tallied the results of the strike, and noted that eight airmen had been rescued by surface craft, with "some others" thought to be in *Tang.* Clearly Task Force 58 did not know how productive the lifeguard mission had been. But O'Kane decided not to radio any clarification. He would hunt around Gray Feather Bank the next morning for possible escaping Japanese ships, and wanted no telltale radio transmission to give away *Tang*'s position.

Any aircrew members who may have been tantalized by periscope watches and midnight food quickly had their bellyful of submarines following a daylight submerged patrol. Stench was one problem, aggravated by an improperly blown sewage tank. Lack of fresh air was another. Toying with them, at 1830—a half hour before surfacing—O'Kane announced that the smoking lamp was lit. Not even a match would ignite in the low-oxygen atmosphere. For three more days O'Kane stayed on station, hunting for shipping, and lifeguarding a Liberator attack on May 5.

Finally, at 0300 on May 6, *Tang* was relieved from lifeguard duty by *Permit,* and Frazee plotted the course for Pearl Harbor. There was frequent air activity, both hostile and friendly, forcing many evasion dives for the next three days. O'Kane and Frazee tried to drum up a neat Morton-style flash about the number of airmen aboard. They finally settled for the simplest message, which had major impact at both Pearl and aboard TF58:

FOLLOWING AIRMEN ABOARD ALL HEALTHY

and listed twenty-two names alphabetically. Admirals Nimitz, Mitscher, and Lockwood were pop-eyed with surprise and pleasure.

The air group commander now came forward with his own message, requesting a rendezvous with TF58 to transfer the recovered air crew to their respective carriers. O'Kane diplomatically gave both messages to the AIC for coding and transmission, with much body English and head nodding. Muttering "Why, that son of a bitch!," the airmen transmitted the messages, but pulled out the antenna trunk lead for the commander's request. He never understood why there wasn't even an acknowledgment of his message.

O'Kane was overjoyed at being able to save these specific men, but resented the fact that his late-model submarine had been diverted to this Good Samaritan task. What O'Kane may have suspected, but did not truly know, was that the Japanese had been steadily losing their irreplaceable aircrews since the Battle of the Coral Sea in May 1942. Their skill loss was now intense. There was nothing terribly wrong with the continuously improved Japanese carrier aircraft—except that there were no experienced pilots to fly them.

By the end of 1943 lifeguard duty had become common in the U.S. Navy; nearly 120 air corps and navy aircrew members, including president-to-be George Bush, would be saved by submarines in just 1944 alone.

Six weeks after *Tang's* record-breaking feat, U.S. Navy airmen would obliterate more than four hundred Japanese carrier planes, manned by inexperienced pilots, in the Battle of the Philippine Sea—the "Great Marianas Turkey Shoot." Because of the late-afternoon launch of the American planes, more than a hundred aircraft were lost in low-fuel, late-night landing attempts. Mitscher employed his floatplanes and destroyers aggressively; nearly 90 percent of the fliers would be saved to fight another day. This willingness to divert critical resources, including submarines, to saving skilled aircrew lives, instead of concentrating solely on a war of attrition, was to prove of great strategic as well as humanitarian value.

Aboard *Tang* the aircrews and submarine crews became uncommonly friendly during the return to Pearl. There were practical consequences to all this camaraderie. For their part, O'Kane and Frazee were shocked to learn that, weeks before, navy air had mined areas where *Tang* had been instructed to patrol—an unusually dangerous breakdown in air-undersea staff communication. O'Kane resolved to bring this little matter to Admiral Lockwood's attention.

For his part Lieutenant Burns, in civilian life a theological student, identified strongly with the six new members of *Tang's* crew who would not receive combat insignia for this patrol since no ships were sunk. He resolved to do something about what he perceived to be a grievous injustice.

Tang eased into Pearl Harbor on May 15 with fewer than two thousand gallons of fuel left. The reception committee was packed with gold braid. Admiral Nimitz was first aboard to greet the aircrews. Lockwood was next and was stopped by the brash young Burns. "Admiral Lockwood, there are some members of *Tang's* crew who joined her at Midway. Is this patrol going to be designated as successful for combat insignia?"

Startled, Lockwood answered, "Why, uh—why, yes, indeed." Burns stepped back, triumphant. Lockwood made good on this extracted pledge. O'Kane returned the favor—though it was certainly earned. He recommended Burns for the Navy Cross for his actions in saving downed aircrew members, including crossing the reef while under enemy fire. Burns got his award. He also requested fighter training, where he was later killed.

Lockwood was enormously impressed with O'Kane's feat and wrote a glowing endorsement for wide distribution, saying, "The remarkable recovery of twenty-two naval aviators . . . is a sterling example. This patrol report should be carefully studied by all COs as a guide for future lifeguard duty."

Lockwood also gave O'Kane and Frazee some bad news. *Grayback*, Frazee's prior submarine, and Johnny Moore were gone. *Grayback* was having a fine tenth patrol, her third under Moore. She had downed two normal-size cargo ships on February 19, while *Tang* was on her first war patrol. On the twenty-fourth *Grayback* sank a third 10,000 tonner, and severely damaged a fourth, the 17,000 ton *Asama Maru*. Moore had radioed Pearl Harbor on February 25, saying he was down to two torpedoes. *Grayback* had been on patrol for only three weeks, but Lockwood ordered Moore to return to Midway. Then—silence.

Grayback must not have received Lockwood's instructions, for she penetrated the Nansei Shoto chain on February 27 to sink the 4,900 ton freighter *Ceylon Maru*. But *Grayback* was caught on the surface after this attack by a land-based Nakajima "Kate," which delivered one 250-kilogram bomb directly on target. Japanese surface ships then piled on, using the air-bubble trail as a marker. In time there was nothing but a lake of oil to mark where the *Wahoo*-trained, extraordinarily aggressive Moore had gone down. The Japanese were able to "lay a glove" on him after all.

In his personal report to Admiral Lockwood, O'Kane was quite critical about *Tang* being sent to patrol waters already mined by navy air. Lockwood was shocked and mused that perhaps this is what had happened to

MAY 1944. Dick O'Kane and twenty-two rescued airmen aboard *Tang*. (National Archives)

Tullibee. Now overdue, she was also patrolling off Palau, having preceded *Tang* into the area by a few weeks. *Tullibee* was truly lost—this was unpleasant news to O'Kane—but only after the war would it be learned that she had been sunk by a circular run of her own torpedo.

For the next few days O'Kane actually relaxed a bit. He had arranged to have Scotty Anderson assigned as navigator of the *Holland,* an old submarine tender that rarely got under way. Frazee felt it was "an ideal job for a guy who needed lots of sleep." Meanwhile, Anderson would stay aboard, watch the refit crew, and have several small alterations taken care of. O'Kane, a powerful swimmer, headed for the waters off the beach at the Royal Hawaiian.

Frazee was left to concentrate on personnel issues, including dealing with Howard Walker, the steward. Somehow Walker had used his card and dice winnings to bribe a five-gallon tin of pure alcohol off the submarine base and into the Royal Hawaiian. O'Kane found his antics amusing. Frazee, who had to work with the real problem of getting this potentially lethal mix diluted so it didn't kill the drinkers, was far from pleased.

On the morning of O'Kane's fourth day off duty, Walker swam out to the second reef to tell O'Kane that his prized "crow's nest" was about to be dismantled to make way for more radio antennas. Without hesitation, O'Kane rushed back to Pearl Harbor. With some care and diplomacy, he got Lockwood to intervene for him. The antennas were installed, but in a way that preserved *Tang*'s unique lookout perch.

That was it for a break. O'Kane began to trim the R&R period so that one officer going to sea on the next patrol would always be aboard and responsible for all repairs to *Tang*. Anderson was eased out, and Bill Walsh was sent to shore duty. O'Kane was itching to get to sea and back into the shooting war.

15

Prize Patrol

... rashness brings success ...

—Phaedrus, Fables

By the close of 1943 even the hardest-headed Japanese Combined Fleet zealot knew that something had to be done to suppress the increasing rate of sinkings by U.S. submarines. Admiral Koshiro Oikawa was now named commander-in-chief of the Grand Escort Command. Admiral Nimitz's Joint Intelligence Center at Pearl Harbor immediately began to track the actions of their opponent.

Oikawa knew he could never muster enough high-speed escorts for the merchant convoys, but he did rush slow, small frigates called *kaibokans* into service. The chief asset of these eight-hundred-ton boats was their huge depth-charge-carrying capacity. If they could just get into action on a sub-merged submarine they could harry it to death or force it to surface. Oikawa tried to organize hunter-killer groups around four escort carriers, but as soon as the aircrews obtained any proficiency they were dragooned into service on the fleet carriers.

Desperate, he proposed to lay a gigantic mine barrier from Japan to Bor-neo behind which Japanese shipping could move with relative impunity. Maddeningly, the Japanese Navy General Staff would not release their ample stock of mines, reserving them for what they believed would be the eventual entry of the Soviet Union into the war. Oikawa was persistent, however, and used a smaller allocation of mines to flank the East China Sea. Lockwood, suspicious of the reason for the recent loss of *Scorpion,* deliber-ately kept all further submarines out of this area.

In February 1944 U.S. Marines captured Majuro, Roi, and Namur, forcing an end to the fighting on Kwajalein. The sudden success of these new conquests brought the U.S. Joint Intelligence Center a mass of captured documents. Among these were many secret "Notices to Mariners"—easily identified by the prominent red border—which established limits of restricted navigation for the minefields.

By June the Joint Intelligence Center had collected sufficient information on Oikawa's mine barriers to map a safe route for submarines to flank the Nansei Shoto and find safe operating areas in the East China and Yellow Seas. Lockwood decided to exploit this intelligence by sending three loosely coordinated, but independently operating, pack boats into these areas: *Sealion, Tang,* and *Tinosa.*

Lockwood had been experimenting with wolf packs since the previous autumn, with mixed success. The late Johnny Moore and *Grayback* had participated in the first wolf pack. Only three ships had been sunk by the pack, all by Moore. In later patrols he was even more successful alone.

German wolf packs were controlled from Doenitz's headquarters in France, and the heavy radio traffic—especially the beacon signals sent by the first U-boat to discover a convoy—inevitably drew countermeasures. The teeming U-boats often were involved in night collisions, many fatal, since they could not communicate with each other.

Lockwood wanted none of that, certainly no central control from Pearl Harbor. Instead, the ability of the submarines to employ short-range voice radio so the captains could talk to each other would be enhanced. Strict rules were to be followed on attack sequences to avoid disastrous accidents. U.S. wolf packs were joint search, not joint attack, units.

The seventh wolf pack, "Blair's Blasters," was now operating in the Marianas. One of the participants was *Shark II,* with its new fourth officer, John "Duke" Griggs, aboard. On May 31 *Shark'*s captain, Ed Blakely, a classmate of Dick O'Kane and a good friend of George Grider, generously yielded a shot to one of his packmates, who also was from the same Academy class. He missed.

Between June 2 and 5 *Shark,* courteous no longer, attacked and sank four ships of nearly 22,000 tons and severely damaged a fifth, 5,000-tonner. These ships were filled with Japanese troops and equipment bound for Saipan and Guam. Their destruction certainly made life somewhat easier for the soon-to-attack U.S. Marines. Blakely received the Navy Cross for his part in these pack attacks.

Griggs was uneasy with Blakely, as he confessed his troubled feelings in a postwar letter. During this patrol, after their success was obvious, Blakely assembled the officers in the tiny "stateroom and with curtains drawn had a drink of whiskey. None for the crew . . . I have always had a sense of guilt about that. Better that no one celebrate if all cannot." Griggs also found him to be a cold fish. "Ed Blakely in his dealings with officers and crew followed . . . the old way. . . . The C.O. was aloof to all, confiding primarily in his Exec, when in port joining other C.O.s."

Ignoring any further relaxation, O'Kane now spent most of his time aboard *Tang* managing the refit and seeing a lot of Lockwood. He quickly learned of his coming assignment and was eager to get another shot at Tung Hai, whose geography was fixed in his mind from navigating *Wahoo* in and out on her fourth patrol. The shallow waters did not trouble him, nor did minefields.

His disdain for minefields was based on prewar experience. In *Argonaut* an attempt had been made to maintain a dummy field off San Francisco. Every storm that swept through the area broke mine cables; the dummies washed ashore from Point Reyes to Half Moon Bay. He was sure the Japanese would have encountered similar problems. Why, therefore, would they lay mines in areas in which live drifters would soon present a hazard to their own navigation? O'Kane didn't think there were any minefields there at all. He thought it was just a ruse, fake information deliberately arranged to fall in American hands, simply to deter U.S. submarines.

O'Kane underestimated his opponent's technology. Japanese mines were very, very good. They were often anchored very deep—a capability unknown to American mine intelligence officers—which protected them from storms, and avoided unwanted surface-ship sinkings but which were lethal to submerged submarines.

What O'Kane feared most was that *Sealion* and *Tinosa* would beat him to the hunting ground and drive all the shipping into hiding. There was no stopping *Tinosa;* she would be on her way, with Don Weiss in command, a day before *Sealion*. Weiss was five years older than O'Kane, and thus senior to him in spite of the fact that this would be only his second war patrol. He had downed four ships on his first outing, and O'Kane was a little anxious about being drawn into Weiss's orbit in a pack situation.

Tang could go out in synchronization with *Sealion*—if the rest period at the Royal Hawaiian, and the ship's refit, were cut to a total of fifteen days. Training would be immediately initiated to break in new crew members. As a reward, each night in port during the training interval most of the crew could return to the hotel instead of sleeping aboard. Frazee and Ballinger were given the chore of bringing the crew around to the fact that they were going to love giving up a week's R&R. This was not entirely successful. O'Kane began to observe a few "reluctant dragons" among the crew.

Preparations roared forward. *Tang* received the new "measure 10" camouflage paint job, which was extremely effective; new communications gear for sub-to-sub talk was sited; and a passive aircraft detection device, the APR-1, was installed. A mix of war shots was loaded: sixteen of the traditional steam torpedoes went to the forward torpedo room, eight of the new Mark 18 electrics, first used by *Wahoo*, went aft.

Time was made for officer recognition. O'Kane received a Navy Cross for *Tang's* first, highly successful war patrol. By the complex rules of navy

MAY 1944. Dick O'Kane after receiving the Navy Cross from Admiral Nimitz. (National Achives)

award policy, O'Kane's award permitted Frazee to receive his well-earned second Silver Star.

At 1330 on June 8—an hour ahead of *Sealion* and Eli Reich—O'Kane backed *Tang* away from her berth at Pearl. He took the con instead of Frazee or another junior officer—the usual departure routine—because if "any possible minor damage [or] . . . any mistakes were made they would be mine." He would be damned if *Sealion* got started before *Tang* did.

Aboard was a new PCO, Mort Lytle. Lytle had been the XO on *Porpoise* the prior year, when it had taken such a vicious beating from Japanese anti-submarine forces that it had to be permanently withdrawn from combat. Lytle wanted a command, of course, but he was no longer enthusiastic about shallow-water combat.

On June 12 *Tang* arrived at Midway very early in the morning, followed a bit later by *Sealion*. As the fuel tanks were topped off, O'Kane sent Walker to *Sealion* to "help" their stewards with the officers' noon meal. Walker was actually spying for O'Kane—something that had been under way using other enlisted men, even at Pearl Harbor.

O'Kane was trying to guess what strategy would be employed by Eli Reich and Don Weiss. From scraps of overheard talk he concluded that his competition for career advancement would conduct traditional, offshore surface patrols, with liberal use of the energy-emitting SD radar to protect themselves from aircraft. O'Kane intended to shut down his SD, go inshore—very close inshore—and stay submerged, hoping the activity generated by *Sealion* and *Tinosa* would drive shipping to *Tang*.

As *Tang* made ready to sortie, a problem with a main motor ground that had manifested itself the previous day threatened to delay their departure. O'Kane suspected a "reluctant dragon" in the crew and announced that *Tang* would depart anyway; the patrol would be conducted using only three main motors. Miraculously, the problem was located immediately. At 1600 on the twelfth *Tang* backed away and headed for the East China Sea. They planned to rendezvous with *Sealion* at Kusakaki Shima in ten days.

The interference-generating SD radar was secured; O'Kane simply pushed more lookouts on duty, including some who could only partly enter the submarine through the gun trunk in case of an emergency dive. The SJ radar was only permitted to search seaward and never sweep across an island that might detect its interference. When close to land thought likely to possess Japanese radar, *Tang* moved at only eight knots, mimicking fishing trawler speed. O'Kane intended to arrive on station undetected.

Because of his familiarity with the area, or perhaps just a desire to retrace *Wahoo*'s route, O'Kane instructed Frazee to plot a course through Colonet

Strait. O'Kane may not have been troubled by potential minefields, but the thought certainly crossed Frazee's mind. The crew was rigid with apprehension, postponing the nightly movie to be near their battle stations during the night transit.

Neither O'Kane nor Frazee had any plan to sleep. O'Kane was troubled because they were late for their rendezvous with *Sealion*. As navigator, Frazee was doubly concerned to plot the right course, and avoid the shoal waters to starboard. The transit was made uneventfully a bit before midnight, and *Tang* slipped into the shallow, dangerous waters. At 0330 on June 23 they met *Sealion* off Kusakaki Shima and, given the late hour, simply communicated a few general patrolling areas and contact agreements to each other by blinker light.

Tang remained submerged through the day except for one short interval when O'Kane decided to break the surface, kick on a diesel, and take a suction through the conning tower hatch to freshen the internal atmosphere of the boat. This close to the equinox the days were very long; evening twilight and surface running would be hours away.

That night, shortly after *Tang* surfaced, Mel Enos decoded an Ultra message addressed to all three submarines. It reported a damaged Japanese battleship coming up from the direction of Okinawa headed for either Sasebo or Kobe sometime in the next thirty hours. Sasebo was fewer than 150 miles away. While Kobe was on distant Honshu, the Japanese might elect to run up the western coast of Kyushu, turn into Tsushima Strait to Shimonoseki Strait, and thus to the Inland Sea.

O'Kane resented the message as evidence of a too-tight rein on his patrol by Pearl Harbor, which might be enforced by Don Weiss. As he feared, within twenty minutes a message arrived from *Tinosa* requesting a three-boat rendezvous at Danjo Gunto, in open, deep water about seventy miles off the coast of Sasebo. Hank Flanagan took the con as they roared toward the rendezvous, while O'Kane, Frazee, and Lytle conferred over possible strategies.

O'Kane was furious, since he believed that Danjo Gunto was the wrong spot to make an intercept. He was sure the battleship—in fact, any Japanese ship—would be hugging the coast and would pass through Koshiki Strait. Since it had a maximum depth of 120 feet, the Japanese would tend to discount submarine attacks in a confined area that narrowed to fewer than six miles wide at its northern, Sasebo end.

O'Kane's instructions to Frazee—who would paddle over to *Tinosa* for the meeting—were clear: one sub in close to Bono Misaki to intercept any traffic headed into Koshiki Strait; one sub ten miles farther to sea to catch the Japanese if they decided not to enter the strait; and the last sub on the northern, Sasebo side of the strait. *Tang* would take any spot assigned by Weiss. This was a sop to appease the other COs. It was made clear to Frazee that his job was to stick to this plan.

Frazee did just that. Neither Weiss nor Eli Reich wanted to go into such shallow water. Weiss became irritated with Frazee's insistence that one sub patrol the Koshiki Island area. After an hour of haggling, Weiss, in anger, finally told Frazee to go patrol "your goddamned islands." *Sealion* and *Tinosa* would head west, to the open sea, and patrol thirty miles apart. As soon as Frazee heard this release, he paddled back to *Tang* in the rubber boat. "The Koshiki Islands," he called to O'Kane on the bridge as he scrambled aboard, and *Tang* was off like a shot, racing toward the coast at flank speed. Weiss and Reich thought O'Kane was nuts.

Free of all restraints, *Tang* plowed forward on the surface, white spray blowing from the cold sea, till well into daylight. At 0808, with a Japanese patrol coming into view, he dove but proceeded at a battery-depleting rate of six knots all day long. Frazee plotted their position and speed and told O'Kane that they could not now make the "ideal" spot. Without missing a beat, O'Kane asked Frazee for a course that would place *Tang* at the shallow, narrow, northern opening of the strait before 2200.

At evening twilight *Tang* was back on the surface, dodging sampans in the dark, running at seventeen knots with two engines on the battery charge. The other two mains, as well as the auxiliary, were on propulsion. O'Kane was itching to fight, and neither he nor Frazee had had any sleep for more than twenty-four hours. None could be expected this night, either.

Frazee watched the water depth recede as *Tang* crossed the two-hundred-fathom curve. At the hundred-fathom mark *Tang* went to three engines on propulsion. Crossing the fifty-fathom curve Frazee, as navigator, was duty-bound to mention the increasingly shallow water to the captain. "No matter, we can still dive in ten fathoms" was the reply, but he did slow the forward speed to six knots. O'Kane intended to get in so close that at periscope depth *Tang* would be rubbing the bottom.

At 2145 Bergman had a convoy on radar. *Tang* would see no wounded battleship. She had come across a bigger prize, and had the targets all to herself. O'Kane radioed a contact report to both *Sealion* and *Tinosa*, who were now far out of position. The convoy was still distant—about eleven miles away—and still forming up after a nearly single-file run through the narrow strait. Gradually a picture developed on radar: six core targets in two columns surrounded by two rings of escorts, twelve guardians.

At 2227 the convoy was fully organized, running northward at twelve knots in the direction of Nagasaki. *Tang* was now very close, well positioned on the port bow of the lead ship. Twice O'Kane tried to penetrate the escort screen by sliding across the stern of a ship in the outer ring, only to be blocked by the bow of an escort in the inner ring. The convoy was passing them by. On a third attempt, now on the convoy's port quarter, O'Kane found a hole in the screen. *Tang* took up a position following the targets, a Japanese escort on either flank, roughly 1,650 yards away.

O'Kane was exultant. This would be his revenge on Pinky Kennedy, who had scathingly, insultingly told him that ships could not be attacked from behind. He eased *Tang's* speed up to sixteen knots, at the edge of creating too much phosphorescence, just below the threshold of the eye-detecting motion that would alert Japanese lookouts to the presence of the wolf among the lambs.

At the differential pace of a fast walk, *Tang* gradually got her bow inside the escorts' sterns, then amidships. They were very nearly equidistant, at about 1,200 yards away. Adrenaline-charged, breathing shallowly, speaking rarely, and then only in whispers, the topside crew watched as *Tang* began to pull forward of the escorts into the convoy itself. O'Kane called Frazee to the bridge to see this electrifying sight with his own eyes.

The evolving plan was to attack from the starboard, or land side, with large gyro angles on the torpedoes, since *Tang* would be unable to bore in on a perpendicular track. O'Kane eased the speed up to seventeen knots, the wash of water down the submarine's sides reminding him that the phosphorescent wake that could reveal their position was increasing. Then, just past Oniki Saki, the convoy slowed to ten knots and turned to true north. With the good fortune that sometimes comes to the truly brave, O'Kane was in perfect position to attack from ten degrees forward of the target's beam.

Unseen, Walker had come to the bridge with coffee for his captain. Riveted by the sight, Walker watched as O'Kane swung *Tang* due west, aiming at the two nearest ships in the overlapping columns. He cut the forward speed to avoid turbulence on the torpedoes; the fire control party plotted zero angle on the bow. Closing at one-third speed, O'Kane would fire all six bow shots at the two nearest ships, leading them like a duck hunter. Frazee's voice floated up from the conning tower with reassurance from the TDC's fire control solution.

Looking through his binoculars mounted on the TBT, O'Kane could see the wire touching the first target's mast. His heart was pounding so loudly its pulse filled his ears, muffling the sound of the diesels.

"Constant bearing—mark!" he shouted.

"Set!" from Frazee.

"Fire!" from O'Kane, who repeated this shot-by-shot interchange with the XO as three torpedoes were individually aimed to hit the bow, center, and stern of each target—six mark!, set!, fire! sequences in all.

As the torpedoes sped toward the targets, O'Kane swung *Tang* north to parallel the convoy. After the hits, and in the confusion of the inevitable counterattack, he would find a way out on the surface. All four engines were ready.

Thirty seconds before the first torpedo was timed to hit, Frazee joined O'Kane—and the quiet Walker—on the bridge. At the calculated instant, the first target was illuminated with "a whack, a flash, and a tremendous rumble. . . ." Walker dropped the captain's coffee cup, which fell into the superstructure. The second torpedo hit "amidships, and her whole side seemed ripped out." Two more timed torpedoes were seen, heard, and felt blasting the second target. The others apparently missed, but O'Kane noted that there were "more tremendous explosions and accompanying flashes . . . not timed as our torpedoes."

At flank speed *Tang* raced for deeper water, her new camouflage paint clearly contributing to the fact that the nearest escort could not see her, even though she passed only fourteen hundred yards away.

When five thousand yards from the attack site, and now clearly unde-tectable, O'Kane gave the con to Lytle and ran for the head in the forward torpedo room. Walker was waiting near the wardroom with a fresh cup of coffee when O'Kane headed back toward the bridge. "How many'd we get, Captain?"

"Why, both of them, Walker. We saw them go," O'Kane replied.

"I think there was more, sir," Walker said, confessing to O'Kane that he had been present on the bridge in the final moments of the attack.

Walker was right. While O'Kane claimed credit for only two sinkings that night, he had just executed the most successful single salvo of the Pacific war. Two of the six torpedoes missed their targets in the near column and plowed into ships in the second. These two damaged ships, one of which was small, collided; four merchant ships in the convoy went to the bottom. O'Kane, and *Tang,* had just sunk 16,291 tons of shipping with six torpedoes.

O'Kane didn't want to quit. Bergman could still see a "decent-sized pip" on radar. Even though the shipyard lights of Nagasaki were now visible, *Tang* bore in to resume the attack. But the rate of closure was too high. The "target" had to be making at least twenty knots. O'Kane executed a ninety-degree turn to avoid running into a destroyer escort out hunting, now only sixteen hundred yards away.

Tang leaped forward at emergency speed, black smoke pouring from the overloaded engines. "Can we dive, Fraz?" O'Kane asked the XO. The answer was negative; *Tang* was too close to the beach. They would have to run for deeper water on the surface. At twenty-two knots the submarine evaded the destroyer escort (DE), which clearly could not see her, but only the smoky trail of their flight. As the Japanese hunter lurched from smoke patch to smoke patch, *Tang* gradually opened the range. At thirty-four hundred yards the DE was using its searchlight but, because of the new paint scheme, still could not see *Tang*. Soundheads raised, O'Kane ordered a dive when the water depth reached seventy-five feet. The Japanese patrol boat raced by, the pings of its echo ranging gear audible, but ineffective at her speed.

Discretion finally became a part of O'Kane's conscious thought. *Tang* listened with the passive sonar, then eased up to permit the SJ radar antenna to break the surface. Deciding they were in the clear, O'Kane ordered a full surface, and *Tang* sped away to the southwest and the sanctuary of deeper water before dawn, fewer than two hours away.

Sleep was impossible for the excited officers. After fixing *Tang*'s exact position off the Koshiki Islands, Frazee joined O'Kane and Lytle in the wardroom. "Well, they sure fell in our lap tonight," Frazee wisecracked to Lytle.

Lytle was not in a joking mood: "If the object is to sink ships and avoid depth charges, then I guess this is all right, but I hate to think it was going to be my steady diet. I'll take a few depth charges out in deep water any old day."

O'Kane privately felt the same way Lytle did, but his sense of mission overcame caution. He believed they should exploit the geography of the Yellow Sea and sink ships, feeling that "this immediate area held everything." At dawn *Tang* dived for the day, but O'Kane was still supercharged, resting very little. By evening a new contact with a Japanese patrol ship, then increasing squalls that might hide the "alerted enemy . . . prevented any solid sleep."

Just after dawn on June 26 a new contact was picked up on radar. The tireless Frazee, already on the bridge, managed the initial positioning while O'Kane drank coffee in the wardroom. The target looked good. O'Kane called for an end-around to position *Tang* for a daylight submerged attack off a natural choke point, Bono Misaki. They would make a stern shot, using their new electric torpedoes.

The approach was textbook. Four torpedoes were fired, which should have guaranteed the target's destruction. But two of the torpedoes broached, running toward the target on the surface, throwing back enormous plumes of spray. The electrics ran at only twenty-seven knots; it would take two minutes for them to reach the target, which easily evaded these highly visible erratic fish. Win some, lose some.

That evening another Ultra arrived, directing a rendezvous with *Sealion* and *Tinosa*. Two shipping lanes were included in the Ultra, which immediately aroused O'Kane's paranoia. Japanese ship movement reports would be unlikely in these waters. How could Pearl Harbor be certain of their authenticity? O'Kane thought the shipping lanes were fakes, deliberately broadcast by the Japanese to lure American submarines to the wrong location. And he was resentful: "The period during which the three submarines were to work together was being prolonged, [and] the dispatch further directed Don Weiss to position us to intercept the enemy." O'Kane wanted to work alone, where he saw fit.

Frazee, in the rubber boat, paddled over to *Tinosa* again. This time he had no specific instructions. O'Kane wanted him to be deliberately vague. Frazee came back soon with the best possible news: "We've been banished." Weiss ordered *Tinosa* into a position south of the shipping lane, in the East China Sea. *Sealion* would be to the northeast, well into Tsushima Strait. *Tang* was ordered to an area commencing forty miles north of the shipping lane. Weiss had not specified any other geographic constraints, and Frazee asked for no clarification. He knew his captain. *Tang* was immediately off to pass west of the Korean coastline. O'Kane believed "That should guarantee ... contacts, and ... hot pursuit had no limit. We had the whole Yellow Sea."

As *Tang* worked her way through the fog patches over the cold waters of this new hunting ground, *Sealion* had some luck in the strait, downing the 2,400-ton *Sansei Maru* on the twenty-eighth. O'Kane was hoping this kind of activity would cause the Japanese to route their shipping along the Korean coastline, weaving in and out of the hundreds of islands dotting the shore.

At midday on the twenty-ninth *Tang*'s search was rewarded with the sighting of a large freighter. They were poorly positioned for a daylight submerged attack, especially in the cold water, which fogged the periscope lens a second after its exposure to the air. The tracking party determined the base course, and *Tang* ran an evasion course away until enough distance had been created for a surfaced end-around.

At 1330 *Tang* surfaced in heavy seas and ran at four-engine speed to get ahead of the target's projected track. Cold spray whipped against the faces of the men on the bridge, and *Tang* twisted uncomfortably in the disturbed ocean. But the bad weather was effective in hiding their small, low silhouette from the target, which was also struggling with the same poor weather conditions, and it virtually precluded air patrols.

At 1600 *Tang* dove nine miles dead ahead of the target, whose speed, track, length, and masthead height were now accurately determined. O'Kane waited, not so patiently, for an hour and a half for the freighter to come within firing range. Because of the choppy seas, the torpedo depth settings were ten feet. Two bow shots were perfectly aimed but too deep, passing under the target without exploding.

The freighter turned toward *Tang*, following the torpedo wakes to the point of fire. Surprised at this aggressiveness, O'Kane took *Tang* to two hundred feet, near the bottom, and moved away at standard speed. The "victim" now unleashed two very close depth charges, startling all of *Tang's* crew.

Fifteen minutes later they were back on the surface in the failing light, following the last known target bearing northward. The remaining torpedoes were checked; the failed attack was analyzed. O'Kane concluded that the ship was virtually unladen, thus drawing only eight feet of water. Dinner was served to all the off-duty crew before radar made contact again.

The target was heading for the ten-fathom curve, sixty feet of water. When submerged, *Tang* could not get both her new radio masts under at this depth. O'Kane decided to go for it anyway, and planned an attack in the lee of Daikokusan Gunto, where he thought the incessant chop would be somewhat reduced. He planned to use shallower depth settings for the torpedoes with this land protection.

Since the ideal firing position was a few hours away, O'Kane decided to get some rest: "Someone had to be cool, calm, and collected." Frazee, who was undoubtedly exhausted, was in charge of the long approach.

Walker awakened O'Kane at moonset with a fresh mug of coffee. As he struggled to clear his brain, the captain decided to revert to a modification of Morton's favorite technique. A single feeler shot, then a salvo if the first torpedo missed. The seas were rougher than he hoped, but O'Kane ordered the torpedo running depth to be set at six feet anyway. He would compensate by closing to point-blank range. Near midnight on June 30 a single, deadly torpedo broke the back of *Nikkin Maru*, and 5,705 tons of Japanese shipping plunged to the bottom of the shallow Yellow Sea.

With the sub running on the surface, most officers turned in at 0130 on July 1. O'Kane slept fitfully, aware of everything going on aboard. Frazee was up a few hours later for the morning stars, and then *Tang* dove at 0540, batteries charged for what he hoped would be a day of rest. But at 0900 Hank Flanagan spotted a Chinese junk. Succumbing to Mel Enos's urging, O'Kane agreed to a battle-surface, gun-pointing drill. Using their practiced technique, *Tang* leaped to the surface with a mighty roar of air and water, followed by the cranking sounds of engine ignition and the scream of high-pressure turboblowers.

The Chinese were scared out of their wits by the sudden appearance of this sea monster alongside their tiny craft, and tightened sails to escape. A few rounds of gunfire caused its crew to douse sails. Language barriers made meaningful communication impossible, but O'Kane decided to pass stray canned goods over to the Chinese crew for their trouble. Suddenly the shout rang out from the crow's nest: "Smoke ho!"

Tang immediately turned toward this unexpected opportunity and worked up to full power in pursuit. As soon as the base course could be established from the pattern of zigs on the increasingly visible targets, *Tang* was off on another end-around. Battle stations were not called; the normal duty crew plotted the interception course.

Three hours later, with a fourteen-knot speed advantage, *Tang* passed the two targets and dove in front of them. O'Kane planned to fire two electric torpedoes from the stern tubes at the smaller ship, which was fitted with both depth charges and a gun mount. Since they were wakeless, and ran slower than the steam torpedoes, he would use this interval to swing *Tang* for a bow shot at the larger, unarmed vessel.

The first electric torpedo missed, but the second detonated the depth charges carried on deck. There was an enormous explosion, which caused the larger target to turn away. The shot spoiled, O'Kane wearily realized they would have another night chase to endure. Before beginning the new end-around, he let many of the crew view the sinking ship through the periscope. O'Kane believed they had sunk the 2,500-ton *Amakasu Maru*. They had actually downed the small, 878-ton *Takatori Maru,* whose short length likely caused the first torpedo to miss. O'Kane's exhaustion may have affected his tonnage judgment.

With O'Kane cautious about potential air patrols this close to the coast, the submerged *Tang* followed the freighter at six knots. The freighter was doing its best to run for safety and at eleven knots was gradually disappearing from sight. By nightfall, when *Tang* surfaced to pursue, the target was only a smudge of smoke on the horizon.

Pouring on the coal, *Tang* raced to overtake the freighter. Dissatisfied with the eighteen-knot speed provided by three engines, O'Kane suspended the battery charge and put the fourth diesel to work on propulsion. With three minutes to spare, *Tang* reached the interception point 1,200 yards north of the target's track.

Two torpedoes were fired with a run length of only 460 yards. The ship blew up with a frightful explosion from the first torpedo. Frazee pushed O'Kane aside for a look at their handiwork, a ship that sank in twenty seconds, wasting the second torpedo. O'Kane and the exhausted tracking party were sure they had sunk the respectably sized, 4,000-ton *Samarang Maru.*

In fact they had downed another tiny vessel, the 998-ton *Daiun Maru*. It was no wonder that one torpedo was enough.

For the next two days the officers and crew rested, not even bothering to examine a few fishing trawlers that came within periscope view. More than two hundred miles away, near the southern entrance to Tsushima Strait, *Tinosa* picked off two ships near midnight on July 3. One was a fine 8,000-ton transport. Pearl Harbor's shipping lane advice had proved to be on the money.

At about the same time that *Tinosa* struck, another rendezvous between *Tang* and *Sealion* was conducted. Once again Frazee paddled over to their packmate partner, with an invitation to Eli Reich to join *Tang* in a foray into the Yellow Sea. Reich declined, preferring to head for Shanghai instead, an area he knew well from prewar duty.

Frazee did learn that *Sealion* patrolled with its SD radar active, and had been driven under repeatedly by air patrols. O'Kane concluded that *Sealion* was undoubtedly broadcasting her presence so that targets would be likely to avoid the submarine. This conclusion reinforced O'Kane's determination not to use the SD radar again.

Reich's refusal in hand, O'Kane immediately headed *Tang* north at eighteen knots, deeper into the Yellow Sea, in order to reach the shallow coastal water off Osei To by dawn. The thirty-fathom line was crossed as they bore in, but poor weather blocked Frazee's attempts to fix their exact location. This was no problem to O'Kane, who simply ordered more lookouts topside.

At 0408 on the fourth of July, before reaching Osei To, a target was sighted coming southward toward them. At full speed *Tang* barreled through dozens of fishing sampans and dove only when the ship's bridge came over the horizon. This target had no intention of straying into deep water and kept turning ever closer to the coastline. *Tang* pursued at high, battery-draining, submerged speed, with O'Kane coaching the diving officer carefully on depth control. Their intended victim was clearly making for the ten-fathom line, not enough water for *Tang* to attack submerged.

O'Kane bore in, with sonar reporting eighteen feet under their keel, and the water depth rapidly diminishing. The final firing setup was nearly complete, at a range longer than O'Kane wanted. A final look was needed to confirm the ship's slower speed, detected by a screw count on sonar. Then, in fifty-eight feet of water, *Tang* rubbed aground. Lying on the conning tower deck to look through the exposed periscope, O'Kane simultaneously called the final firing mark and ordered *Tang* to begin backing full to get off the bottom. Lytle was appalled, possibly believing he was working with a madman.

Moving in reverse, likely unique in submarine warfare, O'Kane fired three torpedoes. Their "zing" was muffled by the mud they passed through during their initial drop after being ejected from the tubes. But all ran "hot, straight, and normal," and two hit the target twenty-five hundred yards away. The 6,886-ton *Asukasan Maru* split in two, the stern sinking quickly.

Tang surfaced in the midst of the fishing fleet, the Japanese cursing and shaking their fists at them. Their Korean counterparts bravely cheered, hands clasped overhead like winning boxers. All engines roaring, *Tang* sped westward as the bow of their latest victim went under. As soon as the fishing fleet, some of whom may have had radios to report *Tang*'s course, were out of sight, O'Kane pivoted the boat, and they resumed their northward course along the Korean coast.

In late afternoon two widely separated targets were detected. O'Kane chose the westernmost one, where an attack might be made in at least a hundred feet of water. At 1953 *Tang* surfaced and O'Kane immediately ordered two engines onto a badly needed battery charge. He was determined to conserve ammunition and sink this ship using only two torpedoes. At 2041, with enough charge to let them maneuver during the attack, *Tang* submerged. Her depth was held to only forty-seven feet, the radar mast jutting out of the water painting the oncoming target.

Following the target zigs with precision, O'Kane positioned *Tang* to fire from either forward or after tubes. He was tired now, not having slept for more than twenty-four hours, and saw that "she was big and broad, a massive, loaded ship, a beautiful ship." It was another 10,000-tonner for sure. Two torpedoes were fired; one was enough. Down went the 6,932-ton *Yamaoka Maru*, on her maiden voyage, in a fearful explosion.

Tang surfaced after this sinking and prowled the wreckage. One very reluctant survivor was spotted whom *Tang*'s crew, after firing their Tommy guns, finally snared in heaving lines. "Firecracker," so named because of their fourth of July successes, was hauled aboard, only to have convulsions at the sight of the red night-light glow emanating from the hatches. He must have thought he was going to be burned alive.

Tang again moved northward, and targets were sighted throughout the daylight hours of July 5, but in water only thirty-six feet deep. Then, just before 2200, a ship was picked up on radar seventeen miles ahead of them. A long end-around was started to put *Tang* ten miles ahead, all out of sight of the target, before it could reach Gaichosan Retto and safety. Frazee, a skilled navigator whose talents O'Kane admired enormously, plotted the course legs and times to pull off this feat. They could make it—barely—if *Tang* immediately went to full power.

Frazee's plot required *Tang* to run for 3½ hours before getting into firing position, with at least another hour to make the attack. O'Kane had rested during the day, and was sorely tempted to stay on the bridge during the end-around. But he decided to let Frazee and the junior officers manage the preliminaries. Instead, he roamed the boat, talking to the crew and trying to stay out of the way of Frazee, Lytle, and Frank Springer.

At about 0200 O'Kane returned to the bridge to find the target astern. Well positioned for a stern shot, *Tang* dove at 0227. O'Kane conducted the final approach, bothered by a periscope lens that fogged almost immediately after being raised from icy water to moist, warm air. At nine hundred yards' range the last two torpedoes, both electrics, were fired from the after tubes at a ship of "conventional size for the China trade," about 4,000 tons. Both hit, sinking the very much smaller 1,469-ton *Dori Go*. There were no survivors. Empty of all torpedoes, *Tang* turned and began the long run home with all four diesels pounding at full power.

Two hours after this sinking, *Sealion* picked off the 1,922-ton *Setsuzan Maru* southeast of Shanghai. Reich, too, had badly overestimated the size of his conquest. These continuing depredations were acknowledged by Tokyo Rose. That night Walker came to get his captain to listen to a funeral march being played for American submarines operating in the East China and Yellow Seas. Walker took this attention personally. "I think we're in the news, Captain," he remarked proudly.

Now unarmed, O'Kane decided to steer clear of the sites of prior attacks and headed for the Hawaiian Islands. Running full speed surfaced at night, and four knots submerged by day, *Tang* reached Nakana Strait on the evening of the eighth. There a line of five of Admiral Oikawa's slow but deadly *kaibokans* awaited her. O'Kane decided not to dive, but literally outran them in a tense fifteen-minute escape.

Now O'Kane abandoned any pretense of zigzagging and went to full power for the run to Midway. As required upon departure from a patrol area, *Tang* reported her results: eight ships sunk. Not till after the war would it be learned that she had actually downed ten. Eight was more than enough for a congratulatory message from ComSubPac.

Behind her the sinkings continued. *Tinosa* gunned under a tiny nineteen-ton fishing boat on July 10. *Sealion* downed two more meaningful cargo vessels in torpedo attacks on the eleventh. At high noon on the 14th *Tang* passed through the Midway reef for two weeks of rest.

16

New Preparations

Readiness is all.

—Shakespeare, Hamlet

San Diego was on full wartime footing. The center of town, Horton Plaza—just "the plaza" to most residents—had a fountain in its center, a last reminder of a less intense peacetime. This tiny oasis was now completely ringed by bars and twenty-four-hour-a-day movie houses, most packed with sailors, marines, and their "girls."

From the Owl drugstore on the corner of Third and Broadway one walked west through a sea of uniforms toward the bay and the start of the camouflage netting and fake farmhouses that covered most of the city near the Consolidated Vultee plant. At Union Station lines of stretchers, filled mostly with wounded marines, lay on the ground by the Santa Fe and Southern Pacific tracks. These were combat casualties being transferred from nearby Balboa Park, where they were temporarily housed in the Panama-California Exposition buildings or in field tents, to hospitals closer to their hometowns.

Navy aircraft roared overhead, those landing on North Island—now connected to the Silver Strand (today's Coronado) by dredging and landfill—so low the pilots' faces could be seen by pedestrians on Washington Street. Farther north, at Mission Beach, hundreds of sailors, each with a precious pass, rode Pacific breakers on their inflated mattress covers. Even the former isolation of La Jolla had given way to the wartime onslaught of military personnel. From its lonely hilltop, the Colonial Inn's sea vista was now marked by young marines frolicking on the narrow beaches in seal-like packs, while destroyers trained to seaward.

A nickel ride on the Coronado Ferry as it picked its way through the fleet was one of "Dago's" diversions. The huge Essex class aircraft carriers always caught the eye first, but soon small, sharklike, purposeful ships retained an observer's interest. These were the submarines. Occasionally a new fleet boat would be spotted, perhaps down from Mare Island on a shakedown cruise. More often they were one of four or five old S-boats, identifiable by their distinctive conning tower shape and seemingly too-large deck gun mounted on the foredeck. One of these was *S-34,* commanded by Lieutenant Roger Paine.

Life as captain of an S-boat had zero glamour. *S-34* would pull out of San Diego early every Sunday morning and head to sea for training exercises with destroyers. She would return late Friday night. Saturday was spent reprovisioning the boat. Paine's time with Bebe and Roger III was nearly nonexistent, especially during one eleven-week stretch of this activity. One-third of the crew was rotated each week to train new officers and men, but the captain, of course, was never given relief.

Living conditions aboard *S-34* were miserable. The boat had been built by Union Iron Works in 1918, before air conditioning was thinkable for ships. Steady condensate soaked the four bunks for six officers, so hot bunking on damp mattresses was the norm. But to Paine she was "all mine," and he loved the tired old boat.

There was another, secret activity going on in San Diego, unknown to most civilians. The University of California's Naval War Research Laboratory had been pursuing the possibilities of a new FM sonar for nearly two years. During the second week of April 1943 Dr. G. P. Harnwell had invited Lockwood to a prototype demonstration while the admiral was at Coronado visiting his family. Bobbing around in a small boat, Dr. Harnwell had the instrument display shoals on either side of the channel, and nets at the entrance, on a PPI scope. When a passing surface ship came within its range the device emitted a clear, ringing echo.

Lockwood was not much interested in an FM sonar device to locate enemy harbor entrances. He considered other possibilities and ultimately came to this question: Could this device, which responded to a passing ship, become a mine detector? In time the answered seemed to be yes.

In early 1944 Paine's *S-34* was selected for the first submarine trials of FM sonar. There was no time to build a unit that would have the ultimate physical shape. The trial unit was simply mounted on *S-34*'s deck. Submerged, Paine began testing its capability with a dummy mine field laid down for this purpose.

As would be expected for a prototype, the unit was often out of service. This crucial fact was sometimes undetectable to *S-34*'s crew. When operational, the FM sonar unit did not have the hoped-for 700-yard range, but about 85 percent of the time it could detect a mine at 450 yards. Then it would emit its characteristic ringing sound, quickly dubbed "hell's bells." The real problem was that the other 15 percent of the time the unit gave no indication that a mine was present, even if *S-34* bumped into it. Clearly, this was not confidence-inspiring technology.

On June 6, 1944, the new-construction boat *Hawkbill* entered the Mississippi River at Lockport, Illinois, bound for New Orleans. The ship was built at Manitowoc, Wisconsin, and her new executive officer was George Grider. During the construction phase Grider had been offered command of an existing submarine. He declined, happy to be in the States with Ann and their young son Billy. Grider also remembered how bone-tired he had been at the end of his tour on *Pollack*. He was not yet rested from eighteen months of steady combat. Grider also did not yet feel quite ready to be a captain. One more patrol as XO should be just about right.

After an all-out farewell party in New Orleans, Grider reluctantly said good-bye to Ann, with whom he had driven all the way down from Manitowoc. On June 16 *Hawkbill* departed for Balboa and new-boat training.

There Grider was given multiple opportunities to conduct attacks on destroyers used for training. On two separate attempts the depth-keeping mechanism on the dummy torpedoes failed. But Grider's eye was on, and the dummy shots hit the targets amidships instead of passing beneath, penetrating their plates and doing serious flooding damage. In mid-July, training completed, *Hawkbill* set sail for Pearl Harbor and a resumption of the war.

On July 10, as *Tang* was heading home from her record-breaking third patrol, *Shark*, and John Griggs, departed from Midway for her second. The two submarines passed each other as *Shark* continued on to the Bonins. On July 19 Blakely was again on the attack, damaging a freighter.

At Midway O'Kane immediately stepped up his intensive training for Frank Springer. O'Kane expected to lose Murray Frazee at the conclusion of the next patrol, and had to make sure this reservist could do the job. Springer responded well, and after successful practice approaches and torpedo firings O'Kane declared him "qualified for command." O'Kane also collaborated with the division commander to hold up Springer's paperwork so he would not be faced with the problem of losing both Frazee and Springer at the end of the next patrol. A new diving officer, Larry Savadkin, fresh from submarine school but experienced in combat from his destroyer time in the Atlantic and Mediterranean, also joined the boat.

For his part, O'Kane was dissatisfied with the kind of advanced base that Midway had become. The enlisted men now had the resources of a full-fledged "recreation department" to take them sport fishing on boats manned by navy specialists, a fact that irritated him. Worse, submarine captains were expected to use the new "senior officers' bar" and set themselves apart from the junior officers. "Those who had seen to this construction had unwittingly undercut the finest war patrol school in existence." O'Kane went to the Gooneyville anyway, to work the occupants of the corner room for their patrol experiences.

There was also an awards ceremony, with medals awarded to Frazee, Hank Flanagan, Bill Ballinger, and Bill Leibold, among others. O'Kane received his third Silver Star for his last patrol in *Wahoo*, and a Legion of Merit for picking up the twenty-two aviators during *Tang*'s second patrol. He accepted these well-deserved honors graciously.

But mostly *Tang*'s crew worked. Frazee later wrote that O'Kane was always eager to get to Midway "just so he could load up more torpedoes and get back out there—sink more ships, kill more Japs. That did not thrill many people in the crew."

On July 30 fourteen steam torpedoes were loaded in the forward torpedo room, ten electrics in the after room. This mix of torpedoes made the TDC setups difficult, but there were not yet enough electrics to fully load every boat. O'Kane was itching to go; after all, he had been onshore, excluding time at sea for training, for sixteen days. Their destination: Honshu.

Tang's departure time was scheduled for 1500 on July 31, but was delayed. Steward Howard Walker was not yet aboard. Exasperated, Frazee sent shipmates to retrieve him. They knew just where to look and Walker was hauled back, his hands filled with his gambling winnings. At 1555 the shore party took in the lines and *Tang* eased away from the dock on her way to Japan, and a cruise in "Ashcan Alley."

17

Torpedo Troubles in Ashcan Alley

I was not in safety, neither had I rest; yet trouble came.

—Job 3:26

"I counted them from the start, and I figure I was subjected to about 500 depth charges during the war on 11 patrols. Those 500 are counting the ones relatively far away, the ones when we said, 'Ha ha, listen to the stupid bastards! They're going the wrong way!' Half of the total came on the first ten patrols. The other half came on the fourth patrol of *Tang*." Thus wrote Murray Frazee fifty years after this noisy, frightening, frustrating patrol in an area some grim-humored wags dubbed "Ashcan Alley."

Tang's destination was Honshu, where Admiral Lockwood had been disappointed in the poor results of three prior submarines operating in Japanese home waters. Lockwood gave Dick O'Kane a private note that laid out his expectations: the prior "boats report . . . a dearth of shipping. [But] Intelligence reports indicate that merchant traffic must be there, and I am certain that *Tang* can rediscover it." To O'Kane this meant get in close, in shallow water, and locate the tonnage that must be hugging the coastline.

O'Kane shared this note with Frazee, who never scared easily. "It requires nothing we wouldn't do anyway," the XO remarked, clearly understanding the personal fearlessness of his captain.

To have everyone mentally prepared for the pending action, O'Kane dismissed potential captain's mast late-for-duty charges against Walker, writing it off to "crew recreation." Walker responded instantly for his captain: "Never had a cup of coffee at just the right temperature, hot, been served more quickly."

O'Kane secured the SD radar on the way to the home islands so the Japanese could not pick up its transmissions; *Tang* would rely solely on the APR-1. He also introduced a new speed estimating tool: an ordinary metronome he had picked up in San Francisco. Now, instead of the sound man counting propeller turns with stopwatch in hand, he simply tuned the beat of the metronome to match the churn of the enemy screws. When they pulsed in synchronism, O'Kane had the turn count depicted as beats per minute.

As they neared Honshu, O'Kane had Chief Quartermaster Jones plot all known ship sightings recorded in prior patrol reports. The median search line passed north to south between two island specks about fifty miles off the coast. *Tang* proceeded along this line during daylight on August 9, submerged, but often with twenty-six feet of shears and scope exposed, creeping slowly closer to the shore. The pace picked up during the night as the surfaced submarine rolled along while charging batteries. At dawn on the tenth *Tang* dove, fifteen miles west of the Omae Saki peninsula, three miles off the beach.

In this area the seas washing against mountainous terrain quickly shifted from shallow to deep. O'Kane intended to attack in shallow water, then escape seaward to the hundred-fathom curve, a position *Tang* could reach in fifteen minutes even while submerged. A gunboat had already been sighted, and O'Kane fretted that *Tang* was too far offshore. Frazee resisted the pressure to move shoreward in a "cooperative but frank" exchange, telling O'Kane "I like just what we're doing. . . . That PC could have spoiled our whole day. We're not rushed."

Early that morning a junior officer missed seeing a target that, O'Kane noted, was running "unbelievably close to the beach." When spotted, it was too late to fire. Now even more alert, at midmorning Frazee personally picked up an air patrol and the returning escorts protecting a single tanker.

O'Kane bore in till there was only twelve feet of water beneath *Tang* and fired a three-torpedo spread at close range. There were no hits, but O'Kane could see the target suddenly reverse course. She had seen, or heard, something. As *Tang* moved away the submarine suddenly grounded, but bounced off the rocky bottom and kept going. An intense postmortem led to the inescapable conclusion that they should have registered at least two hits on this target. There had been some sort of torpedo failure.

Tang moved westward after this failed attack, running on the surface as soon as the skies darkened. At 0418 on August 11, in sweltering humidity and self-generated heat from the battery charge, *Tang* dove off Miki Saki, a pronounced coastal promontory fifty miles southwest of inland Osaka. It had been too hot to sleep; O'Kane and Frazee spent their four free hours talking, trying to relax, and eating freshly baked apricot turnovers.

Patrol craft were constantly in sight a thousand yards off the point, and steady sonar search pinging could be heard. Japanese listening, or passive, sonar was quite good, and U.S. submarines had been remarkably silenced since 1942 to offset this enemy capability. But Japanese active sonar was never better than fair. It was often in the sonic range, clearly detectable by the human ear as opposed to the supersonic gear used in the U.S. and British Navies. The noisy search sonar so clearly located the patrol craft (PC) that *Tang* was easily able to keep turning, presenting a small silhouette and avoiding detection.

At least one target slipped around the bend inside this PC screen. O'Kane pushed his submerged ship in to two thousand yards off the point, continually adjusting *Tang's* position to offer a small sonar echo. Managing *Tang's* motion was made much more difficult by the three-knot Kuroshio current, which seemed always to work against them, but Frazee was ready. He smiled as he commented "This is the spot, Captain."

One potential attack was foiled when an escort turned toward *Tang* and bluffed Hank Flanagan on the periscope into moving the submarine away. A second target slipped to safety behind this skilled escort. O'Kane seethed. It would not happen again: "Next time we would turn toward [the escort] and go under the SOB." It was clear that this little craft knew that *Tang* was watching, having sighted her periscope during one too-long exposure.

After twelve hours submerged in this cat-and-mouse game, two columns of smoke were sighted toward nearby Owashi Wan. O'Kane moved *Tang's* speed up to standard and commenced a thirty-minute run toward the track of the last target that had eluded them, hoping to leave the persistent escort searching in the wrong location.

After twenty-five minutes of blind running, O'Kane slowed *Tang* to one-third speed and made his first periscope observation. He saw two freighters and two escorts, one the gunboat that O'Kane and Frazee had spotted the previous day. The targets could be reached in fewer than ten minutes of high-speed underwater running. Course adjusted, *Tang* moved quickly to the firing spot, outer torpedo tube doors open.

Just as O'Kane ordered the scope up for the final bearings, Caverly, on sound, reported fast screws approaching. O'Kane swung to Caverly's bearing and saw their friend the gunboat, less than a thousand yards away and throwing back an enormous bow wave. In his mind O'Kane calculated that the gunboat would take "... over a minute to reach us; continuing with the attack was automatic."

Urgently, O'Kane called the angles for both targets and fired a spread of three torpedoes at each one before turning back to the gunboat. "With the scope in low power she filled the field. I had misjudged her range or speed," he later wrote. But the captain of the gunboat made a judgment error as well. Probably assuming the enemy submarine would be heading seaward, the gunboat raced toward *Tang*'s projected location but could not pick up a sonar echo. The Japanese ship wheeled to make a second pass. The gunboat now would be visually aided by the convergence of *Tang*'s torpedo wakes, at least one of which was an arrow to a target that had been struck and exploded.

As the escort bore in again, O'Kane gave the orders: "Flood negative. Take her deep. Rig for depth charge." Seven more tons of incoming seawater aided *Tang*'s descent to 180 feet, virtually all the water they had to work with. The submarine was rapidly buttoned up and quieted for the coming assault. The attacker came in on *Tang*'s stern at slow speed, sonar pings reverberating inside the submarine. The churning screws could be heard throughout *Tang*. Suddenly the gunboat speeded up and turned away. All knew that she had dropped her first depth charges.

In a furious cacophony of underwater explosions *Tang* was straddled by violent detonations. O'Kane was later to confess that in ten patrols "that lousy gunboat laid them down faster and closer than any I had experienced before." Savadkin, who had been on the giving end in his prior destroyer assignment, was shocked by the furious assault as twenty-two close charges, and many more less accurate, rained down with incredible violence. The gunboat made repeated passes, its deadly missiles slamming men against solid objects, bursting lightbulbs, filling the compartments with dust and cork.

But by the fifth pass the explosions were shoreward of the escaping *Tang*. Lacking good search sonar, the Japanese were simply unable to hunt *Tang* to exhaustion. Watertight doors were opened so the crew could move between compartments once more.

O'Kane dropped down into the wardroom and found a disturbed Savadkin and a poker-faced Frazee. Savadkin spoke first. "Captain, if I had known that depth charges would be like those, I might just have stayed in surface ships."

O'Kane began to con the junior officer. "Larry, they seemed close because you're not used to them. When we get some that are really close, these won't seem too bad." Frazee sat listening, straight-faced. Then O'Kane burst out laughing and confessed that it was the worst attack he had ever endured, and that without *Tang*'s extra-thick skin he believed the submarine now would be in grave trouble.

Frazee left to visit every compartment and returned with the time-honored hand-to-mouth gesture suggesting that all hands be given a shot of brandy: "depth-charge medicine." O'Kane nodded his assent, believing that most of the sailors would toast the sinking of the target and not just calm themselves.

O'Kane thought they had sunk two ships, but since no one had seen the second ship go down, he only claimed damaging it. The sunken vessel was about 5,500 tons, he felt, a Biyo Maru class freighter. Actually they had sunk *Roko Maru*, of 3,328 tons. This was not a good enough start for O'Kane: nine torpedoes expended, only fifteen left, and only one positive sinking claim.

On the surface again, *Tang* headed east, away from the coast, rumbling depth charges annoying her and searchlights scanning the horizon as in a surrealistic movie premiere. For the next few days both air and surface ship patrols were always in sight, and random depth charges were dropped, as *Tang* prowled south of Tokyo Bay. But no reachable targets were closed, even though they searched down the Nampo Shoto chain.

On August 14, frustrated, O'Kane employed the old *Wahoo* technique to suddenly, surprisingly, battle surface. He let the gun crew fire eighty-eight rounds at a small boat fitted with large-caliber machine guns and multiple radio antennas. This little ship was tough, maneuverable, and fought back, always keeping *Tang* at least 2½ miles away. Only eight hits were registered, and O'Kane broke off the attack to conserve the remaining ammunition for an emergency.

More empty days dragged by in relatively open sea before *Tang* headed for the coastal waters near the entrance to Kii Suido and the Inland Sea. Frazee, relatively well rested, reacted positively to O'Kane's orders to the navigator: "Fraz, let's head in and get a ship." He plotted a course that would have *Tang* in good firing position by nightfall on the nineteenth.

Ignoring patrol craft and sampans, the first escorted target was sighted just after breakfast on the twentieth. *Tang* was submerged in ninety feet of water; the target and her protectors were inshore, in much shallower depths. Two torpedoes were fired. The first seemed to run normally, but exploded beyond the target. The second made no pretense of normal operation, sinking to the bottom with a disheartening thud.

During the attack *Tang* had crept into eighty feet of water. She turned for a run to the deep, but the first Japanese counterattacks occurred while they were at periscope depth. Fortunately the small escorts did not have a good position fix, and had limited depth-charge-carrying capability. Thirty explosives were dropped in single attacks, but *Tang* safely made it to deep water.

The next day, under similar conditions, an attack was made in which O'Kane purposefully injected a wide spread into the tracks of the three torpedoes fired. All ran up on the beach and exploded. They must have run deep. Now *Tang* had only ten torpedoes left of the original twenty-four. The inevitable Japanese counterattacks included twenty not particularly threatening depth charges, which were largely ignored.

Frustrated and resentful, his pride damaged, O'Kane planned a torpedo inquisition. The first step would be controlled test firings against a vertical cliff, in a location free of the Kuroshio current. Frazee determined the spot: inside the bay of Owashi Wan. *Tang* entered on the surface at midnight. O'Kane was astonished to find their nemesis, the gunboat from the August 11 counterattack, anchored, its crew apparently sleeping. To hell with the cliffs. They would coolly, deliberately sink this slumbering antagonist.

Sliding quietly in on battery power, avoiding all noise or even diesel odor, O'Kane swung *Tang* to the dark shore, silhouetting the gunboat against the sea. The stern tubes were aimed. Depth setting: three feet. Range: twelve hundred yards. Gyro angle: zero. Target speed: zero. Own speed: zero.

The first electric, wakeless torpedo ran a hundred yards before sinking to the bottom with only a detonator rumble. There was no giveaway explosion. The second electric torpedo ran straight for the target. All hands topside, including Frazee, who sprang up the ladder as an eager witness, braced for the explosion; the torpedo ran below the target and out to sea.

O'Kane then turned *Tang* around. A third, steam, torpedo was fired from the bow tubes. It jogged left a hundred feet and boiled past the stern of the anchored target. Now there was some stirring of activity from the Japanese crew. Men could be seen moving about with flashlights, probably wondering what was causing all the swishing, gurgling noises. Whales? Dolphins?

The fourth torpedo also jogged left, but not far, and O'Kane could see that it was headed straight for the target. At his call, *Tang*'s fire control party clambered to the bridge just in time for the most intense explosion they had ever seen. Every depth charge on the gunboat went up in an incandescent column of flame climbing five hundred feet into the sky. *Nansatsu Maru 2*, 116 tons, had evaporated. With an abundance of failure characteristics recorded, *Tang* headed to sea to become an interim torpedo repair facility. O'Kane hit the sack as the submarine raced eastward sixty miles before diving.

While O'Kane slept, the torpedo crews worked on the remaining six fish. Three were quickly spotted with identifiable defects: depth-keeping rudder throws that ensured they would run below their depth settings. Other potential problems would be discovered in the daylight hours.

What *Tang* was experiencing was the result of the failure of the Newport Goat Island torpedo facility to keep up with the navy's wartime production needs. The National Defense Research Committee broke Newport's monopoly and expanded production through industry manufacturing sub-contracts as well as the use of government-owned, contractor-operated facilities. Production leaped, with many more than half of all torpedoes now coming from sources other than Newport.

But this quantity advance was decidedly a mixed blessing. The hand-built, Swiss watch qualities of the Newport units permitted them to function beautifully—if one ignored their grievous design errors that, after all, were not the fault of manufacturing personnel. The industrial production units delivered to *Tang* had rough edges, sticky differential valves, high-friction control engines.

All day long *Tang*'s torpedo men worked on the remaining units, hand-lapping edges, wearing in valves with repeated actuations, "firing" with compressed air as the fish swung suspended inside the torpedo rooms, test-ing, testing, skipping meals to get it right. By nightfall on the twenty-second they were ready. *Tang* surfaced and O'Kane pounded back to the coast off Omae Saki, the site of their first failed attack. Here, seventy-five miles southwest of the entrance to Tokyo Bay, navigation lights still burned.

Frazee had been up all night in anticipation of antisubmarine patrols. The first aircraft were spotted at daybreak, followed quickly by surface ships. The first target candidates appeared during breakfast. O'Kane joined Frazee in the conning tower, where both were succored by Walker and his ever-ready coffee.

In a high-speed underwater run, *Tang* slipped beneath a ring of three small escorts to come into shooting alignment with three freighters. But the freighters zigged, and *Tang* was now faced with a new problem. She was being tracked by an old echo-ranging destroyer, supported by five aircraft.

The antisubmarine aircraft may have been dropping sonobuoys, for some Japanese units now possessed this capability. But *Tang* was twenty decibels quieter than its 1942 predecessor *Wahoo*. In the arcane world of audio log-arithms, this is a 99 percent reduction in sound intensity. The average sonobuoy detection range was thus reduced to only 50 to 160 yards. In con-trast, German U-boats could be detected at 1,600 yards. In reality, Japanese aircraft were now only really useful for visual sighting. To this end O'Kane made sure that *Tang*'s depth changes had very gradual angles, and speed changes were modest, to avoid swirls of water from the props.

Outer doors open, ready to fire if necessary, O'Kane kept *Tang* slowly turning counterclockwise, her nose pointed at the destroyer, which circled, pinging noisily. It was often as close as 500 yards but could not pick up the submarine that it must have believed was there. The tension inside *Tang* was palpable. O'Kane took frequent water-lapping looks in low power, calling angles and ranges should they be forced to shoot. Caverly kept the metronome ticking in time with the destroyer's screws, whose swishing noise was broadcast throughout the boat. Savadkin held the depth oh-so-steady. Slowly the destroyer's maneuvers dragged *Tang* seaward, away from the potential cargo traffic.

After an hour the destroyer moved away from the constant circling and moved slowly out to sea. Pushing the periscope up a bit higher, O'Kane spotted the masts and part of the superstructure of an oncoming ship. He perceived it to be similar to a 10,000-ton Buenos Aires Maru class vessel, a "big naval transport" with many escorts. *Tang* was hurriedly moved toward a firing position inshore, and three torpedoes were unleashed. At least two hit. O'Kane was exultant. He was sure they had sunk a really big vessel. Immediately after the war JANAC credited him with the 8,135-ton *Tsukushi Maru*. But in 1952, IJN records indicated that the tonnage attribution was incorrect. It was *Tsukushi Maru*, all right, but only 1,859 tons.

No matter. It was an exceedingly daring, persistent attack, and O'Kane and the crew of *Tang* almost ignored the steady diet of depth charges and sonar pinging as they spent two hours moving to deeper water at sea.

Changing stations to confuse the Japanese, *Tang* returned to the Shiono Misaki area on August 24. Before noon an attack was begun on two freighters in shallow water, under tight escort from five PCs, which blocked *Tang*'s retreat to deep water. In a candid admission O'Kane said, "Fraz, this situation stinks!" Frazee could not have agreed more, and jerked his thumb seaward. In a rare retreat, O'Kane turned *Tang* and at relatively high submerged speed dove below a five degree temperature gradient, which would deflect sonar. *Tang* then passed beneath a searching PC and escaped seaward.

While this patrol was still young, Frazee would only be happy when they expended their last three torpedoes and returned to Pearl Harbor. The waxing moon was now becoming bright enough to hinder the escape of a surfaced submarine trying to make a run for it. Attack and be done with it. The sooner the better. He plotted a return course to the Miki Saki area.

On their way *Tang* encountered a surfaced Japanese submarine eleven hundred yards away. Both subs turned away from the other. After an hour's wait for a possible shot, *Tang* resumed her move to the target area. Frazee remained awake the rest of the night, too keyed up to sleep, and responsible to manage *Tang*'s landfall on these unfriendly shores.

Submerging at dawn, *Tang* immediately encountered considerable traffic. Frazee, who should have turned in, stayed up for the coming action. Escorts were everywhere, some pinging with uncommon vigor that sounded like pile drivers inside the hull of the submarine. During one particularly noisy patch *Tang*'s officers almost convinced themselves that some escorts were dragging chains along the bottom to snag *Tang*.

A marginal attack possibility was passed up as not optimal for the last three torpedoes. Finally, a "medium-sized" tanker, protected by five escorts, was spotted, to seaward of *Tang* because the submarine had crept so close to shore. *Tang* was actually running parallel to the tanker, on opposite courses. They would depend on the umbilical cord to set the TDC-generated gyro angles on the torpedoes, which would turn toward the target after firing. And they would be close. Unlike the steam torpedoes, the Mark 18 electric torpedoes armed within two hundred yards of firing. O'Kane would fire at six hundred yards.

With all the incessant pinging sound clutter, O'Kane was not afraid to check the tanker's range by sonar. Three torpedoes were fired. The one set to lead the target was also aimed to run in the midst of the escorts. One could always hope! Two torpedoes hit the tanker, which sank uncommonly quickly. O'Kane believed he saw one of the escorts explode as well.

Frazee remembered the attack and getaway slightly differently. "We were 1,000 yards off the coast . . . running submerged, and it was just turning dusk. We had torpedoes only in the stern tubes, for one ship and two escort vessels we had spotted. They were hugging the coast . . . and we were between the target ship and the beach, less than 1,000 yards point-to-point. . . . I was getting no reading on the fathometer. Just as we were about to go aground, we fired the torpedoes, sank the ship, and turned out.

"Submerged speed depended on the charge of the battery, and we had a fairly full charge. So we ran at six knots for three hours. Depth charges were going off everywhere. 'Hell, they can't hear us,' O'Kane said, 'They don't know we're here.' . . . typical Dick O'Kane."

Tang surfaced at 2039 that evening, as soon as a cloud obscured the moon. The escorts were still visible in the distance, but now the submarine was making more surface speed than they could likely muster. As they drew away from their pursuers and began to settle on a course for Pearl Harbor, celebratory steaks were broken out of the freezer. After chow the crew watched the umpteenth showing of *Flying Down to Rio* in the forward torpedo room.

O'Kane was enormously pleased. He believed he had just sunk a modern new tanker of 5,000 tons as well as a 600-ton escort. JANAC was to give him no postwar credit, but in 1952 it was learned that one ship was sunk that night, the 834-ton civilian tanker *Nanko Maru 8*. After his miserable experience with torpedoes, O'Kane believed he had salvaged the situation by sinking five ships for 22,500 tons. *Tang* actually downed four for a total of 6,137 tons.

After the evening meal Savadkin reported the fuel status to O'Kane. Since the patrol had been a short one, they were flush. O'Kane decided to let the auxiliary engine charge the batteries. The four main diesels were to be kept on propulsion as *Tang* roared back to Pearl Harbor. And there were to be no true dives. Once a day *Tang* was dipped till the decks were awash, then immediately returned to the surface. For their part, the crew was thrilled at the prospect of liberty in Pearl Harbor, and happy to gorge themselves every day on straight cholesterol—steaks and fries—which they had no intention of returning to the base commissary.

As *Tang* neared Hawaii, days ahead of schedule, she overtook *Rasher*, with the senior Hank Munson in command. Munson was finishing an outstanding patrol, one that would turn out to be the second best of the Pacific war in terms of gross tonnage sunk. He had just downed the escort carrier *Taiyo* and four large tankers and freighters.

Munson, a patrician man, grandson of an admiral, and proud of his lineage, which included a signer of the Declaration of Independence, wanted to be first at ten-ten dock. *Rasher* was flying a new battle flag hand-sewn during their return. He "wanted to make a splash . . . with a full section of his crew at quarters on deck and himself in crisp khakis and black tie." To him, allowing *Rasher* to have the right of way was a simple courtesy that should be extended to the senior commander.

Munson had continuous searchlight signals sent for *Tang* and *Pompon*, which was also in sight, to fall in astern. *Pompon* complied. O'Kane had no intention of giving an inch to Munson or, for that matter, to any "staff nitpickers" who might criticize the fuel consumed in his high-speed return. He wanted to "be able to depart on patrol again just that much sooner."

O'Kane instructed his signal man to respond to Munson with a continuous string of repeats, interrogatories, and verifies until *Tang* charged ahead and reached ten-ten dock first. But Lockwood understood this boorish act. He refused to board *Tang*, and waited for *Rasher*, conned by a furious Munson, to pull in. Then the admiral and his staff went aboard *Rasher* to congratulate Munson "for one of the greatest submarine patrols ever conducted."

For his part, O'Kane may have been jealous of Munson, already a full commander with two Navy Crosses to his one. Munson had graduated sixteenth in the 1932 Annapolis class, was a Rhodes scholar and a brilliant mathematician and had the height, physical bearing, and demeanor that commanded respect and loyalty.

As a submarine commander, O'Kane had nothing to be jealous about. Munson had "a reputation for driving his repair crews hard to get the boats refitted and back at sea as quickly as possible." *Rasher*'s average turnaround time between patrols was 27 days, roughly the staff goal. But *Tang*'s average was only 18 days. *Rasher*, a fine submarine, had been commissioned 4½ months ahead of *Tang* but had made only one more war patrol. Clearly nobody drove refit crews as hard as O'Kane.

Shark II, with John Griggs aboard, had arrived at Pearl Harbor five days before *Tang*, but O'Kane would nearly overtake Blakely in the refit cycle. The two submarines would depart on their next patrols one day apart. Griggs would not be going with *Shark*. He had made seven war patrols on multiple boats. On September 12 he was rotated to relief crew work at a new refit facility in Majuro. Griggs was tired and ready for a break. He also didn't care much for *Shark*'s CO, whom he found "aloof to all."

At San Diego Roger Paine received orders to report to *Tinosa*, then under refit at Hunter's Point, as the new executive officer. For a few days his skipper was Don Weiss, O'Kane's imagined competitor in the East China and Yellow Seas. Weiss was later replaced by Dick Latham as *Tinosa*'s new mission became clear. She would take the first production FM sonar unit into Nansei Shoto to map Japanese minefields. Paine was obviously a natural for this task.

Many of *Tinosa*'s crew had been aboard for all seven of her war patrols and believed that the U.S. refit was the end of the war for them, at least for a very long time. They hoped for, or dreamed of, an assignment to new construction, perhaps at the notoriously slow Cramp Shipbuilding in Philadelphia. Latham found the crew hostile to the FM gear and its obvious purpose. They felt this new, inexperienced skipper would get them all killed.

The crew's resistance intensified as *Tinosa* was sent to San Diego for mine detection training in the dummy minefield Paine had come to know so well. Bebe was pregnant again and very close to her delivery date. Paine "managed a couple of brief train trips south from San Francisco before the end of the overhaul and the beginning of our refresher training in San Diego." On September 12, the same day that Griggs transferred from *Shark*, Bebe gave birth to a baby girl. Refresher training in San Diego gave Roger a chance for a few glimpses of his new daughter.

As O'Kane feared and expected, but fully understood, after eleven war patrols Murray Frazee was to be transferred. Both men were "tired, exhausted, worn out," but O'Kane felt it was "nothing that a few days or possibly weeks would not rectify." Frazee, however, had had it. O'Kane recommended him for PCO school in New London, but that was not approved. Instead he was given thirty days' leave in the States and told to return to Pearl for a new assignment on the staff of ComSubTrainPac.

Frank Springer, who had been performing admirably as acting XO during the refit, was formally appointed second in command. At the top of the first "ninety-day wonder" class, Springer was the senior V-7 in the navy and one of the first reserve officers to attain such a position.

On September 22 Admirals Nimitz and now Vice Admiral Lockwood came aboard *Tang* to award the submarine a coveted Presidential Unit Citation, to give O'Kane his second Navy Cross and Frazee his third Silver Star. Frazee left for the mainland the following day. O'Kane had spent much of his political time during refit maneuvering to avoid assignment to a wolf pack. His wish was granted. On September 24 Lockwood came aboard, drank Walker's coffee, then caught the bowline as the submarine backed away from the dock. *Tang* sailed for Formosa, alone.

18

Fortune's Crest

The most successful patrol ever made by a U.S. submarine.

—Vice Admiral Charles A. Lockwood

The Pacific typhoon season struck early and hard in the fall of 1944. During the third week of September, before *Tang* departed Pearl Harbor, a number of boats already on patrol were fighting the weather as well as the Japanese.

Four days out of Midway and a few days ahead of *Tang*, *Sterlet* encountered a typhoon. Paul Schratz wrote later that the "beam end seas caused heavy rolling and pitching, making the bridge extremely wet and uncomfortable. One gigantic comber overwhelmed us and sent a twenty-five-inch pillar of solid green water down the hatch to the control room. . . . The bridge was an overflowing bathtub." This was just the beginning of weather impact on patrol operations.

On September 15 *Pampanito* encountered a crude group of life rafts crammed with surviving Australian and British prisoners of war, originally 2,100 in number, who had been adrift at sea for three days. These were the accidental victims of *Pampanito*'s and *Sealion*'s earlier depredations in Luzon Strait. The two submarines packed in 128 POWs and radioed for help.

Barb and *Queenfish,* ordered by Admiral Lockwood to proceed westward at flank speed to help in the rescue effort, encountered a rich war prize first: a modern convoy, escorted by destroyers employing the latest German radar and sonar and fully aware that U.S. submarines had already downed the POW ships. At convoy HI-74's center was the large fleet tanker *Azusa Maru* and the escort carrier *Unyo,* "Falcon of the Clouds." In a daring attack

Barb evaded the escorts and sank both ships before surfacing to resume her run to the POW raft area.

Gene Fluckey, *Barb*'s captain, was uneasy with the sea conditions. The sky "was unusually clear, the horizon too distinct, the air hot and oppressive . . . *Barb* carved the oily waves. The light breeze that had been slowly backing counterclockwise died. A long, low swell came from the southwest, barely rolling us . . . TYPHOON!"

On September 17, in steadily rising seas, *Queenfish* recovered eighteen wretched prisoners, *Barb* fourteen more. By then *Barb*, as Fluckey later wrote, "kept reducing speed as the waves pooped us, breaking over the stern. . . . We were down to four knots, barely enough to quarter the seas. The conning tower hatch was frequently slammed closed to avoid having water cascade below. The bridge became a bathtub as twenty-foot waves swept across us. . . . The bow came completely out of the water when we crested a gigantic wave. As we tipped over and plunged down, the propellers whirred when they broke the surface.

"With darkness, the rains came. In torrents. I felt the heavens were being flushed along with me." *Barb*'s OOD, a veteran of four patrols, was too seasick to stand watch. Still, Fluckey refused to dive, fighting it out on the surface, using the searchlight in a vain attempt to spot more survivors.

The prewar U.S. Navy had been dependent on weather reports from the now Japanese-held regions. That easy advantage was gone. But the Japanese still maintained a weather presence in the Pacific. *Barb*, now struggling toward Saipan with her terribly ill cargo of POWs, received a message on September 23 that direction finders (DFs) had located a Japanese weather ship close to her track. Why not sink it, and deprive the Japanese of some of this valuable information? *Barb* diverted but found only a patrol plane. Fluckey concluded that the navy had likely DF'd a weather plane, not a ship.

Early on the morning of September 27 *Tang* was approaching Midway. Floyd Caverly was wearing a kid's potty on his belt, his "retch receiver." For whatever reason, perhaps a sensitive inner ear, Caverly was especially vulnerable to seasickness when *Tang* was surfaced in brisk seas. *Tang* was in just that position now, perhaps from the remnants of the storm that had plagued *Sterlet*.

O'Kane had to make the decision to bypass Midway and go on patrol with the fuel on hand, a realistic option, or risk entering the dredged northbound channel with wind and seas from the south. O'Kane gambled and *Tang* ran in at surprisingly high speed, pushed along by the following seas which were accelerating on the shelving bottom. *Tang* yawed thirty degrees to each side of north as the helmsman struggled to dampen her motion. At the last moment, with O'Kane gritting his teeth, *Tang* steadied and shot up the center of the channel. Five hours later, tanks topped off, *Tang* was through the channel, pounding toward Formosa through heavy seas.

For the next three days *Tang* struggled through eight-foot waves at two-engine speed, in a determined effort to reach Formosa prior to Task Force 38's October 12 air strike. On September 30 the seas abated long enough for Caverly, and some other of the crew, to overcome their seasickness. A third engine went on line to make up some of the lost time.

An inspection of the boat was scheduled to make sure that *Tang* was ready for expected heavy weather, which would follow this temporary breather. O'Kane began his portion in the forward engine room. Taking a salute from his officers, he stepped forward, head held high, and plunged five feet through an open hatch into the lower half of the engine room.

It was a sharp, embarrassing fall, and O'Kane's left foot was broken by a ladder rung at the bottom of the pit. He was the farthest thing from a baby, but could not rise because of the pain and nausea. Sweating profusely, he was hauled up from below; then he hobbled to his cabin. Paul Larson, the chief pharmacist's mate, straightened the foot out—in effect, setting it— and told O'Kane it was now up to nature to fix.

For the next four days O'Kane was bedridden; Frank Springer ran the boat. Naturally O'Kane kibitzed mightily, issuing commands from the squawk box. On October 4 an Ultra arrived that pointed out the existence of a weather ship, just as *Barb* had been told two weeks earlier. O'Kane got up long enough to help Frank Springer plan an approach, but it was his intent to let Springer make the attack on this nearly stationary target, perhaps with a single torpedo, perhaps by deck gun.

By now the weather was foul again, and rapidly worsening. The barometer had fallen to 941 millimeters of mercury, already a class 4 on today's Saffir-Simpson scale, an "Extreme" classification. The long, easy swell from the southwest intensified as wind increased to fill the atmospheric vacuum. The waves soon caught up with the advancing wind velocity and began to grow exponentially, doubling in height every hour.

O'Kane lay in his bunk listening to the screaming wind and crashing seas on the Voycall. He ordered the lookouts below, leaving only Savadkin, the OOD, who was partially protected by the bridge cowling. But soon mountains of green water washed over the bridge, and *Tang* began sledding down the seas sideways. O'Kane ordered Savadkin below, the hatch sealed, engines stopped. *Tang* would run slowly before the storm on battery propulsion so the air-hungry diesels would not suck seawater through the manifolds. Ever hungry for combat, O'Kane would not order a dive. He was determined that his crew find the elusive Japanese weather ship by periscope search while *Tang* struggled on the surface.

Simply running before the storm was not enough to reduce its ghastly effects. *Tang* rolled horribly, dumping O'Kane over the guardrail on his bunk and onto the deck. Springer, whose prior experience had been on the battleship *Maryland*, had his hands full and called for assistance. Chief Larson went forward and injected a painkiller directly into O'Kane's foot. The ever caring Walker laced the broken foot tightly into a size 14 sand shoe, and O'Kane hobbled to the control room with Springer.

The moment they stepped over the watertight doorsill *Tang* rolled violently to starboard. O'Kane was thrown forward onto the high-pressure air manifold and saw that the inclinometer read an eye-popping seventy degrees. *Tang* had been knocked down by the storm and hung there, with no apparent righting moment. Thoughts of capsizing flooded O'Kane's mind and he involuntarily cried, "Jesus Christ, is she ever coming back?"

Springer, entangled in the open knife switches of the IC switchboard, responded with uncommon equanimity, "Sometimes they don't, you know!"

Gradually *Tang* began to right herself in spite of the blows from successive rollers. Both men could now make their way up into the conning tower. O'Kane's first sight through the periscope, its head fifty-five feet above the nominal water surface, was looking UP at a monstrous wave with breaking crests that instantly engulfed the scope in solid green seas. Repeated, quick exposures of the scope let *Tang* be maneuvered so that her stern was pointed directly into the wind. The oscillations now dampened to forty-five-degree rolls.

Tang should have dived long before and run under the storm, but that option was now foreclosed. Any attempt to dive now could be fatal. As the seawater tried to flood the tanks, *Tang* could be caught in a roll. Then the downside tanks would fill more rapidly than those facing the sky, accelerating the roll and capsizing the boat. They would have to tough it out. *Silversides*, not far away, had long since dived. She had been caught in a typhoon the previous year, and her crew remembered rolling twenty degrees even when submerged.

As the wind speed picked up, and O'Kane believed they were now blowing 150 knots, the fury of the waves, whose energy rises to the fourth power of wind speed, became breathtaking. The general rule of fluid dynamics is that an object in the water, in this case *Tang*, tends to do whatever the water it replaces would have done. There was no question but that they were caught in the wrong semicircle of this advancing storm. *Tang* was quite likely being pushed along at storm speed and might strike the Ryukus to the north. *Silversides* had been pushed into a landlocked harbor the prior year and narrowly escaped destruction. At the very least *Tang* could be carried along with the storm for days, and there wasn't enough battery power to endure that eventuality. They would have to turn into the seas and escape.

The turn would place *Tang* "beam-to" the heavy seas, with at least some waves nearly a hundred feet high, for at least thirty seconds. While a submarine sits low in the water, a definite help, any boat broadside to the waves is vulnerable to capsizing. Even aircraft carriers, with enormous power reserves to accelerate their turn, are at risk when they are beam-to heavy seas. *Tang* would have to make her maneuver quickly, with only battery power to spin the propellers.

Timing was everything, and O'Kane called the shots. As the boat temporarily returned to a twenty-five-degree heel, a following wave of manageable size could be seen through the scope. At full power the rudder was put hard over in a right turn. The turn was accelerated by the next wave, which struck the starboard quarter, rolling *Tang* horribly but twisting her in the right direction as well. Fortunately *Tang*'s low freeboard did not let the bow catch the wind, which would have driven her to leeward. The next wave caught *Tang* on the starboard bow and very nearly capsized her, but her turning momentum prevailed. Skillfully the helmsman met the oncoming waves, and *Tang* was steadied on the reverse course, bow facing the seas, moving away from the storm's direction of motion.

For five hours paired helmsmen, using the motors and props as well as the rudder, and coached by O'Kane and Springer on the scope, kept *Tang* on her new heading. "It was a wild, plunging roller coaster," O'Kane wrote later. And suddenly they were free of the worst of it. There were still torrential rains and monstrous swells, but *Tang* was pulling clear. Or were they? Could they possibly be heading into the eye of the storm?

An attempt was made to crack a hatch to obtain a new barometer reading. It was impossible. The hatch was sealed shut by the now higher atmospheric pressure outside, a good sign. High-pressure air was bled into the boat to equalize the pressure, and the hatch cracked. The new reading was 962 millibars, still a Saffir-Simpson category 4, but just barely. They had survived.

At 1700 O'Kane was confident enough to start the diesels. At dawn on October 7 the bridge watch was stationed, but Springer could not get navigational star shots till evening. They had been blown sixty miles off the position shown on the dead-reckoning indicator. A new course was plotted for Formosa, and *Tang* was on her way using four engines. The weather ship was forgotten.

Now O'Kane could reflect on the state of his foot and found it was much better. Larson's pain-killer had worn off, yet O'Kane felt no undue discomfort, and the tightly laced sand shoe was no longer tight. Walker now trussed him in a size 12 sand shoe to keep the compression going.

At noon on October 10 landfall was made on Formosa's high mountains. Using four engines, *Tang* left the Philippine Sea, made a semicircle around the northern coast of the island, and headed into the much calmer waters of Formosa Strait. Before 0400 on the eleventh her crew had a target in sight behind them, technically only two hours after reaching their patrol station.

O'Kane saw this ship as a 7,500-ton diesel freighter, a "big freighter," a "good-sized ship" making her way toward the Tamsui River, which led into the capital, Taipei. The speed of the target was high, 14 knots. The depth of the water was "good" for the captain, 120 feet. *Tang* ran on the surface with the target until past dawn, slowly letting the distance between them close.

With the sun beginning to rise, *Tang* dove to 45 feet, keeping the SJ radar antenna out of the water, watching for a zig, which occurred. O'Kane conned *Tang* in on a compensatory track, with Springer doing a superb job of managing the fire control party. O'Kane fired three fish with a torpedo run of only 570 yards. Two hit, and the boat sank virtually instantly. *Tang* surfaced at once and cruised through the wreckage, looking for survivors. There were none.

O'Kane had just sunk the small 1,658-ton freighter *Josho Maru*. Her sudden disappearance convinced the Japanese that she had struck a mine. They were not yet aware that *Tang* was in the strait. Springer had questions about the rapid sinking, perhaps suspicious of the target size estimate. But O'Kane was adamant. "She had only a few feet of freeboard and our torpedoes exploded at six feet below the waterline. They just plain blew out her side and the tops of her cargo holds, and engine spaces, too." It was settled. This was a good-sized ship for *Tang* to claim.

The submarine boldly cruised southwestward on the surface in the early-morning light, partially obscured by the high mountains, which still blocked the sunrise. O'Kane was looking for more game, but prudently let *Tang* slide beneath the waves when the first air patrol was sighted.

At noon, still on the eleventh, O'Kane went to the conning tower, where Hank Flanagan had just made a periscope search. "It's all clear, Captain," he said, only to have O'Kane spot the mast of a ship when he double-checked. This one could also be making for the Tamsui River. *Tang* followed at a relatively high underwater speed of seven knots, with the intent to make a night surface attack before the target could reach sanctuary.

O'Kane called off the details to the identification party, who reported that it was an Aden Maru class freighter of 5,824 tons. Surfacing at twilight in steep waves and flying spume, *Tang* slowly overtook the target. O'Kane conned her into position for a stern shot.

"Big and black," this "400-foot ship looked enormous . . ." he wrote years later. But he may have sensed she was actually much smaller. Only a single torpedo was fired, a distinct departure from O'Kane's usual practice, with a run of only 450 yards. "Her boilers . . . exploded . . . sending a pillar of fire and illuminated steam skyward. . . . [Few of the fire control party] saw much of the ship, for she sank almost immediately." He had just downed the tiny, 711-ton *Oita Maru*.

For the next twelve days *Tang* roamed between the Chinese mainland and Formosa, sometimes in response to Ultra tips, sometimes prepared to act as lifeguard for Task Force 38's air strikes, once in visual contact and fruitlessly chasing a high-speed cruiser, once a hospital ship, always avoiding new radar-equipped Japanese escorts. O'Kane tired from the prolonged time awake to complete the last two sinkings, and this constant searching exhausted him. Catch-up sleep was impossible when there was a possibility of sighting a carrier, or a Japanese task force, as Ultra informed him. He was still worn from the broken foot and the experience of the terrible typhoon. Quite rarely for him, he yearned for rest. "We'd all just as soon call off the war games for a day," he remembered thinking years later.

Eight hundred miles to the northeast, events were unfolding that were to engulf O'Kane and *Tang*. On October 18 a major Japanese convoy, MI-23, with fifteen merchant ships and seven escorts, departed Imari Bay near Sasebo, bound for Borneo. On October 20 they anchored in a bay off South Korea; by the twenty-second they were halfway to Formosa, anchoring at Shushan, east of Shanghai. They would be coming *Tang*'s way, hugging the China coast, by the twenty-fourth.

Meanwhile, on the night of October 22, with the first sweep of the SJ radar after it had been repaired, Caverly picked up a cluster of pips in the strait. The range was at 14,000 yards, and Savadkin had already turned *Tang* toward the contact by the time a newly awakened O'Kane reached the conning tower. This was convoy U-03, which O'Kane remembered as ten ships, half of which he expected to be escorts. It actually contained six ships, two of which were authentic destroyers, *Hasu* and *Tsuga*.

O'Kane weighed their options, involuntarily shuddering at the prospect of another night surface attack with its attendant requirement to penetrate an escort screen. But in the end, this course was chosen. The convoy was in midstrait with no quick escape to a shallow water haven, and the night offered the prospect of multiple strikes.

Walker, who had a standing call to be awakened anytime his captain was roused, was ready with the coffee as O'Kane maneuvered to avoid an exceptionally alert escort. Just after midnight of the twenty-third *Tang* penetrated the screen by stopping ahead of the convoy while it came on, zigzagging constantly. As the targets closed, the aggressive escort took off on a precautionary sweep, leaving a temporary hole. O'Kane pivoted the boat by going ahead two-thirds on the port propeller, while backing two-thirds on the starboard. He intended to put torpedoes into two columns of "large ships" whose "little freeboard . . . marked them as tankers," using both bow and stern tubes.

O'Kane opened fire at exceptionally close range, with five bow torpedoes fired at three ships in the starboard column. The Japanese reported that "at 0136 the second ship in the column, [the 1,915-ton] *Toun Maru*, was hit by a torpedo, [and] fires broke out. One minute later the [1,944-ton] vanguard ship *Tatsuju Maru* . . . was attacked. The first two tracks seen coming in from sixty degrees ahead to port were avoided, however another two missiles struck her stern in the region of the coal bunker. Her boilers and engine rooms were destroyed and steam gushed out. Flooding occurred and a few minutes later *Tatsuju Maru* sank with the loss of two soldier-passengers and five crewmen."

In the confusion of explosions that began almost immediately, O'Kane raced to the after part of the bridge to set up the stern shot. Focused on the new target, he was unaware that a transport from beyond the first column was coming in to ram. Chief Leibold yanked O'Kane's arm, pulling him away from the after TBT, and forced him to look at the oncoming transport menace. It was the 1,920-ton *Wakatake Maru*, the third ship in the column, which had spotted *Tang* about four hundred meters ahead on her port bow. The Japanese later wrote that "*Wakatake Maru* dashed forward at full speed with the intention of ramming."

There simply was no time to dive. Orders for flank speed were rung up, and *Tang* moved forward belching clouds of diesel smoke, but it was not enough to get clear. O'Kane thought the transport was going to plow into *Tang*'s port side just behind the conning tower. The sound of small-arms fire from the Japanese crew was audible, adding to the confusion.

In desperation O'Kane screamed for left full rudder, hoping at least to avoid a direct hit from the sharp bow of the oncoming transport. *Tang* pivoted nicely and the two antagonists, as O'Kane remembered, scraped by each other, close enough to pass hand lines between ships. The Japanese gave the encounter a bit more space, reporting that "when the distance had closed to 100 meters, the enemy turned away to port and successfully evaded. . . ."

Now came the order to clear the bridge in preparation for a crash dive. But O'Kane, the last man to go below, believed he saw that a transport, in disorder, was going to strike *Wakatake Maru*. He immediately counter-manded the order. "Hold her up! Hold her up!' he screamed, and *Tang* bobbed back to the surface after only her decks had been awash.

Returning to the after TBT, O'Kane called out a quick setup on the two entangled Japanese merchantmen. Four torpedoes were fired into the con-fused mess. At 0140, the Japanese reported, two of them struck *Wakatake Maru*, the first in "the rear part of her engine room . . . on the port side. Twenty seconds later, a second torpedo hit amidships. *Wakatake Maru* quickly broke in two and forty seconds later disappeared," taking "128 men of a salvage unit, 7 other passengers, 11 ship's gunners, and 30 crewmen" with her. This snapshot stern salvo also appears to have hit and sunk the 1,339-ton *Kori Go*. *Tang* sped away past the bewildered escorts, who were now shooting at each other in confusion.

O'Kane was absolutely convinced he had sunk three large tankers, a transport, and a freighter. At some risk to his boat, he circled the area of the sinkings to confirm his impressions and found nothing afloat. In fact, he had done extraordinarily well, low JANAC credit notwithstanding. He was far too high on his tonnage estimates, but he had destroyed all four cargo-carrying ships in the convoy. The small tanker *Toun Maru* had not gone down immediately, but burned out and drifted ashore on the Pescadores, where it was abandoned.

O'Kane and Springer conferred. There was likely to be little traffic in the center of Formosa Strait for the next several days. Perhaps it was time to head to the shallow waters of Turnabout Island, immediately off the coast of mainland China. O'Kane discounted the possibility of minefields in the area because of disruptive typhoon activity and because he incorrectly believed that "the sea, though shallow, was much too deep for magnetic mines."

And so it was that at 2242 on the night of October 24, south of Turnabout Island, *Tang* detected southbound convoy MI-23, which had passed Gyoshan To at 2030. The Japanese escorts were extremely jumpy, having dropped depth charges on a phantom submarine contact six hours before. But *Tang* moved in undetected toward the projected attack point off Oksu Island. O'Kane later remembered that there were fourteen large pips and twelve smaller ones, twenty-six ships in all, on the radarscope. It was actu-ally seventeen ships, since three transports and two escorts had peeled off earlier to cross the East China Sea to Takao. But it was still one of the largest convoys he had ever seen.

At 2315 *Coast Defense Ship 46* detected the oncoming submarine. By blinker light and short bursts of antiaircraft fire it advised the rest of the formation of the contact. The *Japanese Wartime Ships History* records that all ships "made a simultaneous right turn and headed away at full speed." This brought the formation even closer to the China coast, and the hoped-for protection of shallow water. But the signaling searchlights illuminated the convoy for O'Kane and *Tang*'s bridge watch, helping them select the best candidates for attack, the first of which was a large, three-decked transport.

Just after midnight on October 25, at 0008 local time, the seven thousand-ton *Ebara Maru* took a torpedo hit in the port side near the stern. The engine room was destroyed, and she shuddered to a stop.

What O'Kane remembered as happening next does not precisely conform to the Japanese convoy accounts but remains an epic battle. O'Kane reported a full bow salvo at three different targets, followed by a gradual, then a hard right turn of *Tang* to bring the stern tubes to bear on two additional ships. He was enormously excited, as who would not be, by the streaks of metal flying his way, "a holocaust of antiaircraft and horizontal gunfire . . ." that started before the first torpedo struck home.

O'Kane believed that all six torpedoes found their intended targets as he heard "a slow-motion string of monstrous firecrackers." Range corrections were coming in from Frank Springer, and from this close distance "on near ninety-degree tracks, verifying bearings were unnecessary. Neither was there time, for salvos from the escorts . . . were splashing uncomfortably close."

In this violent arena O'Kane now saw "coming into my binoculars' field of view from the right was the bow of a large destroyer escort, or perhaps a full-fledged destroyer." The oncoming enemy ship fired "a well-placed large-caliber salvo," which must have affected O'Kane's concentration. *Tang*'s stern tubes were fired with two hits, O'Kane believed, the second completely obliterating the DE.

In fact, there was no DE or destroyer accompanying convoy MI-23, only small coast defense ships and patrol boats. But the 7,024-ton *Matsumoto Maru* had turned toward *Tang* to ram just after *Ebara Maru* took the first torpedo. *Matsumoto Maru* had two machine-gun mounts on the bridge, and they were blazing away at the submarine. The Japanese reported that "by bad luck one of the torpedoes . . . struck the onrushing *Matsumoto Maru*'s no. 1 hold. Immediately her bow plunged under and she came to a halt." O'Kane could see that the last target "was at least stopped."

This same attack also seems to be the one in which the Japanese reported that "a second torpedo struck [*Ebara Maru*'s] no. 3 hold, violent flooding ensued, and she started to go down by the stern with a starboard list. Soon her bow stood up at an angle of about sixty degrees, she sank at about 0020 with a loss of eleven of her crew and three of her guard force."

Confusion reigned. The Japanese were absolutely certain that multiple submarines were involved. False sonar contacts were abundant, as were the depth charges that rained down on them. But *Tang* had moved seaward to load her last two torpedoes to finish off the cripple.

19

Catastrophe

All tragedies are finish'd by death.

—Lord Byron, "Don Juan"

With the final two torpedoes loaded in tubes 5 and 6, *Tang* moved in to finish off the damaged, now-stopped transport. Floyd Caverly, operating the SJ radar in the conning tower, called out "range: fifteen hundred yards." *Tang*'s speed was reduced to dead slow. This would be a classic ninety-degree shot, with no fire control problems to solve. Slowly the range closed. At nine hundred yards O'Kane, on the bridge, gave the order to fire. It was 0230 on October 25, 1944.

The first torpedo, the next-to-last on *Tang*, shot from the tube straight at the transport, its wake clearly visible in the phosphorescent sea. Again "Fire," and Frank Springer's palm struck the firing plunger for the final shot. In the conning tower Larry Savadkin heard someone call out "Let's head for the barn."

But torpedo 24, like a crazed porpoise, broached immediately in front of *Tang*'s bow. It turned sharply left and repeatedly broke the surface, leaping in and out of the water as it circled back toward the submarine.

"All ahead emergency! Right full rudder!" O'Kane screamed. *Tang* began to turn, but acceleration of fifteen hundred tons of surfaced submarine is not instantaneous. The deadly torpedo came abeam and started in for the kill at a speed approaching thirty knots. "Left full rudder!" O'Kane called, desperately trying to swing *Tang*'s stern away from the murderous weapon, now turned against her. He thought it would be close.

In the forward torpedo room a jubilant Pete Narowanski had just finished venting the tube. He slammed his fist into the palm of his left hand and called out "Hot dog, course zero nine zero, head her for the Golden Gate!"

In the after engine room nineteen-year-old Jesse DaSilva, not normally a coffee drinker, had just received a watch relief. He was on his way forward, had passed through the crew's quarters, and had one leg in the mess area when the torpedo hit the stern.

The Mark 18 torpedo, carrying 565 pounds of Torpex, slammed into *Tang's* after torpedo room, near the maneuvering room bulkhead, with indescribable violence. On the bridge O'Kane saw the tops blow off the after ballast tanks. Throughout the boat high-pressure lines were ruptured and deck plates lifted. Inside, men were thrown against sharp, hard-metal edges of tables and bulkheads. As far forward as the control room, severe injuries occurred for anyone not holding on to something solid: John Accardy fell through the open hatch from the conning tower, breaking his arm when he struck the control room deck; another man's leg was broken; the chief of the boat, Bill Ballinger, was knocked unconscious; and Lieutenant (J. G.) Mel Enos's head was split and bleeding. Jesse DaSilva grabbed the ladder leading to the access hatch to steady himself as *Tang* was whipped violently "like a giant fish grabbed by the tail." He had heard no alarm.

The sternmost three compartments, including the after engine room just vacated by DaSilva, flooded instantly, drowning everyone not killed outright in the explosion. Mortally wounded, *Tang* sank by the stern like a great pendulum, bow in the air, stern resting on the bottom some 140 to 180 feet below.

As the water rushed toward the bridge O'Kane cried out "Close the hatch!" followed by "Do we have any propulsion?" Floyd Caverly jumped up the ladder from the radar to deliver the report. With that, the water swept over the bridge, washing O'Kane, the OOD Lieutenant (J. G.) John Heubeck, Chief Bill Leibold, and Caverly into the sea. There were also four lookouts topside, but as the boat suddenly fell backward they were tossed against the periscope shears. Entangled in the customized guardrails around the lookouts' platform, none reached the surface. Leibold remembered lookout Charles Andriolo in a death grip on the rail as they both plunged below the surface of the sea. Leibold was conscious of being deep under water, rigid with fear, when a second "explosion," likely *Tang's* stern hitting bottom, knocked him free.

After reaching the surface Leibold struggled to breathe, paddling slowly.

Initial Position: Sunken Tang

1 - Flanagan
2 - Narowanski
3 - Trukke
4 - Savadkin
5 - Decker
6 - DaSilva

X = torpedo impact point
[shaded] flooded compartments

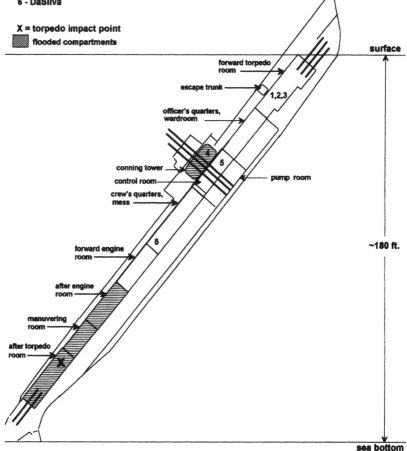

In the pitch darkness he could see no one else till John Heubeck swam by him in "a beautiful Australian crawl," headed for *Tang*'s bow, which still jutted out of the water. Heubeck was never seen again. Leibold could hear the voices of Sidney Jones and Darrell Rector yelling back and forth to each other. Then, silence. Now the utter loneliness began to frighten Leibold. He was overjoyed when he encountered Floyd Caverly, a poor swimmer, thrashing in the sea. Caverly gasped that he could not swim. Leibold, not wanting to lose his companion, said "Hell, you can float!" Soon the two of them were doing just that, floating, trying to conserve energy, waiting for daybreak.

Perhaps eight men were left inside the conning tower after Caverly's exit and Accardy's fall. Savadkin, responding to O'Kane's propulsion inquiry, stepped away from the TDC to look at the pit log. Simultaneously the lights went out and water began to pour through the open hatch. The conning

OCTOBER 25, 1944. Bill Leibold was washed from the bridge into the sea when *Tang* was sunk. He swam for hours and was rescued by the Japanese, spending ten months in a POW camp. (Courtesy William R. Leibold)

tower lurched backward as *Tang* sank by the stern. The sea poured through the open hatch, drowning at least five men, including Frank Springer.

In pitch darkness Savadkin held on to the no. 2 periscope shaft as men and loose equipment swirled by him in the rush of water. He instinctively rose up along the periscope shaft and found an air bubble just large enough for his nose and mouth in an indenture where the scope passed through the hull. *Tang* was quiet now, and Savadkin was totally disoriented. In the blackness he believed that *Tang* was upside down; to follow the scope upward would trap him in the pump room.

Savadkin gasped for air in the tiny bubble, thinking of his wife and parents. Where was he? He had to position himself. Nose pressed against the cork insulation, he took a last breath and ducked out, treading water, groping for a familiar object. Suddenly he hit a larger air bubble; his whole head and face were out of the water. His hand touched the engine room telegraph handle, then the bridge ladder with its encircling trunk. He hoped that there would be another air pocket above him, since the hatch opened up beneath the overhanging bridge cowling. Gambling, he pushed off and swam free of the conning tower tomb.

Savadkin's luck held. In utter darkness he popped out of the water into an air pocket below the cowling. Startled, he heard another human voice ask: "Who is it?" Bergman, the sonar operator posted beside the TDC, also had made it into this fast-disappearing haven.

"Do you know where we are? What are you going to do?" asked Bergman. Savadkin replied that they had to get out and reach the surface. He volunteered to help Bergman: "Hold on to my legs." With Bergman in tow, Savadkin ducked under the cowling and pushed for the surface. Bergman, possibly confused, possibly dreading to leave the air pocket for the long ascent, let go. He was never seen again.

Savadkin swam for the surface with both hands. Believing he was at least fifty feet underwater, he continuously exhaled to ease the pressure on his lungs. Just as he had nearly reached his limit, he burst free. Savadkin also tried to swim toward *Tang*'s bow, which was submerged as far as the anchor windlass, the forward torpedo room hatch underwater. He needed something to hang on to, if only for a minute. But the current was against him, and he knew he had to adopt an energy-conserving strategy if he were to live.

In San Diego Savadkin had attended survival school, where he learned the trick of turning long trousers into a life preserver of sorts. Unlike the other officers, who wore shorts, Savadkin preferred long pants. This bit of sartorial choice saved his life. He successfully made his jury-rig preserver and floated, shivering—alone in the night. His cries unanswered, Savadkin thought he was the only survivor.

OCTOBER 25, 1944. Ed Bergman escaped from *Tang's* flooded conning tower, but drowned in his attempt to reach the surface. (Courtesy William R. Leibold)

When *Tang's* open conning tower hatch dipped below the waves, the rushing water poured through into the control room as well. In the mad scramble the hatch to the conning tower was closed, perhaps by an escapee from above, but the wooden handle of the lanyard caught in the hatch seat. It would not seal firmly. Water continued to stream in and after a few minutes reached the lighting motor generators.

Mel Enos had shaken off the blow to his head and instructed the men with him to try to blow the tanks dry to raise the stricken submarine. It was hopeless.

In the after part of the boat the watertight door between the engine rooms had been closed, but not before the forward engine room was badly flooded. Water poured over the sill of the control room door into the crew's mess. DaSilva and two others struggled to close the half-ton watertight door between compartments, forcing it upward against the rush of high-pressure air and incoming water. They succeeded, sealing themselves and fifteen to twenty others into compartments with no escape hatch.

There were about ten men in the forward torpedo room, and they could hear air being vainly blown into the ballast tanks. Further, they could also distinctly hear the sea outside lapping against the sides of their compartment. It might be possible to escape through the torpedo tubes; it had been done before, when *S-48* sank in 1921. However, the Japanese were still depth charging in the area. The trapped men feared that the protruding bow would soon be discovered and shelled. Leland Weekley, the chief torpedoman, crawled up into the escape trunk and opened its lower hatch—the only other way out of *Tang*.

Back in the flooding control room, a last attempt to blow the ballast tanks, heard in the torpedo room, was tried. The effort failed; the enormous flooding damage to *Tang* could not be overcome. Clayton Decker believed the only hope of escape was via the forward torpedo room escape trunk. He reasoned that a successful breakout would not be possible with *Tang* at such a sharp up-angle. There was no hydraulic pressure left in the boat, but Decker opened vent no. 2 with sheer brute strength. Air began to bleed out of the forward ballast tanks, and *Tang*'s bow began to settle. The possibility of escape via the torpedo tubes was gone.

Now those in the control room began to move forward. Decker virtually attached himself to Chief Ballinger, whom he greatly respected. Ballinger had made five war patrols on *Tunny* before coming to *Tang* as chief of the boat. Decker believed Ballinger was the perfect cool, experienced head for this terrible predicament. Wherever Ballinger went, Decker wanted to be with him. They immediately encountered Mel Enos, who was in the officers' quarters area burning codebooks in a metal wastebasket. Ballinger stopped him and dropped below into the forward battery compartment, where the codebooks were immersed in battery acid.

At about 0245, roughly fifteen minutes after the sinking, the first party of about fifteen men, including Ballinger, Decker, Enos, and the ship's steward, Howard Walker, joined the men already present in the torpedo room. The difference in air pressure between compartments literally blew the newcomers through the watertight door, which was dogged again. Hank Flanagan and Ballinger began to issue Momsen lung personal escape devices and life jackets. Flanagan, who was originally an enlisted graduate of the submarine school, gave a refresher course on the use of the lung, along with the necessary cautionary advice.

It was quickly apparent that half the men had no idea how to use the escape devices. In the urgent press to churn out new submariners, escape tank training was no longer required at submarine school. Some of these young men had made short escapes from ten-foot depths. But the long ascent that now faced them, under adverse physical conditions, was a very different matter. There were also disagreements about how to operate the escape trunk, especially since ruptured air lines made it impossible to blow the chamber clear of water after use; it had to be drained into the steadily filling bilge.

DaSilva and the twenty or so men trapped in the galley area also had to reach the torpedo room to have any hope of escape. To do this they would have to pass through the control room. The eye port in the watertight door was already flooded, but a check of the ventilation piping via the bulkhead flapper showed no sign of water; there was likely at least *some* air in the control room. They would have to risk opening the door again.

But first they got ready for the expected rush of seawater. DaSilva opened the lower-deck freezer locker to act as a sump for the flood. Most men climbed on top of the mess tables to keep from being swept away. Gambling they were right, the others cracked the door. Water rushed past, but stabilized; the men were able to make a knee-deep transit through the slowly flooding control room. DaSilva was relieved to see that the high-pressure air tank was fully charged. The stored air meant suffocation was still hours away.

The men making their way from the after part of the boat found the watertight door between the battery and torpedo rooms closed. The voice communication systems between compartments was out of action, and men on both sides tried to signal their intent to each other by tapping. Torpedoman Hayes Trukke knew that broken high-pressure air lines meant that there was an enormous pressure difference between compartments. He and Walker tried to convey the idea that the door should be opened slowly to equalize the pressure.

But those now caught in the battery room, having already escaped one trap, feared they were being purposely blocked; they pushed with all their strength. They were aided by a level boat and the two-hundred-pound-per-square-inch air-pressure tanks that had been released into the compartment. The door blew open, smashing Walker full in the face, splitting his lips, breaking his nose and flattening it to one side, and blackening his eyes.

It was now about 0315. Between forty and forty-five survivors, at least two with broken limbs, were now packed into a narrow semicircular compartment whose usable length was less than thirty feet. Pharmacist's Mate Paul Larson was caring for the wounded with emergency supplies stored in the torpedo room. The air was foul from heat and smoke, some from runaway bow plane rigging motors that had run uncontrollably until finally burning out. The lights were gradually dimming as seawater found its way to the batteries, shorting out cells one by one. Still, most of the survivors seemed confident that they would escape; some intended to make their way to the China coast, ten miles away.

A disagreement over escape alternatives now occurred. Mel Enos believed that *Tang* might yet be blown to the surface. If that failed, it still might be possible for some crew to escape via the gun access hatch. With a party of six men he started for the control room. When the watertight door leading from the torpedo room was cracked, a blast of black smoke poured in, probably from a battery fire. The smell of burning insulation and rubber sickened many men; some vomited. The alternative escape attempt was abandoned, but the damage was done. The air was now so foul from chemical smoke that the Momsen lungs had to be intermittently used just to avoid gagging. The lights failed; battle lanterns were used but made only a feeble glow in the smoky compartment.

At 0330, about an hour after the sinking, the first escape party was organized. There were to be three escapees: Mel Enos, armed with two pistols, bandoleers of ammunition, and a bayonet; Bill Ballinger; and Torpedoman First Class (TM1c) John Fluker. A rubber life raft, in lieu of a fourth escapee, was jammed in beside them. The hatch to the torpedo room was closed below them, and the escapees locked inside the trunk. The plan was to don lungs, flood the chamber, open the side door to the outside, and escape up a buoyed rope to the surface. The last man out would tap on the hull. The men trapped inside the torpedo room would then close the exterior door with an interior lever, drain the accumulated water from the escape trunk into the bilges, and reopen the lower hatch for the next try.

Things immediately went wrong. Precious time slipped away as the men argued over the mechanics of escape trunk operation. As the trunk flooded, the great sea pressure proved to be exceedingly difficult to endure. Breathing became panting, voices became high-pitched and surrealistically squeaky. Air was compressed in the escape trunk as the water became the piston in the cylinder; the temperature climbed; senses were blurred. It was maddeningly difficult just to think how to attach the buoy to the escape line in the tightly jammed trunk. Mel Enos bolted, diving out the side door into the superstructure without waiting for the line to be rigged. He was never seen again, perhaps dragged to the bottom by the weight of armament on his body. Forty minutes had passed since the escape attempt had begun.

Inside the torpedo room, Flanagan could not imagine what had gone wrong. He closed the external door and drained the trunk. Still inside were Ballinger and Fluker—and the rubber boat. Ballinger was near exhaustion, but willing to try again. Fluker needed to rest first; the first aura of probable death entered the trapped men's minds.

Flanagan decided to personally lead the second attempt, which was started at about 0415. Dumping the rubber boat, five men were jammed into the trunk: Flanagan, Ballinger, Decker, Ensign Basil Pearce, and—there is some disagreement here—Weekley. Decker's friend George Zofcin tended to Decker. As the new Momsen lung was slipped over Decker's head, Zofcin noted a wire packaging clip on the lung's discharge valve and removed it. Decker pleaded with Zofcin to come with him. They were close; even their wives shared the same apartment in Richmond, California. Zofcin declined. He didn't know how to swim. Decker tried to persuade him that he could use the Momsen lung as a flotation device. "Maybe I'll try it later," said Zofcin, and turned away.

This time in the chamber, Ballinger took control. As the water flooded in and reached shin level, he had Decker duck under and test his Momsen lung operation. Decker was instructed to deploy the escape buoy, and counted knots on the line as the soccer-ball-size float headed for the surface. No one noticed that the unraveling line had pinned Flanagan to the wall of the trunk. Decker cut the line free from the spool and tied it in several locations, including the first rung of the escape ladder.

Then Ballinger gave the nod to Decker, who went out the side door and up the rope. His ascent was smooth, and he could see the water growing lighter as he neared the top. He broke the surface, wiping blood from his face. Superficial blood vessels in his nose and cheeks had burst from the pressure change, but there was no pain. A few minutes later Ballinger broke the surface, screaming. His nose clamp was off, his mouthpiece out. He was in mortal agony, two to three feet away, and Decker was afraid to touch him, afraid he would be pulled under by Ballinger's pained grasping. Decker later came to believe that Ballinger's Momsen lung discharge valve may also have been clipped shut. Unnoticed, it would have caused a lung embolism.

In the torpedo room below, another forty minutes had passed with no signal to those waiting their turn. It was now nearing 0500. The men in line pressed their ears to the side of the escape trunk. Moaning voices could be heard. Once again the exterior door was closed and the trunk drained.

Inside the escape trunk Hank Flanagan was unconscious. He was cut free from the escape line, carried to a bunk, and covered. Pearce was also still in the trunk. He was badly shaken and announced he would make no further attempt to escape. Determination to break out began to wane; discipline began to fray. It was now impossible to get the men to stop talking when Japanese ships passed over. Many took to the bunks, including George Zofcin. Only those determined to escape stayed on their feet, working for themselves.

Acrid smoke continued to seep into the compartment through a devious route: from the sinks in the officers' quarters above the burning battery, it was pressure-driven into the sanitary tank, then through the sink drain in the torpedo room. Cutoff valves were closed, to no avail. Even wooden plugs hammered into the drain did not stop the deadly smoke. Meanwhile, the Japanese escorts on the surface made a new depth-charge attack on the sunken *Tang*. The men were badly shaken, though no serious damage was done. During the attack the men could not speak or move for fear of making noise detectable by the enemy. Tensions rose as the air grew fouler.

Lacking an officer, Hayes Trukke organized the third attempt. Four enlisted men went into the trunk: Fluker (his second try), Pete Narowanski, Trukke, and a fourth motor machinist's mate (MoMM) unknown to the eventual survivors. This was not Narowanski's first brush with death. Two years before, he had been in the surface navy when a German U-boat torpedoed his ship, *Hugh L. Scott*, off Casablanca. He had survived that sinking; he was determined to survive this one.

Since the buoy line had been cut to free Flanagan, they expected to have to free-float to the surface. A souvenir life ring, retrieved from a Japanese ship sunk earlier, was taken along so the survivors would have something to cling to. After flooding the trunk there was a problem freeing the outer hatch, which finally yielded to their hammering. It was then discovered that the oxygen used to charge the Momsen lungs was depleted. Trukke knew that oxygen was not critical to the escape; filling the artificial lung with their own breath would suffice. Still, the others hesitated. Fifteen minutes had passed since they entered the escape trunk, some of the time spent in attaching the life ring to the escape line, which they later learned that Decker had providentially secured outside the trunk.

Trukke was dizzy, close to passing out. He ducked out of the trunk carrying the ring attached to the escape line and began to rise rapidly. Narowanski jerked on the line as a signal to slow down, dislodging Trukke's Momsen lung. He continued to free-float to the surface, exhaling all the way to equalize the pressure of the air expanding in his own lungs. He reached the bright sunlit surface exhausted, sick, and vomiting, to join Decker. Trukke was to live.

In the sunken *Tang* Narowanski closed the exterior hatch and rapped on the trunk as a signal to start drainage. Fluker and the unknown MoMM were through. Stepping down into the torpedo room, they announced they would not try again. Narowanski stayed in the trunk and asked that the last oxygen valve be opened so that Momsen lungs could be charged from inside the trunk. He was going to make a second attempt.

Hank Flanagan was now awake. On his feet again, he joined the fourth escape party being organized by Narowanski. Smoke from the battery fires in the adjacent compartment was now beginning to seep around the seal of the watertight door; paint was blistering and peeling on the bulkheads from the intense heat.

Jesse DaSilva, standing near the torpedo tubes, was attracted by the activity underneath the escape trunk hatch and moved beneath it. Flanagan called down for two more men. "Hell, I'm not afraid to try" said DaSilva to his friend, who refused to go and was replaced by another volunteer. In the torpedo room most men were now lying in bunks, talking quietly about their families and loved ones. Some seemed unconscious.

As Narowanski began to flood the trunk, the sharp increase in air pressure sent stabbing pain through everyone's ears. They held their noses and blew in an attempt to equalize the pressure. The temperature in the trunk soared, breathing became a shallow pant—which induced feelings of suffocation panic, and voices rose in pitch as the men squeaked words to each other.

Narowanski went out first, making it to the surface without incident, followed at three-minute intervals by Flanagan and DaSilva. The fourth man did not appear. The five survivors now on the surface held on to the buoy and recovered their strength.

Existence of a fifth escape attempt was flagged when Larson suddenly broke the surface, blood spurting from his nose; he was unconscious. The men took turns holding his head above water so he would not drown. Five minutes later Walker broke the surface, more than fifty feet away. He had lost his grip on the line and was not wearing a lung. His ruined nose must have presented a practical obstacle to pressure relief in the trunk and precluded a proper fit of the lung clips. DaSilva, a good swimmer, started toward him. Walker was in agony, and his arms flailed for a few moments; then his head sank in the water and he drifted away—probably the victim of an air embolism. Struggling against the current, DaSilva barely made it back to safety.

Six men were now clustered around the rescue buoy and the life ring which had been tied to it. They could see the coast of China, and the wreckage of the Japanese ships they had sunk the previous night. About a mile away the masts of two ships protruded from the water, along with the bow of a third. Some thought was given to the idea of swimming to the wrecks, but the tidal current and their weakened condition ruled that out. They waited for rescue.

Larry Savadkin had been floating for hours, replenishing his homemade pants life preserver with air every fifteen minutes or so. During this time the Japanese surface patrols made several depth-charge runs on *Tang*. Savadkin anticipated the explosion of each charge by arching his back out of the water. In the darkness he tried to swim west, but his in his condition he could not steer by the stars and was pushed in circles by the current.

As it grew light, Savadkin could make out both the China coast and the searching Japanese ships. At first he tried to avoid being seen. By 1000 he was suffering from hypothermia and knew that he must be picked up to live. He began to yell and splash water; the crew of the Japanese escort *P-34* spotted him, and he was hauled aboard.

About thirty minutes later the *P-34*, sweeping for Japanese survivors in whaleboats, came across Leibold and Caverly. They had been floating and paddling nonstop for eight hours. The Japanese crew were puzzled at these Caucasian faces. Apparently there had been Germans aboard the convoy's ships; their rescuer asked them a question that contained the word "Deutsche." "Hell, they think we're Germans," said Caverly, who turned to his rescuer and said, "Heil Hitler."

Temporarily satisfied, the Japanese continued their search and spotted Dick O'Kane swimming gamely toward the China coast. As the whaleboat pulled alongside, Leibold said, "Good morning, Captain. Do you want a ride?" The Japanese crew understood the word "Captain." As soon as Leibold and Caverly hauled him out, O'Kane was placed in the stern sheets of the whaleboat. The Japanese had tumbled to the identity of their captives.

Finally the knot of men clustered around the rescue buoy were spotted. Larson was in desperate shape, convulsing. The Japanese slapped his face in an effort to revive him, then threw him into the sea. The other five were hauled aboard and transferred to *P-34*. There all nine received their first beatings and began ten months of hellish captivity. All would narrowly survive.

For *Tang* and its crew, the war was over. At war's end every single officer, living or dead, was decorated with the Silver Star, Navy Cross, or, in O'Kane's case, the Congressional Medal of Honor. Every enlisted man known to have reached the surface after the sinking also was awarded the Silver Star—save one: the "negro steward" Howard Walker, who received no commendation.

20

Submarine Sweep

> . . . the iron hand of fate.
>
> *—Kipling, "An American"*

Tang did not sink without trace, the fate of so many submarines. The same codebreakers who knew that *Ebara Maru* went under also knew that *Tang* was down—and that there were survivors, including Dick O'Kane. The news was ordered tightly held because of the risk of exposing the incredible secret that the Japanese naval codes had been broken.

But the word leaked out. Ned Beach wrote in 1946, without attribution, for the naval code secret was maintained for another quarter century, that "after a few months some rather odd stories began to be bruited about. . . . But all stories seemed to agree on three particulars—great damage to the enemy, shallow water, and Dick O'Kane in a Jap prison camp!"

Murray Frazee learned the news as soon as he returned to Pearl Harbor from his California leave. "I was told very confidentially by a senior officer, who got the word from the intelligence staff at commander in chief, Pacific, that the *Tang* had been sunk by her own torpedo, only nine of the eighty-seven-man crew survived, and that O'Kane was a prisoner of war." He wanted desperately to tell Ernestine, but did not. "All I could do was bite my tongue. . . . If the Japanese ever suspected that [we were breaking their codes], they would have changed everything, and we would be back at square one. So Ernie O'Kane . . . had to suffer."

Tang was not the only submarine lost during the third week of October. *Escolar*, so long delayed by the slow construction cycle and shoddy workmanship at the Cramp yard, finally had departed Pearl Harbor on

September 18, six days before *Tang*. Fertig Krause, long O'Kane's trusted enlisted sideman on *Wahoo*, now served a new skipper, "Moke" Millican, the bantamweight fighter who had done so well on *Thresher*, then run afoul of Admiral Christie in 1943, and replaced because of his written criticism of U.S. torpedoes.

Millican now had a second chance under Admiral Lockwood, and led a wolf pack named after himself: "Millican's Marauders." On October 17 Millican reported to his packmates in the East China Sea that he was on his way into the dangerously mined Tsushima Strait, the southern entrance to the Inland Sea. And then *Escolar* vanished. Krause's luck, and that of every man aboard *Escolar*, ran out—perhaps on the same day as *Tang*'s. Lockwood was certain that *Escolar* had struck a mine, and bore down ever harder on the experiments being done aboard *Tinosa*.

Dave McClintock, who had been OOD of *Plunger* when she was strafed by the Japanese float plane on December 7, was now *Darter*'s commanding officer. On October 21 McClintock and *Darter* were roaming the shoal waters of Balabac Strait looking for any Japanese fleet units that might be on the move to repulse the American landing on Leyte.

Darter made contact with several Japanese warships moving at a speed so high that she could only radio their oncoming rush to headquarters. Early on the morning of October 23, patrolling literally side-by-side with *Dace*, with whom she had rendezvoused, *Darter* picked up a slow-moving radar contact. McClintock and *Dace*'s CO exchanged quick plans by megaphone, and *Darter* was off on the chase.

At 0533 McClintock put four torpedoes into the flagship of Vice Admiral Kurita's main body, the heavy cruiser *Atago*, forcing Kurita, his flag, and the emperor's portrait to transfer to the destroyer *Kishinami*. In the same attack McClintock sent two more torpedoes into the cruiser *Takao*, which was slightly larger than *Atago*. The torpedoes blew off *Takao*'s rudder and two propellers and flooding three boiler rooms. *Dace*, not to be outdone, sank the heavy cruiser *Maya* with four devastating torpedo hits. Two hours earlier, *Bream* had severely damaged the heavy cruiser *Aoba* with two hits. These four attacks, with their attendant need to divert escorts for the cripples, were a stunning, ruinous, early blow to the Japanese attack force in what became the decisive Battle of Leyte Gulf.

Darter lay doggo for a few hours until McClintock discovered that *Takao* was not sunk like *Atago* and *Maya*, only damaged. *Takao* was surrounded by destroyers who were attempting to salvage her. McClintock struggled unsuccessfully to get *Darter* in position for a day shot. After dark he made an end-around at seventeen knots to get into firing position. His navigator, who had not made a position fix for more than a day, was confident of their location, based primarily on the dead-reckoning indicator. But there were strong currents in Balabac Strait.

At 0005 on October 25, while *Tang* was making her attack on *Ebara Maru*, *Darter* slammed so hard onto Bombay Shoal she completely left the water and lay fully aground like some gigantic, stranded fish. The XO could not believe it, continuing to insist to McClintock that "the nearest land is nineteen miles away." *Darter* was a total loss. McClintock and the crew were ultimately saved by *Dace*.

Nine hundred miles to the north, in Luzon Strait, and due south of *Tang*, *Shark II* was on her third patrol. On that same October 24 her packmate, *Seadragon*, received a radio message from Ed Blakely that *Shark*, the pack leader, had spotted a lone freighter and was going in to attack. The freighter was either not alone, or Blakely made an identification error. The Japanese destroyer *Harukaze* detected *Shark* and began dropping depth charges. On her second run the sound contact was unusually good, and *Harukaze* dropped a string of seventeen. A great deal of "bubbles, heavy oil, clothes, and cork" came to the surface. *Shark* was gone, with all hands.

Three weeks later the U.S. commander, Naval Unit China, reported that a ship carrying eighteen hundred American prisoners of war from Manila was sunk by an American submarine on October 24. Only five of the prisoners were able to survive long enough to reach the China shore. At least six Japanese ships were reported sunk that day near *Shark*'s position, but none of the attacking submarines reported seeing prisoners in the water. Was there a seventh ship, and was its sinking the work of *Shark*, attacking the lone freighter? Was *Harukaze*'s contact so very good because *Shark* had surfaced to rescue prisoners?

No matter. *Shark* was gone.

Jack Griggs heard the news about *Shark*'s loss aboard *Picuda*. He had departed Majuro and refit duty for his eighth war patrol. His new skipper, Ty Shephard, tried to make light of Griggs's second narrow escape. Griggs later wrote that "the loss of *Wahoo* and *Shark* weighed on me, but it didn't help when Shep in a jocular fashion said that the only way I could leave *Picuda* was after he did."

Picuda, called "Peculiar" by the crew, had a hot patrol in the East China Sea. On November 17 she damaged the 6,925-ton *Awagawa Maru* with stray torpedoes from a six-torpedo spread that missed the primary target. The primary, the 9,433-ton transport *Mayasan Maru*, went down from the other three hits. Both ships were packed with members of the Japanese 23rd

Infantry Division, which had been withdrawn from Manchuria in a losing effort to bolster the defense of the Philippines.

Six days later, *Picuda* penetrated a convoy screen close to the Korean coast and sank both the 6,933-ton *Shuyo Maru* and the 5,293-ton *Fukuju Maru*. With these attacks, Griggs had participated in the sinkings of at least twenty-five Japanese ships. Low on torpedoes after this nearly 30,000-ton foray, *Picuda* returned to Apra, Guam, on December 2 for replenishment. The American submarine bases had begun moving far forward in a tightening choke hold on the empire.

On October 31, in Fremantle, Australia, George Grider was not yet aware of how difficult the month had been for U.S. submarines. Instead, his attention was diverted to the fact that he formally replaced Reuben Whitaker as CO of *Flasher*. Normally *Flasher*'s longtime XO would have succeeded Whitaker, but both men had returned from *Flasher*'s third patrol physically and mentally drained. Whitaker had reached the point where he had to force himself, with dread, to attack. Nevertheless, he took *Flasher* out for a fourth patrol, his tenth, while the XO requested, and received, a transfer to New London. On this patrol Whitaker sank four more Marus for 25,131 tons, against a claim of only 24,000 tons. He also damaged a fifth ship.

On October 20 a thoroughly exhausted Whitaker returned *Flasher* to Fremantle with nearly dry fuel tanks containing fewer than 4,400 gallons of oil. *Hawkbill*, with Grider aboard as XO, had arrived three days earlier. Admiral Christie had decided to replace Whitaker the day *Hawkbill* arrived with a capable, qualified-to-command Grider aboard.

Flasher's new XO was the experienced Phil Glennon, a *Flasher* plank owner who also had served as XO on the fourth patrol. Glennon was extremely aggressive. Whitaker said "Hell! That guy was the goddamndest tiger at sea I ever saw! I don't think he knew he could get killed." Glennon also was going with an Australian woman and hoped to marry her at the conclusion of the next patrol.

At the start of her wartime service *Flasher* had a reputation as "a boat built by women." This notorious, and irrelevant, claim was true. She had been built at Electric Boat's "Victory Yard" by an all-female construction crew, and it was widely booted about in Groton that *Flasher* was a boat headed for certain disaster. Instead, she had racked up an outstanding record, the hottest boat based in Australia.

As Grider nervously prepared himself to replace the revered Whitaker and try to make this fine boat better, he was unnerved to see *Dace* coming staggering into Fremantle with the rescued crew of *Darter* aboard. All 165 men had sustained themselves in 2,500 square feet of space by eating mushroom soup and peanut butter sandwiches. Grider found himself "caught up in sudden doubts that I could ever match their aggressive spirits when I went out on my own."

He need not have worried. Grider's even-tempered personality was a welcome break from the demanding Whitaker, who once was described, ironically, the same way. Tom McCants, a junior officer, told Whitaker, "You know, Captain, you're the most even-tempered man I've ever known." As Whitaker warmed to this compliment, McCants added, "You're always mad."

Grider was the opposite. He never assumed, as Whitaker did, that the officers and crew *knew* what he wanted; he explained it. Perhaps taking Morton as a model, Grider was very accessible, far less demanding, much more forgiving. He exploited the night order book not just as a way of explaining what he wanted, but also as a mechanism for passing on key information to all the crew.

A constant worrier himself, Grider was very involved with his XO and did not simply leave the worrying to him. The new captain was extremely restless and had difficulty sleeping while onboard, another departure from his predecessor. He would eat a can of peanuts and a candy bar to put himself to sleep, then awake worried both about gaining weight and having insufficient energy to conduct a patrol. If he slept soundly, he worried that he would not awaken promptly in an emergency.

But all this fussing and fretting was offset by admirable humility. Grider did not insist on changing the boat to suit him. Instead, he adopted *Flasher's* fire control procedures instead of the ones he had developed for *Hawkbill*, believing it was unwise to tamper with proven, established techniques on an already successful boat. It helped that Grider had the confidence of a good shot. He also adopted Whitaker's practice of short watches for lookouts, a procedure to which the crew had become accustomed.

Grider was a joker. He wrote both bylined and anonymous poems for *Flasher's* newspaper *The War Shot News*, some in awful "pig German." He also livened patrol reports with deadpan commentary. Early on, after he came aboard, *Flasher* got an SJ radar contact just two miles off the starboard beam, on a southerly course, at twenty knots. Grider wrote that *Flasher* "finally slowed down and let pass what the executive officer believes was an ionized sea gull." He was a good ship handler, often taking risks to impress the crew while simultaneously frightening the officers. In short, Grider was accepted.

His confidence grew during successful prepatrol training exercises. "It was a glorious feeling to stand on the bridge and look at the *Flasher*, and know that she was all mine," but given Grider's personality, "it was also a lonely feeling and a disquieting one."

NOVEMBER 14, 1944. George Grider (second row, center) and the officers of *Flasher.* (Photo courtesy of William R. McCants)

Tinosa was not quite ready for combat use of the QLA mine detector. She departed San Diego bound for Pearl Harbor and further testing on November 7. Don Latham and Roger Paine, CO and XO, respectively, had a near-mutinous crew on their hands. Half the crew wanted off, but Latham rejected all requests for transfer until the submarine reached Pearl Harbor a week later. In transit, Latham radioed Pearl that morale was rock bottom, and requested a rate-for-rate exchange. This included a few junior officers and some chief petty officers normally thought to be "key men."

At Pearl Harbor Paine worked with SubPac staff on the replacement problem. Fortunately, the candidate pool was rich with prospects. Many men who had spent the war in two-week relief duty were "gung-ho to get to war." Thirty-three crew, three officers, and thirty enlisted men were transferred out; thirty-two new men reported aboard. This was far more than the usual ten- to fifteen-man turnover, and Paine was pleased to see that "morale went from bad to excellent in a matter of days." He wrote later that "experience loses much of its value when tempered by a persecution complex growing out of being retained on board too long as 'indispensable.' Ship spirit was increased markedly by the leaven of new personnel and the elimination of experienced malcontents. . . ." The new crew did not seem troubled at the possibility of a mine detection patrol.

That settled, *Tinosa* received a new "rate." Admiral Lockwood temporarily joined the boat "to participate in what was becoming my favorite hobby— locating mines with the FM sonar. . . . I missed no opportunity to observe this equipment in operation and to study its capabilities. *Tinosa's* perform- ance that day was excellent and, beaten down though I was with worry over our losses . . . I went back to base with a song in my heart."

But Lockwood was realistic enough to be cautious. *Tinosa's* first patrol, scheduled to depart December 4, would be a conventional one in the Nansei Shoto–Formosa area. Latham was not to deliberately probe for minefields, but simply leave the FM sonar turned on to see what developed.

On November 15 a completely overhauled *Flasher* departed Fremantle bound for Darwin, then a long northern run through Makassar Strait to her patrol area in the South China Sea. She had new propellers to quiet her fur- ther, and was loaded with new electronics, including one of the first LORAN receivers, and VHF radios and IFF gear.

Flasher also got an APR-1 aircraft detection radar that *Tang* had had for months. Grider had a simple signaling rig installed for the APR operator. Based on a subjective judgment of signal strength, if the operator thought an aircraft was within a five-mile radius of *Flasher*, he sounded a buzzer on the bridge. The OOD was to dive the boat, no questions asked. Grider delighted in testing his new toy, and forced a few quick dives.

On her outbound leg *Flasher* burned up a TDC motor, a rare event on this reliable unit. Grider was crushed, envisioning a flop for his first patrol. In despair he radioed headquarters, asking if there were any southbound submarines from which he could bum a replacement motor. Incredibly, *Hardhead* was not far away. In four hours they met and the motor was installed. In his lighthearted way Grider wrote in the patrol report, "That's better service than one gets alongside the tender."

On December 4, two hundred miles west of Luzon, *Hawkbill* tipped off her prior XO that a convoy was headed his way, about thirteen miles distant. *Hawkbill's* CO closed his transmission with "YOU TAKE THE ESCORTS, WE'LL TAKE THE GRAVY."

Grider ran to the conning tower, turned the surfaced *Flasher* toward the contact, and ran the periscope up to its limit. Almost immediately he could see the tips of masts, like sticks on the surface of the sea, coming toward him. They were still invisible to the lookouts.

Grider was in internal turmoil. He felt the gaze of every officer and crewman, trying to take the measure of this stranger who was about to endanger their lives. Grider felt stiff and red-faced. He ordered *Flasher* to dive on an interception course, then saw that rain squalls were going to deprive him of periscope observations. But the sonar sweeps from the approaching destroyers, and then the beat of propellers, could be heard.

The rain suddenly cleared enough for Grider to see a target. The exact sequence varies by teller, but Grider wrote that he saw a destroyer first, fired at it, then saw a large tanker a few minutes later and put torpedoes into her. McCants's memory is that Grider saw the tanker first, and focused on it with single-minded intensity. Glennon, the XO, kept asking Grider where the escorts were located. Finally he grabbed the periscope and forcefully turned it, Grider still attached and peering through the lens, till he saw a large Asashio class destroyer. McCants's account seems possible, given Grider's similar performance on *Pollack*.

In any case, the destroyer was attacked first, at 0915. When finally seen, it was close to passing them. Grider ordered the rudder hard over, stopped the starboard screw, and gave full power to the port screw to increase *Flasher*'s swing rate. It wasn't enough, and Grider decided to fire a spread of four with *Flasher* still turning, gambling that his range knowledge was so good that at least one of the torpedoes would hit.

He then focused on the tanker, which he would shoot from the stern tubes. The TDC was already cranking on a solution, which suggests that Grider really had seen her before. But he had only one look through the periscope to verify the speed and range, and thought the TDC calculation was marginal. Meanwhile, two torpedoes struck the destroyer, and the other escorts changed direction toward *Flasher*.

Turning to Glennon, Grider asked his XO, "You think we ought to shoot, Phil? It's a beauty, but it's a lousy setup."

The steely Glennon did not hesitate. "Yes, let's try it, Captain."

Grider put the scope up again, lined its marks on the middle of the tanker, and shouted "Fire seven!"

The diving officer, who was already having depth control trouble as the result of the weight loss of the earlier four torpedoes, lost it when the fifth torpedo sprang from its tube. *Flasher*'s periscope ducked under, and Grider could no longer see the target. They needed more forward speed, which Grider ordered. Waiting for his "eye" to reappear, Grider ordered the second after torpedo fired by TDC spread calculations.

When the periscope broke the surface again, Grider saw that the tanker was turning away and ordered "Check fire!" to avoid wasting torpedoes in a hopeless cause, then "Flood negative! Take her deep! Rig for depth charge!" The escorts were upon them.

But, stunningly, through their fear, they heard the sound of their two snapshot torpedoes plowing into the tanker. This should not have happened. Grider's "feel" for the untrustworthiness of his single periscope observation had been correct. The target speed estimate was too low; the TDC setup was wrong. But as the tanker turned away, its effective forward speed slowed. *Flasher*'s two torpedoes had hit her in the stern. "Verily, we smell of the rose," Grider wrote in the patrol report.

The escorts came in with a vengeance. Another Grider entry in the patrol report: "At 0931 heard screws through the hull. Executive officer: 'If he drops now, they're gonna be close.' At 0932 four depth charges. They were."

Exploiting the quietness of American submarines and working under a well-defined temperature gradient, *Flasher* stole away. The escorts were simply unable to hear her.

A few hours later, Grider discovered what he believed to be another destroyer, stopped, apparently attending the stricken tanker. He sank this new ship. At nightfall he finished off the tanker as well. In his first attack as CO, Grider had sunk the 10,022-ton *Kakko Maru*. He also definitely sank the 2,077-ton destroyer *Kishinami*, which had rescued Admiral Kurita from the water after *Darter* sank the cruiser *Atago*. Earlier in the year, *Kishinami* had destroyed the U.S. submarine *Trout*, so there was a certain unknown retribution in this sinking.

Flasher also was credited by JANAC with sinking a second destroyer, *Iwanami*. This is probably untrue, since no *Iwanami* existed in the Japanese Navy. In *kanji*, the pictographs for the two names are very similar. It is likely that Grider simply had finished off a crippled *Kishinami*, which he truly believed to be a second ship. He got postwar credit for two destroyers anyway.

Grider was overjoyed. "A feeling of exaltation, like nothing I had ever experienced before, swept over me. By heaven I had paid my way as a skipper now. . . . Filled with a tremendous exhilaration, we slipped away. . . . My attitude had deteriorated from humility and exultation to downright cockiness."

Flasher continued to patrol on the surface until Admiral Christie ordered her to Manila Bay to conduct a blockade. Grider thought this ridiculous. "Manila Bay is a very large body of water, far too large for one small submarine to keep an eye on." Glennon was pleased, however. He hoped they would have many contacts, fire all their torpedoes, and get back to Fremantle in time for a Christmas wedding. Grider, cheeky as ever, sent an on-station report to the admiral that read, "Conducting our paper blockade as ordered."

Manila Bay was no picnic. Escorts hounded *Flasher* constantly, making it hard to even to get in a battery charge. Grider was sleepless for two nights before being ordered to Camranh Bay, instructions that were followed with alacrity. Grider fell into his bunk and slept till midafternoon.

Flasher patrolled these shallow waters without reward along with several packmates. The weather was poor, with heavy seas left over from a vicious typhoon that had already sunk Third Fleet ships in the Pacific. There were sightings, but the huge waves and fast currents made it impossible to close on them. Then *Dace* was damaged in a grounding. *Flasher* replaced her and began to search in the uncomfortably shallow waters around Hon Doi Island.

On the morning of the twenty-first, in high seas and spray, an escort was spotted. Grider automatically ordered *Flasher* to move seaward to avoid it. After *Flasher* got completely out of the way, five large tankers were seen following, extremely close to shore. It was convoy HI-82. Grider was frantic, "cursing myself, my lack of aggressiveness, and my bad judgment, as the stark realization mounted that the choicest target I would probably ever see had passed me because I had given in to a momentary weakness."

But then his pride and natural aggressiveness asserted itself. "For the rest of my life I would hate myself as a coward unless I surfaced, made an end-around, and redeemed myself." Struggling to regain her lost position, *Flasher* surfaced and ran north, parallel to the targets. The poor weather held their speed to only 12½ knots and they were fighting a 3-knot current. The convoy's speed was estimated at 8½ knots; *Flasher* was barely gaining ground.

All day, and into the night, *Flasher* plodded on. Because of the poor weather no lookouts could be placed in the shears. Waves swept over the bridge. The hatch to the conning tower was closed every time a roller washed over Grider and his bridge watch, forcing them to drink seawater. And they lost the convoy. Probably it had holed up somewhere, but it was impossible to see, even though the weather was moderating. At 2200 Grider wrote that "our spirits began to droop" and resolved to call off the pursuit if no contact was made by 0100 on the twenty-second.

At midnight on the twenty-second, during the watch change, the signalman advised his relief to watch Tortue Island with the words "something isn't quite right." They did. Just before the reverse-course hour, the watch party summoned Glennon to the conning tower. The island was in motion.

At that moment Grider hoisted himself into the conning tower. "The relief that swept over me was tremendous. I felt like a prisoner who has been reprieved on his way to the death chamber. This time . . . I was going to damage that enemy convoy or die trying. This time no one could say or even think that Grider's hesitation had lost the opportunity for us."

And so began one of the most daring attacks of the war. The convoy was escorted by a radar-equipped destroyer that continually interposed herself between *Flasher* and the tankers. Finally, Grider decided to run ahead of the convoy, cut across its bow, then attack from the land side. He was gambling that the Japanese radar would lose *Flasher* with a landmass behind her. But this meant an attack from uncommonly shallow water, fewer than a hundred feet, a thought that made even Glennon recoil.

Flasher ran ahead, radar sweeping, then cut across and waited. The diesels were turned off; all maneuvering would be by battery-powered motors. One officer manned the TBT, giving a steady stream of bearings. Radar was returning excellent range information, and plot had a terrific fix on the convoy's speed. The TDC had its "correct solution" light-illuminated. Grider passed the word to Glennon: "Fire when ready."

At 0446 the exec fired three torpedoes at the lead tanker, three more at the second. Then Grider ordered *Flasher* to swing right to bring the stern tubes to bear on the third tanker in line. At that moment the sky erupted in flames. Grider gasped, writing later, "In the brilliant surge of light we stood out like actors on a stage. The escorts, the trees on the beach, the very rivets on the targets were like floodlit props about us. And there in the center was *Flasher*, its deck bathed in light so brilliant it was almost blinding."

In a desperate attempt to shorten tanker routes, the Japanese had begun to use unrefined Borneo crude to fuel their ships. But Borneo oil comes from the ground lighter and cleaner than most naval fuel oil, and laced with many volatile elements that lead to the formation of extremely explosive vapors. It was this unstable mixture that *Flasher* had ignited.

As *Flasher* swung for the stern shot, the TDC solution light went out. The spindles were not yet set in the torpedoes. Grider may have thought better of using his last shots on the tanker while illuminated perfectly for an avenging destroyer. Perhaps he wanted to save the torpedoes to use in a getaway. In any case, Grider ordered "Check fire!"

At that moment the TDC gave an excellent computer-generated solution for Glennon. One of the fire control party shouted, "Gyros matching aft, Phil! Jesus Christ, let's shoot!" Glennon may have been influenced by his urgent desire to head for Australia. Without hesitation he ordered the four stern torpedoes, nos. 20 to 23, launched. All hit. The flames grew higher. Grider never complained about the unauthorized shots.

Now it was time for *Flasher* to escape. A struggle between competing interests developed between Grider and Glennon. Glennon was truly concerned about running aground and wanted to turn toward the destroyer and deeper water. But Grider could see that the destroyer had its forward gun unlimbered; he had no intention of turning toward her. For two miles both ships raced along, with Glennon pleading for Grider to turn. He would not. And then the destroyer turned—away. *Flasher* eased toward deeper waters. Perhaps the destroyer had never even seen *Flasher,* so good was her camouflage.

At daybreak Grider sent a message to Admiral Christie, then dived for the day. He slept till 1600. When he awoke there was a message waiting for him from the admiral:

WONDERFUL CHRISTMAS PRESENT.

CONGRATULATIONS TO YOU ALL.

COME ON HOME. REUBEN IS GOING

TO BE PROUD OF HIS OLD SHIP.

During this attack *Omurosan Maru, Otowasan Maru,* and *Arita Maru,* totaling 28,736 tons, went to the bottom. Including the tanker sunk three weeks before, *Flasher* had sunk more fuel-carrying tonnage on a single patrol than any other submarine. In terms of total tons sunk, Grider had just turned in what would be the third-best patrol of the Pacific war.

While *Flasher* was patrolling Indochina waters, *Tinosa* departed Midway Island on December 9 in foul weather. Still in the channel, with the forward torpedo room hatch open, she took a wave over the bow that soaked the Mark 18 electric torpedoes below. About half a gallon of seawater had to be flushed from each of them.

Weather conditions worsened. By the twelfth the forty-knot winds had kicked up seas so high that *Tinosa* "took two green ones over the bridge. [We] received about one foot of water in the conning tower and the port lookout was knocked out." By the fourteenth she was staggering along, making only eight knots, slowed by solid water over the bridge.

On the seventeenth, at 0335, C. H. Wagner Jr., a TM3C, was washed from his perch on the starboard high lookout station and landed on the main deck. The OOD ordered "All stop" as Wagner struggled to make his way back to the conning tower ladder. He grasped it, but a second wave slammed into *Tinosa* and swept him away. Desperate, flailing, Wagner hung up on the lifeline. Once again he fought his way to the conning tower ladder "and was hauled to safety by eager hands."

On this same day a great typhoon struck Admiral Halsey's Third Fleet, which was supporting MacArthur's Mindoro landings. Three destroyers went down with great loss of life, an event that would cause Halsey to be brought before a court of inquiry. He was held culpable, but punishment was withheld. There were no targets for *Tinosa* in such hideous weather, only the sight of dislodged, floating mines and Japanese ships aground on the rocks. The typhoon was nation-impartial.

By the morning of December 22 the sea had calmed. That afternoon *Tinosa* was experiencing calm and pleasant seas for the first time on this patrol. Latham and Paine were in the conning tower when, at 1502, Latham wrote, "[Roger] and I each looked at the other. There was an unmistakable and beautiful bell-like tone with a small persistent spot on the scope at 1400 yards, bearing 10°." The FM sonar had detected a mine.

"[We] closed to 1,000 yards, still with a good echo. Came left full rudder. Wiped off perspiration and calmed down. Decided to try again. This attempt was made with forced cheerfulness." The situation worsened. They had three mines, though only by "Hell's Bells," not with an accompanying pip. Latham and Paine had planned to back out of such a situation, but Latham now feared they couldn't maneuver well enough in reverse. He turned away from where he believed the minefield to be; *Tinosa* got a fourth contact.

Latham was now sweating bullets. "The current here . . . made it difficult to position ship . . . and also added zest to evasive maneuvers. . . . The nervous strain imposed on personnel during an FM search for suspected mines is intense. When a contact is actually found, endurance of personnel reaches a limit rapidly." *Tinosa* turned, as Latham shuddered with the thought of how close one of the mines was, and escaped.

Thousands of miles away, Lockwood was overjoyed at the contact report. His pet project was working! He began to lay long-range plans for a major penetration of the Sea of Japan, not visited since *Wahoo's* loss, which, Lockwood erroneously believed, was from mines. More surprising was the fact that *Tinosa* detected the mines in six hundred feet of water. Clearly the Americans had underestimated Japanese mine capability.

Lockwood now ordered *Tinosa* to make a full sweep of Okinawa, searching for minefields. Latham closed to two miles of the beach and began to search. He was abnormally keyed up. "Talk about alert! I could feel, see, hear, smell, and taste better than an Indian or a wolf." The slow searching went on for weeks. *Tinosa* would not return to Pearl Harbor until January 30, 1945. The tension and length of this patrol, fifty-eight days, were extremely wearing; no new minefields were detected.

As *Tinosa* prowled the Okinawan coastline, *Flasher* began her return to Australia, dodging—sometimes sinking—drifting mines along the way. She went through the South China Sea into the Java Sea, to penetrate the Malay Barrier via the Lombok Strait. Both Bali and Lombok, which the strait separated, were held by the Japanese. They were acutely aware that U.S. submarines used it as a highway to and from Australia, and patrolled accordingly.

On Christmas Day, while in the shallow Karimata Strait approach, *Flasher* was slowly overtaken by *Barbero*, also headed for Fremantle. *Barbero* had attacked three ships in a convoy the previous day, sinking one 4300-ton cargoman and a patrol craft. *Barbero* was hurrying home, and stirred up a hornet's nest in Lombok Strait on the twenty-seventh. An alert air patrol dropped a bomb while *Barbero* was at periscope depth. It struck very close aboard aft, wrecking the port reduction gear and nearly destroying her. Her tough HST hull allowed *Barbero* to survive, but the badly damaged submarine crawled home to Fremantle, out of the war for good.

Grider appears to have witnessed this attack. Running on the surface, at 1615 *Flasher*'s lookouts spotted a black RUFE, a Japanese float plane, headed for Lombok Strait, where *Barbero* lay. Grider ordered *Flasher* down, then watched through the periscope as the RUFE "made several dips and circles . . . over the strait . . . until 1655."

Flasher was on the surface by 1700, but dove again as the RUFE returned at 1730. Grider was uneasy with this activity, and decided to wait until dark to make a night transit. At 1835 *Flasher* was back on the surface, running for the strait's opening, when, at 1909, the lookouts and the SJ radar simultaneously spotted a Japanese PC. Grider was determined not to submerge and take a depth-charge pounding. Instead, he rang up flank speed and poured on the coals to outrun the PC. The Japanese ship was poorly conned, missing the opportunity to cut off *Flasher* in her high-speed flight. Nevertheless, the range closed steadily as the submarine tried to run right around her opponent.

At 1930, at 4,860 yards' range, the PC began to fire twin twenty-millimeter cannons at *Flasher*. Grider forcefully ordered all lookouts and the OOD below, conning the submarine alone from a position halfway inside the conning tower hatch, a spot that gave him some protection from the incoming enemy fire.

Flasher's crew had earlier built two decoy devices for just such an eventuality as this. The first was a false radar return apparatus trailed by a helium balloon, a device that was useless given that the PC could clearly see them in the bright moonlight. The second was a decoy explosive that would burn in *Flasher*'s wake, hopefully drawing gunfire. Grider was afraid to use it, fearing it might simply sharpen the PC's aim.

At 1950 the range to the PC had contracted to 4,500 yards, but *Flasher*'s flank speed had permitted her to get around the escort. They were now headed for the middle of the strait, with the PC astern. At 2020 the range had opened to 7,050 yards, and the PC was observed sending visual signals to Bali, reporting the imminent escape of another submarine. Confident now, Grider called the OOD back to the bridge. At that moment they saw a second PC headed toward them, at 5 miles' range. The signaling had meant something after all.

There was no hope for it now. *Flasher* would have to dive. As they slid under the waves, the enormous heat built up in the engines from their 1¼-hour-long flank speed run overwhelmed men in the engine rooms. Throttlemen collapsed at their stations and had to be carried to a cooler spot in the boat. Grider took *Flasher* under a sharp temperature gradient present at 250 feet and silently slid away. Though both PCs conducted sonar searches, they never made a solid contact and never dropped a depth charge.

Grider's boylike spirits returned with the long swells of the Indian Ocean. Since he had always had navigation trouble himself, he decided to relieve the XO of that responsibility and let the third officer gain some experience in the task. He did not tell him that he had discovered a trick. If *Flasher's* periscope controls were carefully set between low and high power, an illusion of breakers in the water could be created at the prism junction. Grider kept this trick secret until the right moment.

The navigator-victim faced several practical problems besides Grider's antics. First, he was a "mustang," a former enlisted man, and had never had formal navigational schooling. Second, *Flasher* was extremely low on fuel; there was no hope of making Fremantle directly. He would have to plot an exact, precise, no-mistakes course due south to Exmouth Gulf for an emergency topping if they were to make it home. Third, the onboard navigational tables were incomplete. The full set only ran through December 31. After that the navigator could not take a star sight, and would have to rely solely on the sun and the dead-reckoning indicator. He had to have a precise fix by New Year's Eve.

As the victim sweated out these authentic problems, Grider toyed with him. One noon, as the January 1 event approached, the navigator reported *Flasher's* position to Grider, who pressed him for confidence levels. "That's our exact position. I got a fine fix this morning, and I've got a morning sun line and now a noon fix. I know exactly where we are."

Then Grider asked him if there was enough fuel to make Exmouth Gulf, a calculation the trainee was also making as engineering officer. "We'll just barely make it to Exmouth Gulf."

And then the trap was sprung. A messenger hurried forward. "OOD reports they have sighted land through the periscope."

Grider looked disdainfully at the navigator, as if dismissing his earlier assurances. "No, sir!" the navigator responded with some heat. "It couldn't be land!" Some of the participants remember that the navigator shouted, "All stop!"

Grider replied, "Maybe it's a mirage. Let's go take a look."

In the conning tower Grider and Glennon hogged the scope, describing breakers, buildings onshore, and other landfall sights; the all-business quartermasters recorded their observations. By the time the falsely tuned eyepiece was finally relinquished to the unfortunate mark, he was nearly in a state of shock and vulnerable to seeing the "breakers" himself. He immediately called for a fathometer reading, so deeply had he been hooked. But the fix was in. The report was of shallow water. And then the lookouts on the bridge reported that they could see land as well. The hapless navigator raced up the ladder to the bridge and saw—the Indian Ocean. Grider nearly collapsed in glee.

On New Year's Day no. 3 engine failed completely, her exhaust valves probably pushed over the edge by the long flank speed run to Lombok Strait. But *Flasher* pushed on at 17.5 knots, took on 22,800 gallons of fuel at Exmouth Gulf, and arrived at Fremantle on January 2. Of their forty-nine days on patrol, only one had been spent entirely submerged. She was met by Admiral Fife, who had just replaced the summarily relieved Admiral Christie, and the endorsements were glowing.

Glennon had his wedding, not much delayed after all. The groom's party included *Flasher*'s officers. Grider acted as a surrogate father for his XO, telling appropriate stories to all the guests. Then Glennon left on his honeymoon, while the remainder of *Flasher*'s crew left for R&R at Perth. Fife had been ordered to move SubSoWestPac headquarters forward to Subic Bay as the Japanese maritime empire contracted. Grider expected that this next patrol would be his leave-taking from Australia.

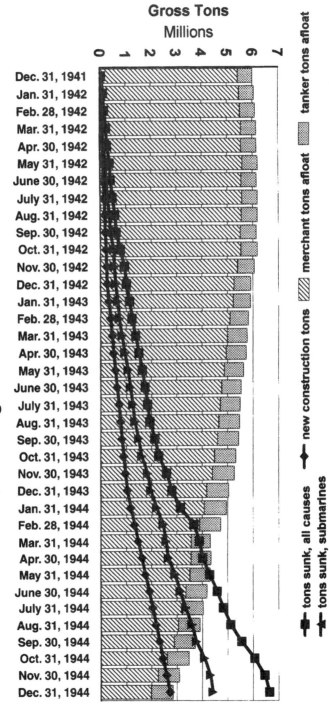

Accelerating War of Attrition: Year End 1944

Gross Tons
Millions

Dec. 31, 1941
Jan. 31, 1942
Feb. 28, 1942
Mar. 31, 1942
Apr. 30, 1942
May 31, 1942
June 30, 1942
July 31, 1942
Aug. 31, 1942
Sep. 30, 1942
Oct. 31, 1942
Nov. 30, 1942
Dec. 31, 1942
Jan. 31, 1943
Feb. 28, 1943
Mar. 31, 1943
Apr. 30, 1943
May 31, 1943
June 30, 1943
July 31, 1943
Aug. 31, 1943
Sep. 30, 1943
Oct. 31, 1943
Nov. 30, 1943
Dec. 31, 1943
Jan. 31, 1944
Feb. 28, 1944
Mar. 31, 1944
Apr. 30, 1944
May 31, 1944
June 30, 1944
July 31, 1944
Aug. 31, 1944
Sep. 30, 1944
Oct. 31, 1944
Nov. 30, 1944
Dec. 31, 1944

tanker tons afloat

merchant tons afloat

new construction tons

tons sunk, all causes

tons sunk, submarines

21

Final Victory

The atomic bomb was the funeral pyre
of an enemy who had been drowned.

—Theodore Roscoe, United States Submarine
Operations in World War II

In the cold, wintry hills an hour's bus ride from Yokohama, Jesse DaSilva
struggled to stay alive inside the deadly naval intelligence prison at O'funa.
He had been beaten badly and repeatedly from the moment of his rescue
from the sunken *Tang*, at the temporary camp at Takao, southern Formosa,
and later in the medieval Spanish jail at Kiirun in the north, where the
survivors had been taken by train. Rations were at starvation level—three
hundred calories per day—and DaSilva was rapidly shedding weight.

At least at O'funa he had been given a shirt and pants. It was a cold winter
in Japan, and DaSilva had been wearing only the shorts he had on when he
escaped from the torpedo room. But the Japanese had issued no suitable
shoes; their absence was to freeze all feeling from DaSilva's feet for more
than four months.

Soon after their capture, *Tang*'s enlisted men had been separated from the
surviving officers: O'Kane, Hank Flanagan, and Larry Savadkin. Taken to a
destroyer for transport to Japan, the officers had been decently treated; the
enlisted men were placed in the forward hold of a cruiser along with sacks
of cane sugar. They endured a rough voyage in heavy seas that made more
men than just Floyd Caverly deathly ill.

At O'funa the thrashings intensified. The dreaded Gunrabo, the Japanese
rough equivalent to the German Gestapo, delivered ritualistic beatings to
near death of the previously captured officers of *Grenadier;* this was done as
an example to *Tang*'s crew. Four of *Grenadier*'s captured sailors were to die
in O'funa from their harsh treatment. At night, gangs of sadistic thugs

would set upon prisoners at random, beating them with clubs as soon as they could no longer hold their position in the "O'funa crouch"—on the balls of their feet, knees half bent, arms raised above heads.

O'Kane was discouraged by what he had seen in his travel to the camp: ". . . the fast loaded trains, the hydroelectric lines coming down out of the mountains . . . the buzzing industry . . . [and] factories . . . booming like Kaiser's shipyards." He came to believe that Japan was not near the edge and "could be defeated only by invasion."

At this low ebb came two small rays of hope. B-29s were observed bombing Yokohama and, more practically useful, the arrival of Red Cross food packages, which the Japanese distributed as a Christmas 1944 present. DaSilva carefully guarded his box of soap, cigarettes, gum, chocolate bars, powdered milk, dried prunes and raisins, canned fish and meat, a small block of cheese, and canned butter. He would not participate in the often fatal prisoner ritual of trading food for cigarettes.

Leibold was not so lucky. The Japanese let the American prisoners out of their cells on Christmas Day. After some welcome socializing, Leibold returned to his cell to find that his Red Cross food package was missing. The Japanese rewarded his complaints by issuing him two baked sweet potatoes.

As the Japanese Empire contracted, targets for U.S. submarines grew ever harder to find. One area that remained productive was Formosa Strait, where *Tang* had gone down. The Japanese were desperately trying to supply the Philippines down this shallow-water corridor and had organized true convoys to protect the precious cargo from marauding submarines.

Four days after the *Tang* survivors received their Red Cross parcels a three-submarine wolf pack departed Guam to patrol the China coast from Wenchow south to where a U.S. blind bombing zone and Japanese mine-fields combined to close Formosa Strait to submarine operations. Led by *Queenfish*, the other two boats were again *Barb* and *Picuda*, now on her fifth war patrol. It was Jack Griggs's ninth patrol.

With a short run to empire waters, it was only three days later—New Year's Day 1945—when *Queenfish* and *Picuda* encountered a small patrol boat, which they decided to attack on the surface. After an hour of four-inch and automatic-weapons fire it was a three-hundred-ton ruined hulk. The wreck was temporarily saved by the arrival of a Japanese patrol plane, which drove the two submarines under.

Barb, sixty miles behind, came upon this burning ruin later in the day and sent over a boarding party to obtain legitimate war matériel, not knowing there were still live Japanese aboard. *Barb*'s crew also stole every souvenir they could lay their hands on: binoculars, radios, rifles, compasses, barometers, signal flags, and the Rising Sun flag. After the boarding party cleared the derelict, *Barb's* four-inch gun crew were ordered to sink it. The patrol report recorded that "When the diesel tanks caught fire, the eight or nine Japs came running out . . . on deck. They stopped for a minute and our four-inch crew, being very bloodthirsty at that time, landed a shot right in their midst, which blew them all apart."

Six days later the wolf pack struck pay dirt, sighting two independent convoys. The first, HI-87, consisted of ten tankers, the escort carrier *Ryuko*, and the navy ship *Kamoi*, protected by four destroyers and six frigates. The massive size of this convoy was not understood till after the war. *Picuda* made the initial contact and flashed the alarm to her packmates. *Barb* was unable to get into firing position because of heavy seas and rain squalls, but *Picuda* penetrated the escort screen. Shephard put four torpedoes into the only target he could see in the foul weather, the 10,045-ton tanker *Munakata Maru*, but *Picuda* was nearly sunk herself by a freighter coming in to ram. The tanker survived—temporarily. It was towed into Keelung Harbor, only to be sunk by carrier aircraft two weeks later.

The wolf pack members cursed their bad-weather luck. *Picuda's* attack caused the convoy to scatter to harbors along the Formosan coast, with some damaging collisions between ships. The submarines withdrew toward the Chinese mainland. The next day, January 8, the wolf pack picked up the second convoy, Mo-Ta 30, with seven important ships protected by four frigates and four sonar-equipped patrol craft.

Exactly what happened next, "Who struck John?," may never be satisfactorily sorted out. The three submarines conducted a series of slashing attacks that so confused the Japanese that they believed they were under air assault and elevated their guns to fill the sky with metal. What is also certain is that at least six, and possibly all seven, Japanese ships were unable to deliver their cargo. They were either sunk outright or severely damaged and beached.

Barb, in the shallowest water, struck first, hoping to drive the convoy toward her packmates. Her first three torpedoes, fired while submerged in the pale afternoon light, caused such a fearful explosion that *Barb* was driven sideways and twenty-two feet deeper into the depths, ducking the periscope. Canned goods inside the torpedo room burst from the impact; parts of the superstructure above the after engine room were ripped away. Fluckey believed this was the 9,256-ton *Anyo Maru* exploding, but it may have been the 6,892-ton ammunition ship *Tatsuto Maru*, which Fluckey thought he destroyed with the second batch of torpedoes from the forward tubes. A third, overlapping ship was hit by a torpedo that missed its primary target in this melee.

As the winter night darkened the skies, all three submarines surfaced to conduct serial attacks. Three times they mistook each other for an escort or a target, nearly causing a catastrophe. *Picuda* slipped between escorts to get a hit in the 2,854-ton *Hikoshima Maru*, which slowed to last place in the starboard column but kept going. "*Peculiar*" was immediately set upon by the convoy's protectors in a battle sequence that the *Barb* crew could follow on their radarscope.

Barb attacked again to take pressure off *Picuda*, coming from behind at escort speed to mask her presence. She also got hits in *Hikoshima Maru*, that eventually forced that unfortunate vessel to run aground in Tunghsiao Bay. Another torpedo slipped by the primary target and damaged *Meiho Maru*, which eventually fell out of line and beached herself to avoid sinking.

Barb continued up the line of ships in her lamb's cloth disguise as an escort. Three torpedoes were placed in *Sanyo Maru*. Fluckey wrote that they "were followed by a stupendous eruption that far surpassed any Hollywood production. The rarefaction that followed the viselike squeezing, first-pressure wave wrenched the air from my lungs. . . . The high vacuum in the boat made people in the control room feel like they were being sucked up the hatch. Personnel in the conning tower who didn't have their shirts tucked in at the belt had them pulled up over their heads."

Queenfish now put torpedoes into *Manju Maru*, the sole survivor of the convoy's starboard column, and possibly the overlapping *Meiho Maru*, already damaged by *Barb*. *Manju Maru* was seen to settle by the three submarines, but there are other reports that she, too, was beached by her crew.

Only one ship remained of the convoy, *Rashin Maru*, which had detached herself and run ahead to the safety of the minefields. *Picuda* daringly followed her and got in a damaging hit. *Rashin Maru* was beached but later salvaged.

After this night of devastation *Queenfish* departed for Pearl Harbor. *Barb* and *Picuda* moved into the very shallow water near Shanghai, where coast watchers reported that a long intracoastal shipping channel had been dredged. Fluckey found convoy Mo-Ta 32 holed up in Namkwan Harbor for a safe night's sleep. He determined to go in on the surface, down a twisting, rocky channel in only thirty feet of water to fire eight torpedoes into the anchored mass. He invited Shephard in *Picuda* to go in with him, but Shephard's radio response was unequivocal: "DROP DEAD."

Fluckey went in anyway and likely sank four ships and damaged three others. However, JANAC only gave him credit for sinking the 5,244-ton *Taikyo Maru*. *Barb*'s escape was perilous, backtracking down the channel at high speed, governors tied down and engines operating at 150 percent overload; for forty minutes a speed of 23.5 knots was achieved. *Barb* escaped to two hundred feet of water. Most navy personnel considered this a U.S. kamikaze attack. It earned Fluckey the Congressional Medal of Honor.

Picuda was now detached for lifeguard duty. In the early-morning darkness of January 29 a convoy was sighted in the rain. Shephard set up on a troop transport and overlapping freighters. The transport absolutely received one torpedo hit, and *Picuda*'s bridge watch could see her dead in the water, blowing her shrill whistle. One of the freighters, the 5,497-ton *Clyde Maru,* went down, but *Picuda* was blocked from making a *coup de grâce* on the transport by the arrival of Japanese aircraft, which drove her under.

Torpedoes expended, *Picuda* returned to Saipan on February 5, then on to Pearl Harbor for refit. Griggs was beginning to show obvious signs of too much war. His weight had dropped to 130 pounds from his Naval Academy graduation level of 166. He had changed very much in the past 2½ years, but had not yet come to grips with the magnitude of that change on his own personality.

On January 27, two days before *Picuda*'s last convoy attack, George Grider took *Flasher* on her sixth war patrol. Grider knew that the final destination for this patrol was California. The very prospect of a thirty-day leave in the States with Ann, and perhaps avoidance of the need to return to war, made him cautious. "Be careful. You're going home when this is over."

After passing through Lombok Strait on February 2, this time without incident, Grider found a perceptibly different war. The Japanese had been virtually swept from the seas; no targets were to be found in the waters between Malaya and Borneo. On the other hand, contact with American submarines was almost continuous. On February 4 they passed *Bluegill,* inbound to Australia after a target-free patrol.

Grider grew uncommonly bored. There was very little for a CO to do on a submarine whose crew was as well trained as that of *Flasher*'s. He fretted about his terrible eating and sleeping habits, skipped rope on the cigarette deck to control his weight, read Civil War biographies repeatedly, and was stirred into curious attention only by the presence of drifting mines. These were destroyed with all manner of small-arms and light-weapons fire in little marksmanship contests.

It was not until February 21 that Grider saw his first "pathetically small" targets. They were little sea trucks. "This late in the war the Japanese had become so desperate for bottoms that they were using wooden ships powered with diesel engines . . . that would carry a few men and some oil in drums." Grider called in nearby *Bashaw* to participate in this monotony-breaking exercise. *Bashaw* expended two torpedoes, one of which disintegrated a sea truck while Grider watched. But the second missed, and expending a third torpedo seemed wasteful. Since *Bashaw*'s deck gun was inoperable, Grider stirred himself to action.

Flasher's four-inch-gun crew lobbed in its first shell from the safe distance of fifteen hundred yards. Receiving no counterfire, Grider closed up to five hundred yards and the gun crew fired about one per minute until ten hits from twenty-six shots caused the little boat to capsize. About a dozen survivors clambered up the keel.

Grider felt sorry for these pitiful creatures in the cold water and tried to entice them aboard with phrases from a Japanese-language phonetic manual. There were only two takers, both teenage Chinese (Grider learned later) boys who had been pressed into the Japanese Navy. Both grabbed *Flasher*'s bow as it slowly backed from the wreckage, and struggled to climb aboard. They were quickly helped by pistol-packing crewmen and hustled below.

The terrified teenagers were chained. Grider put on an impressive khaki dress shirt with insignia, but promptly failed in his Japanese-language interrogation attempt. It was then that the quaking boys revealed that they could speak fragmentary English, taught them as orphans at St. Anthony's in Hong Kong. The chains were removed, but the captives were separated, one to each torpedo room.

The prisoners disclosed that the sunken sea truck had a Japanese captain and about fifteen Japanese troops aboard, but half the crew were Chinese. The truck was also loaded with empty oil barrels. The Japanese were desperately scrounging for oil anywhere they could find it.

As had happened so many times before, the "prisoners" quickly became pets of the crew. Showered, shaved, with new clothes—and especially new shoes—donated from the smallest members of *Flasher*'s crew, the two youths instantly accepted any chore given them. They would not stop cleaning the boat until the rags were physically taken from their hands. The shower revealed large welts on their backs, souvenirs of the Japanese, which further softened the Americans' hearts. Quick learners, they were taught the best American vulgarities. With little prompting, the accommodating boys dumbfounded the cook with the put-up expression "Piss-poor chow."

For the next few days *Flasher*, still employing the electronic-noise-generating SD radar, roamed the deserted seas, prudently diving at every airplane contact. On February 25 a Chidori escort and small target approached from astern, chased toward them by failed attacks of *Bashaw*. Grider elected a night periscope attack, a difficult choice given the poor optical characteristics of American periscopes.

The range estimate was seven hundred yards, but a single sonar ping said the distance was more like nine hundred yards. A compromise value of eight hundred yards was used in the TDC, and three stern torpedoes were fired at right angles to the target's track. Hearing no hits, Grider glumly began to swing for a bow shot when, quite belatedly, all three torpedoes plowed home. The actual range had been twenty-two hundred yards. The hits occurred only because there was no gyro angle computation to complicate the run. Grider called over the newest junior officer and said, "Bob, it ain't always that easy."

Grider had just sunk the 850-ton *Koho Maru*. He did not then realize that when the war's final counts were tallied, *Koho*'s sinking placed *Flasher* above the 100,000-ton mark in confirmed sinkings—and the record for most tonnage sunk by a single submarine.

Try as he might, Grider could find few worthwhile targets. Two sampans were sunk by gunfire. But the personal nature of what amounted to close-range murder of the crews sickened Grider. He had no blood lust and was forever troubled by the eyes of his victims as they fell, wounded, into the sea.

The patrol droned on, extended by Admiral Fife's order, inadvertently suggested by Grider, to refuel in Subic Bay and patrol for two more weeks. Grider later wrote, "I could have cheerfully cut my own throat." The Chinese prisoners were put ashore dressed in the newest dungarees, with "Dolphins" hand-sewn on their shirtsleeves by the crew. During the three day mini-overhaul stay at Subic Bay, the crew visited the boys in prison camp, bringing them supplies and chocolate candy. Many of the officers and crew also got roaring drunk.

Departing Subic Bay on March 8, Grider wrote that they "stayed on the surface night & day . . . feeling quite cocky in our virtual ownership of the Ocean." At last, on March 24, Grider received orders to head for Saipan and ongoing transit to the United States. They rolled merrily along, sniping at loose mines all the way, and exchanging greetings with a continuous stream of outbound submarines. One of these was *Snook,* which soon vanished forever into the seas east of Formosa, possibly the victim of a Japanese submarine.

The harsh winter had been extremely punishing to the *Tang* survivors held in O'funa. DaSilva, still essentially shoeless, exercised with the others by endlessly walking the compound wrapped in a blanket. He wrote, "During this winter we experienced at least two feet of snow on the ground. There was no heat in the cells and, in fact, you could see right through the cracks in the walls, so we talked the guards into letting several of us get together in one cell. This way our body heat would at least make it a little warmer. We would sit around in a circle and talk about food, food, food. . . ."

All of the prisoners had diarrhea, and many, DaSilva among them, had beriberi, with its attendant symptoms of thiamin deficiency: fatigue, disturbed sleep, memory loss, and abdominal pain.

The guards seized on every infraction as an excuse to beat the prisoners. Some Red Cross parcels had not been distributed by the Japanese but, instead, were stored in a room at the end of the barracks. A few of these parcels "went missing," and all prisoners were forced to stand at attention all day, outside, until someone confessed. By evening, having had no success, the guards forced everyone into a push up position. With every quiver of a prisoner's arm a club was slammed against his buttocks. By nightfall the beaten men had admitted nothing and the Japanese stopped the torment.

Air raids now became frequent. The prisoners knew that was a sure sign that the vise was closing on Japan, because many of the aircraft were from carriers. At the same time, there was a real possibility that they would be killed in these raids, as bomb fragments often whistled through the wooden barracks. Increased air activity brought more American prisoners, especially B-29 crews.

O'funa was filling up and, in the first week of April 1945, the Japanese were compelled to transfer *Tang*'s enlisted men, and thirteen others who were judged still capable of work, to the army prisoner-of-war camp at Omori, a nearby island in Tokyo Bay. O'Kane and the other two *Tang* officers were held back. "Pappy" Boyington, who had been a prisoner since he was shot down over Rabaul on January 3, 1944, was required to lead the work brigade on Omori.

DaSilva found conditions at Omori somewhat better. There were far more prisoners, so they were not singled out for individual "attention" by sadistic guards. Boyington persuaded the Japanese to shift the work detail to the digging of vegetable gardens in the bombed-out areas of Yokohama. This provided opportunities for pilfering, and DaSilva would wolf down small vegetables and eat them raw when the guards were not looking. He also became skilled at scrounging garbage behind occupied buildings. These scraps were added to the tea to make a kind of soup. At one low point a stray old dog wandered up to the toiling prisoners. Neither DaSilva nor anyone else could bring themselves to kill and eat the poor animal.

Clay Decker became Boyington's roommate. As was the Japanese custom, U.S. officers were given their equivalent monthly pay in yen. Boyington generally used this currency to make cigarette paper, but once pressed a handful into the fist of a quaking civilian in exchange for a fish. He and Decker ate it raw, Decker's only fish—he had no meat—during captivity.

While *Tang's* prisoners were being transferred to Omori, *Tinosa* departed Saipan's Tanapag Harbor, in the Marianas, on March 17. This ninth war patrol was another "special tests" mine detection mission in Nansei Shoto. *Tinosa* would also perform reconnaissance and lifeguard duty. The QLA was still temperamental; it could not be relied on as a clear indicator of the presence of mines.

Paine, *Tinosa's* XO, also found a far different war. American submarines were everywhere, and *Tinosa* passed nine of them in transit. The radio was used freely, in contrast to prior patrols. No targets were sighted, but as *Tinosa* went deeper into the East China Sea, the depredations of prior submarines and carrier air strikes were obvious. On March 28 *Tinosa* began to swim through virtually continuous oil slicks. Swollen bodies, some in full army equipment, bobbed in the fouled sea. Nosing through debris, Paine quickly counted thirty bodies before putting his mind on other matters.

That afternoon they sighted a lifeboat with a sail deployed. Pulling alongside, Paine tallied seventeen Japanese military personnel in a variety of uniforms. *Tinosa's* captain wanted prisoners, but the Japanese refused to cooperate, all but one lying face down in the lifeboat. Then one of the junior officers fell down "by the torpedo room hatch accidentally placing a couple of shots from his .45 quite close," as was drily recorded in the patrol report.

Now all the Japanese wanted to come aboard, and Paine was able to be selective. One with three stars on his uniform, another with a single star, apparently aviators, were chosen. The others were set adrift again in their sailboat. When the new prisoners were examined they were found to have terrible trench mouth, and the pharmacist's mate put them on an oral cleansing regime, including twice-daily tooth brushing.

The evidence of carnage continued in the following days. Only the more unusual bodies were recorded now, such as the aviator dead in the sea, parachute still attached. There was some possibility that this was an American, but *Tinosa's* captain chose not to investigate the awful corpse.

Tinosa was fighting a mechanical problem first encountered on March 23. The bow planes refused to rig fully out. There was a broken shear pin, all right, but something else was wrong that did not lend itself to repairs at sea. Once they attempted to anchor in 444 feet of water, but lost their anchor and chain after deploying 450 feet. It turned out there was little need to dive—only three patrol days were spent submerged—but a bow plane problem precluded a quick dive should it be necessary. The patrol was truncated, and *Tinosa* reached Apra, Guam, on April 9.

There Paine received wonderful news. He was detached from *Tinosa* and sent to Groton, Connecticut, as captain of the new-build boat *Cubera*. He was twenty-seven, had survived the war, the loss of so many friends, and soon would see Bebe again.

Dave Connole, Paine's watch relief on December 7, was not so lucky. On March 28, while Paine was encountering the floating gore in the East China Sea, Connole and *Trigger*, which he now commanded, was spotted by a Japanese airplane fairly near *Tinosa*. The plane bombed *Trigger*, and got a very good location fix. Surface escorts were quickly vectored in and began relentless depth-charging. After two hours of this punishing attack, *Trigger*'s thin-skin hull was breached. Oil gushed to the surface to add to the disgusting pools already present. Connole, and eighty-eight other officers and crew, vanished forever.

The day after *Trigger*'s loss, already suspected by Pearl Harbor because of her failure to respond to *Tirante*'s rendezvous call, *Picuda* left Apra, Guam, for Kii Suido. It was John Griggs's tenth war patrol, and he yearned for the end of the war. No shipping could be found.

On May 6, after a mind-numbing patrol, *Picuda* rendezvoused with the lifeguard boat *Scabbardfish* and took on five B-29 crew. Five days later they were in Saipan, where the airmen reported to another 21st Bomber Command plane. There Griggs heard welcome news: *Picuda* would depart for the States for a shipyard replacement of her noisy reduction gears.

Griggs, too, had made it—but not without cost. When examined by navy doctors in Portsmouth, the diagnosis was combat fatigue. He was also temporarily sterile. Griggs was sent on rest leave, where he ended the war regaining his health.

Flasher, also bound for the States, pulled into Pearl Harbor on April 13 after a seventy-seven-day patrol. Because of the lack of targets, she had a full load of unexpended torpedoes. At Pearl Grider and crew learned the sobering news of President Roosevelt's death. To men so young Roosevelt was essentially the only president they had ever known, and there was some unease about his successor.

Flasher would be ready to depart for San Francisco in four days, but Grider was shaky. "My nerves were shot, my sleeping and eating habits more irregular than they had ever been." With a prearranged code Grider conveyed a message to Ann before departing. They would arrive at the Golden Gate on April 26—and Ann and several other wives she secretly tipped off would be waiting. Those who went to the bridge to wave at the incoming submarine were completely stymied by the pea soup mist.

The docking at Hunter's Point was rich with emotion. McCants's wife was there, along with the son he had never seen. Grider ordered McCants down the gangplank first to meet them. The infant held out his arms and said "Hello, Daddy" in a loving greeting that tore at all their hearts.

While officers and crew scattered on richly deserved leaves, *Flasher* was completely upgraded for the new maritime war with Japan. Everything on the ship was repaired, repainted, or replaced. There were ninety-three equipment upgrades, from radar mounted inside the periscope heads, to a double-speed TDC, to an enormous upgrade to her surface armament: a five-inch gun replaced the 4-inch, and two forty-millimeter Bofors displaced the less effective twenty-millimeters, which were displaced to the cigarette and main decks.

Most troubling to Grider was the installation of the QLA FM sonar mine detection gear. *Flasher* would be returning to war, and Grider hated the thought of minefield penetration, especially with the QLA's lousy reputation for accuracy. He ". . . looked forward to this assignment with something less than enthusiasm."

Grider, too, yearned for the end of the war. On May 7 Germany surrendered, and the full attention of the U.S. military began to be fixed on Japan and the Pacific. The end felt so close, and yet. . . .

In June O'Kane, Savadkin, and Flanagan also were transferred to Omori, a move that probably saved their lives. O'Kane was in sharply declining health. He had been beaten for asking permission to feed an airman named Hunt. The flier had two broken arms and was unable to feed himself. O'Kane was also developing hepatitis, probably from a single needle used to inoculate everyone against dysentery.

At Omori the food was improved a bit. There was real rice, and a worthwhile, if disgusting-looking, soup. O'Kane actually had a manageable working assignment stacking sheet metal and roof tiles that were left over from bombing raids. He also began to run into sympathetic Japanese civilians who would smuggle prisoners handfuls of soybeans, at the risk of beatings from the guards.

Back in Washington, O'Kane's old friend Dusty Dornin, who knew that O'Kane was alive, could stand it no longer. Dornin sent a letter to Ernestine, who remembered, "He wrote that a garbled message had been received via radio listing some men as present in a prison camp in Japan. Among the names was a Jed O'King and the only person the U.S. files could come up with was . . . my husband." Now, at last, Ernestine had a slender ray of hope.

Barb and Gene Fluckey were still at war. Fluckey had received the Congressional Medal of Honor for his Namkwan Harbor penetration, and Admiral

Nimitz assumed that he had been rotated to safe duty. But Fluckey had extracted a promise from Admiral Lockwood to conduct a last "graduation" patrol of his own choosing. Since shipping had essentially vanished from all but the Sea of Japan, Fluckey chose a new, maximum-harassment approach. He had *Barb* fitted out with a deck-mounted five-inch rocket launcher, and obtained all manner of supplementary weapons from the marines, including demolition gear and rifle grenades. *Barb* also took on a full complement of new evasion devices. To supplement the Mark 18 electrics, she was also equipped with three Mark 28 and several Mark 27 acoustical homing torpedoes, known as "cuties."

Fluckey's plan was to patrol between northern Hokkaido and southern Sakhalin, creating the biggest uproar possible. The timing meshed well as a diversion for Lockwood's long-planned penetration of the Sea of Japan by a wolf pack of nine QLA-equipped submarines.

For more than a month, from June 21 till July 26 with a one-week patrol extension requested by Fluckey, *Barb* roamed the shallow waters from Patience Bay in the north to Abashiri Bay in the south. No real effort was made to conceal her presence; *Barb* often was in fist-shaking sight of Japanese civilians onshore. Fluckey wanted to create the impression that multiple submarines were operating off La Pérouse Strait.

The rocket attacks that began at Shari on Hokkaido and quickly switched to Shikuka, Shiritori, and Kashiho on Karafuto (Sakhalin), were devastating to the Japanese. The hits on Shiritori were particularly bad. Fluckey let all members of the crew come on deck as gasoline drum explosions burned out three miles of the factory city. When rockets were inappropriate or expended, Fluckey conducted bombardments of Kaihyo Island, Chiri, and Shibertoro, destroying seal oil stations, canneries, sawmills, and small boatyards with dozens of trawlers on the ways.

Fluckey even put a party of saboteurs ashore, the only Americans besides POWs to land on Japanese soil during World War II. A former railroad electrician was among the group, and he cleverly engineered a track-mounted demolition device. Activity along the rail line was brisk enough to interrupt the saboteurs in their work. The unfortunate following train came along while the men were furiously rowing back to *Barb,* waiting only six hundred yards offshore. The explosion was stupendous, with a string of cars plunging down the embankment after the engine blew up.

The Japanese were uncertain about the source of some of these assaults, attributing the night rocket attacks to carrier air strikes. These events, along with counts of many civilian casualties, were broadcast and picked up by American news agencies, which concluded that Halsey was striking farther north than ever before. Through this secondhand source Nimitz learned that Fluckey was not in some safe assignment, but was on a single-submarine rampage. He began to press Lockwood to bring *Barb* home before Fluckey got killed. Nimitz was also uncomfortable that all this press attention might not please the prickly Admiral Halsey.

Hydeman's Hellcats, *Tinosa* among them, were simultaneously operating in the Sea of Japan. *Tinosa* snagged a mine cable, QLA notwithstanding, but survived. The nine boats completed an extraordinarily successful twenty-eight-ships-sunk foray on June 24. Without *Bonefish,* which was sunk by the Japanese, eight boats exited La Pérouse Strait, with *Barb* presenting plenty of diversions. After that Lockwood, too, became nervous that Fluckey would overreach, but refrained from ordering *Barb* home for another three weeks.

Fluckey actually made ship contacts as well, but was dismally let down by the Mark 18 electrics. They may have run slowly in these cold waters; they certainly ran much deeper than set. Fluckey, an outstanding shot, had thirteen consecutive misses before sinking the 2,820-ton *Sapporo Maru 11* on July 5. Two weeks later Fluckey also downed the 940-ton frigate *CD112,* with the carefully reexamined Mark 18 torpedoes.

In all this uproar the Japanese sent an experienced air-sea search team, equipped with MAD gear, after the marauder. *Barb* was relentlessly pursued, and severely depth-charged. She fought back, but all the new Mark 28 torpedoes proved to be duds. *Barb* finally escaped by using the whole panoply of new evasion devices, including Pillenwurfer bubblers and gassers as well as swim out beacons, to render the Japanese sonar totally useless. Once again the American technology was one step ahead of its enemy.

Reacting to a bet from one of his junior officers, Fluckey determined to put fifteen ships of any size on the bottom. One small ship was sunk with a cutie acoustical torpedo. A motion-picture photographer was aboard *Barb* and filmed everything. The chart house broke free, and *Barb*'s crew recovered many precious charts and plenty of souvenirs as well, including the ship's running lights. Alas, there was to be no JANAC credit for this well-documented sinking.

Because of the poor torpedo performance, most of *Barb*'s pirate war was fought with deck guns in very shallow water. This activity began with the sinking of a lugger as soon as *Barb* got on station, on June 21. A continuous string of gun actions and boardings followed. Trawlers, luggers, and sampans all came under the gun and were dispatched as economically as possible, preferably with a single five-inch shell to the waterline. One already holed trawler was sunk by roaring past at high speed, swamping the unfortunate vessel with *Barb*'s bow wave.

On the last patrol day Lockwood, sensing evasion on Fluckey's part, decisively ordered *Barb* home. There was no more ammunition aboard for the twenty-millimeter, forty-millimeter, or five-inch guns. Fluckey attacked the fifteenth ship, a trawler, with the marines' rifle grenades. Having no luck, he rammed the trawler, riding up on top of her and sinking her at once.

All throughout these gun actions *Barb* had been picking up prisoners. The rescued men were very close to home. Fluckey could often see their simple fishing shacks onshore. But these men were exhausted and through with war. It was an interesting indicator of the decline in the Japanese will to resist. As usual, the crew got along well with their captives.

On his way back to Midway, Fluckey wrote an amazingly prescient analysis of the future of submarines and missiles: "The torpedo has fulfilled its purpose. Its day in . . . war is passing. . . . In the near future . . . [we must] look to a new main battery—rockets. The rocket is not a toy. Its possibilities are tremendous, strategically and tactically, but not beyond comprehension." Fluckey had laid the groundwork for the missile-carrying submarine of the future.

The same day that *Barb* withdrew from the Hokkaido-Karafuto area, July 24, George Grider and *Flasher* arrived at Pearl Harbor. They immediately began to practice with the QLA mine detection gear, with lackluster results. Mine cables in the test field would scrape across the hull without being detected. Sometimes the fouling was worse. Grider wrote that "Every night we went into drydock so the snarled mine cables could be cut off our propellers. It was a little unnerving."

Flasher's crew, like *Tinosa*'s some months before, began to fret. They believed Japan was on the ropes. Why should they die in a minefield trying to use this worthless piece of junk? While Grider and his new XO were away from the boat for an evening meal, a near-mutiny occurred. Tom McCants, the third officer, was awakened with the news, put on his dress uniform, and came up on deck. Most of *Flasher*'s crew was assembled and told McCants of their fears and misgivings. They intended to submit a petition not to go on patrol until their concerns were addressed, a notion that McCants skillfully put to rest. It took much talking for the remainder of the night, but the crew finally dispersed. Not one asked for a transfer.

Grider, gloomy about the future, still had a plan for a later practical joke. Two close pilings were located off to one side of Pearl Harbor's main channel. Secretly he sent his XO and two men over to measure the clearance between the pilings, and the depth of water beneath them. This information was filed away for future use.

On August 6 the stunning news of Hiroshima reached Grider. The next day the Soviet Union declared war on Japan and quickly and cheaply occupied much nearby territory, including all of Sakhalin Island. On the following day came news of the atomic bombing of Nagasaki. On August 11 a false rumor of Japan's surrender swept through Pearl Harbor, and Grider exuberantly fired flares from *Flasher*'s signal gun into the night air.

On August 14 Japan's legitimate verbal acceptance of the surrender terms was accompanied by new orders for *Flasher*. She and several other submarines were to proceed to Guam, with orders to penetrate the Sea of Japan if the surrender fell apart. Grider was heartsick, but "in a bitterness of spirit" backed *Flasher* away from her mooring to begin the seventh war patrol.

On August 15 O'Kane and Leibold were at work digging caves to use as bomb shelters when the emperor's voice came over the radio. Now crudely able to understand a few words of Japanese, O'Kane heard "The war is over." To punctuate this startling news, the Japanese guards butchered an old horse, packed up the meat, and left.

Jesse DaSilva, too ill to dig, woke up to discover that the Omori POW camp was deathly still. There was only one guard, and he told DaSilva and his fellow prisoners the news. Without hesitation the prisoners took over the camp and cooked up the butchered horse's intestines—their first meat in ten months—with field corn.

Markers were spread out on the ground, and soon American aircraft found them. Food began to rain from the skies, sometimes crashing through the roofs of the buildings. The prisoners put up signs asking the fighter pilots and B-29 crews to drop the food away from the barracks.

On August 24 *Flasher*, in company with several other submarines in transit to Guam, intercepted and decoded a message addressed to the officer in tactical command of their group. While not directly addressed to them, *Flasher*'s officers decoded it immediately. It read "RETURN TO PEARL HARBOR." Without hesitation, Grider sliced out of formation and ran at flank speed all the way back to Pearl. Seeing this maneuver, the closest boat flashed "WHERE ARE YOU GOING?" Grider responded "BREAK YOUR MESSAGES" and beat all of them back.

This was the perfect moment to spring the long-planned boat-handling joke. As *Flasher* moved up the Pearl Harbor channel, the two secretly measured pilings came into view. McCants wrote: "Grider began a dramatic speech. Solemnly, and pursuant to official navy procedures, he announced to the officers present that they were all witnesses, that he was formally relieving the officer of the deck, that all but Grider himself were fully absolved of any liability in the matter, and that he was taking complete responsibility for whatever might happen to seven million dollars' worth of official government property. . . ."

"Grider skillfully maneuvered *Flasher* to the pilings. The boat slid slowly through with minor clearance to each side and without grounding, to the relief of the worried officers topside, all obviously concerned except for the cool, confident Grider."

On August 28 Grider, "cocky as a lord," and *Flasher* departed Pearl Harbor for a joyous trip home. He had lived after all.

Thousands of miles away, at dusk on that same August 28, perennial presidential-candidate-to-be Captain Harold Stassen anchored his destroyer division off Omori. He came ashore to make preparations for a rescue the next day, but was galvanized into a night rescue by the sight of the Allied prisoners. O'Kane was near death, his weight less than 100 pounds, with a high fever. Stassen had him placed in an isolation area of the hospital ship *Benevolence,* and he was quickly airlifted to Pearl Harbor.

DaSilva, in spite of food from the airdrops, was in a similar state, his weight hovering at about 100 pounds, down from his normal 170. He was put to bed, given whole blood and medication, and started on that old American cure-all, bacon and eggs.

Accompanying Stassen was a reporter from *Time* magazine whose New York editor was also from Dover, New Hampshire. He knew of O'Kane; his brother still lived in their common hometown. He reacted instantly to the news and had the on-the-spot reporter wire Ernestine directly from Japan. O'Kane was alive! She had never given up hope.

The voyage and recovery at home would be long and hard but, against all odds, O'Kane had lived. Nearly fifty years later, the emotional impact of that day was still vivid. He summed it up simply: "I know I was so very fortunate, so many lost their loved ones. . . ."

On September 2 Japan formally surrendered aboard the battleship *Missouri.* Twelve submarines and the tender *Proteus,* commanded by Roger Paine's first CO, Lew Parks, were present in Tokyo Bay. Parks had already seized the Japanese submarine base at Yokusuka and, accompanied by two of his officers, became the first U.S. military force to set foot inside Japan.

At the ceremony Admiral Lockwood was given a place in the solid front rank of the conquerors. There were gaps in the Japanese line, including Vice Chief of the Naval General Staff Takijiro Onishi. In on the planning of both Pearl Harbor and the invasion of the Philippines, Onishi had created the kamikaze from his naval fliers. He decided to follow them in death after the emperor's surrender broadcast, committing ritual *seppuku* by slitting open his abdomen, then stabbing himself in the chest and throat.

AUGUST 29, 1945. "Happy Day"–prisoners repatriated from Omori. Clay Decker with "x" on chest. (Clay Decker)

The ceremony was short but impressive. MacArthur gave, arguably, the best speech of his life. Shelley Mydans, Carl's wife and a former prisoner of the Japanese, thought it "Olympian. He is thinking in centuries and populations." The Japanese were deeply impressed. Toshikazu Kase, representing the Foreign Office, wrote and wondered "whether it would have been possible for us, had we been victorious, to embrace the vanquished with similar magnanimity."

MacArthur himself concluded, "And so my fellow countrymen, today I report to you that your sons and daughters have served you well and faithfully. . . . They are homeward bound. Take care of them."

AFTERWORD

The arrival of Harold Stassen's rescue team was just in time to save the lives of several faltering survivors. O'Kane was so near death that he was quickly sedated by the doctors to block his courageous attempts to remain functional, then flown to Pearl Harbor. All of the other officers and crew, save Jesse DaSilva, who preferred to return by ship to fatten up before seeing his family, were airlifted back to the States, though not on the same plane. At least one of the rescued stood in the open doorway of the aircraft after take-off and urinated on the burned-out city of Tokyo beneath him.

A member of Admiral Lockwood's staff was present at every refueling stop—Kwajalein, Johnston Island, Pearl Harbor, wherever—in the middle of the night, if that was when the plane arrived, to greet the rescued submariners. At Pearl the officers were given rolls of cash and taken to tailors for new, very tight-waisted, uniforms befitting starved men. Some, and this included O'Kane, elected to interrupt their journey at Pearl Harbor until they could recover enough health not to frighten their loved ones with their haggard appearance. Others could not wait to get back home.

The enlisted men tended to be through with the navy. After partial recovery on *Benevolence*, Jesse DaSilva was transferred to the hospital ship *Rescue* for a twenty-one-day return trip. He arrived in the States on October 25, 1945, two years to the day he left, and one year to the day from *Tang*'s sinking. He chose to be discharged in February 1946 and resumed civilian life as a press man for the *Los Angeles Times*. His wartime service was the central event of his life. He ultimately became the active national president of the U.S. Submarine Veterans of World War II during 1993 and 1994. He died in 1999; I was privileged to have received wonderful details on *Tang* and Jesse's later captivity from him before his death.

Clay Decker's prison dream of reuniting with his family was quickly dashed. Airlifted home to California with his cellmate Pappy Boyington, Decker learned that his wife, Lucille, who worked in the Kaiser shipyard in Richmond, had assumed he was dead. She had remarried, and another man was a replacement father for his three-year-old son.

Decker's divorce was followed by happier times. He returned to his home area of Denver and, in 1946, married his current wife, Ann. They celebrated their fifty-third year together in 1999. Decker toyed with the idea of finishing college but went to work for Skelly Oil instead to provide for his new

Clay Decker received the Silver Star. Decker was the first man ever to escape from a sunken submarine using a Momsen lung and live. (Clay Decker)

and growing family. After fifteen years he left Skelly to establish a successful trash business. When he sold it years later, the business had forty employees, fourteen trucks, and ten routes.

As the years passed, the many beatings administered by the Japanese took their toll. CAT scans of his lungs revealed scar tissue reminiscent of a serious automobile injury. Decker is now on full disability and 100 percent oxygen, round-the-clock. But this constraint has not blocked his traveling, especially to World War II submarine conventions. He simply obtains an advance list of where oxygen can be obtained, and he and Ann jump in the car. His voice is strong and robust, his enthusiasm for life undiminished.

Bill Leibold elected to stay in the navy. This skilled man became a warrant officer and was a witness in the war crimes trials in Japan where, he noted, "most Japanese being tried or interrogated had very poor memories." Subsequently he entered the LDO program and was commissioned an ensign. During the next ten years he served under O'Kane again and, over the years, became a close friend of the aging warrior. Leibold definitely has a life beyond *Tang*, and never joined any World War II commemorative organization where, he felt, the stories tended to grow a bit larger and more imaginative with each passing year.

While still in the submarine force—he served on snorkel boats—Leibold gradually began to specialize in deep submergence and submarine rescue programs. He had numerous shore commands and came to be captain of his own ship, *Volodar*. He rose to the rank of commander before retiring in 1969 after thirty years' service, and now lives on top of Mount Palomar. He is strong and youthful in appearance, thoughtful and diplomatic in his speech, and was particularly helpful in catching errors in the late stages of this manuscript.

Larry Savadkin chose to make the navy his career. A graduate of the wartime V-7 program, Savadkin in 1946 was sent to PCO school, where he qualified in submarines for the first time! He rotated between sea and shore duties for the next ten years. In addition to stints at the General Line School and the Naval War College and its staff, he was the XO of *Seadog* and brought *Sabalo* back in commission in June 1951.

Savadkin did not remain locked to submarine duty, even doing a tour aboard the Essex-class carrier *Valley Forge*. He was assigned to Istanbul, was an officer in the Unconventional Warfare Department, and served in Belgium with four Allied nations planning access to Berlin. He retired in 1972 to a lovely home on a golf course in San Marcos, California. A very private man, he is a gracious host in a den lined with photographic memories of his career. He made seventy-two written comments on the manuscript—a record for all reviewers; I think I've got it right this time.

Murray Frazee, not technically a "*Tang* survivor" but treated as one by the surviving crew, also stayed in the navy. The man whom Bill Leibold describes as having "the pulse of the boat" took over as CO of *Gar* when *Tang* put to sea for her last patrol. *Gar* was an old Tambor-class submarine and no longer served in a combat role.

The month the Japanese surrendered, the navy sent Frazee to George Washington University Law School. He studied in the mornings, and spent the afternoons in the judge advocate general's office until he graduated, with honors, in May 1948. Instead of using his new skills for some form of legal duty, the navy made him aide and flag secretary to ComSubPac, where he was promoted to the rank of commander.

For two years ending in July 1951 he was CO of the new *Greenfish*, a boat that had been converted to a snorkeling, large-battery Guppy (Greater Underwater Propulsion). He was once again Pearl Harbor–based. For the next four years Frazee rotated between Pentagon assignments and sea duty until, in July 1955, he became commander of ComSubDiv 24, a fleet of five boats based in New London.

In June 1956 Frazee returned to Washington, D.C., as the Bureau of Naval Personnel's submarine placement officer, responsible for the assignment of all submarine officers, from commanding officer down—a job in which he "got more Christmas cards than I needed." In this assignment he was promoted to captain. His sea duty days were over.

After a year at the National War College, Frazee received the finest assignment of his career: flag officer submarines, Royal Navy. He was based in Gosport, Hampshire, England, at Portsmouth Harbour. The only American on the staff, he was accepted as if he were British. Frazee's oldest son went to Gordonstoun and was a classmate of Prince Charles.

In 1962 Frazee returned to the United States and shore quarters in Charleston as ComSubRon 4, the commander of twelve submarines, a tender, and a rescue vessel—about two thousand men in all. In 1963 he returned to George Washington University and this time earned an M.A. in international relations. The navy used this education in his final assignment as head of the Europe and NATO Branch, Political-Military Policy Section.

In July 1966 Frazee retired after thirty years in the navy. Five days later, partly as a lark, he took and passed the Pennsylvania bar exam "to the huge surprise of myself and many others." He practiced law in Gettysburg for the next fifteen years, including service as a public defender, where he discovered he liked courtroom appearances.

Frazee remains active in Gettysburg, serving on the Borough Council and other community functions, enjoying his four children and eleven grandchildren. He was a close, avid reader of the manuscript, correcting several areas of fact. He is also a mean copy editor; the legal training did nothing to harm his command of the English language!

Dick O'Kane recovered very slowly from the effects of Japanese imprisonment, at the Naval Hospital in Portsmouth, New Hampshire. On March 27, 1946, Commander O'Kane received the Congressional Medal of Honor from President Harry Truman at a White House ceremony. In September and October of 1947 he testified at the war crimes trials in Tokyo.

O'Kane served in several postwar assignments, including commander of Submarine Division 32. In 1952 he became officer in charge of the submarine school at Groton and was promoted to the rank of captain. He later became the commander of Submarine Squadron 7.

In 1956, after tours at both the Armed Forces Staff College and the Naval War College, O'Kane was assigned to the Navy Department in Washington, D.C., as a member of the Ship Characteristics Board, an assignment he

MARCH 27, 1946. Dick O'Kane receives the Medal of Honor from Harry Truman. (U.S. Navy)

detested. In the spring of 1957 he decided to take early retirement and gave an interview to Hanson Baldwin that appeared in the *New York Times*. His severe criticism of a job with "too narrow an interpretation of service loyalty, and above all a sense of a job worth doing . . ." enraged Admiral Arleigh Burke.

Burke ordered O'Kane's friend from *Argonaut* days, Pete Galantin, to get to the bottom of O'Kane's retirement decision. Galantin found that "O'Kane was a pragmatic innovator, impatient with routine and scornful of any rigidity in planning or procedure. In a Pentagon assignment that was little more than clerical . . . he was completely miscast. In his words, 'What I have accomplished in one year could be done in one month.'"

Because of his combat decorations, O'Kane was permitted to retire with the "tombstone" rank of rear admiral, which he did. However, his pension was not increased, and O'Kane retired on just $358 per month, not counting the special allotment given to Medal of Honor winners. To earn a living he worked for Great Lakes Carbon in New York for three years.

In 1960 he and Ernestine moved to Red Hill Horse Ranch in Sebastopol, California, where he finished *Clear the Bridge* in 1977. This best-selling account of his experiences aboard *Tang* was followed in 1987 by a second popular book, *Wahoo*.

O'Kane was readily approachable and provided small bits of colorful detail about *Tang*, its survivors, and the wives and children of the lost men. He also kindly steered me toward other *Wahoo* men, most importantly Roger Paine. O'Kane's love for Ernestine was evident in every letter. He was proud of their union, ending each note with a mention of the number of years they had been married.

His last book seemed to cement an obsession to gain the recognition for Mush Morton that he felt had been too long denied. The greatest barrier to a Medal of Honor for Morton, he felt, was the January 26, 1943, gun action against the lifeboats of *Buyo Maru*. At the close of 1990 his letters to me began to take on a hard edge: he was furious with Clay Blair's ". . . sensational writing [which] emphasized the hearsay and omitted the truth." Soon he denied Sterling's account "whose battle station was on sound in the conning tower." Further, "George Grider, being engineer, was below decks during the action. . . ."

I knew the Sterling/Grider assertions were incorrect. I did not realize that O'Kane had begun his last fight with an enemy he could not defeat: Alzheimer's disease. Bill Leibold made the journey from Mount Palomar to Sebastopol, but his captain could no longer recognize "Boats." O'Kane died on February 16, 1994, a few days after his eighty-third birthday, and was buried in Arlington National Cemetery. In December 1994 the Navy named its newest destroyer, *DDG-77,* ironically of the Arleigh Burke class, the *U.S.S. O'Kane.*

Those men still living who served aboard *Wahoo* also had interesting, sometimes sad, postwar lives. Forest Sterling made it to stenography school and completed the courses that permitted him, in time, to become a chief petty officer. He transferred temporarily to the surface navy after steno school and served aboard *Comet* at the landings at Saipan, Tinian, Guam, and Leyte Gulf.

Sterling returned to the submarine service at Pearl Harbor in 1945. He retired in 1956 after twenty-six years of service, and wrote the moving *Wake of the Wahoo.* This mood piece is still in print nearly forty years later. Sterling now lives at the U.S. Naval Home in Gulfport, Mississippi. At midnight on January 1, 2000, he planned his own private salute to the crew of the *Wahoo,* whose fate he so narrowly escaped so long ago.

In April 1944 Marvin "Pinky" Kennedy got a second chance at combat, as CO of the destroyer *Guest.* He earned a Silver Star for his performance in the sea battles at Guam, Palau, and the Philippine Sea. By 1948 he was the commander of Destroyer Division 112 and rose to the rank of captain. In 1951, at age forty-six, Kennedy suffered a disabling stroke and retired from the navy with the rank of rear admiral. He lived quietly until his death on February 9, 1997, at age ninety-one.

After the war Jack Griggs served as engineering officer on Roger Paine's, then George Grider's new submarine *Cubera.* Griggs finally became executive officer of *Sirago* in March 1948, about four years after some of his classmates. He got his first command, the submarine rescue vessel *Greenlet,* in December 1951. In 1953, at age thirty-three, in a reflection of the slower pace of the peacetime navy, he received his first submarine command, *Tilefish.* Captain Griggs would never become an admiral. He retired in February 1965 and died in 1994 at age seventy-four.

George Grider spent a tranquil seven months after the war slowly moving *Flasher* toward her March 1946 decommissioning. He was then ordered to Key West to take command of *Cubera* from his old shipmate Roger Paine. Jack Griggs was the engineering officer.

Grider, like many combat veterans, grew increasingly annoyed with the navy's return to peacetime bureaucracy. In September 1947, at age thirty-five, he had a serious heart attack and elected to retire with the rank of captain. He then earned a law degree at the University of Virginia and went into private practice in his hometown of Memphis.

In 1958 Grider, with Lydel Sims, wrote his memoir *Warfish.* He was elected to the U.S. House of Representatives in 1964, but was unseated after one term. Grider continued to practice law in Memphis until his full-time retirement, and he died on March 20, 1991, at age seventy-eight.

Roger Paine commissioned *Cubera* three months after the formal Japanese surrender ceremony. He remained in command for only four months before being replaced by George Grider. Paine was being groomed for greater things and would reach flag rank in the coming years.

Paine was first tapped for advanced education in the new atomic age. He attended both the navy's postgraduate school at Annapolis and MIT, where he earned a master's degree in nuclear physics in February 1949. Subsequently he worked directly with Norris Bradbury, Edward Teller, Raemer Schrieber, and Hugh Paxton on both A-bomb and H-bomb development at Los Alamos until August 1951.

The next two years were a detour at sea, including five months in the Korean War theater, in command of the destroyer *Cowell*. In September 1953 he returned to the atomic weapons area, for which he had been trained. As chief of the Analysis Branch, he participated in all nuclear weapons tests that were conducted from 1954 to 1956, in Nevada, Bikini, and Eniwetok. Paine managed the analysis of all test data.

MARCH 16, 1946. *Flasher's* decommissioning at Groton. George Grider is at the right. (Photo courtesy of William R. McCants)

After a year at the Naval War College Paine assumed command of the four destroyers of Division 282 in July 1957. His specialty was an area he knew well: antisubmarine warfare.

In November 1958 Paine began a three-year tour of duty at the Bureau of Ordnance—later the Bureau of Naval Weapons—in Washington, D.C. He became director of the Missile Guidance and Airframe Division and was responsible for research, development, test, and evaluation of a host of missiles.

After another year at sea in command of the guided missile cruiser *Topeka*, Paine returned to Washington in November 1962, first as head of the Surface Warfare Branch, then in the office of the secretary of defense, Harold Brown. There Paine testified extensively on Capitol Hill in support of defense, not just naval, research program spending. He was awarded the Joint Service Commendation for this complex military, technical, and political role.

In 1966, days after his forty-ninth birthday, Paine was promoted to rear admiral. Then it was back to sea as commander, Cruiser-Destroyer Flotilla 10, where he directed a fleet of twenty-one cruisers and destroyers. In the spring of 1967 he moved to the Mediterranean as commander of an attack carrier strike group, flying his flag in the aircraft carriers *Shangri-la* and *Saratoga,* and the guided-missile cruiser *Galveston.*

In 1968 he returned to Washington as director of the Information Systems Division, responsible to procure, maintain, and operate all of the navy's computers, an assignment that was not even imagined a few years earlier. Paine finished his active duty as commander of the Pacific Fleet's Training Command with facilities in major navy installations from Japan to the West Coast. In the summer of 1972 Paine, with Bebe, retired to their El Cajon home. It had been a remarkable career.

Roger Paine befriended this author, guiding him into membership in the Naval Submarine League, directing him to other *Wahoo* survivors, and answering scores of questions. When just our correspondence reached the one-inch-thick mark, I thought it time to try to record some of what I had learned. Paine read multiple drafts of the manuscript, enriching much of the text with personal stories. This book would not exist without his encouragement.

Nor can we forget the remarkable commander of this successful fighting force, Charles A. Lockwood. The rapid demobilization of the navy at war's end finished Lockwood's dream of commanding a strong peacetime submarine force. He was further deeply disappointed in the inspector general assignment given him by his longtime friend Admiral Nimitz. Lockwood skillfully persuaded the secretary of the navy to create a job as deputy chief of naval operations for submarines, but Nimitz dug in hard, as did Nimitz's successor. Discouraged, Lockwood retired from the navy on September 1, 1947, at age fifty-seven. Twenty-three years later, Lockwood's proposal was accepted.

Lockwood moved to Los Gatos, California, to a ten-acre tract he named Twin Dolphins. He began to write about submarine life, including his own, with considerable success. In 1967 his last book, *Down to the Sea in Subs,* was published, but Lockwood did not live to see it, dying that June at age seventy-seven.

The fate of a few submarines may be interesting, covered here in alphabetical order. After the war *Barb* went in and out of commission three times during the next decade. In 1954, in spite of her age (thirteen years), thin skin, and possible battle stresses, she was converted to a large-battery, smooth-superstructure, snorkel submarine—a Guppy. In her new configuration she served the U.S. Navy for only four months before she was given to Italy and rechristened the *Enrico Tazzoli.* After eighteen years as an Italian boat, she was retired on October 15, 1972. Without the knowledge of Gene Fluckey or *Barb*'s wartime crew—who would have attempted to purchase her for a museum—she was sold for a hundred thousand dollars and scrapped.

George Grider took *Flasher* on a leisurely voyage home, with long stopovers in New Orleans, Mobile, and Key West. As the weeks, then months, went by, more and more of the crew were discharged. Only a skeleton force was aboard when she reached Philadelphia, and her batteries were stripped from their compartments. She was towed to New London, and the Bureau of Ships decided that her hull had been weakened by too many depth charges. On March 16, 1946, she was formally decommissioned in the presence of a teary-eyed Grider.

Flasher was laid up in the Thames at Groton for sixteen years, but on June 8, 1963, she was sold for scrap for forty-one thousand dollars. Veterans of her crew tried to save her, to no avail. Only the skin surrounding the conning tower, which made up the bridge and fairwater, along with her periscope tubes, radar antenna, and conning tower armament, were saved. This section sits today at the northern end of Thames Street, nearly under the newer I-95 bridge, near Electric Boat and the river where she first felt water.

Surrounding the bridge structure is an impressive memorial to the lost submarines of World War II. This location is lovingly maintained by a veteran of nine patrols, four of them on *Flasher.* The memorial is used by submarine veterans for special ceremonies to mark the passing of aging crew members.

On the bottom at 24° 36' N, 121°25' E, *Tang* rested unseen and forgotten by all except survivors and their families until the outbreak of the Korean War. With the entry of Chinese ground forces into that peninsular campaign, the U.S. Navy moved into the Strait of Formosa. They were determined to block any possibility that Chiang Kai-shek might use this opportunity to attack the mainland. They were equally concerned that the Chinese Communists might attack Formosa, which the Joint Chiefs of Staff thought a "likely" target.

In a state of war readiness, the destroyer *Higbee* detected a submarine on the bottom of the strait during the night of December 27, 1951. For seventy-two hours this stubborn assailant was pounded with depth charges until word was relayed from the Pentagon that their target was, in all probability, the sunken *Tang*.

After that date there were desultory efforts by a few parents of young men killed aboard *Tang* to investigate the hulk. All foundered amid the Cold War tensions surrounding the role of China. She still rests where she sank in 1944.

A refitted *Tinosa* embarked on her twelfth war patrol on August 11, 1945. Japan's surrender truncated this mission, and by August 26 she was on her way from Midway to San Francisco. She operated as a West Coast boat until June 1946, when she was placed in reserve status, then into mothballs in January 1947.

Taken out of storage because of the Korean War, *Tinosa* was recommissioned in January 1952 and served until December 2, 1953. Her name was struck from the navy list on September 1, 1958, and her hulk became an antisubmarine-warfare target. In November 1960 this gallant ship was scuttled in deep water, escaping an ignominious scrapping.

A century of distrust causes the new Russian Federation to maintain strict controls on vessels transiting La Pérouse Strait on its side of the border. Nevertheless, Japanese fishermen do ply these waters, and their nets have entangled *Wahoo*'s wreckage often enough for the location—45° 42' N, 142° 24' E—to appear in local "Notice to Mariners" reports.

Wahoo is a lure for those who would love to retrieve souvenirs or at least photograph the ruined hulk. To date, Russian insistence on high "fees"—often more than fifty-thousand dollars—simply to lower a camera overboard have discouraged all such expeditions. Even the Wahoo Peace Memorial ship was required to stand off from the site of the sinking, coming no closer than 45° 34.06' N, 141° 54.327' E during the ceremonies. To date, *Wahoo* sleeps on alone and unseen in the icy Sea of Okhotsk.

Finally, research into the geography of Wewak Harbor led to an unexpected discovery. Following *Wahoo*'s penetration of the roadstead, the Japanese began to strengthen "fortress Wewak." Heavy artillery was sited on most of the coastal islands, with a battery of naval guns on Kairiru. Extensive defensive positions were dug in all along the Wewak coastline, and bunkers and natural caves were used to provide strong overlapping fire points. The Japanese 41st Infantry Division provided the troops, which were well supplied with stores.

In early 1945 the task of taking Wewak was assigned to the Australians, mostly to the 16th and 19th Brigades as well as the 2/6 Commando Regiment. The advance began on April 27 and was marked by particularly heavy, stubborn fighting, with progress marked in yards. The Japanese fought to the death, and had to be eliminated one-by-one with coordinated ground flamethrower attacks supported by Australian naval and RAAF units.

The Aussies misjudged the strength of the garrison on Mushu Island, and the party of special troops who landed to capture it were annihilated. Unable to get back to their boats because of the aggressive Japanese counterattacks, there was only one survivor. The Australians then brought up 155-millimeter Long Toms to pound Mushu's defenses.

On May 11 Wewak and its airstrip were declared secure, though extremely bitter, bloody fighting continued in the surrounding area until the Japanese capitulated in August 1945. With a no-surrender strategy, almost no Japanese prisoners were taken. They were slowly destroyed, often sealed in caves.

After the war the eastern half of the island on which Wewak is located became Papua New Guinea, an Australian mandated territory. The fierce tribesmen were gradually turned from their normal pursuits of headhunting. Australian-style civilization was slowly imposed. The Japanese erected an important memorial to their war dead, but the only other signs of their occupation are the ruined gun emplacements. Most skeletons were taken from Wewak's graves and caves to shrines in Tokyo.

Today Wewak is the capital of East Sepik, Papua New Guinea's second-largest province. It is an attractive town with beautiful white sandy beaches and lush tropical vegetation. It is the most visited of Papua New Guinea's provinces, partly because of its convenient airport, and there has been steady pressure to make it a tourist hub. In spite of the fear of destroying the livelihood and culture of the indigenous people, seven important hotels were operating in 1999, with a decided lure for snorkeling and scuba diving vacations.

A P P E N D I X   I

Top Skippers of World War II: Tonnage Credited

Skipper	Tons
Richard H. O'Kane	227,800
Eugene B. Fluckey	179,700
Roy M. Davenport	151,900
Slade D. Cutter	142,300
Henry G. Munson	113,400
Reuben T. Whitaker	111,500
William S. Post Jr.	110,900
Charles E. Loughlin	109,400
Walter T. Griffith	106,300
Edward E. Shelby	106,200
Thomas W. Hogan	105,500
Eli T. Reich	101,400
Dudley W. Morton	100,500
Bernard A. Clarey	98,600
Robert E. Dornin	96,500
Anton R. Gallaher	94,000
Norvell G. Ward	90,200
Gordon W. Underwood	89,600
Charles O. Triebel	83,300
Henry C. Bruton	82,600
Samuel D. Dealey	82,500
William T. Kinsella	80,500
Royce L. Gross	80,500
Frank G. Selby	78,600
Thomas M. Dykers	77,900

Skipper	Tons
Lawson P. Ramage	77,600
Thomas B. Klakring	76,900
Louis D. McGregor	74,600
John E. Lee	74,100
John S. Coye Jr.	71,700
Creed C. Burlingame	71,700
Charles H. Andrews	71,500
Glynn R. Donaho	71,400
Raymond H. Bass	70,300
George E. Porter	70,300
Lowell T. Stone	68,600
Donald F. Weiss	67,100
William C. Thompson Jr.	66,300
Robert J. Foley	66,000
Russell Kefauver	64,000
William B. Sieglaff	63,500
John A. Moore	63,500
Vernon L. Lawrence	62,200
Duncan C. MacMillan	61,400
Enrique D. Haskins	61,200
Willard R. Laughton	60,200
Malcolm E. Garrison	60,100
John A. Tyree Jr.	55,900
Joseph H. Willingham	55,500
Ralph M. Metcalf	54,800
James C. Dempsey	52,100
Thomas L. Wogan	51,700
John C. Broach	51,400
Eric L. Barr	51,200
Thomas S. Baskett	50,700
Walter G. Ebert	49,000
Robert H. Rice	49,000
Philip H. Ross	45,400
James W. Coe	45,300
Charles C. Kilpatrick	44,600
George W. Grider	43,800
William H. Hazzard	43,100
William J. Germershausen	42,300
William J. Millican	40,000
Robert D. Risser	33,500
Joseph F. Enright	28,000

APPENDIX II

Top Skippers of World War II: JANAC Assessment

	Tons	
Skipper	**Credited**	**JANAC**
Eugene B. Fluckey	179,700	95,630
Richard H. O'Kane	227,800	93,824
Gordon W. Underwood	89,600	75,386
Slade D. Cutter	142,300	72,000
Henry G. Munson	113,400	67,630
Royce L. Gross	80,500	65,735
Reuben T. Whitaker	111,500	60,846
Eli T. Reich	101,400	59,839
Joseph F. Enright	28,000	59,000
Charles O. Triebel	83,300	58,837
Charles H. Andrews	71,500	57,243
Dudley W. Morton	100,500	55,000
Robert E. Dornin	96,500	54,595
Henry C. Bruton	82,600	54,564
William S. Post Jr.	110,900	54,213
Samuel D. Dealey	82,500	54,002
Creed C. Burlingame	71,700	46,865
Thomas L. Wogan	51,700	46,730
Eric L. Barr	51,200	46,212
Walter T. Griffith	106,300	45,874
John A. Moore	63,500	45,757
Edward E. Shelby	106,200	45,613
Louis D. McGregor	74,600	44,637
George W. Grider	43,800	43,718
Bernard A. Clarey	98,600	42,956

Skipper	Tons	
	Credited	JANAC
Thomas M. Dykers	77,900	42,417
Charles E. Loughlin	109,400	41,718
Robert D. Risser	33,500	40,931
Ralph M. Metcalf	54,800	40,040
John A. Tyree Jr.	55,900	39,371
Norvell G. Ward	90,200	39,302
Lowell T. Stone	68,600	39,266
Robert H. Rice	49,000	39,100
Donald F. Weiss	67,100	39,047
John S. Coye Jr.	71,700	39,000
Willard R. Laughton	60,200	38,340
Frank G. Selby	78,600	38,159
Raymond H. Bass	70,300	37,977
John C. Broach	51,400	37,923
Malcolm E. Garrison	60,100	37,368
Lawson P. Ramage	77,600	36,681
William C. Thompson Jr.	66,300	36,062
Thomas W. Hogan	105,500	34,329
Vernon L. Lawrence	62,200	34,199
Walter G. Ebert	49,000	34,108
William T. Kinsella	80,500	34,101
Thomas B. Klakring	76,900	33,122
William B. Sieglaff	63,500	32,886
George E. Porter	70,300	30,940
James C. Dempsey	52,100	30,794
Glynn R. Donaho	71,400	29,870
Roy M. Davenport	151,900	29,662
John E. Lee	74,100	28,562
Thomas S. Baskett	50,700	27,273
Robert J. Foley	66,000	26,235
James W. Coe	45,300	26,130
Joseph H. Willingham	55,500	25,636
Enrique D. Haskins	61,200	25,400
Philip H. Ross	45,400	23,226
Russell Kefauver	64,000	23,081
Charles C. Kilpatrick	44,600	22,749
Duncan C. MacMillan	61,400	22,277
William J. Millican	40,000	21,525
Anton R. Gallaher	94,000	20,181
William H. Hazzard	43,100	18,087
William J. Germershausen	42,300	16,277
Totals	5,083,100	2,760,058

APPENDIX III

Top Skippers of World War II: Tonnage Percent Overestimated

Skipper	Tons Credited	Tons JANAC	Percent Over/Under
Joseph F. Enright	28,000	59,000	47.5
Robert D. Risser	33,500	40,931	81.8
George W. Grider	43,800	43,718	100.2
Thomas L. Wogan	51,700	46,730	110.6
Eric L. Barr	51,200	46,212	110.8
Gordon W. Underwood	89,600	75,386	118.9
Royce L. Gross	80,500	65,735	122.5
Charles H. Andrews	71,500	57,243	124.9
Robert H. Rice	49,000	39,100	125.3
John C. Broach	51,400	37,923	135.5
Ralph M. Metcalf	54,800	40,040	136.9
John A. Moore	63,500	45,757	138.8
Charles O. Triebel	83,300	58,837	141.6
John A. Tyree Jr.	55,900	39,371	142.0
Walter G. Ebert	49,000	34,108	143.7
Henry C. Bruton	82,600	54,564	151.4
Samuel D. Dealey	82,500	54,002	152.8
Creed C. Burlingame	71,700	46,865	153.0
Willard R. Laughton	60,200	38,340	157.0
Malcolm E. Garrison	60,100	37,368	160.8
Louis D. McGregor	74,600	44,637	167.1
Henry G. Munson	113,400	67,630	167.7
James C. Dempsey	52,100	30,794	169.2
Eli T. Reich	101,400	59,839	169.5
Donald F. Weiss	67,100	39,047	171.8
James W. Coe	45,300	26,130	173.4

| Skipper | Tons | | Percent |
	Credited	JANAC	Over/Under
Lowell T. Stone	68,600	39,266	174.7
Robert E. Dornin	96,500	54,595	176.8
Vernon L. Lawrence	62,200	34,199	181.9
Dudley W. Morton	100,500	55,000	182.7
Reuben T. Whitaker	111,500	60,846	183.2
Thomas M. Dykers	77,900	42,417	183.7
John S. Coye Jr.	71,700	39,000	183.8
William C. Thompson Jr.	66,300	36,062	183.9
Raymond H. Bass	70,300	37,977	185.1
William J. Millican	40,000	21,525	185.8
Thomas S. Baskett	50,700	27,273	185.9
Eugene B. Fluckey	179,700	95,630	187.9
William B. Sieglaff	63,500	32,886	193.1
Philip H. Ross	45,400	23,226	195.5
Charles C. Kilpatrick	44,600	22,749	196.1
Slade D. Cutter	142,300	72,000	197.6
William S. Post Jr.	110,900	54,213	204.6
Frank G. Selby	78,600	38,159	206.0
Lawson P. Ramage	77,600	36,681	211.6
Joseph H. Willingham	55,500	25,636	216.5
George E. Porter	70,300	30,940	227.2
Norvell G. Ward	90,200	39,302	229.5
Bernard A. Clarey	98,600	42,956	229.5
Walter T. Griffith	106,300	45,874	231.7
Thomas B. Klakring	76,900	33,122	232.2
Edward E. Shelby	106,200	45,613	232.8
William T. Kinsella	80,500	34,101	236.1
William H. Hazzard	43,100	18,087	238.3
Glynn R. Donaho	71,400	29,870	239.0
Enrique D. Haskins	61,200	25,400	240.9
Richard H. O'Kane	227,800	93,824	242.8
Robert J. Foley	66,000	26,235	251.6
John E. Lee	74,100	28,562	259.4
William J. Germershausen	42,300	16,277	259.9
Charles E. Loughlin	109,400	41,718	262.2
Duncan C. MacMillan	61,400	22,277	275.6
Russell Kefauver	64,000	23,081	277.3
Thomas W. Hogan	105,500	34,329	307.3
Anton R. Gallaher	94,000	20,181	465.8
Roy M. Davenport	151,900	29,662	512.1
Totals	5,083,100	2,760,058	184.2
			(average)

Wahoo Sinkings
and
Tang Sinkings

Wahoo Sinkings

	Kennedy (1,2)/Morton (3-7)			JANAC			IJN			Alden		
Date	Ship Type	Sunk	Tons	Name	Sunk	Tons	Name	Sunk	Tons	Name	Sunk	Tons
9-20-42	cargo	1	6,500									
12-10-42	cargo	1	5,600	Kamoi Maru	1	5,355	Kamoi Maru	1	5,355	Kamoi Maru	1	5,355
12-14-42	submarine	1	2,000									
1-24-43	destroyer	1	1,685									
1-26-43	cargo	1	7,200	Fukuei Maru 2	1	1,901	Fukuei Maru 2	1	1,701	Fukuei Maru 2	1	1,901
1-26-43	transport	1	7,200	Buyo Maru	1	5,446	Buyo Maru	1	6,446	Buyo Maru	1	5,446
1-26-43	oiler	1	6,500	unknown Maru	1	4,000						
1-26-43	cargo	1	9,500									
3-19-43	cargo	1	4,100	Zogen Maru	1	1,428	Zogen Go	1	1,428	Zogen Maru	1	1,428
3-19-43	cargo	1		Kowa Maru	1	3,217	Kowa Maru	1	3,217	Kowa Maru	1	3,217
3-21-43	cargo	1	7,200	Hozan Maru	1	2,260	Hozan Maru	1	2,260	Hozan Maru	1	2,260
3-21-43	cargo	1	6,500	Nittsu Maru	1	2,183	Nitu Maru	1	2,183	Nitu Maru	1	2,183
3-23-43	cargo	1	2,400	unknown Maru	1	2,427						
3-24-43	oiler	1	7,500	unknown Maru	1	2,556						
3-25-43	cargo	1	2,600	Takaosan Maru	1	2,076	Takaosan Maru	1	2,056	Takaosan Maru	1	2,076
3-25-43	cargo	1	1,000	Satsuki Maru	1	830	Satsuki Maru	1	830	Satsuki Maru	1	830
3-27-43	patrol	1	100									
3-28-43	sampan	1	50									
3-28-43	sampan	1	50									

Date	Type	#	Tonnage	Ship	#	Tonnage	Ship	#	Tonnage	Ship	#	Tonnage
3-29-43	cargo	1	5,200	Yamabato Maru	1	2,556	Yamabato Maru	1	2,556	Yamabato Maru	1	2,556
5-7-43	cargo	1	5,700	Tamon Maru 5	1	5,260	Tamon Maru 5	1	5,260	Tamon Maru 5	1	5,260
5-9-43	oiler	1	9,500	Jinmu Maru	1	1,912				Jinmu Maru	1	1,912
5-9-43	oiler	1	9,500	Takao Maru	1	3,204	Takao Maru	1	3,204	Takao Maru	1	3,204
8-18-43	sampan	1	30							sampan	1	30
8-20-43	sampan	1	25							sampan	1	25
8-20-43	sampan	1	—							sampan	1	—
9-21-43										Hokusei Maru	1	1,394
9-25-43										Taiko Maru	1	2,958
9-29-43				Masaki Maru 2	1	1,238	Masaki Maru	1	1,229	Masaki Maru 2	1	1,238
10-5-43				Konron Maru	1	7,903	Konron Maru	1	7,903	Konron Maru	1	7,903
10-6-43				Kanko Maru	1	1,283	Kanko Maru	1	1,283	Kanko Maru	1	1,283
10-9-43				Hankow (Kanko) M.	1	2,995	Hankow (Kanko) M.	1	2,995	Hankow (Kanko) M.	1	2,995
Totals		25	107,640		19	57,035		15	46,911		21	52,459

Tang Sinkings

Date	O'Kane			JANAC			IJN			Alden		
	Ship Type	Sunk	Tons	Name	Sunk	Tons	Name	Sunk	Tons	Name	Sunk	Tons
2-17-44	Mansei Maru	1	7,770	Gyoten Maru	1	6,854	Gyoten Maru	1	6,854	Gyoten Maru	1	6,854
2-17-44							Kuniei Maru		5,184	Kuniei Maru	1	5,184
2-22-44	Kenyo Maru	1	6,486	Fukuyama Maru	1	3,581	Fukuyama Maru	1	3,581	Fukuyama Maru	1	3,581
2-23-44	Arimasan Maru	1	8,663	Yamashimo Maru	1	6,777	Yamashimo Maru	1	6,777	Yamashimo Maru	1	6,777
2-24-44	Tatutaki Maru	1	7,064	Echizen Maru	1	2,424	Echizen Maru	1	2,424	Echizen Maru	1	2,424
2-25-44	naval tanker	1	12,000	Choko Maru	1	1,790	Choko Maru	1	1,790	Choko Maru	1	1,790
6-24-44	Genyo Maru	1	10,000	Tamahoku Maru	1	6,780	Tamahoku Maru	1	6,780	Tamahoku Maru	1	6,780
6-24-44	Aobasan Maru	1	7,500	Nasusan Maru	1	4,399	Nasusan Maru	1	4,399	Nasusan Maru	1	4,399
6-24-44				Tainan Maru	1	3,175	Tainan Maru	1	3,175	Tainan Maru	1	3,175
6-24-44				Kennichi Maru	1	1,937	Kennichi Maru	1	1,937	Kennichi Maru	1	1,937
6-30-44	Tazan Maru	1	5,464	Nikkin Maru	1	5,705				unknown	1	5,705
7-1-44	Amakasu Maru	1	2,000	Takatori Maru	1	878				Takatori Maru	1	878
7-1-44	Samarang Maru	1	4,000	Taiun Maru	1	998	Daiun Maru	1	998	Taiun Maru	1	998
7-4-44	Kurosio Maru	1	16,000	Asukasan Maru	1	6,886	Asukasan Maru	1	6,886	Asukasan Maru	1	6,886
7-4-44	Ama-Auka Maru	1	7,000	Yamaoka Maru	1	6,932				Yamaoka Maru	1	6,932
7-6-44	Osaka Maru	1	4,000	Dori Maru	1	1,469	Dori Go	1	1,469	Dori Go	1	1,469
8-11-44	Biyo Maru	1	5,425	Roko Maru	1	3,328	Roko Maru	1	3,328	Roko Maru	1	3,328

Date	Type	No.	Tons	Ship	No.	Tons	Ship	No.	Tons	Ship	No.	Tons
8-22-44	patrol boat	1	1,500				Nansatsu Maru 2	1	116	Nansatsu Maru 2	1	116
8-23-44	transport	1	10,000	Tsukushi Maru	1	8,135	Tsukushi Maru	1	1,859	Tsukushi Maru	1	1,859
8-25-44	tanker	1	5,000				Nanko Maru 8	1	834	Nanko Maru 8	1	834
8-25-44	Kushiro Maru	1	600									
10-11-44	freighter	1	7,500	Josho Go	1	1,658	Josho Maru	1	1,658	Josho Go	1	1,658
10-11-44	Aden Maru	1	5,824	Oita Maru	1	711	Oita Maru	1	711	Oita Maru	1	711
10-23-44	tanker	1	10,000	Toun Maru	1	1,915				Toun Maru	1	1,915
10-23-44	tanker	1	10,000	Tatsuju Maru	1	1,944				Tatsuju Maru	1	1,944
10-23-44	tanker	1	10,000									
10-23-44	transport	1	7,500	Wakatake Maru	1	1,920	Wakatake Maru	1	1,920	Wakatake Maru	1	1,920
10-23-44	freighter	1	7,500				Kori Go	1	1,339	Kori Go	1	1,339
10-25-44	transport	1	10,000									
10-25-44	transport	1	7,500									
10-25-44	tanker	1	10,000	Matsumotu Maru	1	7,024	Matsumotu Maru	1	7,024	Matsumoto Maru	1	7,024
10-25-44	tanker	1	10,000	Kogen Maru	1	6,600	Kogen Maru	1	6,600	Ebara Maru	1	6,957
10-25-44	destroyer	1	1,500									
10-25-44	transport	1	10,000									
Totals		31	227,796		24	93,820		23	77,643		28	95,374

CHAPTER NOTES

Prologue

Fewer submarine attacks have such a rich array of source material. The attack was not only well reported in *Wahoo*'s patrol report, it also was recounted in detail by participants such as George Grider *(Warfish)*, Dick O'Kane *(Wahoo)*, and Forest Sterling *(Wake of the Wahoo)* in their own books. Providentially, Roger Paine, who manned the TDC during the attack, was available to lend his memories when the four written versions were organized in sequence and written into a new narrative. This powerful combination was used in all chapters dealing with *Wahoo*.

Chapter 1

The sudden impact of war distorted the memories of virtually all the participants. Roger Paine, for example, thought that *Pompano* was only eighteen miles away from Pearl Harbor when the attack began; he remembered Diamond Head in sight. But an examination of the original deck logs of all four P-boats showed that this was impossible. This timeline reconstruction was confused by the fact that most boats had not set their clocks to Hawaiian time.

Years after the war, some of the participants polished their stories a bit. Slade Cutter, in an otherwise highly useful account of *Pompano*, wrote in *Naval History*, April 1987, page 73 that ". . . we got attacked by the first wave of planes, and were strafed." But there is absolutely no evidence that there was more than one attacker and, in any case, *Pompano* was submerged when the strafer came in; Cutter could have seen nothing. In no way is this meant to detract from Cutter's personal courage, since this man went on to win four Navy Crosses and two Silver Stars. He sank nineteen JANAC-credited ships—second only to O'Kane. It's just that one must be careful when the memories are forty-five years old.

Information on the miserable performance characteristics of *Argonaut* come from a variety of sources, such as the writings of Admiral I. J. "Pete" Galantin and Dick O'Kane (who were shipmates aboard her), as well as more engineering-oriented references, such as Norman Friedman's *U.S. Submarines Through 1945*.

Chapter 2

Patrol reports served as the principal sources of information for the activities of *Argonaut* and *Pompano*. The *Gudgeon* sections were enriched with material first reported in W. J. "Jasper" Holmes's *Undersea Victory*.

Attack results (or lack of them) were cross-checked with John Alden's "United States and Allied Submarine Successes in the Pacific and Far East During World War II," prepared in October 1999. Commander Alden also kindly read the manuscript to ensure that I had not slipped up. His work is used as a source throughout this book.

Conditions aboard *Dolphin* were made clear from the diary of Bob Logue, which his brother George generously copied for me. Murray Frazee, who served in Naval Personnel, clarified what happened to the unfortunate "Dizzy" Rainer.

Information on early, disappointing torpedo results came from Dr. Frederick J. Milford, who also gave me a copy of a 1991 master's thesis written on this subject by John David Hoerl. Statistics from Dr. Milford's work are used throughout the remainder of the book.

The TDC information came from my own study of the subject (I spent thirty-two years in product design with IBM), including copies of the technical manuals made for me by the Force Museum in Groton.

Chapter 3

In addition to the sources already mentioned, information on the German attacks comes from three books: Clay Blair's *Hitler's U-Boat War* (volume I), Michael Gannon's *Operation Drumbeat*, and Terry Hughes/and Michael Costello's *The Battle of the Atlantic*.

The failure of U.S. submarines to make any contribution to the Battle of Midway was galling to ComSubPac. In a defense against criticism, Bill Brockman's patrol report of his daring, persistent attack on a damaged Soryu-class carrier, and its subsequent sinking, was accepted at face value. A stirring Fred Freeman painting, completed in 1949, shows *Nautilus*'s periscope observing hits in what was now accepted as *Soryu* herself. A copy of the painting is prominently displayed in the Force Museum at Groton. A gripping account of the attack was written by Theodore Roscoe in the same year, based on the official operational history compiled by Captain R. G. Voge's ComSubPac staff.

But in his 1966 book *Undersea Victory*, page 143, Jasper Holmes, a respected member of Voge's staff, clearly identified the ship that was attacked as *Kaga*, and recorded the middle torpedo's failure to explode even though it struck its target. *Nautilus* did not sink a carrier. In 1967 Walter Lord pushed a bit farther in *Incredible Victory*, discovering Yoshio Kunisada, who had used *Nautilus*'s torpedo as a life raft. By 1975 Clay Blair was able to report in his book *Silent Victory* the results of a careful postwar analysis by the navy that substantiated the assertions of Holmes.

The *Nautilus* vs. *Soryu* myth persists, unprofessionally propagated by the Force Museum, whose personnel know better.

Chapter 5

The unique sections on Morton vs. Kennedy were recorded by John Griggs III and sent to the University of Wyoming along with the "Blair Papers." I recovered all of Griggs's handwritten notes and have used them throughout the book, including those portions that deal with *Shark II* and *Picuda*.

I also obtained Marvin "Pinky" Kennedy's papers from Wyoming, including the transcript of an interview he gave on December 5, 1943, nearly a year after being relieved by Morton. Morton was already dead, but Kennedy did not know it. He was remarkably generous in his comments saying, "I was relieved. On [Morton's] next patrol he set quite a record with *[Wahoo]*. . . . Lieutenant Commander Morton [is] probably [one of] the outstanding commanding officers of today."

Kennedy also singled out Paine for special notice. "There is another officer [who] was on board the *Wahoo* who will probably be heard of before the war is over. That is Lieutenant Roger Paine. He ran the torpedo data computer during our trips. Extremely level-headed, intelligent, cool person, nothing ever bothers him, he acted very well under fire. He is now in command of *S-34* and, unless I miss my guess, he will eventually have one of the big boats [and] probably go around and set a record for himself. . . . He is the youngest officer at the moment we have in command of any submarine."

Kennedy never made a reference to Dick O'Kane.

Chapter 7

One problem with reconstructing the events surrounding the destruction of *Buyo Maru*'s boats is the plethora of conspiracy theories, mixed with exaggerated tales of savage brutality. There are any number of submarine devotees who believe that Morton was sent on a secret mission by Douglas MacArthur simply to destroy *Buyo Maru* and kill all her "troops." Missing deck logs are taken as evidence that *Wahoo*'s batteries were not really low, that it was just an excuse for surfacing and opening fire. Some of the more lurid tales involve Filipino stewards heartlessly spearing helpless Japanese while they struggled in the water.

The secret-mission theory is not worthy of Oliver Stone at his worst, and has been decisively rejected. The Japanese Diet Library was the first to inform me that most of the victims of *Wahoo*'s gun attack were Indian prisoners of war, not Japanese soldiers. They even provided the exact location of the records in the U.S. Archives. After obtaining these reports, known to very few people, I decided that their testimony provided eloquent witness to what it felt like to be on the receiving end of *Wahoo*'s wrath. No spear wielding stewards are required to dramatize the tale.

An oddity remains. British captain A. K. Daw, one of the POW swimmers in the water, testified at the war crimes trials that: "The submarine was quite close as I could see the painted number on it. . . . I did not have my spectacles with me otherwise I could have known the number of the submarine."

The navy began to obliterate painted numerals on submarines operating in the

Pacific as early as October 1941. The navy photo of Wahoo departing Mare Island for the first time shows no numerals on the port side of the conning tower. Photographs of *Wahoo* arriving at Pearl Harbor after the *Buyo Maru* action show a number-free starboard side. It seems that Captain Daw, without his spectacles, and looking at a submarine five hundred yards away, only thought he saw numerals. None could have been present.

The seemingly superficial Japanese effort to save prisoners of war by trailing ropes and nets in the water should not be judged too harshly. This technique was standard policy in the British Navy at the outbreak of the war, and the Japanese Navy adopted most British practices. However, the British soon dropped even this halfway measure during the Battle of the Atlantic. German survivors in the water, whether from capital ships or U-boats, were routinely left to perish. American aircrews who forced U-boats to the surface during an attack generally dropped life rafts to the helpless men below. However, surface ships were rarely diverted to rescue them. The resulting loss of life was staggering.

Chapter 8

It seems likely that Dick O'Kane's memories of some of the activities that occurred during the Midway refit cycle grew more dramatic with the passage of time. He reports (*Wahoo,* page 249) that he conned Wahoo "through the slot in the reef into the angry seas" during the emergency drill. Roger Paine, who was acting XO, does not remember them leaving the lagoon (personal correspondence). Forest Sterling (*Wake of the Wahoo,* page 158) writes that they stayed at the dock. During the later awards ceremony (*Wahoo,* page 250) O'Kane said that all "hands broke out their whites . . . for inspection." Contemporary photos (see figure 8) show a far more relaxed form of dress for the officers. Sterling reports (*Wake of the Wahoo,* page 162) that he was wearing "my old ragged clothers and out-of-shape moccasins."

O'Kane was hardly the only one to remember events a bit more dramatically twenty-five years later. In John Griggs's written memoirs is a faintly bitter reference to the fact that he was given only a twenty-four hour respite when he made his one-time patrol in *Seal.* In fact, *Seal*'s arrival at Midway is well documented. Griggs actually had twelve days' rest. Not a lot, but better than one.

Chapter 10

Dick O'Kane, in his excellent book *Wahoo* (page 287), reported that Roger Paine developed appendicitis while at sea. This is a dramatic story, but inaccurate. According to Paine, who was there (O'Kane was in the States), the appendicitis developed three days after *Wahoo*'s arrival at Pearl Harbor.

Chapter 11

My reconstruction of *Wahoo*'s loss is based on the Japanese Attack Report 17, translated in August 1995, and by the recollections of Japanese participants, including Suguru Ichida and Sinichi Sabata. My account is totally at odds with the theory postulated by Dick O'Kane, even though the Japanese action report on which his earlier narrative was constructed seems to be similar—if not identical. In my opinion, O'Kane's disastrous experience with a circular run skewed his judgment on the fate of *Wahoo*. It is difficult to imagine how *Wahoo* could have withstood a direct torpedo hit, but this must be accepted if O'Kane's theory is to work. Judging from the horrible damage done to *Tang* by a single torpedo, and the virtually instantaneous extinction of *Tullibee*, which suffered the same fate, the circular-run theory must be rejected. The Japanese account clearly explains what happened after *Wahoo*'s presence was detected.

Chapter 12

The account of *Tang*, covered by patrol reports and ably documented by Dick O'Kane, is buttressed with information from a third source. In the July 1994 issue of *Naval History*, Murray Frazee wrote an account of his service aboard *Tang* titled "We Never Looked Back." This valuable cross-check has been used throughout the *Tang* chapters and is buttressed by additional correspondence with Frazee, who was a close reader of the manuscript.

Chapter 16

The memories of wartime San Diego are my own. I lived in the Gaslamp District; my father was a corpsman at Balboa Naval Hospital.

Chapter 17

In addition to the continuing torpedo information from Dr. Milford, the sound characteristics of U.S. submarines came from Norman Friedman's work already cited in the notes for chapter 1. The O'Kane vs. Munson incident came from many sources; the clearest account is in Peter T. Sasgen's *Red Scorpion: The War Patrols of the U.S.S. Rasher.*

Chapter 18

The accounts of *Barb*'s activities were derived from Eugene Fluckey's *Thunder Below,* and the sinking record cross-checked against Commander Alden's report.

Chapter 19

No single incident was harder to reconstruct than the survivors' escape from the sunken *Tang*. This was partly due to the "Rashomon effect." Those thrown into the sea from the sinking bridge simply did not experience what went on below, yet tended to report on it as if they had. The torpedo room escapees sometimes gave their version of what happened topside, even though they were not present. Further, since the escape from that chamber occurred over a period of some hours, the first ones out of the escape trunk did not experience the steadily deteriorating conditions experienced by the last. Dick O'Kane was required to make an official report on the entire escape in September 1945, immediately after repatriation, and while near death in the hospital at Aiea, Oahu. While short on details, and with a few inaccuracies, it is a marvel that he was able to make such a cogent report given his terrible physical condition.

Other written depositions were gathered by the navy in subsequent months. These were sometimes in conflict but, rightfully so, no pressure was put on any of the survivors to justify their statements or to resolve inaccuracies. It also seems probable that some details were withheld by the survivors, either to spare the emotions of the families whose loved ones did not make it, or to protect the reputations of the very few who flinched in the crisis.

As the years passed, the memory of the horrible event mutated. Four of the survivors who read early drafts of the manuscript provided much detail that was unknown outside of their privileged circle—not all of it in agreement, not all necessarily accurate. In cases where current memories veer from the then nearly contemporaneous written accounts, I have remained locked onto the earliest version.

I have relied on those present on the bridge for the account of who was present there and how they died. For example, Decker is sure that Charles Andriolo was not a lookout, but was in the conning tower manning the sonar. But Chief Bill Leibold clearly remembers Andriolo as the port forward lookout standing a few feet above him, gripping the shears in shock as *Tang* went under. Leibold was there and I believe, and have used, his account. This was an easy decision, given that Larry Savadkin was emphatic—and most believable—that the sonar man he tried to save was really Ed Bergman, not Andriolo.

In the official navy account John Heubeck, the OOD, was ". . . unable to swim." But Bill Leibold, who cross-checked with Floyd Caverly just to be absolutely sure, clearly remembers Heubeck passing them with "a beautiful Australian crawl." Leibold also is the source for the cries in the night of Sidney Jones and Darrell Rector. Leibold could hear them, but never saw them in the inky darkness.

The torpedo room escapee also reported that Savadkin escaped from the conning tower's rear gun access door, not the conning tower hatch. This is certainly incorrect, and is an example of someone reporting an incident he did not witness. Frazee, Leibold, and Savadkin report there was no such door. If *Tang* was built with one, and I truly doubt it, it may have been disabled by O'Kane for safety reasons, especially since *Tang*'s deck gun was mounted ahead of the conning tower.

Additional details on conditions inside the sunken *Tang* were supplied by Jesse DaSilva and Clay Decker. Most written accounts report that the inability to seat the lower conning tower hatch was due to distortion from the force of the explosion. Decker reported that it was a jammed wooden dowel—and he was there. The actions of Mel Enos in destroying ship's papers, and Bill Ballinger's attempt to moderate the smoke damage from that source, also came from Decker.

Topside survivors were irritated that DaSilva could be in the mess area, since *Tang*'s crew were at battle stations. However, DaSilva lived to tell the tale. As a MoMM2c he would have been killed by the torpedo explosion if he had actually been at his station. O'Kane, as XO of *Wahoo*, reported more than once (e.g., in

Wahoo, page 136) that the crew would be "standing easy at battle stations, with normal meals for most . . . served in groups." It is likely that the chiefs in the after part of the boat gave their crew some flexibility and that the topside survivors have now forgotten that possibility.

The exact number of escape attempts from the forward torpedo room will never be known. O'Kane wrote in his final patrol report that "four parties left the ship." The postwar ComSubPac report, in the section titled "Loss of the U.S.S. *Tang*" (starting page 253), lists five escape parties. There may have been six.

The escape sequence and list of participants appear to have come mostly from the testimony of Hank Flanagan and Hayes Trukke. Both are no longer alive; a second chance to talk to them is forever gone. But Decker is emphatic that two men— Robert McMorrow and Leland Weekley—"scooted out" before the first formal escape attempt was organized. In his account they went into the chamber without wearing Momsen lungs, without a buoyed rope, and attempted a free ascent. Decker says one could look inside the chamber through thick glass, and that the escape lever was down, proof that the escape door was open. Neither man was ever seen again. In my judgment it is possible that Weekley could have done this. It is worth noting that the ComSubPac report, relying on Trukke's account, states that ". . . CTM Weekley presumably left the trunk and was not seen again," a curiously oblique reference.

Decker also states that he was in the first official escape party, and is careful to emphasize how he set the escape line and Chief Ballinger coached him through the entire process. My judgment is that he was likely in the second party, which also included Ballinger, then making his second attempt. It was during this second attempt that the rescue line was initially deployed, which conforms to Decker's recollection. Decker also remembers that his escape occurred within "thirty minutes, forty-five minutes, tops" from the time *Tang* was holed. Yet he also remembers the water growing ever lighter as he rose up the escape rope to the surface, evidence that the sun had already brightened the skies. Depending on which clock we wish to use, this undoubtedly meant two to three hours after the sinking.

There are numerous smaller inconsistencies. Example: Decker remembers that Hank Flanagan had the dive; Trukke wrote that Flanagan was the torpedo officer, present in the torpedo room. A long-forgotten narrative of Flanagan's was uncovered that reveals that Flanagan *was* in the torpedo room when *Tang's* last torpedo hit, but went to the control room while Decker was still struggling to level the boat. Thus Decker can easily remember his presence and simply mixed up his role.

Many of the officers who reviewed the manuscript—even those from other boats—took exception to the section on the low level of Momsen lung training. No enlisted men did. Yet multiple ComSubPac documents that summarized the *Tang* disaster make a major point of the low, or nonexistent, level of training for the newest crew members.

The depth of the water where *Tang* sank is open to debate. DaSilva says that when he passed through the conning tower the depth gauge read 180 feet. But Leibold and Savadkin state that that particular depth gauge stopped at 165 feet.

Decker says that he counted knots on the ascent rope and there were 30, spaced one fathom apart. He also cites the reading of the escape trunk pressure gauge, but I find it hard to believe that a conversion from pressure to depth could be made, given Decker's completely understandable focus on escaping. There is some peripheral evidence that *Tang* is down in 140 feet. Forty feet of the stern may have been blown away by the explosion, which would permit both the down angle and the amount of bow exposed to be correct. I have been unable to determine an independent source for the knot spacing on an escape trunk rope. If that interval were actually 5 feet, Decker's count would be on the money.

Decker is certain he had escaped before DaSilva entered the forward torpedo room. I have worked with many possible timeline scenarios. All point to the fact that DaSilva must have arrived before Decker made good his escape.

Some accounts have Fluker giving up after his first attempt to escape. The scraps I can piece together point to two attempts by Fluker before surrendering to certain death.

Most accounts say the rubber boat employed on the first escape attempt was pulled back into the submarine. Flanagan insists the boat was pushed out, but did not make it to the surface. Just another one of those little "Who knows?" points that do not affect the escape narrative.

Finally, mention—or lack of it—of Howard Walker's name in the ComSubPac report is unsettling. While every other escapee, living or dead, is listed by rank and full name, Walker is only referred to as "a negro mess cook" or "the negro" (page 257), and "Negro Cook or Mess Att." or "negro mess attendant or cook" (page 258). Even in death he was denied recognition.

Chapter 20

Flasher's patrol reports, and Grider's own account, were supplemented by material from William R. McCants's book *War Patrols of the USS* Flasher.

Chapter 21

The prison camp accounts came from Jesse DaSilva, Clay Decker, Bill Leibold, and Dick O'Kane.

In Charles Lockwood's *Sink 'Em All* (page 344) he wrote that immediately after the ceasefire "I learned to my surprise that Commander Dick O'Kane was still alive, though terribly ill and emaciated." Lockwood's book was written in 1951, and the breaking of the Japanese codes was still a state secret. He dared not reveal that he had known from the day *Tang* went down that O'Kane was alive.

SOURCES

General Bibliography

The books listed here deal primarily with the history of U.S. submarines in World War II. All of them were useful in the preparation of this book, but particularly valuable were the writings of Clay Blair, George Grider, W. J. ("Jasper") Holmes, Richard H. O'Kane, and Forest J. Sterling.

Alden, John Doughty. *U.S. Submarine Attacks During World War II.* Annapolis, Md.: U. S. Naval Institute, 1989.

————. *United States and Allied Submarine Successes in the Pacific and Far East During World War II.* Pleasantville, N.Y.: privately published, October 1999.

Barnes, Robert Hatfield. *United States Submarines.* New Haven,Conn.: H. F. Morse Associates, 1944.

Beach, Edward Latimer. *Submarine!* New York: New American Library, Signet Books, 1946.

Blair, Clay. *Silent Victory.* Philadelphia: J. B. Lippincott, 1975.

————. *Hitler's U-Boat War: The Hunters.* New York: Random House, 1996.

Calvert, James F. *Silent Running.* New York: John Wiley & Sons, 1995.

Chambliss, William C. *The Silent Service.* New York: New American Library, Signet Books, 1959.

Compton-Hall, Richard. *The Underwater War: 1939–1945.* Poole, Dorset, Eng: Blandford Press, 1982.

Edwards, Bernard. *Blood and Bushido.* New York: Brick Tower Press, 1991.

Fluckey, Eugene Bennett. *Thunder Below.* Urbana, University of Illinois Press, 1992.

Francis, T. L. *Submarines.* New York: Metrobooks, 1997.

Friedman, Norman. *U.S. Submarines Through 1945.* Annapolis, Md.: Naval Institute Press, 1995.

Galantin, Ignatius Joseph. *Take Her Deep.* Chapel Hill, N.C.: Algonquin Books, 1987.

———. *Submarine Admiral.* Urbana: University of Illinois Press, 1995.

Gannon, Michael. *Operation Drumbeat.* New York: Harper & Row, 1990.

Grider, George William. *Warfish.* New York: Little, Brown, 1958.

Holmes, Harry. *The Last Patrol.* Shrewsbury, Eng.: Airlife Publishing, 1994.

Holmes, W. J. *Undersea Victory.* Garden City, N.Y.: Doubleday, 1966.

Hoyt, Edwin P. *Bowfin.* New York: Van Nostrand Reinhold, 1983.

Humble, Richard. *Undersea Warfare.* Birmingham, Eng.: Basinghall Books, 1981.

Kaufman, Yogi, and Paul Stillwell. *Sharks of Steel.* Annapolis, Md.: Naval Institute Press, 1993.

LaVo, Carl. *Back from the Deep.* Annapolis, Md.: Naval Institute Press, 1994.

Layton, Edward T. *And I Was There.* New York: William Morrow, 1985.

Lockwood, Charles Andrews. *Sink 'Em All.* New York: Bantam Books, 1951.

———. *Down to the Sea in Subs.* New York: W. W. Norton, 1967.

Lord, Walter. *Day of Infamy.* New York: Henry Holt, 1957.

———. *Incredible Victory.* New York: Harper & Row, 1967.

Lowder, Hughston E. *Batfish.* Englewood Cliffs, N.Y.: Prentice-Hall, 1980.

McCants, William R. *War Patrols of the USS* Flasher. Chapel Hill, N.C.: Professional Press, 1994.

Mendenhall, Corwin. *Submarine Diary.* Chapel Hill, N.C.: Algonquin Books, 1991.

Miller, David. *Submarines of the World.* New York: Salamander Books, 1991.

Miller, Nathan. *War at Sea.* Oxford, Eng.: Oxford University Press, 1995.

O'Kane, Richard Hetherington. *Clear the Bridge.* Chicago: Rand McNally, 1977.

———. *Wahoo.* Novato, Calif.: Presidio Press, 1987.

Polmar, Norman. *The American Submarine.* Annapolis, Md.: Nautical and Aviation Publishing, 1983.

Poolman, Kenneth. *Allied Submarines of World War II.* London: Arms and Armour Press, 1990.

Preston, Anthony. *Submarines.* New York: St. Martin's Press, 1982.

Rindskopf, Maurice H., and Richard Knowles Morris. *Steel Boats. Iron Men.* Paducah, Ky.: Turner Publishing, 1994.

Roscoe, Theodore. *United States Submarine Operations in World War II.* Annapolis, Md.: United States Naval Institute, 1949.

Ruhe, William J. *War in the Boats.* Washington, D.C.: Brassey's, 1994.

Sasgen, Peter T. *Red Scorpion.* Annapolis, Md.: Naval Institute Press, 1995.

Schratz, Paul R. *Submarine Commander.* Lexington: University Press of Kentucky, 1988.

Sterling, Forest J. *Wake of the Wahoo.* Philadelphia: Chilton, 1960.

Trumbull, Robert. *Silversides.* New York: Henry Holt, 1945.

Submarine Operations

Patrol Reports, Deck Logs, Ships' Scrapbooks

All submarines that completed a war patrol submitted an official report; these form the core sources for this book. Copies of the reports can be examined in many locations. The Force Museum at Groton has fragile paper copies in binders that include all endorsements. Regrettably, over the years considerable pilferage has occurred. Some patrol reports from the most popular boats—and *Wahoo* certainly falls in that category—have been stolen; there appear to be no plans to replace these artifacts. Patrol reports may also be obtained from the National Archives on microfiche. The quality of these images is often remarkably poor. Printouts must be carefully examined and hand-annotated, line-by-line, to get a usable document. Fortunately, some enthusiasts have committed their reconstructions to the World Wide Web. One is now able to read, say, *Wahoo*'s third report at the URL: http.twics.com/~mackinno/wahoo-warrep-3.html, or view other patrol reports at Paul Crozier's web site at www.warfish.com.

Deck logs are also available for some boats. My experience has been that they are useful only to settle timing questions. Many COs—Morton was one — rejected deck logs as unnecessary. Roger Paine has written, "Morton hated paperwork almost as much as the Japanese. Logs were prepared for his signature, but he never got around to reading and signing them. I remember him saying that the patrol reports were enough; that logs would be wasted duplicatory effort." I did retrieve the deck logs of *R-5* when Morton was in command. They consist of page after page of 8½ × 14 sheets, broken down by watch section, saying "no remarks" or—for variety—"war patrol." They are absolutely useless except as a means of gathering many photocopies of Morton autographs.

The ship's scrapbooks at the Force Museum are, however, a rich source of "color" material. They contain newspaper clippings, fading snapshots, and mementos that help the reader relocate to the time and atmosphere of the war years.

Personal Interviews and Letters

Many of the smallest details in this book come from my nine years of personal correspondence and phone discussions with some of the principal characters in this book. In alphabetical order, I treasure the background material that came from Jesse DaSilva, Clay Decker, Murray Frazee, William Leibold, Richard H. O'Kane, Roger W. Paine, and Larry Savadkin.

Third-Party Interviews and Letters

Clay Blair spent three years gathering taped interviews and personal memoirs from scores of participants in the war. Beginning in 1975, this material—and source documents for his other work—were donated to the Archive of Contemporary History, University of Wyoming at Laramie. When I went searching for this treasure trove I learned that it is contained in 225 cardboard boxes and has not been shelved or indexed. But each box has a contents document. For $50 per hour (1999) the staff will search the boxes by officer name and copy the written documentation for $.30 per page. Both Jack Griggs and Pinky Kennedy left their memoirs there. Finding them was an invaluable boost for this book.

Miscellaneous Sources

Many people have given me valuable, sometimes precious, artifacts from the Pacific submarine war. Chief among these is George Logue, who gave me not only the diary of his brother Bob, killed on *Wahoo*, but also the videotape of the September 9, 1995, "USS *Wahoo* Memorial Dedication at Wakkanai, Japan."

INDEX

Accardy, John G., 213, 215
Aden Maru class freighter, 206–207
Air conditioning. *See also* Crew comfort
  S-34, 186
  Tang, 156, 164
  U.S. submarine design, 2–3
  Wahoo, 37, 46
Akagi (Japanese carrier), 18
Akebono (Japanese destroyer), 23
Alcohol, Morton and, 70
Alden, John B., ix
Aleutian Islands, 112
Allied shipping, German U-boats, 38
Amakasu Maru (Japanese escort), 181
Anderson, Bruce "Scotty," 148, 159,
  167–168
Andriolo, Charles, *Tang* sinking, 213
Anyo Maru (Japanese cargo ship), 245
Anzan Maru (Japanese cargo ship), 122
Appel, Jesse, 139
Argonaut (SS 166), 5, 33, 36, 40, 171, 266
  deficiencies of, 26–27
  loss of, 72
  Mare Island repairs, 35
  Pearl Harbor attack, 22, 23–24
  Wake Island patrol, 32
Arimasan Maru (Japanese naval auxiliary),
  153
Arita Maru (Japanese tanker), 237
Arizona (battleship), 17, 25, 57
ARMA Company, TDC development, 28
Army Distinguished Service Cross,
  Morton awarded, 94

Articles of the Government of the Navy,
  147
Asama Maru (Japanese armed transport),
  166
Asashio class destroyer, 59
Asukasan Maru (Japanese cargo ship), 183
Atago (Japanese cruiser), 227, 234
Atom bomb
  Hiroshima, Japan, 256–257
  research in, 268
Australia, 39–40, 41, 63–64, 65, 73, 74
  Japanese attack on, 81
  prisoners of war, 201, 202
  Wewak Roadstead, New Guinea, 272
Azusa Maru (Japanese fleet tanker), 201

Balao (SS 285), 144
Balao class, 2
Baldwin, Hanson, 266
Ballinger, William F., 145, 147, 164
  medal awarded to, 188
  Tang sinking, 213, 218, 220, 221
Bangkok Maru (Japanese armed merchant
  cruiser), 116
Barbero (SS 317), 239
Barb (SS 220), 201, 202, 203
  China coast patrol, 244–247
  fate of, 270
  Hokkaido/Sakhalin patrol, 253–256
Barchet, Stephen
  limits of, 26, 33
  Pearl Harbor attack, 22–23
Bashaw (SS 241), 247–248

Bass, Raymond H. "Benny," 122, 124, 125, 127, 137
Battle of Leyte Gulf, 227
Battle of the Coral Sea, 40
Battle of the Philippine Sea (Great Marianas Turkey Shoot), 165
Beach, Edward "Ned," 10, 12, 132, 159, 160, 226
Bellinger, Patrick, 17
Benevolence (U.S. hospital ship), 258, 261
Bergman, Edwin F., 175, 177, 216, *217*
Biyo Maru class freighter, 193
Blair, Clay, 266
"Blair's Blasters" (wolf pack), 170
Blakely, Edward N., 170, 199
    Griggs and, 170–171
    Shark II and, 228
Blandy, William H. "Spike," 39, 131
Bluegill (SS 242), 247
Bonefish (SS 223), 255
Bose, Subhas Chandra, 65–66
Bougainville. *See* Solomon Islands patrol
Boyington, Gregory "Pappy," 250, 262
Bradbury, Norris, 268
Bream (SS 243), 227
Britain. *See* United Kingdom
Brockman, William, 41
Brotherhood concept, vii
Brown, Harold, 269
Brown, John H. "Babe," 148–149, 158
Buenos Aires Maru class vessel, 196
Bureau of Ordnance, 123, 126, 269
    TDC development, 28
    torpedo problem, 39, 40, 41, 104, 117, 122, 130–131
Burke, Arleigh, 266
Burns, J. A., 162, 163, 166
Bush, George Herbert Walker, 165
Buyo Maru (Japanese transport), x, 66, 77–78, 79, 80, 81, 82–84, 85, 90, 93, 94, 266
Byron, George Gordon, 212

California (battleship), 25
Campbell, John S., 107, *109*
Camranh Bay patrol, *Flasher*, 235–237
Canopus (tender), 55
Captains
    leadership role of, vii
    problems with, 3, 4

statistics on, 273–278
    Wahoo Five, 5–6
Career caution, leadership problems, 4
Caroline Islands patrol, *Tang*, 151
Carr, William J., 82, 123, 124
    career of, 122
    death of, 138
    Morton and, 130
Cassin (destroyer), 25
Casualty rates, U.S. submarine warfare, 5, 6
Caverly, Floyd M., 203
    Formosa Strait patrol, 207, 212
    Japan patrol (Ashcan Alley), 191, 196
    prisoner of war, 243
    rescue of, 224
    Tang sinking, 213, 214, 215
CD 112 (Japanese frigate), 255
Ceylon Maru (Japanese armed transport), 166
Chiang Kai-shek, 271
Chidori class antisubmarine vessels, 8, 9, 11
Chikuma (Japanese cruiser), 21
China Clipper, 105
China coast patrols. *See* Formosa Strait patrols
Chinese impressed seamen, 248, 249
Chiyoda class seaplane tender, 50, 54
Choko Maru (Japanese tanker), 155
Choku Maru # 2 (Japanese armed merchantman), 86–87, 90
Christie, Ralph W., 117, 227, 229, 234, 237
Cisco (SS 290), 97, 138
Clear the Bridge (O'Kane), 266
Clyde Maru (Japanese freighter), 247
Coast Defense Ship 46, 210
Code breaking
    Solomon Islands patrol, 58, 61
    Tang sinking, 226
Comet (AP-166), 267
Congressional Medal of Honor
    Fluckey awarded, 247, 253
    O'Kane awarded, 225, *265*, 266
Connole, David R., 27, 139
    death of, 252
    Marshall Islands patrol, 30
    Pearl Harbor attack, 18, 19, 20
Convoy HI-74, 201–202
Convoy HI-82, 235
Convoy HI-87, 245

Convoy MI-23, 207, 209–210
Convoy Mo-Ta 30, 32, 245, 246
Convoy U-03, 207
Coral Sea, Battle of, 40, 165
Cowell (U.S. destroyer), 268
Cramp Shipbuilding, 144, 199, 226
Crawford, George C. "Turkey Neck," 39
Crew comfort. *See also* Air conditioning
   importance of, 2–3
   S-34, 186
   Wahoo, 37
Cubera (SS 347), ix, 251, 267
Cutter, Slade D., vii, 27, 28–29, 139, 164
   Marshall Islands patrol, 30
   Pearl Harbor attack, 20

Dace (SS 247), 227, 228, 229, 235
Daiun Maru (Japanese cargo ship), 182
Darter (SS 227), 227–228, 229, 234
Darwin, Australia, Japanese attack on, 81
DaSilva, Jesse B., ix
   prisoner of war, 243, 244, 249, 250, 257
   rescue of, 258, 261
   Tang sinking, 213, 218, 219, 223, 224
Daw, A. K., 83, 84, 90, 92
DDG-77 (U.S.S. O'Kane), 267
Decker, Clayton O., ix
   career of, 262–263
   prisoner of war, 250
   rescue of, *259*
   return to U.S., 261–262
   Silver Star awarded to, *262*
   Tang sinking, 218, 221, 223
Decker, Lucille, 262
DeHavilland, Olivia, 69
DeTar, John L., 39, 42
Distinguished Service Cross, Morton
   awarded, 94
Diving
   procedures of, 42
   Wahoo, 73–74
Doenitz, Karl, 3, 38, 170
Dolphin (SS 169), 33, 55, 131
   Pearl Harbor attack, 20
   problems of, 32
Dorado (SS 248), sinking of, 139–140
Dori Go (Japanese cargo ship), 184
Dornin, Robert E. "Dusty," 159, 253
Downes (destroyer), 25
Down to the Sea in Subs (Lockwood), 270

East China Sea patrols. *See also* Yellow Sea
   patrols
   mine defenses, 169, 170
   Wahoo, 96, 98–110
Ebara Maru (Japanese cargo ship), 210,
   226, 228
Echizen Maru (Japanese cargo ship), 153
Edwards, Richard S., 40, 41
Electric Boat's Victory Yard, 229
Electric torpedo design, 131, 136, 188, 197,
   255
Engine problems, submarine develop-
   ment, 1–2
England. *See* United Kingdom
English, Robert H., 55
   death of, 87
   Kennedy and, 44, 45, 54, 56, 57, 65
   Midway Island defense, 40–41
Enos, Fred M. "Mel," Jr., 148, 174, 180
   Tang sinking, 213, 217, 218, 220
Enrico Tazzoli (USS Barb), 270
Enterprise (carrier), 29, 32
Equator, 75–76
Escolar (SS 294), 120, 144, 226–227
Etorufu Strait, 124, 128

Fairbanks-Morse engines, 36, 37
Fiedler, Eugene F., 111
Fife, James, 65, 72, 241, 249
Finnigan, Steve, x
Flanagan, Henry J. "Hank," 148, 174, 180
   Formosa Strait patrol, 206
   Japan patrol (Ashcan Alley), 191
   medal awarded to, 188
   prisoner of war, 243, 253
   Tang sinking, 218–219, 221, 222, 223
Flasher (SS 249), 148
   Australia return voyage, 239–241
   decommissioning of, *268*
   fate of, 270–271
   Grider and, 229–230, *231*
   Indochina patrol, 235–237
   Manila Bay patrol, 234–235
   mine detection gear, 256
   Pearl Harbor return, 257–258
   Sea of Japan patrol, 257
   sixth war patrol, 247–249
   South China Sea patrol, 232–234
   successes of, 249
   U.S. return, 252–253

Fluckey, Eugene B., 202, 270
  Congressional Medal of Honor awarded
    to, 247, 253
  Formosa Strait patrol, 245–246
  Hokkaido/Sakhalin patrol, 253–256
Fluker, John W., 220, 221, 222, 223
Flynn, Errol, 123, *123*
FM sonar mine detection. *See* Mine
  defenses
Formosa Strait patrols
  Tang, 206–211
  U.S. wolf pack, 244–247
France, 2
Frazee, Murray B., ix, 5, 187, 188
  career of, 143, 200, 264–265
  Japan patrol (Ashcan Alley), 189–197
  Koshiki Island patrol, 175–180, 182
  medal awarded to, 188
  Silver Star awarded to, 173, 200
  Tang and, 145–146, 147, 148, 153, 154,
    157, 159, 161, 163, 164, 165, 166–168,
    173–175
  Tang sinking, 226
  Yellow Sea patrol, 183–184
Fresh water, submarine design, 3, 37
Fuchida, Mitsuo, 19
Fuke, unknown first name, 66
Fukuei Maru # 2 (Japanese cargo ship), 77,
    79, 80, 92
Fukuju Maru (Japanese cargo ship), 229
Fukuyama Maru (Japanese converted gun-
    boat), 153

Galantin, Ignatius J. "Pete," 40, 266
Galveston, 269
Gandhi, Mahatma, 65
Gar (SS 206), 117, 264
Gato class (SS 212), 2, 37
General Motors, 2
Geneva Disarmament Conference, 1
Germany
  radar and sonar technology, 195, 201
  submarine strategy, 37, 38, 170
  submarine technology, 2–3, 37, 97
  torpedo technology, 3, 131
Glennon, Philip T., 229, 233–237, 241
Goat Island torpedo facility, 195
Gooneyville Lodge. *See* Midway Island
Goto, Hiro, 66
Grampus (SS 207), 5

Grayback (SS 208), 5, 143, 147, 148, 166, 170
Gray Feather Bank convoy, *Tang,* 151–152,
    164
Grayling (SS 209), 5
Great Britain. *See* United Kingdom
Great Depression, submarine develop-
    ment, 1
Great Marianas Turkey Shoot (Philippine
    Sea, Battle of), 165
Greenfish (SS 351), 264
Greenlet, 267
Greenling (SS 213), 148
Grenadier (SS 210), 5, 243
Grenfell, Elton "Jumping Joe," 32–33
  Kennedy and, 55–56
  Pearl Harbor attack, 18–19
Grider, Ann, 36, 43, 124, 187, 247, 252
Grider, Billy, 43, 187
Grider, George W., vii, x, 5, 42, 43, 56, 76,
    78, 92, *97,* 99, 108, *124,* 135, 170, *231,*
    266, *268*
  Buyo Maru (transport) and, 82, 83, 84
  career of, 36, 267–268
  Choku Maru # 2 (Japanese armed mer-
    chantman) and, 86–87
  destroyer attack on *Wahoo,* 87–90
  Flasher and, 229–230, 232–237, 239–241
  Flasher's sixth war patrol, 247–249
  Hawkbill and, 187
  Kennedy and, 41
  mine detection, 256
  Morton and, 69, 70, 71, 72, 73, 75, 81
  Pearl Harbor return, 257–258
  personality of, 124
  Pollack command, 97, 116
  Sea of Japan patrol, 125, 128–129
  Solomon Islands patrol, 57, 60, 61–62,
    63–64
  successes of, 79, 80
  Truck patrol, 48–49, 50, 51, 52, 54
  Ukishima Maru (Japanese armed trans-
    port) and, 86
  U.S. return, 252–253, 270
  Wahoo, 74
  Wahoo loss and, 138–139
  Wewak Roadstead patrol, 7, 8, 9, 12, 74
Griggs, John B., III, 5, *109,* 187, 199
  Blakely and, 170–171
  career of, 122, 132, 267
  China coast patrol, 244–247

health and personality of, 247, 252
Morton and, 70, 71, 108
Seal and, 111, 112
Shark II, 170
Shark II sinking, 228
successes of, 229
tenth war patrol, 252
Wahoo assignment, 56
Griggs, John B., Jr. (Admiral), 87, 90
Grouper (SS 214), 63
Midway Island defense, 40–41
Guardfish (SS 217), 104
Gudgeon (SS 211), 3, 5, 32, 55
Bungo Suido patrol, 27
Pearl Harbor attack, 18, 22, 23
Guest (U.S. destroyer), 267
Gunrabo (Japanese secret police), 243
Gyoten Maru (Japanese cargo ship), 152

Halibut (SS 232), 5
Halsey, William F. "Bull," 32, 90, 237, 238,
237, 238, 254, 255
Hankow Maru (Japanese cargo ship), 136,
139
Hardhead (SS 365), 232
Harlfinger, Frederick J. "Fritz," 159, 160
Harnwell, G. P., 186
Harukaze (Japanese destroyer), 228
Harusame (Japanese destroyer), 9, 10–11,
13, 75, 92, 93, 104
Hasu (Japanese destroyer), 207
Hawkbill (SS 366), 187, 229, 230, 232
Helm (destroyer), Pearl Harbor attack, 19
Henderson, Richie N., 45, 107, *109*
death of, 138
East China Sea patrol, 99
Heubeck, John H., *Tang* sinking, 213, 214
Higbee, 271
High-tensile steel (HTS) boats, U.S. sub-
marine design, 144
Hikoshima Maru (Japanese tanker), 246
Hiroshima, Japan, atom bombing of,
256–257
Hokkaido/Sakhalin patrol, *Barb,* 253–256
Hokusei Maru (Japanese fishing boat), 135
Holland (submarine tender), 101
Holmes, Wilfred Jay "Jasper," 4, 10, 32, 70, 84
Hoover-Owen-Rentschler (HOR) diesel
engine, 21, 27, 29, 30, 33
Hugh L. Scott, 222

Hydeman's Hellcats, 255
Hydrogen bomb, research in, 268
Hygiene, submarine design, 3, 37
Hypo code breakers, Midway invasion, 40

Ichida, Suguru, 136
I-15 (Japanese submarine), 62
I-58 (Japanese submarine), 95
Imperial Japanese Navy (IJN), 92, 93, 152,
196
Indian National Army (INA), 65
Indian prisoners of war, 65–66, 77, 80,
82–84, 90, 92, 94
Indochina patrol, *Flasher,* 235–237
International law, submarine blockade, 1
I-173 (Japanese submarine), 33
Isokaze (Japanese destroyer), 72
I-2 (Japanese submarine), 62
Iwanami (Japanese destroyer), 234

Jackson, Chandler C. "Chan," *109*
career of, 122, 123
marriage of, 119
Japan
army morale, 160
Indian prisoners of war, 65–66
mine technology, 171
sonar technology, 191, 195, 255
Soviet Union declares war on, 257
surrender of, 257, 258–259
vulnerability of, to submarines, 1, 169
war crimes trial, 263
Japanese coast patrol, *Wahoo,* 113–116
Japanese Diet Library, 94
*Japanese Merchant Ship Recognition
Manual,* 46, 47, 48
Japanese prisoners of war, 251, 256
Japanese Wartime Ships History, 210
Japan patrol (Ashcan Alley), *Tang,* 188,
189–198
Jimmu Maru (Japanese freighter), 115
Joint Army-Navy Assessment Committee
(JANAC), 33, 60, 62, 92, 93, 100, 101,
196, 197, 209, 234, 246, 255
Jones, Sidney W., 190
Tang sinking, 213
Josho Maru (Japanese freighter), 206

Kado, Akiro, x
Kaibokans (Japanese frigates), 169, 184

Kakko Maru (Japanese tanker), 234
Kamikaze, 258
Kamoi Maru (freighter), 60
Kamoi Maru (Japanese cargo ship), 245
Kase, Toshikazu, 259
Kega (Japanese carrier), 41
Keiyo Maru class freighter, 48–50
Kennedy, Marvin G. "Pinky," 39, 45, 76,
    105, 148, 176
  career of, 267
  eccentricities of, 41–42
  Morton and, 69, 71
  O'Kane and, 41, 44, 55–56
  relieved of duty, 65, 69
  Silver Star awarded to, 267
  Solomon Islands patrol, 57–65
  Truck patrol, 45–52, 53–54
  Wahoo and, 36–37, 43, 57
Kenyo Maru class cargo ship, 153
Kettering, Charles, 2
Khan, Abdulla, 82
Khan, Ahmad, 83, 90
Kido Butai (Japanese strike force), 18
Kiirun prison, 243
Kii Suido patrol, *Picuda,* 252
Kilinailau Islands. *See* Solomon Islands
    patrol
Kimishima Maru (Japanese passenger
    freighter), 101
Kimmell, Husband E., 24
King, Ernest J., 40, 41
  torpedo problems, 117, 131
King (destroyer), 35
Kipling, Rudyard, 226
Kishinami (Japanese destroyer), 227, 234
Kleinschmidt stills, 37, 42
Koho Maru (Japanese cargo ship), 249
Konron Maru (Japanese passenger trans-
    port), 136
Korean War, 268, 271
Kori Go (Japanese cargo ship), 209
Koshiki Island patrol, *Tang,* 175–182
Kowa Maru (Japanese cargo ship), 100
Krause, Fertig B., 44, 61, 79, 103, 114, 116,
    119, 120, 144, 227
Kukishima Maru (Japanese armed mer-
    chant cruiser), 81
Kuniei Maru (Japanese tanker), 152
Kunisada, Yoshio, 41
Kure Reef, 116

Kuriles, 112, 124, 125
Kurita, Takeo (Vice Admiral), 227, 234
Kusaka, Ryunosuke, 19

Lahaina Roads, 18, 21, 22, 24
Langkoeas (Dutch cargo ship), 95
La Pérouse Strait, 121–122, 124, 125, 135,
    136–137, 139, 254, 255, 271. *See also*
    Sea of Japan
Lapon, 131
  La Pérouse Strait, 121, 122
Larson, Paul, 203, 204, 206, 220, 223, 224
Latham, Don, 231, 232, 238
Latham, Richard C. "Dick," 199
Lawrence (destroyer), 119
Leadership
  morale and, vii
  problems in, 3, 4
  risk-taking, 4–5
  Wahoo Five, 5–6
Legion of Merit, O'Kane awarded, 188
Leibold, William R., ix, 147–148, *215,* 266
  career of, 263
  Formosa Strait patrol, 208
  Frazee and, 264
  medal awarded to, 188
  Pearl Harbor attack, 19
  prisoner of war, 244, 257
  rescue of, 224
  Tang sinking, 213–214
Leyte Gulf, Battle of, 227
Lifeboats, morality of destruction of,
    94–95. *See also Buyo Maru* (Japanese
    transport); Indian prisoners of war
Lifeguard duty
  Scabbardfish, 252
  Tang, 160–162, *162,* 162–166, *167*
Litchfield (destroyer), 32, 44, 117
Living conditions. *See* Air conditioning;
    Crew comfort
Lockwood, Charles A., Jr., 92, 118, 123,
    158, 165, 201, 227
  career of, 269–270
  command of, 87
  Fluckey and, 254, 255, 256
  Japanese surrender, 258
  Japan patrols, 189
  Kennedy and, 65
  La Pérouse Strait, 121
  Morton and, 107, 138

O'Kane and, 166, 171, 198, 200
  Sea of Japan patrol, 127
  sonar mine detection, 139, 186, 232, 238
  torpedo problems and, 39–40, 41, 104,
      117, 124, 130, 131, 132
  Wahoo loss and, 138, 148
  wolf pack strategy, 170
Logue, George, x
Logue, Robert B., x, 32, 55
  death of, 138
  Pearl Harbor attack, 20
  torpedo expertise, 131, 136
London Treaty (1930), 1
Longfellow, William Wadsworth, 53
Lookout system
  Morton, 71, 73–74
  O'Kane, 146
Lurline (civilian liner), 18
Lytle, Morton H. "Mort," 173, 174, 177,
    178, 182, 184

MacArthur, Douglas, 72, 94, 160, 237, 259
MacMillan, Duncan C., 5, 36
  East China Sea patrol, 99, 102
  Morton and, 105
  O'Kane and, 158
  Thresher command, 111
Magnetic exploder. *See* Mark VI exploder
Maikaze (Japanese destroyer), 72
Manila Bay patrol, *Flasher*, 234–235
Manju Maru (Japanese tanker), 246
Mansei Maru class cargo ship, 152
Manta (SS 299), 144
Mare Island
  Argonaut repairs, 35
  Wahoo refit, 119–120, 122, *123*
Marianas Islands, 160
Mark VI exploder, 34, 38–39, 40, 93–94,
    117, 124. *See also* Torpedoes
Marshall Islands patrols, 38
  Dolphin, 32
  Pollack, 116–117
  Pompano, 30–32
Maryland (battleship), 20, 25, 204
Matsumoto Maru (Japanese transport), 210
Matsuwa airfield, 112, 121
Maya (Japanese cruiser), 227
Mayasan Maru (Japanese transport), 228
McCants, Thomas R., 230, 233, 252–253,
    256, 257

McClintock, David
  Darter and, 227, 228
  Pearl Harbor attack, 21
McFarland (destroyer), 24
Media
  O'Kane and, 266
  Wahoo and, 92
Meiho Maru (Japanese freighter), 246
Midway Island, 202–203
  Argonaut, 26–27
  defense of, 40–41
  Pearl Harbor attack, 23
  Pollack refit, 108
  Tang refit, 158–159
  training at, 187–188
  Wahoo refit, 104–105, *106*, 107–108, 111
Milford, Frederick, x
Millican, William J. "Moke," 117, 227
"Millican's Marauders" (wolf pack), 227
Mine defenses
  East China Sea, 169
  Flasher, 156
  FM sonar development, 186–187, 199,
      238, 253
  intelligence information, 170
  Japanese technology, 171
  Lockwood and, 139
  Tinosa, 251, 255
Minorities. *See* Racism
Misch, George, *109*
Missouri (battleship), 258
Mitscher, Marc A., 160, 163, 165
Mohd, Ghulam, 83
Mohd, Subedar Hussain Shah, 82, 83, 84
Momsen lung, 221, 222, 223, *262*
Montaigne, Michel de, 77
Moore, John Anderson "Johnny," 5, 143, 170
  death of, 166
  Japanese coast patrol, 113, 114, 115
  personality of, 111, 148
Morale
  basis of, vii
  Japanese Army, 160
  submarine crews, 3
  Wahoo, 70, 71
Morton, Dudley W. "Mush," vii, 5, 55, *78,
    91, 93, 98*, 108, 112, 119, 120, *123*,
    143, 146, 147, 152, 153, 230
  Buyo Maru (Japanese transport) and,
      81–84, 94

Morton, Dudley W. "Mush," *(continued)*
  career of, 54–55, 65, 132
  Choku Maru # 2 (Japanese armed mer-
    chantman) and, 86–87
  death of, 138, 140
  destroyer attack on *Wahoo,* 88–90
  East China Sea patrol, 96, 98–104
  Grider and, 97
  health of, 108
  innovations of, 70–71
  Japanese coast patrol, 113, 114, 115–116
  Kennedy and, 65, 69
  Lockwood and, 107
  MacMillan and, 105
  Navy Cross awarded to, 92, 118
  O'Kane and, 266
  personality of, 56, 69–70, 96, 101, 128,
    139
  racism, 81, 101
  Sea of Japan patrols, 124–128, 135–138
  Solomon Islands patrol, 58–59, 60, 63, 65
  Sterling and, 110, 133–134
  strategy of, 72–73, 129–130, 161, 180
  successes of, 78–81
  torpedo design, 131–132
  Ukishima Maru (Japanese armed trans-
    port) and, 85–86
  Wahoo assignment, 56, 57
  Wewak Roadstead patrol, 7–13, 74–76
Morton, Harriett, 119
Munakata Maru (Japanese tanker), 245
Munson, Hank, 198–199
Mutual dependence, morale and, vii
Mydans, Carl, 259
Mydans, Shelley, 259

Nagumo, Chuichi
  Darwin, Australia attack, 81
  Pearl Harbor attack, 19
Nanko Maru 8 (Japanese tanker), 198
Nansatsu Maru 2 (Japanese gunboat), 194
Narowanski, Pete, 213, 222, 223
Narwhal (SS 167), 36
  Aleutian Island patrol, 112
  La Pérouse Strait, 121, 122
Nautilus (SS 168)
  Aleutian Island patrol, 112
  Midway Island defense, 41
Naval War College, submarine develop-
  ment, 1

Naval War Research Laboratory, 186
Navy Cross
  Blakely awarded, 170
  Burns awarded, 166
  Morton awarded, 92, 118
  Munson awarded, 198
  O'Kane awarded, 172–173, 200
  Tang crew awarded, 225
Nevada (battleship), 25
New Guinea, *Wahoo* patrol, 7–13, 74–76
Newport Goat Island torpedo facility, 195
Nikkin Maru (Japanese cargo ship), 180
Nimitz, Chester W., 40, 87, 104, 117, 118,
    124, 160, 165, 166, 169, 200, 253–255,
    269–270

O'funa prison, 243–244, 249, 250
Oikawa, Koshiro, 169, 170, 184
Oita Maru (Japanese cargo ship), 207
O'Kane, Ernestine, 27, 32, 35, 43, 119, 226,
    253, 258, 266
O'Kane, Richard Hetherington, vii, ix–x, 5,
    32, 33, 42, 45, 69, 75, 76, 78, *91,* 92,
    93, 96, 108, *109,* 112, 119, 138, 170,
    172
  aggression of, 26, 27
  Argonaut loss, 72
  Buyo Maru (transport) and, 82, 83, 84
  career of, 115, 265–267
  Caroline Islands patrol, 151
  Choku Maru # 2 (Japanese armed mer-
    chantman) and, 86–87
  Congressional Medal of Honor awarded
    to, 225, *265,* 266
  destroyer attack on *Wahoo,* 88–90
  East China Sea patrol, 100, 101, 102, 103
  failures of, 157, 180
  Formosa Strait patrol, 206–211, 212
  Frazee and, 143–144, 200
  Gray Feather Bank convoy, 151–152
  Japanese coast patrol, 113, 114, 115, 116
  Japan patrol (Ashcan Alley), 188,
    189–198
  Kennedy and, 41, 44, 55–56, 65
  Koshiki Island patrol, 175–182
  Legion of Merit awarded to, 188
  Leibold and, 148, 263
  Lockwood and, 166
  lookout system, 146
  MacMilland and, 105

Midway Island, 107–108, 158–159, 187–188, 202–203
mine defenses, 171
Morton and, 56, 70–71, 74
Navy Cross awarded to, 172–173, 200
Pearl Harbor attack, 22–23, 24
prisoner of war, 243, 244, 250, 253, 257
promotion of, 103
rescue and survival of, 224, 226
rescue of, 258, 261
Sealion/Tinosa rendezvous, 174–175
Silver Star awarded to, 118, 188
Solomon Islands patrol, 57–65
Sterling and, 55, 99, 109–110, 120
strategy of, 147
successes of, 79, 80, 81, 152–155, 158
Tang and, 144–149, 155–157
Tang sinking, 213, 215
Truck patrol, 45–52, 53, 160–166, *167*
typhoons, 203–205
Ukishima Maru (Japanese armed transport) and, 85–86
Wahoo and, 35–36, 74
Wahoo sinking and, 140
Wake Island patrol, 150–151
Wewak Roadstead patrol, 7–13
Withers and, 40
Yellow Sea patrol, 182–184
O'Kane (DDG-77), 267
Oklahoma (battleship), 25, 57, 119
Omori POW camp, 250, 251, 253, 257, 258
Omurosan Maru (Japanese tanker), 237
ONI-208J. See *Japanese Merchant Ship Recognition Manual*
Onishi, Takijiro, 258
Otowasan Maru (Japanese tanker), 237

Pacific Maru (Japanese cargo ship), 77, 79–80, 85, 86, 90, 93
Paine, Isla Rea "Bebe," 17, 18, 27, 35, 43, 129, 186, 199, 252, 269
Paine, Roger W., III, 35–36, 43, 129, 186
Paine, Roger W., Jr., ix, 5, 27, 29, 33, 45, *64*, 76, *78*, 96, *97*, 107, 108, *109*, 117, 123, *123*, 124, 138, 164, 258, 266
  Buyo Maru and, 82, 83, 94
  career of, 17–18, 111–112, 115, 116, 122, 129, 251–252, 267, 268–269
  Choku Maru # 2 and, 86–87
  destroyer attack on *Wahoo*, 88–90

East China Sea patrol, 99, 100
  Japanese coast patrol, 113
  Kennedy and, 41, 65
  Marshall Islands patrol, 31
  Morton and, 71, 72, 73, 130
  Pearl Harbor attack, 17, 19, 24
  S-34 command, 186
  Solomon Islands patrol, 59, 61, 62
  Sterling and, 55
  successes of, 80
  Tinosa, 199, 231–232, 238
  Tinosa mine defense patrol, 251
  Truck patrol, 45, 47, 48, 49, 51
  Ukishima Maru and, 85–86
  Wahoo orders, 35, 36, 37
  Wahoo sinking and, 139
  Wewak Roadstead patrol, 7–13
Pampanito (SS 383), 201
Paramushiru, 112
Parks, Lewis S., vii, 32, 139, 258
  Marshall Islands patrol, 30–31
  Pearl Harbor attack, 19, 20, 21
Patterson (destroyer), 73, 74
Paxton, Hugh, 268
Pearce, Basil C., Jr., 221, 222
Pearl Harbor attack, 1, 5, 17–25, 81
Pennsylvania (battleship), 19–20, 25, 147
Periscope
  optics of, 147
  procedures of, 42–43
Permit (SS 178), 164
  La Pérouse Strait, 121, 122
Philippines, MacArthur's invasion of, 237–238
Philippine Sea, Battle of (Great Marianas Turkey Shoot), 165
Piaanu Pass. See Truck Island patrol
Picuda (SS 382), 228–229
  China coast patrol, 244–247
  Kii Suido patrol, 252
  Pearl Harbor refit, 247
Pierce, John R. "Jack," 72
Pillenwurfer bubbler, 255
Plunger (SS 179), 227
  Kii Suido patrol, 27
  La Pérouse Strait patrol, 121, 122
  Pearl Harbor attack, 17, 19, 20–21
  Sea of Japan patrol, 124, 125, 127–128, 137

Politics
  O'Kane and, 266
  submarine development, 1
  torpedo failures, 3
Pollack (SS 180), 124, 138, 187, 233
  described, 97
  Marshall Islands patrol, 116–117
  Midway Island refit, 108
  Pearl Harbor attack, 17
  Sea of Japan patrol, 125, 128–129
  Tokyo Bay patrol, 27
Pompano (SS 181), vii, ix, 5, 33, 34, 35, 38,
      74, 97, 121, 164
  Marshall Islands patrol, 30–32
  Pearl Harbor attack, 17, 18–25
  problems of, 28–30
  repairs to, 27
  sinking of, 139
  TDC of, 28
  Wake Island patrol, 30–32
Pompon (SS 267), 198
Porpoise (SS 172), 5, 173
Porpoise class, engines of, 2
Praed, W. M., 111
Presidential Unit Citation
  Tang awarded, 200
  Wahoo awarded, 94, 118
Prien, Gunther, 8, 9
Prisoners of war
  American, 224, 226, 228
  Australian, 201, 202
  British, 201, 202
  Chinese impressed seamen, 248, 249
  Indian, 65–66, 77, 80, 82–84
  Japanese, 251, 256
  Tang survivors, 243–244, 249–251, 257,
      258, *259*, 261
Production statistics, submarine develop-
      ment, 2
Proteus (submarine tender), 258
Pruett, Ralph R., 73, 80, 83
P-34 (Japanese escort), 224

QLA mine detection. *See* Mine defenses
Queenfish (SS 393), 201, 202
  China coast patrol, 244–246
  Pearl Harbor return, 246

Racism
  Morton, 81, 101

U.S. Navy, 146, 225
Radar, air conditioning and, 3
Radio devices, air conditioning and, 3
Rainer, Gordon B. "Dizzy," 32, 33
Ramage, Lawson P. "Red," torpedo prob-
      lems, 117
Rasher (SS 269), 198, 199
Rashin Maru (Japanese freighter), 246
Rau, Russel H. "Pappy," 8, 9, 73, 111
Rector, Darrell D., 213
Reenlistment rates, 3
Reich, Eli T., 173, 175, 182, 184
Rescue, 261
R-5 (SS 82), 54–55
RO-class submarines, 9, 161
Roko Maru (Japanese cargo ship), 193
Roncador, 144
Roosevelt, Franklin D., 27, 252
Roscoe, Theodore, 243
Ryokai Maru (Japanese fish factory), 127
Ryujo (aircraft carrier), 51, 54
Ryuko (Japanese escort carrier), 245

Sabalo (SS 302), 263
Saboteur mission, Fluckey, 254
Sakhalin Island, 257. *See also*
      Hokkaido/Sakhalin patrol
Salmon, 5
Samarang Maru (Japanese freighter), 181
San Clement Maru (Japanese tanker), 112
San Diego, California, 185–186
Sansei Maru (Japanese collier), 179
Sanyo Maru (Japanese tanker), 246
Sapporo Maru 11 (Japanese cargo ship), 255
Saratoga, 269
Satsuki Maru (Japanese cargo ship), 102
Saufley (destroyer), 62
Savadkin, Lawrence, ix, 187, 203
  career of, 263
  Formosa Strait patrol, 207
  Japan patrol (Ashcan Alley), 192, 198
  prisoner of war, 243, 253
  rescue of, 224
  Tang sinking, 215, 216
Sawfish (SS 276), 131, 132, 135, 136
S-boat, low endurance of, 1
Scabbardfish (SS 397), 252
Scapa Flow penetration, 8, 9
Schneider, Earle C. "Penrod," 18, 19, 27,
      139, 140

Schratz, Paul R., 156, 201
Schreiber, Georges, 140
Schrieber, Raemer, 268
Scorpion (SS 278), 169
Scott, Walter, 35
Seadog (SS 401), 263
Seadragon (SS 194), 228
Seahorse (SS 304), 144, 164
Sealion (SS 195), 170, 171, 173, 175, 201
  successes of, 184
  Tang rendezvous, 174–175, 179, 182
Seal (SS 183), 108, 111, 112, 122
Sea of Japan, penetrations of, 124–129,
  135–138, 255, 257. *See also* La
  Pérouse Strait
Seminole (U.S. Navy tug), 95
Sen, O. A. V., 66, 82, 83, 84, 94
Setsuzan Maru (Japanese passenger-cargo
  ship), 184
S-48 (SS 159), 218
Shangri-la, 269
Shark II (SS 314), 5, 132, 170, 187
  Pearl Harbor refit, 199
  sinking of, 228
Shaw (destroyer), Pearl Harbor attack, 25
Shephard, Evan T. "Ty," 228, 245, 246, 247
Shibata, Shinichi, 136
Shimazaki, Shigekazu, 19, 20
Shokaku (Japanese carrier), 40
Shuyo Maru (Japanese cargo ship), 229
Sirago (SS 485), 267
Silversides (SS 236), 204, 205
Silver Star
  Decker awarded, *262*
  Frazee awarded, 173, 200
  Kennedy awarded, 267
  O'Kane awarded, 118, 188
  Tang crew awarded, 225
Sims, Lydel, 267
Singapore, 65, 77
Skate (SS 305), 151
Skipper problem. *See* Captains; Leadership
Skjonsby, Verne L.
  Sea of Japan patrol, 126
  Wahoo and, 123, 124, 130, 133
Sleeping facilities, submarine design, 3
Smith, Donald O., *106*
Smith, Edward A., 47–48
S-19 (SS 124), 57
Snook (SS 279), 117, 249

Solomon Islands patrol, *Wahoo*, 57–65
Sonar
  air conditioning, 3
  FM device development, 186–187, 199,
    231–232, 238, 253, 256
  Japanese technology, 191, 195, 255
Southard (destroyer), 62
South China Sea patrol, *Flasher*, 232–234
Soviet Union
  Japan and, 169
  La Pérouse Strait, 121
  war declared on Japan by, 257
Sperry (submarine tender), 65, 133
Springer, Frank H., 148, 159, 184, 203, 204,
  205
  career of, 200
  Formosa Strait patrol, 206, 209, 210, 212
  Tang sinking, 216
  training of, 187
Stassen, Harold, 258, 261
Sterlet (SS 392), 201
Sterling, Forest J., x, 56, *91*, 96, 105, 108,
  116, 122
  Buyo Maru (transport) and, 82, 83, 84
  career of, 55, 108–110, 267
  East China Sea patrol, 100
  marriage of, 119–120
  Morton and, 72, 73, 101, 133–134
  Nimitz and, 118
  O'Kane and, 99, 105
  Sea of Japan patrol, 127, 128
  Skjonsby and, 124
  Solomon Islands patrol, 57, 58, 60, 61,
    62, 64, 65
  Wewak Roadstead patrol, 10, 11, 12, 75
S-34 (SS 139), 139
  Paine commands, 186
Styer, Charles W. "Gin," 65
Submarine blockade, international law, 1
Submarine crews, morale, 3
Submarine development and design
  engine problems, 1–2
  Germany, 2–3, 37, 97
  high-tensile steel (HTS) boats, 144
  political factors, 1
  production statistics, 2
  women, 229
Submarine warfare
  sinkings, summary tables, 34, 66, 140, 242
  U.S. casualty rates, 5, 6

Sunfish (SS 281), 151
Syoyo Maru (Japanese tanker), 102

Taifuku Maru (Japanese cargo ship), 128
Taiko Maru (Japanese auxiliary), 135
Taikyo Maru (Japanese auxiliary), 246
Taiyo (Japanese escort carrier), 198
Takao (Japanese cruiser), 227
Takao Maru (Japanese freighter), 115
Takaosan Maru (Japanese cargo ship), 102
Takatori Maru (Japanese tanker), 181
Tamai Steamship Company, 77
Tambor, 39, 41, 148
Tambor class, 5
Tamon Maru # 5 (Japanese passenger-
    cargo ship), 113
Tang (SS 306), ix, x, 5, 120, 140, 143, *145*,
    170, 187, 198, 227, 228, 232, 244, 266
  Caroline Islands patrol, 151
  commissioning of, 144
  damages to, 155–157
  endurance and shakedown cruise,
    144–146
  failures of, 157, 180
  fate of, 271
  Formosa Strait patrol, 206–211
  Gray Feather Bank convoy, 151–152
  Japan patrol (Ashcan Alley), 188,
    189–198
  Koshiki Island patrol, 175–182
  Midway Island refits, 158–159, 173,
    202–203
  Pearl Harbor arrival, 148–149
  Pearl Harbor refit, 171–173, 199
  Presidential Unit Citation awarded to,
    200
  Sealion/Tinosa rendezvous, 174–175,
    179, 182
  sinking of, 212–225, 226, 282–283
  successes of, 152–155, 184
  survivors of, 223–224, 226, 249–251,
    258, *259*, 261 (*See also* Prisoners of
    war)
  Trigger rendezvous, 159–160
  Truck Island lifeguard patrol, 160–162,
    162, 162–166, *167*
  typhoons, 203–205
  Wake Island patrol, 150–151
  Yellow Sea patrol, 182–184
Tarawa, Battle of, 116–117

Task Force 38, 203, 207
Task Force 58, 160, 164, 165
Tatsuju Maru (Japanese cargo ship), 208
Tatsuto Maru (Japanese ammunition
    ship), 245
Tatutaki Maru class freighter, 153
Tautog (SS 306), 20, 148
Technology. *See* Air conditioning; Mark VI
    exploder; Sonar; Submarine develop-
    ment and design; Torpedoes
Teller, Edward, 268
Tench class, 2
Terukawa Maru (Japanese tanker), 127
Terushima Maru (Japanese frigate), 116
Thresher (SS 200), 117, 148, 227
  MacMillan commands, 111
  Pearl Harbor attack, 24
Tilefish (SS 307), 267
Tinosa (SS 283), ix, 131–132, 170, 171,
    175, 227
  fate of, 271
  FM sonar device, 199, 231–232, 238,
    256
  mine detection patrol, 251
  Sea of Japan patrol, 255
  successes of, 184
  Tang rendezvous, 174–175, 179, 182
  typhoon, 237
Tirante (SS 419), 252
Toilet facilities, submarine design, 3
Tojo, Hideki, 20
Tokyo Rose, 136, 184
Tone (Japanese cruiser), 21
Topeka, 269
Torpedo data computer (TDC)
  air conditioning, 3
  development and operation of, 27–28
  use of, 5
  Wahoo, 37
  Wewak Roadstead patrol, 10
Torpedoes. *See also* Mark VI exploder
  electric torpedo design, 131, 136, 188,
    197, 255
  Gato class capacity, 2
  malfunctioning of, viii, x, 3, 5, 33–34,
    38–39, 41, 46, 93–94, 101, 102, 107,
    113, 114, 117, 122, 124, 125, 130–132,
    167, 178, 187, 190, 193–195, 255
  Tang sinking, 212–213
Toun Maru (Japanese cargo ship), 208, 209

Trigger (SS 237), 10, 27, 102, 139
  sinking of, 252
  Tang rendezvous, 159–160
Trim, procedures of, 42–43
Triton (SS 201), 99, 124
Trout (SS 202), 117, 234
Truk Island patrol
  review of, 53–54, 55–56
  Tang lifeguard duty, 160–162, *162*,
    162–166, *167*
  Wahoo, 45–52
Trukke, Hayes O., 219, 222, 223
Truman, Harry S., *265*
Tsuga (Japanese destroyer), 207
Tsugaru Strait, 124
Tsukushi Maru (Japanese cargo ship), 196
Tullibee (SS 284), 167
Tuna (SS 203), 39, 42
Tunney, Gene, 132–133
Tunny (SS 282), 218
Typhoons, 201, 202–205, 237–238

U-boats
  attacks by, 38
  German-type VII-C, 2–3
  R-5 and, 54–55
U-47 (German submarine), 8
Ukishima Maru (Japanese armed trans-
  port) and, 85–86, 93
Union Iron Works, 186
Union of Soviet Socialist Republics. *See*
  Soviet Union
United Kingdom
  Indian prisoners of war, 65–66
  prisoners of war, 201, 202
  torpedo problem, 39–49
U.S. Marine Corps
  morale and, vii
  successes of, 169–170
U.S. Navy, preparations of, 1
U.S. Navy aircraft
  patrols of, 29
  Pearl Harbor attack, 21
U.S. submarine forces, sinkings by, sum-
  mary tables, 34, 66, 140, 242
U.S. SubVets
  morale of, vii
  quality of, 3
University of California, 186
Unyo (Japanese escort carrier), 201

Unyo Maru # 5 (Japanese escort carrier),
  112
Up Periscope (painting, Schneider), 140
Ushio (Japanese destroyer), 23

Valley Forge (Essex class carrier), 263
Vapor compression stills, submarine
  design, 3, 37
Vladivostok, USSR, 121
Voge, Richard G., 143
Volodar, 263

Wagner, C. H., Jr., 237
Wahoo (book, O'Kane), 266
Wahoo (SS 238), viii, ix, x, 5, 143, 146, 147,
  172, 188, 193, 195, 227, 228, 238
  Aleutian Island patrol, 111, 112
  Buyo Maru (transport) and, x, 66,
    77–78, 79, 80, 81, 82–84
  crew of, *132*
  described, 37
  destroyer attack on, 87–90
  diving ability, 111–112
  East China Sea patrol, 96, 98–104
  Japanese coast patrol, 113–116
  Mare Island refit, 119–120, 122, *123*
  Midway Island refit, 104–105, *106*,
    107–108, 111
  morale on, 70, 71
  Morton captains, 65–74
  officers of, 35–36
  Pearl Harbor refits, 55, *91*, *92*, *93*, 96,
    117
  preparing of, 41–42, 44–45
  Presidential Unit Citation awarded to,
    94, 118
  Sea of Japan patrols, 124–128, 135–137
  shakedown cruise, 43
  sinking of, 135, 137–140, 148, 280–281
  Solomon Islands patrol, 57–65
  successes of, 78–87, 92–93, 100, 101,
    103–104
  Truck patrol, 45–52, 55–56
  Ukishima Maru (Japanese armed trans-
    port) and, 85–86
  Wewak Roadstead, New Guinea, 7–13,
    74–76
  wreckage of, 271
Wakatake Maru (Japanese transport), 208,
  209

Wake Island, 38
  Argonaut, 32
  Pompano, 30
  Tang, 150–151
Wake of the Wahoo (Sterling), 267
Walker, Howard M., 146, 154, 168, 173,
    176, 177, 180, 184, 188, 189, 195, 200,
    204, 208, 218, 219, 223, 225
Walsh, William C., 148
War crimes trial, Japan, 263
Warfish (Grider and Sims), 267
The War Shot News, 230
Washington Treaty (1922), 1
Weekly, Leland S., 218, 221
Weinel, A. F. "Gus," 97, 138
Weiss, Donald F., 171, 173, 174, 175, 179,
    199
West Virginia (battleship), 25
Wewak Roadstead, New Guinea
  contemporary history, 272
  Wahoo patrol, 7–13, 74–76
Whale (SS 239), 36
Whitaker, Reuben T., 148, 229, 230
White, William T. "Bill," 108–109, 133, 138
Winton diesel engine, 2
Withers, Thomas, Jr., 32
  criticisms of, 33–34, 36
  Pearl Harbor attack, 21, 22, 24

relieved of command, 40
strategy of, 37–38
torpedo problems and, 38–39
Wolf pack strategy
  "Blair's Blasters" (wolf pack), 170
  China coast patrol, 244–247
  Lockwood, 170, 227
  "Millican's Marauders" (wolf pack), 227
Women, submarine construction, 229
World War I, 1, 2, 27
World War II, submarine development, 2

Yamanouchi, unknown first name, 66
Yamaoka Maru (Japanese cargo ship), 183
Yamashimo Maru (Japanese repair ship),
    153, 155
Yambato Maru (Japanese cable ship), 101
Yawata Maru (Japanese transport), 33, 38
Yellow Sea patrols. *See also* East China Sea
    patrols
  mine defenses, 170
  Tangs, 182–184
Yokohama, Japan, bombing of, 244
Young, Arthur, 44
YP-284 (U.S. Navy district patrol craft), 95

Zofcin, George, 221, 222